Over the centuries an intriguing collection of thinkers have realized that voting and social choice are not straightforward. Yet despite the work of many distinguished contributors in this area, the subject has only become established in the last few decades. Indeed, many earlier writings were lost and their content forgotten, only to be rediscovered later and then forgotten again. This puzzling saga of intellectual history unfolds in *Classics of Social Choice* through these original writings. The editors have included recently discovered pieces and other major contributions—newly translated where necessary. The introduction explains who each writer was, locates him in a historical context, and analyzes his argument.

The writings of Roman lawyer and senator Pliny the Younger are included here as are those of Ramon Lull, a medieval mathematician, missionary, mystic, novelist, and poet; Nicolaus Cusanus, the son of a fifteenth-century winegrower who became a cardinal; Jean-Charles de Borda, a naval engineer; the Marquis de Condorcet, a mathematician, politician, feminist, and economist who died in the French revolutionary Terror of 1794; and Charles L. Dodgson, who became famous as Lewis Carroll. All had fundamental insight into voting and what is now called social choice.

It was only in the 1940s and 1950s that the theory of social choice was established by Duncan Black and Kenneth Arrow—whose Nobel Prize in Economics was awarded in part for this work. It is now a large and thriving branch of economics and politics. *Classics of Social Choice* will interest anyone working in social choice theory as well as students of medieval thought, the Enlightenment, and constitutions.

Classics of Social Choice

Classics of Social Choice

Edited and translated by
Iain McLean and Arnold B. Urken

With assistance from
Fiona Hewitt, Paul Ingram, John London, James C. McClellan III,
Alexander Murray, Roger S. Pinkham, and Charles Powell

Ann Arbor

THE UNIVERSITY OF MICHIGAN PRESS

Published in the United States of America by
The University of Michigan Press
Manufactured in the United States of America

1998 1997 1996 1995   4 3 2 1
A CIP catalogue record for this book is available from the British Library.

Library of Congress Cataloging-in-Publication Data

Classics of social choice / edited and translated by Iain McLean and
  Arnold B. Urken with assistance from Fiona Hewitt . . . [et al.].
     p.   cm.
  Includes bibliographical references and index.
  ISBN 0-472-10450-0 (alk. paper)
    1. Voting—History—Sources.   2. Social choice—History—Sources.
  I. McLean, Iain.   II. Urken, Arnold B.   III. Ingram, Paul.
  JF1001.C55   1995
  324.6'09—dc20   94-24390
                                                               CIP

Preface

This book springs from two separate sources. In 1987 each of us obtained a grant to translate the work of Condorcet on social choice and the theoretical study of voting. Our first debts are to the National Endowment for the Humanities and to the Leverhulme Trust, which made it possible to start.

When we discovered that we both held grants to do the same thing, we pooled our efforts, and we have been working together since summer 1988. Beginning with Condorcet, we have been led down some paths that were on the map when we started and down some that were utterly unfamiliar. Pliny was well signposted; his work was discussed in one of the first modern classics of social choice, Farquharson (1969). But we have done a little path clearing, in which Chris Pelling was very helpful. Quotations from *The Letters of the Younger Pliny*, translated by Betty Radice (Harmondsworth: Penguin Classics, 1963), copyright © Betty Radice, 1963, 1969, are reproduced by permission of Penguin Books Ltd.

Lull and Cusanus, on the other hand, were quite unknown to social choice theorists, including ourselves, when we started. Grateful thanks are due to Anthony Bonner, Rudolf Haubst of the Institut für Cusanus-Forschung, William Riker, Paul Sigmund, and the staff of the Bodleian Library, Oxford, for helping us over unmapped ground.

Borda's paper and Condorcet's *Essai* of 1785 are very frequently cited but rarely read by those who do not read French. (A work whose full title is *Essai sur l'application de l'analyse à la probabilité des décisions rendues à la pluralité des voix* does not lend itself comfortably to citation even by those who do read French. To understand the meaning of the title already requires some background in probability and social choice.) A version of Borda's paper has been published in English (de Grazia 1953), but there are some inaccuracies in the translation. Very little of Condorcet's *Essai* has been, apart from a few passages in Black (1958) and Baker (1975). The rest of Condorcet's huge output had not been scanned for further insights in social choice; it turns out that there are many, amplifying and sometimes contradicting the *Essai* of 1785. Lhuilier's ([1794] 1976) paper on the defects of Condorcet's practical voting procedure has been known at least since its mention by Montucla (1802, vol. 3, p. 421) but was not rediscovered until 1976, when it was reprinted in facsimile in *Mathématiques et sciences humaines*. Historians including Charles Gillispie and Martin S. Staum knew that Daunou had written about voting and directed us to his work, which Mme Lafitte-Larnaudie of the Archives of the Institut de France helped us to find. As far as we know, Daunou has never been recognized as a social choice theorist, though he was the first to integrate theory and practice at any length. Daunou led us in turn to Morales. In interpreting these works, we have been very much helped by our colleagues in, and associated with, the *REHSEIS* (Recherches épistemologiques et historiques sur les sciences exactes et les institutions scientifiques) research group of the French Conseil National de la Recherche Scientifique (CNRS), who are conducting an impressive research program on the Academies of the eighteenth century and the work done in them. Grateful thanks to Roshdi Rashed, Christian Gilain, G.-Th. Guilbaud, and above all Pierre Crépel, who has been unstintingly generous in sharing his time and his research. We are also very grateful to the librarians and archivists of the Institut de France, the Académie des Sciences, the Bibliothèque Nationale, the Archives Nationales, and the Archives de la Marine.

   Dodgson and Nanson were already known in social choice theory through the work of Duncan Black (1958). This is well described by the words that he used (1958, 189) to describe Williams's (Williams et al. 1979) catalog of the works of Lewis Carroll: "a work which is the product of the most ripe scholarship and love of its subject and which is a perfect model of its kind." However, one of Black's very few misjudgments was to dismiss Dodgson's work on proportional representation as being "of relatively little interest" (1958, 191); consequently, Dodgson's pamphlet has not been studied, except by Black himself (1967), when he later changed his mind. Nanson's work, and in particular his proposed voting procedure, is cited from time to time in the modern literature, but the original is in such obscure places, not to be found even in many research libraries, that we thought it worth republishing. We are grateful, again, to Bodleian Library staff and to Jenifer Hart for their help on our nineteenth-century writers. It is a particular pleasure to acknowledge the help of John Wing of Christ Church Library, Oxford, who had to tolerate one of us (IM) as an undergraduate a quarter of a century ago. The papers of Duncan Black are now safe in the Archives of Glasgow University; the whole community of social choice owes a debt to Richard Alexander of the Royal Naval College, Dartmouth, Devon, and to Michael Moss and his staff in Glasgow for their roles in rescuing them. The section on Dodgson was kindly reviewed by Morton Cohen, editor of *The Letters of Lewis Carroll*, who showed us four important letters to Dodgson from Isaac Todhunter.

We are very grateful also to the Nuffield Foundation and the British Council for financial support; to our universities for facilitating our research; to the British Library, the Library of Congress, the New York Public Library, and the Taylorian Library, Oxford; and to colleagues at seminars at Duke, Harvard, Maryland, New York, Osnabrück, Oxford, Rochester, and Stanford Universities, the *REHSEIS* seminar (twice), the Colloque Condorcet in Paris, the Public Choice Society, and the Society for Social Choice and Welfare, as well as our home campuses, for helpful suggestions. And, above all, to our families, who have tolerated transatlantic research for five years.

Contents

CHAPTER 1

General Introduction

1. What Is Social Choice?

Democracy means rule by the people. But what if the people do not agree? Traditionally, it has been natural for democrats to assume that the majority should prevail over the minority. But *majority* means "more than half." *Majority* and *minority* are fully defined only for binary decisions such as yes or no on a single proposition or a choice between two candidates. As soon as there are three or more candidates, it is of course possible that no candidate gets a majority of (first preference) votes. Social choice is the study of all procedures for producing group decisions from a set of individual preferences, of which simple majority rule is a special—very special—case. Although the institutions and theory of democracy were well developed by the fourth century B.C., social choice was much slower to get going. As a separate academic subdiscipline it dates back only to the 1950s. Thus all the readings presented in this book were written before the emergence of social choice as a separate discipline. All of our authors saw that majority rule was not a simple concept; none of them could get his audience to see the depth of the problems. To begin to see why social choice found it so hard to become established, we must look briefly at the history of democracy, both as an ideal and as a set of institutions.

Democracy—the word—goes back to ancient Greece. Democracy—the thing—is first recorded in the practices of Athens in the fifth century B.C. (Aristotle 1984; Thucydides 1972). Aristotle, or more likely one of his graduate students, wrote a comprehensive history and description of the institutions of Athenian democracy that is supplemented by many other texts (see Rodewald 1975; Finley 1973 and 1983). From these sources we can see that many central institutions of democracy were thought through with remarkable care and detail. But voting procedures were not analyzed. Why? For one thing, the ancient Greek democrats normally took only binary votes: yes or no to the proposition currently before the assembly; yes or no to a proposition to ostracize (that is, banish) a citizen or to punish an officeholder; yes or no to the guilt of a person accused in the courts. And elections were rare as most offices were filled by lot and rotation, not by election. Plato's and Aristotle's condemnation of democracy and its outcomes did not involve the analysis of voting, although *The Constitution of Athens* by Aristotle or one of his students contains detailed descriptions of other aspects of Athenian democracy.

The fact that the problems of social choice are much more obvious in multicandidate elections than in binary votes on propositions may have motivated Pliny the Younger, the earliest known writer (chap. 2) to consider the problem of social choice, because he was faced with a problem in which three options were simultaneously under discussion.

After Pliny, social choice theory did not appear again in the Western world until the sudden emergence of sophisticated themes in the work of Ramon Lull (ca. 1232–1316; chap. 3), a writer working at the frontier of Christian and Islamic scholarship. This raises the possibility that the issue was discussed during the golden age of Arabic scholarship between the seventh and thirteenth centuries A.D.; but we have not found any evidence for that. At least it can be said that progress beyond the point reached by Pliny probably requires algebra and some knowledge of combinations and permutations, and these were Arabic inventions. Medieval Europe saw little discussion of democracy. With the precocious exception of Venice discussed below, medieval discussion of voting seems to have been confined to religious elections, in a binary context. The framework within which people either thought or had to pretend that they thought was one in which a choice either conformed with the will of God or it did not: a binary choice. Lull and his disciple Nicolaus Cusanus (Niklaus von Cues, Nicholas of Cusa, ca. 1401–64) were lonely thinkers in their insight that the case of multiple candidates threw up new problems.

There was a marked revival of democratic thought in the seventeenth and eighteenth centuries. The Reformation may have been a precondition for it. Though Protestant Christianity need be no more friendly toward democracy than had been medieval Catholic thought, its questioning of hierarchy and authority led writers on politics to start from a presumption of equality among humans:

> For Men being all the Workmanship of one Omnipotent, and infinitely wise Maker; All the Servants of one Sovereign Master, sent into the World by his order and about his business, they are his Property, whose Workmanship they are, made to last during his, not one anothers Pleasure. And being furnished with like Faculties, sharing all in one Community of Nature, there cannot be supposed any such *Subordination* among us, that may Authorize us to destroy one another, as if we were made for one anothers uses, as the inferior ranks of Creatures are for ours. (Locke, *Second Treatise of Government*, § 6)

Locke did not draw explicitly democratic conclusions. But there have been many, starting in his own day, who have felt that his theological starting point implied a democratic finishing point. Lockean ideals motivated the political thought of Jefferson, Madison, and a number of the other founders of the United States (despite the ingenious attempt of Wills (1978) to show otherwise).

The eighteenth century therefore saw the first systematic thinking about democratic procedures. However, systematic thought on procedures seems to attract a particular sort of analyst: the meticulous mathematician rather than the speculative philosopher. Montesquieu and Voltaire have nothing to say about procedures for democracy, as far as we know. What Rousseau has to say about procedures in *The Social Contract* is best passed over, since it is incoherent and self-contradictory. Our eighteenth-century writers are mathematicians and engineers who do not make grand claims (the Marquis de Condorcet is an exception, but we print an excerpt from his technical work on voting, not his broader work on democracy or rights). Jean-Charles de Borda was an engineer and active member of the Academy of Sciences in Paris; his work on voting arose from a study of the Academy's procedures for electing new members. The same source gave rise to Condorcet's, Morales's, and Daunou's work: Condorcet, who disliked Borda, was deeply involved in the same elections in his capacity of secretary of the Academy; Morales read about the adoption of the Borda scheme by the Institut de France (successor of the Academy), and worked out an independent justification of it with an analysis of some of its properties, unaware that any similar work had already been done. The man who introduced the Borda scheme was P. C. F. Daunou, another Academy politician; he later dropped his support of the Borda scheme for reasons that he gives in our chapter 11. Lhuilier was a Swiss mathematician with indirect intellectual links to Condorcet (they were both admirers of Leonhard Euler, and both connected with the liberal Polish aristocracy); however, we do not know if they knew each other directly. Lhuilier was drawn into the theory of voting because his native Geneva had adopted one of Condorcet's practical schemes for its elections. All of them look closely at the properties of choice systems in use or proposed and find them to be full of contradictions and anomalies.

Meticulous mathematics and speculative philosophy were closer in the United States than in France. There were close links between Condorcet and Jefferson and weaker links from Condorcet to Madison and John Adams. Unfortunately, Condorcet failed to transmit any understanding of the central problems of social choice down these links (McLean and Urken 1992). However, Jefferson and Alexander Hamilton deserve the credit for originating a subbranch of social choice, the theory of apportionment. Political apportionment is the allocation of an integer number of seats to each of a number of subunits into which a legislature is divided. The theory of apportionment originated with the interpretation of the U.S. Constitution, article I, § 2:

Representatives and direct Taxes shall be apportioned among the several States which may be included within this Union, according to their respective Numbers. . . . The actual Enumeration shall be made within three years after the first meeting of the Congress of the United States, and within every subsequent Term of ten Years, in such manner as they shall by Law direct. The number of Representatives shall not exceed one for every thirty thousand, but each State shall have at least one Representative.

The problem of interpreting this article therefore arose after the first national census, in 1791. Different ways of interpreting it gave different numbers of House seats to various states, some of them relatively generous to large states and some to small states. Hamilton and Jefferson are respectively the fathers of *quota* methods and *divisor* methods to solve this problem, which is politically charged and mathematically surprisingly challenging. The problem of apportionment was discovered independently by a number of European writers on proportional representation in the nineteenth century, unaware (as their successors often are to this day) that they had been anticipated by a century. The debate on apportionment is authoritatively (and wittily) presented in its historical context by Balinski and Young (1982); therefore we do not discuss it in detail. But we note it as one area in which practicing politicians actually developed a branch of social choice.

In the nineteenth century there was a full debate on proportional representation (briefly summarized below), but almost no discussion of social choice. Charles L. Dodgson (Lewis Carroll) and E. J. Nanson are the only writers we have found who understood the central theoretical issues; Dodgson from scratch and Nanson from his reading of Condorcet. Both were mathematicians and university teachers; Dodgson (and possibly Nanson as well) was drawn to the subject by discovering the paradoxes and puzzles of social choice in college voting procedures.

We can now return to a general characterization of social choice. Social choice is the deductive study of decision procedures, especially voting. Its central puzzle is the majority-rule cycle, sometimes called the *paradox of voting*. This is now best known in its minimal form, the three-voter, three-option Latin square pattern:

Voter #	1	2	3
Preference			
Top	x	y	z
Middle	y	z	x
Bottom	z	x	y

In this three-person society, there are majorities for x over y, y over z, and z

over *x* all at the same time. Regardless of the choice the people make, some other choice would beat it by two votes to one. This problem is a central node—the Clapham Junction or O'Hare Airport of social choice. The development of social choice theory either leads to or departs from this problem. It analyzes the properties of different choice procedures, showing how they may produce different outcomes from the same underlying set of preferences. It explores manipulation and proves that choice procedures are either manipulable or dictatorial. It measures the prevalence of majority-rule cycling and finds that it is universal in any complex society. These findings evidently have radical implications. Plott (1976, 511) has put it as well as anybody:

> The subject began with what seemed to be a minor problem with majority rule. "It is just a mathematical curiosity", said some. . . . But intrigued and curious about this little hole, researchers, not deterred by the possibly irrelevant, began digging in the ground nearby. . . . What they now appear to have been uncovering is a gigantic cavern into which fall almost all of our ideas about social actions. Almost anything we say and/or anyone has ever said about what society wants or should get is threatened with internal inconsistency. It is as though people have been talking for years about a thing that cannot, *in principle*, exist, and a major effort now is needed to see what objectively remains from the conversations.

Normative political theory has not yet climbed out of Plott's cavern. The thing that cannot, in principle, exist is the will of the people. Yet millions of words have been written on democratic theory that make no acknowledgement of this problem. Hobbes and Rousseau cannot be blamed for failing to suggest a way out of Plott's cavern, but the many normative theorists writing today who take no account of the literature we discuss certainly can be. Riker (1982 and 1986) has described with care and some relish the view from the bottom of the cavern. For those tempted, as many still are, to dismiss cycles as just a mathematical curiosity, consider the dilemma faced by the three-person society. It must choose something; it cannot cycle endlessly. Whatever it chooses, some other option beats that choice by two to one. The one member who preferred the final outcome to the choice that beats it is thus a dictator in an immediately understandable sense. In his famous theorem, Arrow (1951) shows that given a number of apparently reasonable requirements for a voting procedure, there may always be such a person, who will then be a dictator not just over one pair of outcomes but over every pair. By the time Riker wrote, it was clear that, as well as the hole created by the initial "paradox of voting," two great rockfalls prevented easy exit from the cavern. One blocked the search for a nonmanipulable voting system by proving that any such system must be dictatorial. The other proved that cycles are almost ubiquitous in a society of any size or complexity, such as first-century Rome or eighteenth-century France.

Riker accordingly used the problems of majority rule to argue for a restricted Madisonian conception of democracy as against a populist Rousseauvian one. Rousseau's followers have only just begun to respond to Riker's challenge (Estlund et al. 1989), and they have drawn attention to unexplored implications of Condorcet's probabilistic framework. Condorcet, who in 1785 first discovered cycles, thought he could develop social choice as an application of classical probability theory. His discovery of cycles was a severe blow to this hope, which has led some of his modern readers to regard the probabilistic framework as an enormous distraction surrounding the tiny but revolutionary discovery of cycles. (See especially Black 1958.) But Grofman and Feld (1988) have pointed out that Condorcet's probabilistic theory can be read as an axiomatization of Rousseau. Rousseau argued that a good society would enact the General Will but could not coherently explain what the General Will was or how it was to be calculated. Condorcet, by developing his "jury theorem" (the name given by Black 1958), gave shape to Rousseau's intuition. The jury theorem states that if

1. voters are expressing their considered judgments on whether a claim is true or false (rather than simply voting for what is in their interests);
2. each voter forms his or her judgment independently of the others; and
3. each voter is on the average right more often than wrong, even if only by a small margin,

then, by stipulating the total number of voters and the minimum majority required to pass a resolution, the constitution can ensure that the voters only rarely make incorrect decisions. This theorem, only one of what Condorcet himself conceived of as "hypothetical situations," has been rediscovered by modern social choice theorists (Grofman and Owen 1986; Young 1988).

Most people who are familiar with social choice nevertheless believe that it was born full grown in 1951, when Kenneth Arrow's *Social Choice and Individual Values* appeared apparently from nowhere (for a typical such statement, see the introduction to Elster and Hylland 1986). Arrow's General Possibility Theorem wreaked constructive havoc, first with welfare economics and considerably later with political theory. What welfare economists called the "social welfare function" was designed to bring society to a point on the "production possibility frontier," or Pareto frontier: the best such point was the best of all possible worlds. Under majority rule, this *might* be identical to what political theorists called the will of the people. There is an old and still interesting debate about whether majority rule and maximizing social welfare are identical, similar, or even consistent. This does not concern us here; what does is the different reception of Arrow in economics and in politics. Before Arrow it was widely assumed that the best society was the one that came nearest to realizing the elusive "maximand" (the unique optimum or the will of the people). The discovery that it did not usually exist immediately sent welfare economists off onto different tracks. Political theorists did not come to grips with Arrow until the 1970s but now generally accept that the will of the people is a will-o'-the-wisp. In empirical political science, social choice is a basic component of spatial theories of voting and of the new institutionalism that has led to renewed interest in collective choice rules such as parliamentary procedures and congressional conventions. (For reviews, see Alt and Shepsle 1990, especially the chapter by P. C. Ordeshook.)

As with many intellectual revolutions, Arrow was not in fact alone. Duncan Black was working in parallel to Arrow in Britain and proved his median voter theorem while fire watching in Warwick Castle in 1942 (wartime civil servants had to spend long shifts on watch in historic or important buildings in case a shell or incendiary landed on them). It is a powerful device that allows the preferences of the median voter to stand for those of the whole committee, legislature, or electorate, providing that the number of voters is odd and the structure of opinion is single-peaked (a term introduced by Black). It is now a basic tool of political science. But Black was working in a more hostile environment than Arrow. Both of them got into trouble with their employers for failing to produce publications in a recognized field (would Newton or Leibniz have got tenure in a twentieth-century university?). Black could not get anybody at all in Britain to understand the point or significance of his work, which did not appear in an accessible form until 1958.

Black was one of the first people this century to discover the history of social choice before 1942. In the early 1950s, he showed that majority-rule cycles were first discovered by Condorcet in 1785 and rediscovered independently by Dodgson in the 1870s. The evidence that Dodgson's discovery was independent is particularly neat. Dodgson was a tutor in mathematics at Christ Church, Oxford. The fundamental eighteenth-century papers on social choice are Condorcet's *Essai sur l'application de l'analyse . . .* ([1785] 1972) and a paper of 1784 by Borda, with commentary by Condorcet, in the proceedings of the Paris Academy of Science (see chaps 5 and 6). Christ Church has a complete run of the Academy's proceedings, the most important scientific periodical of the day. But in the volume for 1784, Borda's paper is uncut. So was part of the Bodleian Library's copy of Condorcet's *Essai* when Black inspected it. These are certainly the copies that Dodgson would have consulted.

The rediscovery of Condorcet in France proceeded in parallel. In 1952 G.-Th. Guilbaud published a notable paper that explained the relationship between Condorcet's discovery of cycles and Arrow's Theorem. This was followed by an important monograph on Condorcet's social mathematics by G.-G. Granger (1956). After a further fallow period, French scholars returned to Condorcet, this time concentrating on his long-neglected uses of probability theory (Michaud 1985; Crépel 1988 and 1990; Crépel and Gilain 1989; Monjardet 1990).

Outside of Europe, Condorcet's work was read by Nanson ([1882] 1907) in Melbourne and Collin ([1820] 1885) in Philadelphia, but social choice did not take root in either Australia or the United States. Nanson's interpretation was colored by the negative reading of Todhunter (1865), although Nanson, unlike Todhunter, understood what Condorcet was trying to say about plurality rule. Nanson's acute comments on the defects of Australian systems of proportional representations might have had some impact, but we have no evidence that anybody else understood what he was saying about social choice. Collin reported on Condorcet's 1785 *Essai* to the American Philosophical Society, but evidence has not been found that clarifies his understanding of social choice ideas. (See Urken 1989a and 1991.)

In the last few years, two more facts have become clear. First, that the history of social choice does not begin with Condorcet. The isolated but telling discussion of manipulation by Pliny the Younger was uncovered by Robin Farquharson (1969) and clarified by William Riker (1986). There is more systematic discussion of voting procedures in the work of Lull and Cusanus. Lull proposes both (what are now called) Condorcet and Borda (or perhaps Copeland) procedures, and Cusanus describes and recommends the Borda rank-order count in exact detail. Cusanus was a follower of Lull, "one of the most inspired madmen who ever lived" (Donald Michie in Gardner 1982, ix). The second fact is that the eighteenth-century discovery of social choice was much more comprehensive than even Black and Guilbaud were aware. The chapters of this book show that Condorcet and his contemporaries understood most of what is now known about cycles and manipulation and debated in a sophisticated way what to do about them. But by around 1820 this thread had been lost again.

2. Why "Classics of Social Choice"?

Our title might seem odd. Our classics were all written decades or centuries before social choice established its current identity in university departments of social science and mathematics. Even now, social choice has little or no clear-cut or intuitively recognizable meaning to people outside the field. Nevertheless, our collection represents a coherent set of nonobvious insights into voting processes.

These insights, analytical and normative, are basically subversive. They challenge us to rethink the way we use voting methods and make us think twice (or more) about the meaning of voting outcomes. Although this challenge can be seen as politically disruptive, it can also be seen as part of a scientific, analytical process aimed at probing the meaning of voting. In some situations, voting analysis tries to select a voting system that will enable the members of an organization to achieve commonly held values. In others, the logical relationship between decision-making processes and collective outcomes can be used to manipulate voting outcomes. Both depend on understanding the underlying logic of voting.

To those already familiar with social choice, our classics are intended to show that it did not, after all, begin in 1951. To those not already familiar, they provide a context for learning about social choice theory. We hope that our selections will enable the reader to appreciate how problems are identified and concepts formed in social choice. For although social choice theory is a deductive endeavor, it did not develop as a purely abstract investigation. Analysts often discovered problems and investigated solutions in an idiosyncratic manner, unaware of each other's work. For a delightful example, see the proud boasts of Morales in chapter 10 that he is the first to codify social choice, unaware that he is repeating arguments from Cusanus and Borda almost word for word. And when opportunities arose for sophisticated observers to engage in fruitful debate, social ambivalence and ambiguity and the state of social choice knowledge combined to produce surprising results.

Most voters are unaware of what is going on in a voting process and do not recognize a breakdown when it occurs. You do not need to know any physics to ride a bike, but it helps to be able to understand what will cause you to fall off. However, when you fall off a bike, you know that you have. When a voting system fails (for instance, by failing to choose a Condorcet winner or by failing to reveal that a cycle exists), most participants are normally unaware that it has failed. As Riker (1982, 21) says:

> We do not frequently have persuasive evidence of the defects in voting. When an election or a committee's decision procedure produces an outcome, evidence that another outcome *might* be socially preferred is usually never collected. One can seldom know, therefore, that the road not taken could have led to a better choice.

So learning about the organizational context of abstract argument about voting is important because it makes us more thoughtful, critical, and intelligent participants. It also enables us to scrutinize the implicit and explicit models of voting situations found in modern argument.

3. Why Do They Matter?

In "normal science," the history of a discipline is an unexciting place, inhabited (scientists often suspect) by people who cannot cope with the pace of life at the intellectual frontier. Papers more than a few years old are rarely cited, and the faster a science is moving, the more true that is. Modern molecular biology began almost at the same time as modern social choice, with Watson and Crick (1953). Their paper is a historical landmark but not a signpost in current use. By contrast Arrow (1951) and Black (1958) are both. This reflects a number of differences. Social choice is not big science; it does not appear to save lives (though the jury theorem could). It has remained much more theoretical: experimental social choice is only now beginning to take root after tentative beginnings in the 1970s. Theoretical papers are probably more long-lived than experimental ones.

Some social choice theorists, perhaps eager for their science to become more like molecular biology, share the working scientist's impatience with history. We think our historical discoveries, and those of others that we reproduce, are fascinating; but we have given seminars at which the first question has been "So what?" Did Lull or Condorcet prove any theorems not in the current literature? No. Well, why are you spending your time on them?

For four reasons. Firstly, just to set the historical record straight. That social choice has been invented, lost, and reinvented several times is a fact worth reporting in itself. And we want our authors to get the credit they deserve, even if it is a few centuries overdue. Duncan Black died in 1991, still somewhat embittered at his half-century struggle for recognition. But at the end of his life his contribution began to be recognized, for instance in a festschrift organized by Gordon Tullock (1981); in the award by the American Political Science Association of the Benjamin Lippincott Prize for a work of enduring impact; and in his election as an overseas member of the Accademia dei Lincei and as a Senior Fellow of the British Academy. These distinctions mattered a good deal to him. How much more frustrating it must have been to be Ramon Lull or C. L. Dodgson, whose ideas were evidently not understood at all, or indeed Condorcet, whose ideas were presented to scientific colleagues and politicians, none of whom seem to have appreciated the fundamental implications of his theory for the design of social or political constitutions (Urken 1991; McLean and Urken 1992). Condorcet's devotion to social choice cost him his life: he was outlawed by the Jacobin-dominated National Convention in 1793 for a pamphlet in which he had complained that Robespierre had supplanted his own draft constitution without understanding the principles on which it was based. Though harbored for nine months by a courageous Paris landlady, Condorcet escaped from her house when a decree ruled that those found harboring outlaws were liable to be summarily guillotined. He was arrested soon afterwards and found dead in prison the next day (Badinter and Badinter 1988, 603–13).

Our second justification is that the classics do contribute to issues that are still current, even if not in the form of previously unknown theorems. Borda and Condorcet give clearer defenses of their respective voting systems than most modern attempts to do the same thing. Daunou, a figure unknown to most social choice scientists, provided an excellent review that would not be out of place in a modern scholarly journal. Condorcet and Daunou between them make quite clear what is at stake between the rival Condorcet and Borda principles, and both of them appeal to what is now called Independence of Irrelevant Alternatives. In Borda's rank-order count, the fate of a and b can depend on the relative merits of c and d or on whether c and d happen to be among the candidates or not. To Condorcet and Daunou, such considerations should be regarded as irrelevant to the social choice between a and b. Most modern social choice theorists agree with them. Some, notably Dummett (1984), do not. The issue between Condorcet and Borda is as open as it was 200 years ago.

Thirdly, the repeated appearance, disappearance, and reappearance of social choice prompts the question, why is this such an abnormal science? There are other instances of dead ends in science. A famous one is the use of steam power by Hero of Alexandria to move statues in temples. But we know of no other case where a body of work was codified three times (Lull and Cusanus, Condorcet and Daunou, and Dodgson), and then lost every time so that the modern codifiers started from scratch. It cannot be that it is inherently difficult: even Condorcet, the most inaccessible of the codifiers, was using more elementary mathematics than his contemporaries and friends Laplace and Lagrange, whose work in physical science was immediately recognized as classic. (See the excellent discussion in Daston 1988.)

Our very use of the phrase "normal science" reveals a debt to the influential views of Kuhn (1970). But the failure of social choice to thrive cannot be for the reasons given by Kuhn in his assertion that "normal science . . . often suppresses fundamental novelties because they are necessarily subversive of its basic commitments"(1970, 5). Certainly, social choice is subversive, but it did not subvert the previous science of voting because there was none. Only in the 1940s and 1950s could it be seen as subversive. Economists, faced with overwhelming refutations of the classical framework for welfare economics, did not regard Arrow's ideas as subversive but accepted them as solutions to their problems. Economists were much faster than political scientists to appreciate the power and joy of an impossibility result. If something cannot be had, there is no point in looking for it and a lot of time can be saved: this message has percolated through the world of political theory rather slowly. From this perspective, the growth of social choice theory in economics seems to have followed a Popperian trial and error process, not a Kuhnian scientific revolution. Kuhn's model applies better to Black's unsuccessful attempts to subvert normative *political* theory. But it does not explain (and is not designed to explain) how a body of ideas could be launched into the scientific community four times, the first three of them to sink without trace. Social choice is also subversive in that it challenges the authority of implicit or explicit ideas about the design and evaluation of choice procedures. Arrow's challenge to welfare economics was associated with a critical reconsideration of issues tied to a perceived failure of social welfare policies in Western constitutional governments. This failure created an intellectual crisis that legitimized new viewpoints such as Arrow's. Understanding the history of these problems is essential because it enables us to learn from past mistakes in developing and applying social choice theory. This skill is important if social choice is to grow as a deductive and experimental science (Popper 1959). For example, the scope of voting problems extends to areas in computer science in which analysts, unaware of voting principles, have reinvented the wheel and fallen into traps that a historical appreciation of the theory would illuminate (Michaud 1985; Monjardet 1990; Urken 1988, 1989a, 1989b, and 1991).

This leads to our fourth point. Our authors did not shy away from applications. Indeed, most of them started with applications and moved on to theory. In contrast, modern social choice theorists develop very general models and are consequently reluctant to give advice. To the nonspecialist, the obvious question thrown up by social choice is, What is the best electoral system? This is an urgent practical question all over the world, never more so than since the collapse of communism began in 1989. But whereas theoretical molecular biology has started to play a large role in curing bodily disease, theoretical social choice has played almost no role in curing constitutional disease. Social choice theorists have usually regarded "the earnest efforts of electoral reformers . . . with the same kind of amused contempt as mathematicians in the past reserved for claims by amateurs to have succeeded in squaring the circle" (Barry 1986, 1). Barry continues:

> A few years ago, at a conference on the theory of democracy, a group of five eminent social choice theorists were trying to decide which of several restaurants to dine at. Since each knew the preferences of the others and could immediately compute the outcome to be expected from any proposed procedure, it was impossible to find any agreement on a method of voting. (The impasse was in the end resolved by one of their number setting off in the direction of the restaurant he favored; after he had gone about thirty yards the others fell in behind). (1986, 1–2)

Since 1989, Czechoslovakia, Hungary, Poland, and the three ex-Soviet Baltic republics have all written new voting laws (for a good review of the first three, see Lijphart 1992). Other new democracies, including those in the former Soviet Union, will shortly have to do the same. Even at the peak of the Enlightenment, only three countries (the United States in 1787; France in 1789, 1791, and 1793; and Poland in 1791) wrote constitutions containing voting laws. In two years we have had at least six; but as far as we know, not one of them consulted any social choice theorists. (In 1990 members of the Mongolian legislature asked the president of the Public Choice Society for advice on a new constitution; but we have reason to suspect that the advice he gave them may have been along the lines lampooned by Barry.) It adds up to a lamentable failure of social science. Too much research in social choice has been conducted in the spirit of the pure mathematician's prayer: "May it never be of any use to anybody!" Peter Ordeshook has recently stressed the

important difference between the *scientific* enterprise of uncovering fundamental forces that operate universally and the *engineering* enterprise of using the lessons of theory to model actual or proposed political-economic institutions and processes. . . . political analysis ought to consist of two enterprises. First, it ought to be concerned with uncovering basic laws and forces. For the Founders of the American Republic, these laws took the form of ideas about the permanence of faction, the necessity for a tripartite balance of forces, the inhibiting influence of a bicameral legislature, and the fact that institutions can regulate but cannot eliminate the forces of self-interest. . . . The second enterprise— political engineering—is unfortunately only weakly, if at all, represented in contemporary political theory. . . . a serious attempt to mold theory into being a practical science is far more valuable than deriving with skill that next cute theorem in the context of an otherwise silly model. (1991, 16, 19, 20).

The writers we translate were, every one of them, both scientists and engineers: they not only understood social choice but used their understanding to construct systems of voting.

Even though it has missed its most important opportunity for 200 years, social choice *is* slowly becoming more applied. For instance, social choice theorists have begun to take part in debates about electoral systems (Balinski and Young 1982; Brams and Fishburn 1983; Dummett 1984; Brams and Nagel 1991). In computer networks, voting rules have been used to develop algorithms to manage distributed data bases and to route messages (Urken 1988 and 1991). In fact, Pierre Michaud (1985), one of the champions of Condorcet's theory in France, is developing a Condorcetian approach to network management for IBM in France. And John J. Bartholdi III and colleagues are applying tests of computability both to voting procedures and to the classical impossibility theorems. Some of their findings are encouraging for electoral system designers: such as that strategic manipulation of Single Transferable Vote (STV) is logically possible but computationally infeasible. But likewise, so is Lewis Carroll's proposed voting scheme. ("We think Lewis Carroll would have appreciated the idea that a candidate's mandate might have expired before it was recognized" [Bartholdi, Tovey, and Trick 1989, 161]. The findings on STV are in Bartholdi and Orlin [1991].) As is obvious, we enthusiastically support all these developments because they indicate that historical experience in applying social choice principles continues to generate important insights and raise new questions. We offer our classical predecessors as an encouragement and an example. We turn next to putting each wave of activity into its context and to introducing our writers.

4. Precursors

4.1 Pliny

As we have already noted, there seems to have been little discussion of voting procedures in ancient Greece, among either friends or enemies of democracy. Although the Romans did not copy the Greek experiment in direct democracy, they did evolve rules on voting within committees. The opening paragraphs of chapter 2 reveal that there was a tradition of rules of procedure for the Roman Senate by A.D. 105:

> Thus men learned by example . . . the powers of the proposer, the rights of expressing an opinion, the authority of officeholders, and the privileges of ordinary members; they learned when to give way and when to stand firm, how long to speak and when to keep silence, how to distinguish between conflicting proposals and how to introduce an amendment, in short the whole of senatorial procedure.

The list of subjects is exactly like a contents table for a modern manual such as *Robert's Rules of Order* or Lord Citrine's *ABC of Chairmanship* (Citrine 1952).

Titius Aristo was indeed "an authority on private and public law, including senatorial procedure" (chap. 2), but of course Pliny is not really seeking advice from him but rather trying to justify his controversial actions in a manner under his control and without interruption. Some context on Pliny and his *Letters* is needed to make sense of chapter 2.

Pliny was born ca. A.D. 62 in Comum (modern Como, in the northern Italian lakes). As a teenager, he came to Rome and was befriended by his maternal uncle the elder Pliny, a prolific writer on natural history. The elder Pliny was killed in the eruption of Vesuvius in 79 (his death is vividly described in his nephew's *Letters*) and bequeathed him his estate. This enabled the younger Pliny to lead a successful public career as lawyer, bureaucrat, and politician in imperial Rome. His career culminated in an appointment as a special commissioner for the Emperor Trajan to investigate the province of Bithynia (the part of modern Turkey across the Bosporus from Istanbul). There he had to deal with incompetence, corruption, overspending, and Christians ("I found nothing but a degenerate sort of cult carried to extravagant lengths"). He died around A.D. 113. He collected his letters for publication himself; they reveal a shrewd if smug and self-satisfied personality.

Of the letters dealing with the Senate and its procedures (3.20; see also Radice 1969, 106–8), our chapter 2 is the most important. It is known from an inscription that has been found that Afranius Dexter was found dead on 24 June 105 by our calendar. His slaves would have immediately been executed; this is hinted in chapter 2 and was the normal Roman practice. The debate reported by Pliny was on the fate of Afranius' freedmen (that is, former slaves whom he had freed). Pliny was presiding over the Senate and strongly favored leniency for the freedmen. His was the largest single faction, but it controlled fewer than half of the votes in the Senate. Two other proposals were made: for banishment of the freedmen to an island and for their execution. Pliny used his position in the chair to insist on a ternary vote, taking all three options at once, and argues (unconvincingly, it might be thought) that the procedural rules of the Senate required voters to go to as many different sides of the room as there were options under discussion. However, the leader of the executioners matched Pliny's move by getting his faction to drop their proposal and vote for banishment. On the information given by Pliny and assuming that opinion was one-dimensional, it can be shown that banishment was the Condorcet winner among the three options (Riker 1986). Thus, the sophisticated outcome given Pliny's strategic imposition of a ternary vote was the same as the sincere outcome in conventional binary procedure. In this case, assuming one issue dimension, the conventional procedure with sincere voting would also have chosen the Condorcet winner. (Whichever of acquittal or condemnation survived into the second round would then lose to banishment, which must survive into the second round with sincere voting. The median voter was a banisher.)

The references to "the servitude of former times" and to the former humiliation of the Senate refer to the period of the Emperor Domitian (A.D. 81–96). Pliny was appointed to run the military treasury under Domitian; Radice (1969, 16) asserts that his holding office under a man he repeatedly denounces in the *Letters* shows not that Pliny was "a time-server" but only that "Someone must keep the civil administrative machine working, and it is the Plinys of all times and places who form a civil bureaucracy to carry on while governments come and go."

4.2 Lull

After Pliny, we have found no discussion of social choice for over 1,000 years, until the remarkable Ramon Lull (ca. 1232–1316). Lull was a native of Palma (Mallorca), which in his time was part of an independent kingdom incorporating the Perpignan and Montpellier areas of southern France. Together with the neighboring kingdom of Aragon on the Spanish mainland, it formed a Catalan economic empire with tentacles reaching all over the western Mediterranean, including mainland Spain, then recently under Islamic rule, and north Africa, still under Islamic rule. Lull thus lived at the frontier of Christian and Islamic civilization. He wrote copiously in Catalan, Arabic, and Latin. At the age of about thirty he became a devout Christian and devoted the rest of his life to missionary work and theology. He turned all his polymathic talents to this end, writing poetry, producing a novel (the first in any Western European language), and copious writings in mathematics and logic. In his autobiography, written in 1311, he wrote that when he was converted he had a vision that God had called him to write "a book, the best book in the world, against the errors of unbelievers" (Lull 1311, 15). This was to be the *Ars Generalis* with which Lull struggled for the rest of his life, in between courageous but doomed journeys to North Africa to convert the Moors and equally unsuccessful visits to successive popes urging them to set up language schools for missionaries. He frequently introduced mathematical arguments for the truth of Christianity into his theological works. His theory of voting appears in at least two places: the pioneer novel *Blanquerna*, written in Catalan between 1282 and 1287, and a short paper entitled *De Arte Eleccionis*, written in 1299.

The eponymous hero of *Blanquerna* is the beloved son of Evast and Alona. When he reaches the age of eighteen, he decides to become a hermit despite his mother's anguished pleas to stay with his parents. She sets her friend's daughter Natana on him in the hope of persuading him to stay; instead, he converts Natana to the ideal of renouncing her possessions as well and entering a nunnery. In due course she becomes the abbess; meanwhile, Blanquerna becomes successively a monk, an abbot, a bishop (reluctantly), and the pope, before renouncing everything again and becoming a hermit. The story gives Lull the opportunity to introduce dialogs illustrating the deadly sins and the virtues of the Christian life. It also includes homely pieces of practical advice. For instance, Alona feeds the infant Blanquerna on nothing but milk until he is a year old, because "bread sopped in milk or oil" and other common baby foods make babies ill (Peers 1926, 38).

Lull's voting procedure is slipped in with similar insouciance. The Abbess has died, and the nuns are deciding what to do.

All the sisters wanted to elect their abbess by their usual electoral method, but Natana said that she had heard of a new electoral method, which consisted in art [in other words, Lull's General Art, the method he believed could solve all mathematical, moral, and theological questions] and figures; this art follows the conditions laid out in *The Book of the Gentile and the Three Wise Men*, which follows *The Art of Finding Truth* [two of Lull's earlier works].

What Natana told the sisters, and what happened next, forms the first of the Lull extracts in chapter 3. The theory of elections recurs in later chapters of *Blanquerna*, as when Blanquerna is elected abbot "according to the manner of election whereby Natana had been elected abbess." Later still, he is proposed for a bishopric. He does not want it because it would mean giving up the contemplative life. Most of the electors nevertheless vote for him on the advice of the retiring bishop, but his enemy the archdeacon leads a faction who do not want him because he might forcibly turn them from secular to regular clergy (i.e., members of one of the monastic orders, bound by its Rule to poverty, chastity, and obedience). The archdeacon "opposed the holding of an election according to the art." One takes place "without the art," but it leads to a dispute, the majority electing Blanquerna and the minority the archdeacon. Both sides go to Rome, where the pope rules in favor of the reluctant Blanquerna. Thus people who oppose the correct art of elections come to a suitably sticky end (Lull 1285, chaps. 24, 60, and 67).

Lull visited Paris four times, trying (vainly on the first two visits) to teach the General Art to the students of the University of Paris and to anybody else who would listen. The electoral procedure in *De Arte Eleccionis* was devised, Lull tells us, at Paris on 1 July 1299. (Is it anachronistic to imagine the scholar sitting down to a serious research paper now that summer has arrived and the tiresome business of trying to teach people who do not understand is over for a few months? In his autobiography he complained that nobody understood him when he lectured in Paris because of his "Arabic way of speaking" (Bonner 1985, 1:29, 38).) *De Arte Eleccionis* begins with a long explanation of why the Church needs honest elections and then proceeds direct to a proposed method of election.

Lull's two election methods have much in common; in particular, both apply the principle of the selection of pairs of objects from a larger set, a technique that fascinated Lull. However, they are not the same. The electoral method in *Blanquerna* is a two-stage procedure. Like Condorcet and the

Federalists five centuries later, Lull seems to wish to compromise between democracy and giving a more decisive voice to better qualified electors. The election is to be made on multiple (four) criteria. It cannot be proved from the text but is at least possible that Lull realized that multiple-criterion decision making can lead to difficulties in aggregating from individual to social orderings. Third and most important, it is a method of exhaustive pairwise comparisons. The thirty-six *cambres* (compartments or cells) represent the thirty-six combinations of two candidates from nine—as it would now be written, $n(n - 1)/2$ for $n = 9$. But note that Lull does not advocate the choice of the Condorcet winner but rather states that "the candidate to be elected should be the one with the most votes in the most compartments" (chap. 3). How is this phrase to be interpreted? We believe that there are two natural interpretations, one of which makes *Blanquerna* an anticipation of Borda and the other an anticipation of Copeland.

On the first interpretation, the phrase "in the most compartments" is redundant, since each candidate will have votes in just eight compartments. These votes are simply summed, and the candidate with the highest aggregate is elected. This is, as is now well known, exactly a Borda count in which zero points are awarded for a last place, one for a second-to-last, and so on up to $n - 1$ for a top place. Borda pointed out this equivalence in his paper of 1770 (chap. 5). On this interpretation, the following passage about ties refers to ties in the Borda count:

> One of the sisters asked her, "If it turns out that some candidates have as many votes as each other in the compartments, what procedure does the art recommend?" Natana replied, "The art recommends that these two or three or more should be judged according to art alone. It should be found out which of these best meets the four aforementioned conditions, for she will be the one who is worthy to be elected."

In support of the Borda interpretation, we can note that the preliminary election of electors relies on a procedure that does not count the number of majorities but aggregates votes.

The Copeland rule has regard to the number of majorities each candidate has, not to their size, individually or in aggregate. It selects the candidate who wins the largest number of contests. If there is no cycle, the Copeland winner is the same as the Condorcet winner. If there is a top cycle, there is no Condorcet winner and a set of Copeland winners numbering three or more. Is this what Lull meant? On this interpretation, "in the most compartments" is not redundant. The whole phrase, "The candidate to be elected should be the one with the most votes in the most compartments," is then an exact instruction to select the Copeland winner, reading the first "most" as "more." On this interpretation, the passage about ties is an instruction on how to select a unique winner from the Copeland set if that contains more than one member. But note that the Copeland set cannot contain just two members unless there are ties on individual pairs arising from abstention, individual indifference, or an even number of voters, none of which Lull seems to allow since he seems to insist on an odd number of voters, each with a strong ordering.

Therefore, on either interpretation of Lull's meaning, there is some obscurity. There is no such obscurity in *De Arte Eleccionis*. The procedure Lull recommends here, unlike that described in *Blanquerna*, is a Condorcet pairwise comparison procedure. It somewhat resembles the successive voting rule used in, for instance, the Norwegian parliament (Rasch 1987). It uses matrix notation, previously thought to have been first used by Dodgson nearly six centuries later. Because the winning candidate must have beaten at least one other, it cannot select a Condorcet loser, and if a Condorcet winner exists, it will select him or her. However, it cannot detect the existence of cycles because not every comparison in the matrix is actually used in selecting the winner.

These works show that Lull does not deserve the scornful treatment he gets in modern histories of mathematics and logic. He was obsessed with comparisons of objects in pairs. The properties of the formula for the combination of two objects from a larger n, which he was probably one of the first mathematicians in the West to import from the Arab world, fascinated him endlessly and fueled the magnificent but impossible dream of the General Art. Lull believed that applying successive pairwise combinations of virtues could lead one to "demonstrating the truth of the holy Catholic faith through the use of necessary reasons to those who are ignorant of it" (Bonner 1985, 69). This is what led Donald Michie, the eminent computer scientist, to label Lull "one of the most inspired madmen who ever lived" (Gardner 1982, ix). Martin Gardner has written that Lull's life was "much more fascinating than his eccentric logic. . . . Lull's mistake . . . was to suppose that his combinatorial method had useful applications to subject matters where today we see clearly that it does not apply" (Gardner 1982, xiv, 18). However, the application to voting rules is perhaps Lull's most fruitful use of the principle of pairwise combination. Unlike others it is an entirely appropriate application of the mathematics of combinations, not repeated until 1785.

4.3 Cusanus

Lull appears to have been too far ahead of his time to have made any impact. But at least one person read *De Arte Eleccionis* and may have been the transcriber of the only known copy: Nicolaus Cusanus. Cusanus was born in 1401, the son of a boatman and vineyard owner on the river Moselle. He studied first at Heidelberg, then at Padua, where he gained his doctorate in 1423, then at Cologne. Padua was one of the leading intellectual centers of Europe, and Lull's mathematical, as well as his theological, works were on the curriculum there (Sigmund 1963, 22–35). Elsewhere in western Europe, Lull had a dangerous reputation: anybody whose ideas were as hard to follow as his ran the risk of being suspected of heresy. But the intellectual climate in northern Italy was more open than elsewhere. Cusanus was active in the conciliar movement of his time. The Council of Constance (1414–17) was convoked to try to end the Great Schism in the papacy that had lasted since 1378; it succeeded in ousting all three of the current contenders for the title of pope and electing one of its choice. Its voting procedures were contentious and included a weighted voting scheme (voting by nations) to ensure that the Italian electors did not carry the day by sheer force of numbers. (Most council members were bishops, and Italy had the largest number of bishoprics.) Thus questions of voting procedure were part of the political agenda of the day.

Cusanus's main work of political theory, *De concordantia catholica*, was written while he was attending the Council of Basel, which opened in 1431; Cusanus was an active member from 1432 to 1434. The Council aggressively asserted its superiority to the pope (Sigmund 1991, xiv). *De concordantia catholica* accordingly defends the rights of councils to elect popes, and it discusses voting procedures in chapters 36 to 38 of Book III. These chapters deal with the election of a Holy Roman Emperor rather than a pope: they were added to the earlier discussions in late 1433, when the emperor was actually in Basel (Sigmund 1991, xvii). Cusanus first discusses the need to prevent "*practicas absurdissimas et inhonestissimas*" (the most absurd and dishonest practices) and notes that because particular electors come from particular "towns and camps of the empire," "*turpiter foedatae electiones per iniustas pactiones fieri dicuntur*" (elections are said to be disgracefully rigged by means of unjust pacts). He then describes his procedure in chapter 37 (chap. 4 in this book).

Cusanus's scheme is just the Borda count, giving 1 for a last place and so on up to n for a top place. It should be regarded as independent of Lull's proposal of (what may have been) the Borda count, because although Cusanus knew of the existence of *Blanquerna*, he had probably not read it. A mention of it exists in a handlist of Lull's work in Cusanus's library (Honecker 1937b, 570–71), but the work itself does not, and the library is believed to have survived complete. The only known copy of *De Arte Eleccionis* comes from this library, transcribed in what is believed to be Cusanus's handwriting. Thus the scheme of Lull's that Cusanus certainly knew was a Condorcet scheme of public voting, and Cusanus proposed instead a Borda scheme with secret voting (despite the statement in Sigmund 1991, 304n.1). Was this simply because he failed to understand the merits of Lull's scheme (cf. Kallen 1964,

448 fn. to chap. 37)? We think not. Cusanus's own words quoted above, together with the high intellectual regard for Lull reflected by his collecting, and probably transcribing, *De Arte Eleccionis*, suggest that he considered Lull's scheme and rejected it. Neither writer gives an explicit mathematical or logical justification for his scheme: such justifications had to await Condorcet and Borda. But there are arguments in favor of both the Condorcet and the Borda principles, and the debate between them is open to this day. We infer that Cusanus rejected Lull's scheme on principle and not out of misunderstanding.

This conclusion derives in part from the phrase that we have translated as, "For this method takes account of all comparisons of candidate to candidate— in whatever groupings or combinations—that any elector can make," toward the end of chapter 4, in Cusanus's paragraph 540. The Latin runs, *"quoniam omnes comparationes omnium personarum et omnes mixturae et syllogismi per unumquemque ex electoribus factibiles in hoc modo includuntur."* The use of *syllogismi* in this sense is highly unusual. But note that a syllogism involves at least three elements (major premise, minor premise, and conclusion). In using the word, Cusanus may have had in mind that a voter's transitive ordering of three elements (I prefer *A* to *B* and *B* to *C*; therefore I prefer *A* to *C*) is fully captured by the Borda count but not necessarily by other schemes, including that of *De Arte Eleccionis*. The theory of voting involves pairwise comparisons, as Lull had seen. But it does not only involve pairwise comparisons.

The issue between secret and open voting is also still open. Both writers wish to eliminate strategic voting, but they make opposite recommendations. That is because they are discussing different situations. Lull is concerned with the members of a cathedral or abbey chapter voting to select their own leader. In this case, the electors are all known to each other and must continue to live together after the vote. Thus it is reasonable to demand open voting: a voter will then be constrained by his fellow voters' knowledge of his preferences. In general, this is the argument for open voting in committees where the members must trust one another if business is to be done. It is an argument traditionally accepted in the direct democracy, with open voting, of some Swiss cantons (Barber 1985). Cusanus is concerned with a body of electors meeting once only and suspicious of one another's strategic voting intentions before the election starts. He had firsthand experience of this at the Council of Basel, and it was a well-remarked feature of the conciliar movement. In this case, increasing the amount of information about others' votes available to each voter *increases* the opportunities and incentives for strategic voting of a logrolling kind. It was presumably in part to prevent this that the Council of Constance had voted by nations.

In the following chapter of *De concordantia catholica*, Cusanus goes on to show that his method may also be applied to votes on propositions when more than two possibilities exist and contrasts it with the simple binary procedure in use in Venice for yes or no propositions and for elections (par. 580; Sigmund 1991, 307). The Venetian procedure for electing a doge, fully specified by 1268 and in use until the Venetian republic was suppressed by Napoleon in 1797, has been recently analyzed (Lines 1986). It has always been regarded as famously, magnificently, or ridiculously complicated. Lines, however, shows that the complications apply only to the first phase of the election. A total of eight iterations by lot or election were needed to derive the final body of forty-one electors of a doge from the initial assembly of 1,500 or so members of the Great Council. Thus "a great deal of the tedious complication . . . served only to ensure the impossibility of forecasting just who would be in the Quarantuno [the forty-one electors]" (Lines 1986, 156). Lines describes the actual election stage as approval voting with a lower bound. The electors voted on each of the ten candidates separately and could vote in favor of or against as many as they chose; the winner would be the candidate with the most favorable votes, as long as he got more than twenty-five. (Because of the option of casting negative votes, the Venetian scheme was not identical to approval voting, for which see Brams and Fishburn 1983, but it was kindred in spirit.)

Thus we find three of the main solution concepts of modern voting theory—the Borda rule, the Condorcet principle, and approval voting—in use in medieval Europe. We should not be surprised to find intelligent discussion of voting schemes first appearing in the West in the Middle Ages. As already noted, the ancient Greeks thought deeply about democracy but much less about elections; the Romans thought about parliamentary procedure, but nobody followed up Pliny's insights. By contrast, elaborate electoral schemes were required to elect popes, doges, and Holy Roman emperors. The experience of the Great Schism in the papacy between 1378 and 1417, when there were two and at one point three claimants to the papacy, showed that elections could not be restricted to two candidates. All orders of monks, nuns, and friars had to make their own rules for electing their superiors; since they were entirely separate from the ordinary parish clergy, there was no hierarchy except their own to choose their leaders. This is the situation addressed by Lull. Among the most elaborate of these electoral rules are those of the Dominican Order (Galbraith 1925, especially 5, 33, 46, 64, 103, 114, 226–36), but a cursory inspection of them suggests that they do not go as far as Lull into the case of more than two candidates for a post. Many other Italian city-states also had elaborate electoral rules (Murray 1978; Ruffini Avondo 1927).

Much remains tantalizingly unknown. Lull was deeply learned in Arab thought, and he no doubt got some of his mathematical ideas from this source. One Arabic writer he is known to have read was the logician al-Ghazzali

(Bonner 1985, 20). Should we look to the Arab world for the origins of social choice as well as of algebra?

5. The Golden Age

5.1 Introduction

After Cusanus, social choice returned to its slumbers. We have found no sensitivity to it in the classical political writers of the sixteenth and seventeenth centuries. Its reemergence in the late eighteenth century can be ascribed to three factors: politics, the organization of science, and the growth of classical probability.

Politics is the most obvious but the last in time of these factors. Once the French, Polish, and American revolutions were under way, there was an urgent need to think through detailed provisions for majority rule and their implications. But this spur to thought did not occur until social choice was already formulated. Condorcet did not become a democrat until 1791, when the French Revolution was well under way (Badinter and Badinter 1988, chap. 7). In a more general way, it is true that social choice was a product of the Enlightenment, which was marked by questioning of all forms of tradition and intellectual authority. But the reasons it arose in France in the 1780s are more specific.

By the late eighteenth century, the French model for the organization of science was widely admired and widely copied. The Paris Academy of Sciences had been founded in 1666 and its rules codified in 1699 (Hahn 1971; Baker 1975, 1–2; McClellan 1986); it was the undisputed world leader in science and mathematics. Academies organized in imitation of it had been founded in a number of other capitals, often by reforming monarchs like those found in St. Petersburg and Berlin. At least one of its imitators (the American Philosophical Society, founded by Benjamin Franklin in Philadelphia in 1743) was a private foundation. The academies formed an intellectual network around which the leading ideas, papers, and people passed freely: leading thinkers could move around in a human capital market at least as open as the modern tenure system. (For instance, the reason that the St. Petersburg Paradox in decision theory is so called is that Nicholas Bernoulli, who propounded it, and his cousin Daniel, who first resolved it in 1738, had been b(r)ought by Peter the Great to add lustre to the new academy in the new Westernized capital of Russia.) The one scientific academy to stand apart from the French model, the Royal Society in London, was scorned by Condorcet and his contemporaries as no better than a gentlemen's club.

This organization had two consequences: that the internal politics of electing members was intense, and that whoever controlled the intellectual agenda of the Paris Academy was the most influential director of research in the Western world. In the royal academies, the king, or the executive, typically wanted to elect people who would be useful or to repay favors to courtiers—generally, to use academy membership as a political bargaining chip—while the scientific members of the academies wished to be free as far as possible to elect their own peers. Borda, to judge by his career and the records of his service that survive, was in the first camp. Condorcet, who saw the application of scientific ideas as a positive force for restructuring French institutions, was emphatically in the second (Baker 1975, chap. 1).

Condorcet became assistant secretary of the Academy in 1773, largely through the adroit manipulation of ministers by Condorcet's patron, d'Alembert (Baker 1975, 39–40), and succeeded as perpetual (permanent) secretary in 1776. He held that post until he was driven from power in 1793. As perpetual secretary, Condorcet was forceful and interventionist. As a pure mathematician, he was at home with colleagues such as Lagrange, de Laplace, and Euler and had little sympathy for experimental scientists such as de Buffon and (as we shall shortly see) Borda. As secretary, he had a number of platforms from which to advance his view that the growth of classical probability was the central development in mathematics and science and that natural and social science should be developed as a set of applications of probability. In particular, he controlled the Academy's proceedings (*Histoire et mémoires de l'Académie Royale des Sciences*. These were published, in Condorcet's day, as annual volumes three years in arrears. The *Histoire* (*HARS*) was a review of the year's most important papers, written by Condorcet himself, while the *Mémoires* (*MARS*) were the actual papers. This model for the organization of a scientific journal is followed to this day by journals as diverse as *Nature*, the *British Medical Journal*, and the *Economist*).

5.2 Borda

Borda's paper proposing the rank-order count—now always called the Borda method although perhaps it should be called the Cusanus method—was delivered orally to the Academy in 1770. The occasion was one of the Academy's periodic bouts of introspection and infighting over election procedures, reflecting the tension between the Academy's wish to be a self-governing and self-reproducing intellectual elite and the wish of the king or the government to advance their nominees. The Academy commissioned, as was its normal practice, a report on Borda's paper, but none appears to have been made. Shortly afterward, on 30 June 1770, an election took place "*selon la forme ordinaire*",[1] a formula that suggests that if Borda's method was considered, it was rejected.

Borda was, in Condorcet's contemptuous description, "what they call 'a good Academician,' because he talks in Academy meetings and likes nothing better than to waste his time drawing up prospectuses, examining machines, etc., and especially because, realizing he was eclipsed by other mathematicians, he abandoned mathematics for petty experiments (*la physicaille*). . . . Some of his papers display some talent, although nothing follows from them and nobody has ever spoken of them or ever will" (letter to Turgot 1775, in Henry 1883, 214–15; our translation). This description reflects the contempt of the theoretical mathematician for the practical engineer, sharpened by a fight on whether 12,000 livres that the king owed the Academy should be spent on Condorcet's salary or on the support of experimental research (Baker 1975, 42). In 1767 Borda had conducted experiments on fluid resistance and had found that the formulas of Newton, Euler, and Johan Bernoulli all failed to match the results he obtained, so he derived a formula from his results: not a procedure calculated to impress Condorcet.

Born in Dax, in southwestern France, in 1733, Borda entered the Academy in 1756 and progressed up its grades to become a *pensionnaire* in the mathematics section in 1775. His work on ballistics drew him to the attention of Louis XV, who chose him to improve the scientific competence of the Navy. This took him away from Paris for long periods, including a period of service as a naval captain in the West Indies during the American War of Independence. He was captured by the English in 1782 and returned to France on parole, where he returned to his measurements: he "worked much and published little" (obituary notice in Borda papers, Archives Nationales). In 1784 he was appointed principal of the royal School for [military] Engineers: a letter to the king urging his appointment describes him as "a mathematician who is both profound in theory and well versed in naval construction, who has learnt to apply scientific practice at sea." He kept his head down during the revolution, which, unlike Condorcet, he survived: an obituarist suggests that he tried unsuccessfully to save Condorcet's life during the Terror of 1793–94 but succeeded only in antagonizing the ruling Jacobins, who suppressed some of his work in return. The personnel records of his service in the navy include a letter from him expressing his "entire devotion to my country and my King" in March 1792, followed quickly by a series of payslips from the "French Republic, one and indivisible" from September 1792 on. At the

---

1. This and (unless otherwise noted) all other references to the *procès-verbaux* of the Academy are due to Pierre Crépel, from a presentation made to the REHSEIS Seminar, Paris, March 1992.

height of the Terror he was dismissed, but in April 1795 he was reinstated as principal and his arrears of salary paid. He died still in office, in 1799.[2]

Borda thus probably played little or no role in having his 1770 paper published. Condorcet mentions it in the *Essai* of 1785, stating that he had heard of it orally but that it was not published until after the *Essai* was in press (Discours préliminaire, clxxix). This is misleading because it fails to reveal that it was Condorcet himself who published it. Condorcet had started thinking about applying probability theory to the evaluation of evidence in 1782 when, as secretary to the Academy of Sciences, he had to write the scientific obituary of Daniel Bernoulli (partly translated in Sommerlad and McLean 1989). This drew him to read and criticize Bernoulli's work on social applications of probability and seems to have been the seed from which the vast *Essai* arose within three years. On 14 July 1784, Condorcet presented the *Essai* to the Academy, which appointed a committee that reported favorably on it on 17 July (The *Essai* is 495 pages long!). On 21 July, a paper by Borda "on the probability of elections [*sic*]" was read to the Academy. It is not known whether this was the same as his paper of 1770. However, Condorcet immediately added Borda's paper to *MARS* for 1781, which he was then seeing through the press, with a commentary by himself in *HARS*. These two works form our chapter 5. (The commentary in *HARS* is unsigned, but the production of these editorials was part of Condorcet's job; part of the manuscript of this one, in Condorcet's hand, survives in the Condorcet manuscripts in the Institut de France.)

Condorcet's maneuver gave the impression, intentionally or not, that Borda's paper was written in 1781, which has misled some modern writers. It implies that Condorcet immediately recognized Borda's method as an important challenge to his own. He comments that Borda's "observations on the drawbacks of the election method used almost everywhere [viz., plurality rule] are very important and totally original" but does not comment on the merits of the Borda method. In the *Essai*, he limits himself to showing that the Borda method does not always choose the Condorcet winner; this follows immediately on a passage that Black (1958, 177–78; cf. Condorcet [1785] 1972, clxxvii—clxxix, 295–96) found impenetrably obscure. He makes an axiomatic argument that is not elaborated against Borda voting. We shall argue below that the obscurity is penetrable and the passages were probably linked in Condorcet's mind. By 1788 he was to articulate the differences between his method and Borda's much more clearly.

The main arguments of Borda's paper and of the sections on social choice of Condorcet's *Essai* have been fairly familiar since the 1950s (de

---

2. The facts on Borda in this paragraph are from various sources collected in his *dossier individuel*, Archives de l'Académie des Sciences, Paris, and his *dossier*, Archives Nationales, Paris, call number Marine C/7/37.

Grazia 1953; Black 1958); we therefore summarize quickly, pausing on the more recently cleared ground. Borda opens by showing that the plurality winner of a three-candidate election may well be the absolute majority loser; this is implicitly to appeal to the Condorcet criterion that the winner in exhaustive pairwise comparisons ought to be chosen. He goes on to propose the general rank-order count in which each voter awards a points for a last place and b (> 0) for each interval above the last place. Ranks are summed, and the resulting vector of collective rankings provides a social ordering and a social choice. Borda uses an argument of equiprobability (or insufficient reason) to insist that b must be the same for each interval and for each voter, referring to the "supposed equality between the voters" (i.e., anonymity, in May's [1952] terminology). He goes on to show that an exhaustive pairwise comparison of the candidates, with the scores for each candidate against the others being aggregated, is identical to a Borda count with $a = 0$ and $b = 1$. Borda finishes by establishing the necessary and sufficient condition to guarantee that the majority winner of a multicandidate election is actually the Borda winner. For an m-candidate election with E voters, the threshold y that guarantees that the majority winner is the Borda winner is

$$y > E \left(\frac{m-1}{m} \right)$$

If the number of candidates equals or exceeds the number of electors ($m \geq E$), this reduces to $y > E - 1$. In other words, only a unanimity rule will guarantee that the majority winner is the Borda winner in elections in which every voter is also a candidate. This was to cast an unexpected light on the notorious unanimity rule, the *liberum veto*, of the Polish Diet ("this surprising result justifies the way in which one of the Northern nations elects its kings"). Borda's reasoning was later to be paralleled independently by Morales (chap. 10) and criticized by Daunou (chap. 11) and Nanson (chap. 14). Liberals, including the Poles who wrote their short-lived constitution of 1791, regarded the *liberum veto* as a disastrous institution. Every nobleman was a potential candidate as well as an elector to the monarchy; each could therefore veto any choice unless satisfied. It followed that elections were long-drawn-out and that kings were weak. Therefore, rather than justifying Borda's method, Daunou argues that Borda ought to have rejected a method with such a dangerous consequence.

5.3 Condorcet's *Essai* of 1785

The main theme of Condorcet's *Essai* of 1785 is as given by its title: it concerns the probability that a plurality of the independent observations of a number of imperfectly accurate observers are correct. Condorcet's basic jury theorem establishes that if h observers are in the majority and k are in the minority, the probability Π that the majority decision is correct is given by

$$\Pi = \frac{v^{h-k}}{v^{h-k} + e^{h-k}}$$

where v (for *vérité*, assumed > 0.5) is the probability that a juror is correct on any one judgment and e (*erreur* $= 1 - v$) the probability that he or she is mistaken. This function is increasing in both v and $h - k$.

We agree with Grofman and Feld (1988) that the jury theorem may be read as an axiomatization of Rousseau's General Will. There are few explicit references to Rousseau in Condorcet's work,[3] but the Rousseauvian phrase *volonté générale* and synonyms occur quite often in Condorcet. In 1785 Condorcet was not yet a democrat: in a letter accompanying a copy of the *Essai* presented to Frederick the Great of Prussia, Condorcet wrote:

> [T]he procedures for taking decisions cannot themselves guarantee the fulfilment of the necessary conditions, unless decisions are taken by very enlightened men. Hence we must conclude that the happiness of the people depends more on the enlightenment of their rulers than on the form of their political constitution. (Sommerlad and McLean 1991, 24)

No doubt we should expect a letter to an enlightened despot to praise enlightened despotism, but this and other evidence suggests that until ca. 1791 Condorcet was more concerned to increase the trustworthiness of decisions by increasing v than by setting a threshold for $h - k$. However, the two are complementary. The first drove Condorcet's work as an educational reformer (he was one of the originators of the French system of national education); the second drove his work on the design of constitutions.

5.4. Condorcet's Choice and Ordering Rules

Black (1958, especially 163) complained, "in the case of elections . . . the phrase 'the probability of the correctness of a voter's opinion' seems to be without definite meaning." Black continues (1958, 163–64): "[Condorcet's] real theory is a system of formal reasoning that is quite independent of the theory of probability. . . . where he does introduce the theory of probability, he explicitly rejects its findings in favor of what he calls 'straightforward

---

3. But an interesting early one is in a letter to Turgot on 8 April 1770: "A state is lost, according to Rousseau, as soon as anyone believes that it is clever to be dispensed from obeying the laws" (Henry 1883, 8).

reasoning'." Black's first point is certainly correct; the second underestimates the extent to which probability and social choice remained entwined in Condorcet's mind: one cannot say that the social choice arguments are Condorcet's "real theory." Three writers (Michaud 1985; Young 1988; Monjardet 1990) have recently reconstructed Condorcet's intended general procedure for deriving a social ordering from a set of individual orderings. The procedure is obscurely stated in the *Essai* (Condorcet [1785] 1972, 119–26), and Condorcet's verbal and symbolic presentations do not match. The following paragraphs attempt to reconstruct Condorcet's argument.

Condorcet discovered a problem when he attempted to apply his model to cases with more than two alternatives. Condorcet requires each voter to rank the options. From the rank-ordering, each voter's preferences over each pair of candidates can be inferred. The majority for each individual proposition of the form "*A* is better than *B*," or simply "*A* > *B*," is calculated. With the size of the majority $h - k$ known for each proposition in the system of propositions—also called an opinion—the probability of the overall system is the product of the probabilities of each component proposition. One of Condorcet's own examples shows why this confronts him with a serious problem.

There are three candidates, *A*, *B*, and *C*, and the electors have ranked them as follows, where the number at the head of each column is the number of electors who have voted for that system or opinion:

13	10	13	6	18
A	A	B	B	C
C	B	C	A	B
B	C	A	C	A

C is the Condorcet winner, beating *A* and *B* by a margin of thirty-one to twenty-nine in each case. "The system with plurality support" is *CBA*, which "embodies a vote in favor of *C*." *B* beats *A* by thirty-seven to twenty-three, and loses to *C* by twenty-nine votes to thirty-one. *But Condorcet's probabilistic formula does not necessarily choose* C. The probability that *C* is the best is the joint probability that "*C* is better than *B*" and "*C* is better than *A*" are true. From the formula

$$\prod = \frac{v^{h-k}}{v^{h-k} + e^{h-k}}$$

we derive

$$\prod(C) = \frac{v^2}{v^2 + e^2} \cdot \frac{v^2}{v^2 + e^2} = \frac{v^4}{v^4 + 2v^2e^2 + e^4} \tag{1}$$

for the probability that C is the best. The probability that B is the best is the joint probability that "B is better than C " and "B is better than A" are true. This is given by

$$\prod(B) = \frac{v^{14}}{v^{14} + e^{14}} \cdot \frac{e^2}{v^2 + e^2} = \frac{v^{14}e^2}{v^{16} + v^{14}e^2 + v^2e^{14} + e^{16}} \qquad (2)$$

However, for values of v not much greater than 0.5, (2) is greater than (1). Quite generally, as was shown first by Black (1958, 169–71) and more fully by Young (1988, 1238), when v is close to 0.5, the most probable candidate is the one who scores the largest total number of votes: in Condorcet's example, B, who scored $29 + 37 = 66$ votes, as against C's $31 + 31 = 62$. But this is precisely the winner of the Borda count, in Borda's second interpretation, where a candidate's score represents the number of times he beats other candidates. When v is close to 1, the most probable candidate is the one who wins his closest fight with the largest number of votes—in other words, the Condorcet winner, if one exists.[4]

At this point Condorcet's argument takes a sharp turn. He points out that "Candidate A clearly does not have the preference," because he is a Condorcet loser. Therefore the choice is only between B and C; as C beats B, it would be perverse to choose B: "it seems that the results dictated by the calculus of probabilities contradict simple reason . . . . As soon as A is excluded, it is natural to prefer C to B" (Condorcet [1785] 1972, lxv).

This is a momentous move. The case for excluding A is that he should be regarded as irrelevant to the comparison between B and C. So Condorcet's move already implied a principle of Independence of Irrelevant Alternatives, although he was not to put this clearly until 1788. Faced with a contradiction between the calculus of probabilities and simple reason, he chose the latter, even though at the outset (Condorcet [1785] 1972, ii) he had declared that "almost everywhere we shall find that our [probabilistic] results correspond to the dictates of the simplest reasoning." Young (1988, 1238) suggests that Condorcet "apparently realized" that his argument pointed to the Borda, not the Condorcet, rule for low v, and that his abrupt shift arises from his con-tempt for Borda.

If Condorcet had not made this shift, he would have been unable to deal with the discovery for which he is best known, that of cycles. Whenever there

---

4. Readers might be puzzled that Black, Young, and we ourselves, expounding the identical passages in Condorcet, each give different values in the equations. The reason is that Black, who uses the same formula as we do, takes the numbers from the equivalent passage in the main *Essai*, where they differ from those in the *Discours préliminaire*, while Young, who uses the same source as we do, uses a different, though algebraically equivalent, version of Condorcet's formula.

are more than two candidates or options, in Condorcet's language a *system* or *opinion* is made up from each of the pairwise *propositions* it contains. For three candidates, there are thus $2^3 = 8$ *systems*, disregarding ties. But there are only $3! = 6$ strong orderings of three candidates. Hence two of the eight possible systems are contradictory. In general, for n candidates, there are $2^{n(n-1)/2}$ systems, of which only $n!$ are noncontradictory. What are we to do if voting reveals a cycle? Condorcet deals first with the three-candidate case:

> Now, imagine that the three propositions with plurality support form one of the two contradictory systems: if there is no need to elect someone immediately, then we should consider that no decision has been reached. If, however, an immediate decision is necessary, then we must take the results of the two most probable propositions. (Condorcet [1785] 1972, lxvii)

"The results of the two most probable propositions" is an innocent-looking formula that has caused endless trouble. Condorcet does not mean "choose the candidate whose propositions have the highest combined probability," because that would take him straight back to Borda. Rather, he recommends excluding the candidate with the smallest plurality. While this gives a direct and intuitive resolution of three-candidate cycles, it does neither in the general case. His general ordering rule is given as follows (Condorcet ([1785] 1972, 126):

> If, once each voter has given his opinion by indicating the order of merit he attributes to the candidates, we then compare them two by two, for each opinion we shall have $n(n-1)/2$ pairwise comparisons to consider separately. Taking the number of times that each is contained in the opinion of one of the q voters, we shall obtain the number of votes for each proposition.
>
> We shall form an opinion out of the $n(n-1)/2$ winning propositions. If this opinion is one of the $n \cdot n - 1 \ldots 2$ possible ones, then we shall consider the candidate to whom this opinion gives the preference to be elected. If this opinion is one of the $2^{n(n-1)/2} - n \cdot n - 1 \ldots 2$ impossible opinions, then we shall successively exclude from it the propositions with the lowest plurality, and adopt the opinion formed by those that remain.

Young (1988) shows that this can be made coherent by deleting from "then we shall successively . . . " to the end, and substituting "then we shall successively reverse in it the set of propositions with the lowest combined plurality, and adopt the opinion formed by those that remain." This is Condorcet's ordering rule, which selects from the allowable strong orderings the maximum likelihood ordering, given a set of paired comparisons that contains at least one cycle. It has been rediscovered many times since (see Michaud 1985 and especially Monjardet 1990) as a method of deriving the median ordering from a set of individual orderings.

Condorcet's *ordering* rule is thus securely reestablished. However, note two problems:

1. If the ordering is to be interpreted in its original "jury-theoretic" way as "the one with the maximum likelihood of being correct," that likelihood will typically be low if only because the average likelihood of any strong ordering of n objects can only be $1/n$! This problem does not arise if the Condorcet ordering is simply interpreted as the median ordering.

2. However, the Condorcet ordering rule is in the class of problems known to mathematicians as NP-complete. This means that any given instance of the problem may take an arbitrarily long time to solve, however much computational power is brought to bear on it. Bartholdi et al. (1989, 161) say of Lewis Carroll's rule, in words equally applicable to Condorcet's, "We think Lewis Carroll would have appreciated the idea that a candidate's mandate might have expired before it was ever recognized."

Where does this leave Condorcet's *choice* rule? Still ambiguous, because the choice rule consistent with the ordering rule ("Select the candidate with the maximum likelihood of being the correct one") is not the same as the choice rule embodying the Condorcet criterion ("Select the Condorcet winner if there is one"). Condorcet never resolved the tension between probability and social choice in his writings on elections during the last nine years of his life.

5.5 Condorcet and an Independence Axiom

In both the *Discours préliminaire* of the 1785 *Essai* and the body of the *Essai* itself, Condorcet's demonstration that the Borda rule is not Condorcet-efficient follows an extremely obscure passage in which Condorcet argues that, given that a voter has expressed the preferences (in Condorcet's notation) $A > B$, $B > C$, and $A > C$, there is no reason to argue that $A > C$ is "more probable" than the other two opinions (see Condorcet [1785] 1972, clxxv—clxxvii; 294–95; Black 1958, 177–78). We believe that in these passages, which differ between themselves, Condorcet is groping toward an axiom of Independence of Irrelevant Alternatives, which he connected (although not yet explicitly) with his succeeding criticism of the Borda rule. In the appendix to his *Essay on the Constitution and Functions of Provincial Assemblies* (chap. 7), Condorcet makes the connection explicit.

This essay is a product of Condorcet's association with the reforming minister Turgot, whose aide he had been in 1775. The idea of a set of provincial assemblies throughout France, with roughly equal populations and with equal powers in place of the chaos of overlapping jurisdictions that was characteristic of the *ancien régime*, was due to Turgot, and Condorcet backed it enthusiastically when Louis XVI announced his intention of introducing provincial assemblies in 1788. Condorcet's essay, an enormously long and detailed constitutional scheme, was the result. However, before it was even published, Louis XVI abandoned the idea of provincial assemblies and decided to call the Estates-General for 1789 instead (for more detail, see Doyle 1989; Schama 1989; McLean and Hewitt forthcoming). Therefore Condorcet's *Essay on the Constitution . . .* was ignored and not noticed by social choice theorists until recently. But it is vital to understanding the evolution of Condorcet's thought.

He begins the section on Independence by repeating from 1785 his example of a case in which the Condorcet winner is not the Borda winner and his demonstration that any ranking method must select B (Paul) unless it awarded a higher score for a second place than for a first (table 1.1).

TABLE 1.1. Divergence of the Condorcet and Borda Winners: Condorcet's Example (1785, 1788)

Number of voters	30	1	29	10	10	1
Favorite	A	A	B	B	C	C
Middle	B	C	A	C	A	B
Least-liked	C	B	C	A	B	A

A = Peter, B = Paul, C = James

Pairwise comparisons:

$A > B$ (41/40)
$A > C$ (60/21)
$B > C$ (69/12)

Borda count ($a = 1$, $b = 1$)

$A = 182$
$B = 190$
$C = 114$

The new argument in 1788 runs thus:

But how is it that Paul is not the clear winner when the only difference between himself and Peter is that Peter got thirty-one first places and thirty-nine second, while Paul got thirty-nine first and thirty-one second? Well, out of the thirty-nine voters who put Peter second, ten preferred him to Paul, whereas only one of the thirty-one voters who put Paul second preferred him to Peter. The points method confuses votes comparing Peter and Paul with those comparing either Peter or Paul to James and uses them to judge the relative merits of Peter and Paul. As long as it relies on irrelevant factors to form its judgments, it is bound to lead to error, and that is the real reason why this method is defective for a great many voting patterns, regardless of the particular values assigned to each place. The conventional [plurality] method is flawed because it ignores elements which should be taken into account and the new one [Borda] because it takes into account elements which should be ignored.

This seems a plain statement of Arrow (or perhaps Nash) Independence, which goes to the heart of the dispute between the Condorcet and Borda principles in a way that is choice-theoretic, not probabilistic. As we have seen, when v is not much greater than 0.5, the Borda rule is more likely to select the correct winner than is a search for the Condorcet winner, because Paul's total score counts for more than Peter's precarious and unreliable majority over him. However, in the 1788 *Essay on the Constitution . . .* , Condorcet uncompromisingly judges other voting procedures by the Condorcet criterion and boldly says that the Borda method "will always [*sic*] give the wrong result" in cases like that of table 1.1.

5.6 Condorcet's Practical Proposals

Condorcet's work on social choice (1785–1794) spans the most active constitution-making era in Western history until then, and the most active ever until 1989. Constitutions for the United States, Poland, and France were written, and Condorcet was connected with all three.

The *New Haven Letters* (Condorcet 1787; McLean and Hewitt forthcoming) are Condorcet's main attempt to influence the ratification of the U.S. Constitution. He believed that bicameralism was inferior to a qualified majority rule. He shared with the American Federalists a belief that a direct democracy would not produce good (correct) decision making. In some respects his scheme resembled theirs: in particular, all his proposed constitutions for France involved the indirect election of executives, along the lines of the U.S. Constitutional provision for an Electoral College. In *The Federalist* No. 68,

Alexander Hamilton justifies the Electoral College in Condorcetian terms: Electors to the presidency are supposed to be people of superior wisdom who will therefore choose a better president than the people left to themselves would do. The people are entitled to elect electors, but not the president directly. In Condorcet's language, the electors have higher v than the people at large; therefore, they will more probably elect the correct president. (That this has not turned out the case might be because electors pledged in advance to a particular candidate emerged first in 1796 and almost no unpledged elector has ever been elected since then.)

However, Condorcet diverged sharply from the Federalists on bicameralism. "It is easy to see[5] (and this can be rigorously proved) that increasing the number of legislative bodies could never increase the probability of obtaining true decisions, and that this advantage can be obtained more simply and more certainly by requiring a fixed plurality in a single body" (near the beginning of New Haven Letter 4, McLean and Hewitt forthcoming). Here Condorcet is recommending setting a threshold level for $h - k$ such that the probability of coming to an incorrect decision is held acceptably low. However, the New Haven Letters had almost no influence in the United States; few people read them at all, and of those who did, both James Madison and John Adams reacted with hostility (Urken 1991; McLean and Urken 1992; Cappon 1959, 322).

The New Haven Letters are the only text in which Condorcet proposes that elections should actually be conducted by a direct search for Condorcet winners. The extract below explains how each district assembly should select two of its own members to serve on the higher-tier legislature. The number of candidates should first be restricted to twenty; thereafter

each elector would form a list, ranking them in order of merit. We would then examine first whether a plurality declared one of the twenty candidates superior to each of the nineteen others, in which case he would be elected, and second, whether a plurality also declared some other candidate superior to the eighteen others, in which case he would be elected.

If no candidate is pronounced by a plurality to be superior to the nineteen others, then we would try to find a candidate declared by a plurality to be better than eighteen of the others, and worse than just one, and we would elect these candidates in order, beginning with those for whom the total number of votes judging them better than one of the nineteen others was the greatest. (Condorcet 1787, as translated by McLean and Hewitt forthcoming)

---

5. A phrase that in Condorcet usually introduces something that is not in the least easy to see.

It is interesting that the second paragraph of this extract amounts to proposing the Copeland rule, with the Borda count as a tie-breaker among the Copeland winners.[6] Condorcet then goes on to propose a sampling procedure to avoid having to count the 190 pairs on each of the 3,000 ballots that would be submitted in his proposed districts. Both of these proposals disappear from Condorcet's later writings on voting: perhaps he realized that they fitted neither his probabilistic nor his choice-theoretic framework.

Condorcet took an active part in the French Revolution, tirelessly proposing voting schemes. The first of these ("On the Form of Elections"; McLean and Hewitt forthcoming), written in 1789, opens with an important distinction: "Elections which should in theory express a judgment in practice only express a will." The probabilistic ("jury") theory of voting applies only to independent observers trying to form a judgment of an unknown fact and not to the expression of preferences. Condorcet's admission here marks a step in separating his two theories, where he writes that a good choice procedure should secure "that the result of the election conforms with the will of the plurality of the voters" (McLean and Hewitt forthcoming): an aim compatible with social choice theory but not with the calculus of probabilities. He goes on to admit that a direct search for a Condorcet winner in a twenty-candidate election would be "very time-consuming," and rejects the Copeland/Borda scheme mentioned in the previous paragraph. He then details an elaborate procedure that he clearly intended to be the best approximation of a Condorcet-efficient one, although he still recommends using "the rigorous method" to begin with and his preferred method as a Condorcet-completion scheme. Since it is complex and he dropped it in later writings, we do not discuss it further here.

In 1792, Condorcet was made the chairman of a committee to draw up a constitution for France. His draft (chap. 8) envisaged that for each election to fill n places, a mechanism would ensure that the number of candidates was restricted to exactly $3n$. (He discusses the case of fewer than $3n$ nominations, but only perfunctorily.) Each voter partitions the candidates into three lists of equal size: an election column, a supplementary column, and the remainder. Votes in the election column are counted, and if at least n candidates each get a majority of the votes cast, they are elected; the top n are elected if more than n each get a majority. If the election cannot be completed in this way, votes in the supplementary column are brought in and counted equally with those in the election column; again, the top n of those who get over half of the votes are elected. If the election is completed from the votes in the election column,

---

6. Or, depending on how one interprets the slightly odd phrase "judging them better than one of the nineteen others," ordering the members of the Copeland set in descending order of votes achieved against the one candidate who beat them.

all those elected are "necessarily judged by the majority to be more worthy than the other candidates"; if it has recourse to the supplementary column, "the candidates then elected will not have such strong majority support, but they will have more support than the remaining ones." Thus the intention of this scheme was to ensure that every elected candidate was a majority winner in some sense.

With the help of the Paris crowd, the Jacobins staged a coup d'état on 1 June 1793; Condorcet was out of power. His constitution was dumped in favor of one drawn up in great haste by Robespierre, which dropped all Condorcet's voting schemes. An outraged Condorcet published a pamphlet denouncing the Jacobin Constitution, for which he was proscribed and eventually outlawed. He hid in the house of a courageous Parisian landlady in the rue des Fossoyeurs (Gravediggers' Street).[7] In the spring of 1794, the National Convention decreed that not only any outlaw but also anybody found harboring one would be summarily guillotined without trial if discovered. To save his host's life, Condorcet escaped, was refused refuge in the house of some pre-Revolutionary friends, was captured when he turned up, exhausted, in a village inn that happened to be run by a Jacobin informant,[8] and was found dead in prison two days later. By not revealing who he was, he may have saved the lives of his family and his landlady. He is the only person so far to have died for social choice.

Just before the Jacobin coup, Condorcet and some friends had founded a *Journal d'instruction sociale*, intended to keep the flag of enlightenment flying. It lasted only a month, during which it published part of Condorcet's last word on elections. Pierre Crépel (1990) has reconstructed the unpublished remainder from Condorcet's manuscripts, and the whole has been recently translated (McLean and Hewitt forthcoming). Condorcet was evidently not yet satisfied that he had found the ideal choice procedure: "I have far from exhausted the subject." He explains the existence of cycles, adding "this only occurs in situations where it is certain that the majority has been mistaken at least once" (McLean and Hewitt forthcoming). This indicates that he was swinging back toward a probabilistic view of elections and away from the social choice view found in the essay of 1788 (our chap. 7). He repeats that "there is only one way of obtaining a true decision" (viz., pairwise comparison and the Condorcet ranking procedure) and that any practical substitute must come as close to this as possible. Here the printed text breaks off. The

---

7. Now rue Servandoni, near the Eglise de St.-Sulpice. The house is marked by a plaque.

8. According to his daughter, he aroused suspicion because, when asked how many eggs he wanted in his omelette, he replied, "a dozen," revealing his unfamiliarity with the cuisine of the working class. However, there is no record that she ever met his captors, so the story cannot be verified. For all this, see Badinter and Badinter (1988).

manuscript continuation is scrappy and inconclusive (not surprisingly, since the author was hiding in fear of his life). Only one firm conclusion can be drawn from its inconsistencies, false starts, deletions, and reinstatements: that Condorcet was not satisfied that he had solved the problem of social choice. Social choice and probabilistic arguments clash violently in this, his last word on elections.

5.7. Lhuilier, Morales, and Daunou

Simon Lhuilier (1750–1840) was from a French Protestant family that had emigrated to Geneva. A mathematician in touch with the latest developments, he had worked in Poland from 1777 to 1788 and had won a prize of the Berlin Academy of Science in 1786 for an essay on the theory of infinity. In 1794 he had only just returned to Geneva after a spell teaching at Tübingen, where according to a biographer, he had gone "fearing revolutionary disturbances" at home in 1789. He was a professor of mathematics at the College of Geneva from 1795 to 1823 and was an active member of the legislative council, presumably until its suppression by Napoleon in 1798.

Lhuilier's "Examination" (chap. 9; see further Monjardet 1976) reveals that Condorcet's procedure from chapter 8 had been adopted in Geneva. Using an ingenious methodology of inferring unknown individual preference orderings from known aggregate totals of election column and supplementary column votes,[9] Lhuilier is able to show that Condorcet's procedure is not Condorcet-efficient and that it produces an arbitrary winner in the cyclical case. He also shows the nonmonotonicity, and hence the manipulability, of Condorcet's procedure. The note of triumph in Lhuilier's introduction is unmistakable:

> I have no doubt whatsoever that when he saw the certainty of the principle on which my examination is based, and the necessary link between this principle and the results I have obtained, Condorcet would have rejected his own work.

Lhuilier had convicted Condorcet of the same failing as Condorcet had Borda in chapter 7: of sometimes failing to select the Condorcet winner.

Lhuilier explains that "Advocate Devégobre, a member of the national assembly" had suggested modifying Condorcet's method by weighting sup-

---

9. The Postscript is particularly ingenious. Using the limited degrees of freedom present in Condorcet's system, Lhuilier lists exhaustively the possible permutations of individual preferences in a given vote outcome and, assuming an impartial culture (i.e., that all orderings are equiprobable), calculates probability ratios for them. This is to start down the road not taken again until the 1960s, when analysts started to compute the probability of cycles given an impartial culture.

plementary votes at half. This is of course to reinvent the Borda count. Lhuilier thought it was "very suitable for the case of three candidates, but . . . too arbitrary for elections in which a great many places are to be filled at once" because the information from strong orderings of many candidates is unreliable for candidates far down a voter's preference ordering.

The most disappointing part of Lhuilier's paper concerns his positive proposal, which ultimately relied on plurality votes if too few candidates could get an overall majority. It is inconceivable that a writer of Lhuilier's sophistication was unaware of the drawbacks of this procedure. Nevertheless, his paper overall is a remarkable contribution.

J. I. Morales was a Spanish mathematician whose eye was caught by a newspaper report that the Institut de France (the Academy of Sciences and the other academies, reconstituted after the Terror in 1795) had adopted the Borda rule for its internal elections. By his own admission unaware of any literature on the subject, Morales thought through a justification of the Borda method (chap. 10), which he sent to the Institut in 1797. His arguments are sometimes parallel to Borda's, particularly in calculating how large a qualified majority is needed to ensure that a majority winner is also a Borda winner. Near the end of chapter 10, he draws a sharp distinction between elections of people and votes on propositions, arguing that the Borda procedure was appropriate for the first but that binary procedures were appropriate for the second.

P. C. F. Daunou (1761–1840) was a historian and literary critic. His earlier scholarly work was on the great French literary figures of the seventeenth century, who frequently appear in the examples he gives. He had both political and intellectual associations with Condorcet in the early 1790s. For example, Condorcet and Daunou worked on a constitutional plan for the republic. Like Condorcet, Daunou was expelled from the National Convention after the Jacobin coup in 1793 and imprisoned for some months. However, he survived and gained prominent political offices after the fall of the Jacobins on the 10 Thermidor an III (July 1794). He was responsible for having Condorcet's *Esquisse* ("Outline for a history of the progress of the human mind"), which had been written in hiding in the rue des Fossoyeurs, published at public expense in 1795. He was also a prime mover in the renaissance of the academies as the Institut de France, and he was on the committee that drafted its constitution. This constitution instituted the Borda rule in 1796, the event that caught Morales's eye. However, the Borda rule was abandoned following what is said to have been Napoleon's only intervention in the affairs of the Institut. Napoleon became First Consul, and effectively ruler of France, by the coup d'état of 18 brumaire an VIII (9 November 1799). He was promptly made president of the Institut de France and its constituent academies. On the 6 germinal an VIII (27 March 1800), he proposed a commission to examine "whether it was appropriate to reform" the Institut's election procedure. A three-member commission including Laplace proposed the system criticized by Daunou in chapter 11 in which candidates for a vacancy in one of the academies must obtain an absolute majority of the votes and the place remain unfilled if no candidate did so. In spite of Daunou's opposition, this system did indeed supplant the Borda count in 1804. No doubt it was difficult to hold out for a rule that had been criticized by the First Consul, now the all-powerful chief executive of France. But Daunou had lost faith in the Borda system. One reason for abandoning it was its susceptibility to manipulation. The records of votes that have survived in the archives of the Academy show that voters had found how to manipulate the Borda rule: not only by putting their most dangerous rival at the bottom of their lists, but also by truncating their lists. "My election method is only for honest men," said Borda when the possibility of manipulation was pointed out.[10] In the second place, Daunou had come to see that the Borda and Condorcet principles pointed in different directions, and by 1803, although he probably was the author of the Borda scheme in the constitution of the Institut, he preferred to go with Condorcet.

Daunou's attack on the Borda count opens by showing that a voting system cannot measure the degrees of intensity of preference sincerely held by the voters. Therefore, rank orderings, as in the Borda count, cannot be held to be measures of intensity. The thrust of this is toward reasserting the Independence of Irrelevant Alternatives. Borda (and Laplace—see Black 1958, 181–82) wishes to claim that if, say, A is six places ahead of B on one ballot paper and B is one place ahead of A on another, that is some evidence that A is socially preferred to B. Condorcet, Daunou, and all those who believe that a choice system should respect Independence, deny the claim.

Daunou goes on to analyse existing and proposed procedures. He gives plurality and runoff methods very short shrift: "I do not consider it necessary to prove" their defects but discuss them "only because we constantly resort" to them. He rejects Condorcet's supplementary list scheme on the same grounds as had Lhuilier, though without reference to him. He points out that qualified-majority schemes can be minority veto schemes. He confirms that the Borda count had been "abused" in the Institute by voters' "deliberately ranking [their favorite's] most dangerous opponents last." Like Condorcet, he points out that the Borda count violates (Nash) Independence and expansion-consistency:

> But how can the intervention of another candidate alter or reverse the relationship established by the voters between . . . two candidates? . . . [as if to] say "if the choice is between just A and B, then we categorically prefer A, but if it is between A, B, and also C, then we consider that B beats not only C, but A as well."

---

10. The original source for this much-quoted remark is *Eloge de Borda* by S.-F. Lacroix, in dossier Borda, Archives de l'Académie des sciences, Paris.

Discussing Borda's proof that only a unanimity rule would guarantee that a majority winner was also the Borda winner, Daunou argues that this should have caused Borda to reevaluate a method that had such a perverse implication: "we must judge the method by the maxim, and not the maxim by the method." He continues boldly by attacking "Citizen Laplace . . . this wise teacher," who had justified the Borda count from a more explicit axiom of equiprobability than Borda's (Black 1958, 181–82). Laplace's justification produces a geometrical, not arithmetical, progression of numbers, and there can be no reason to regard this progression as a measure of the unmeasurable "true" intervals between candidates in voters' minds. The only merit Daunou now sees in the Borda count is that the Borda loser cannot be the Condorcet winner, as he demonstrates. Next, Daunou makes clear what was only reintroduced into social choice by the papers of Michaud (1985), Young (1988), and Monjardet (1990): that Condorcet's ordering procedure is one of choosing the "most probable" system, which does not lead to the same result as ranking the candidates in the order of their aggregate votes in pairwise comparisons (i.e., Borda's second method). He concludes by warning the Institute (vainly, as it turned out) against reverting to runoff majoritarian methods of election.

6. The Nineteenth Century

6.1 Social Choice Theory Lost Again

Nowhere are the breaks and discontinuities in the history of social choice more remarkable than in the nineteenth century. In the nearly seventy years between Daunou and Dodgson, we have found only one writer who approached the theory of voting in an axiomatic way. As we will explain below, we do not even know who this was, as we have only a second-hand report of the criticisms this writer made. Several distinguished writers entirely failed to understand social choice.

Why was the theoretical work of the period 1770–1803 not developed? The immediate reason is that neither politicians nor mathematicians understood it. Although Condorcet intervened in the writing of the American and French Constitutions and the Polish Constitution of 1791 was written by friends and admirers of his (for which see Marchione 1983; Libiszowska 1991), our study of the documents in all three cases has failed to reveal that anybody except Lhuilier understood Condorcet's arguments about cycles and their implications. Among mathematicians, understanding of social choice died out with Condorcet's pupil S.-F. Lacroix (1765–1843), whose grasp of social choice was never secure. Although his *Elementary Treatise on the Calculus of Probabilities* went through many editions as a standard text, nobody followed up his brief and confusing references to social choice. As to probability, the "jury theorem" was discussed by S. D. Poisson and A. A. Cournot with minimal reference to Condorcet, and the idea of even investigating the probability of a judgment was rejected as absurd by every intervening generation of mathematicians until our own. As Poisson and Cournot were mathematicians of stature, nobody went behind their work to its source in Condorcet nor troubled to understand what Condorcet was really trying to say. Condorcet's ideas did not find a place in nineteenth-century French mathematical curricula (Crépel and Gilain 1989, 16–18; Daston 1988, chap. 6, especially 342 ff.; for Lacroix, Cournot, and Poisson, see also Sommerlad and McLean 1991, part V).

The mathematician who gave most currency to Condorcet's *Essai* was not French. Isaac Todhunter (1865), a diligent writer of textbooks, analyzes Condorcet's arguments in great detail. But in the view of his biographer in the *Dictionary of Scientific Biography*, Todhunter was "not an original mathematician." In 1873 Todhunter wrote:

> If he [a schoolboy] does not believe the statements of his tutor—probably a clergyman of mature knowledge, recognized ability and blameless character—his suspicion is irrational and manifests a want of the power of appreciating evidence, a want fatal to his success in that branch of science which he is supposed to be cultivating. (Quoted from Gillispie 1981, 13:427)

He was apparently not being sarcastic. With such an attitude toward science, it is not surprising that he failed to see Condorcet's originality. While he gives a clear account of Condorcet's probabilistic reasoning, he is thoroughly impatient with Condorcet: "we believe that the work has been very little studied, for we have not observed any recognition of the repulsive peculiarities by which it is so undesirably distinguished" (Todhunter 1865, 352). He spectacularly fails to understand the sections of the *Essai* dealing with social choice. After setting out one of the examples of a cycle from our chapter 6, Todhunter says:

> Unfortunately these propositions are not consistent with each other. Condorcet treats this subject of electing out of more than two candidates at great length. . . . His results however appear of too little value to detain us longer. (Todhunter 1865, 375)

Unlike Condorcet, Dodgson, and Nanson, who used mathematical models to describe insights into voting processes in scientific or academic organizations, Todhunter was not interested in empirical aspects of modeling. His "life was mainly that of the studious recluse" (Gillispie 1981, 13:427), and there is no evidence that he took any part in college or university politics at Cambridge.

As we have seen, the development of social choice in the eighteenth century was hindered by the confusion, engendered largely by Condorcet, between the probabilistic and social choice bases of argument. Todhunter missed the social choice arguments and was scathing about the probabilistic ones, which Nanson therefore did not consider. In the nineteenth century, the development of social choice theory was limited by an equally deep confusion that arose between the majoritarian principle and the proportional principle. Proportional representation was independently developed by numerous thinkers, many of them committed and energetic but few of them capable of expressing their principles clearly and only two—G. C. Andrae, a Danish mathematician and politician, and Charles L. Dodgson—trained in axiomatic reasoning. We shall see that this confusion bedeviled discussion of social choice in both Britain and Australia. It still does.

The oldest usage of the verb *to represent* is literally to "re-present" the characters in a play through the actors or the sitter through a portrait. From this conception naturally flows the microcosm ideal of political representation, expressed at the end of the 1780s by John Adams in America and by Mirabeau in France. Adams said that the legislature "should be an exact portrait, in miniature, of the people at large, as it should think, feel, reason, and act like them" (quoted by Pitkin 1967, 60). Mirabeau said, "The Estates are to the nation as a map is to its physical extent: whether in whole or in part, the copy must always have the same proportions as the original" (quoted by Nohlen 1984; our translation). In the sixteenth and seventeenth centuries two other meanings were added: "to act for, by a deputed right" (as when a lawyer represents a client), and "to be accredited deputy or substitute for . . . in a legislative or deliberative assembly; to be a member of Parliament for" (*Oxford English Dictionary*: *represent*, senses 8 and 8b; also *representation*, senses 7 and 8). From these senses flow the principal-agent sense of representation. Each legislator represents the voters of one district: the legislator is an agent, the voters are the principals.

These two senses of *represent* are both in general use. However, not only are they not the same, they can be inconsistent. There is no reason why legislators elected by a system that somehow maps the people in Mirabeau's sense should individually regard themselves as agents, still less that they should in aggregate and, conversely, no reason why legislators who are agents of the people should be a microcosm of them. To some people, the first conception seems the only natural sense of *representation* and to others, the second one does. The first leads obviously to proportional representation (PR) and to multimember districts (since exploring PR soon reveals that Adams's and Mirabeau's ideals cannot be achieved in a system of single-member districts). The second leads to majoritarianism: an individual legislator is a true agent of the voters if and only if he or she represents the majority of them, and a legislature is representative in aggregate if it is accepted by a majority of all the electors.

Of our authors, perhaps only Nanson was at home with both sets of ideas, although all except the last sentence of "Methods of Election" deals only with majority rule. Dodgson was primarily concerned with majority rule: his scheme of PR presupposes two parties in England. Thus arguments about majority rule and arguments about PR did not so much confront one another as sidle past one another.

6.2 Proportional Representation and the Victorians

Curiously, the first rigorous discussion of proportionality was initiated not by either Mirabeau or Adams but by two of Adams's fellow founders: Thomas Jefferson and Alexander Hamilton. As already noted, they were faced with the interpretation of article I, § 2 of the U.S. Constitution, which lays down a rule for the apportionment of House seats to the states after each decennial census. Jefferson proposed a divisor system that was biased toward large states (such as Virginia). This was adopted after President Washington (from Virginia) rejected Hamilton's scheme on the advice of Edmund Randolph (Virginia) and James Madison (Virginia). The later history of apportionment in the United States is irrelevant here (see Balinski and Young 1982) except to note that in 1832 Daniel Webster (from New England, which contained no large states) proposed a modification of Jefferson's scheme that removed its bias toward large states. The Hamilton apportionment scheme is mathematically identical to what is known as the greatest-remainder scheme for PR, the Jefferson scheme to the d'Hondt system, and the Webster scheme to the unmodified Ste.-Laguë system.

However, although the problem of assigning an integer number of House seats to each state is mathematically identical to the problem of assigning an integer number of seats in a multimember district to each party, no nineteenth-century writer except Dodgson seems to have been aware of the parallel. Thomas Gilpin gave a paper to the American Philosophical Society in 1844 that proposed what amounted to a cruder version of the Jefferson divisor system for PR, but his contribution was not noticed at all until it was reprinted in 1872, and then barely until it was again reprinted in a scholarly journal in 1896 (*Proceedings of the American Philosophical Society* 4:81; James 1896). It cannot have influenced the writers we are about to discuss, including Dodgson. The origins of the English-language literature on PR lie mainly with two energetic self-taught men, Thomas Hill (1763–1851) and Thomas Hare

(1806–1891). We shall show that it took several decades for their schemes to reach a form that was practically workable and mathematically defensible; that two other forms of minority representation, the limited vote and the cumulative vote, were introduced through odd combinations of self-interest and misunderstanding; and that politicians consistently failed to understand the issue, even when their vital interests were affected. This background (for which we rely heavily on the indispensable work by Hart 1992; all facts not otherwise credited in this section are due to her) might explain both how Dodgson's and Nanson's work came to be written and how it came to be ignored.

Hill is a Socratic figure: his work comes down to us only through his disciples, including his son Rowland (the inventor of the penny post and the postage stamp). The story goes that Thomas Hill, a schoolteacher, observed that boys in a school playground formed teams by grouping their friends and followers about them and reasoned that voters might group themselves around candidates for office in a similar way. The first Hill scheme to be published was for South Australia, to whose Colonial Commissioners Rowland was secretary in 1839. The scheme provided that

> the municipal elections may be so conducted that a majority of the rate-payers may not have the power to exclude the minority from returning their due proportion of members. . . . [T]he electors shall, by voluntary classification, form themselves into as many equal electoral sections or quorums as there are members to be elected; and each of these electoral quorums shall, provided they can agree upon a unanimous vote, return one member to the Common Council. (*Third Annual Report of the Colonial Commissioners for South Australia*, 19, in Great Britain, *Parliamentary Papers*, 1839 vol. 17, pp. 708–9. This series hereafter cited as *PP*, year, vol. no., pages. Quoted in part in Hart 1992, 8.)

The Hill scheme was put into effect in Adelaide, South Australia, and thus gave rise to an Australian tradition to which we will return in discussing Nanson.

Thomas Hare was the illegitimate son of a Dorset farmer who rose by the sort of self-help often praised (but rarely achieved) in Victorian England to be an officer of the Charity Commission. His background hindered his political and social advancement (he did not become a Charity Commissioner until 1872) but not his inexhaustible campaigning. His scheme, first adumbrated in 1857, was proposed in great detail in 1859 in *The Election of Representatives* . . . (we cite the 1873 edition). Like Hill, Hare began with the root idea that where V votes have been cast and there are S seats to fill, each group is entitled to as many seats as it can obtain quotas, each of size V/S. The details of

Hare's scheme need not detain us. It treated the entire country as one constituency, was designed to enable like-minded groups of voters to combine together from anywhere in the country to make up a quota, asked voters for a strong ordering—that is, a ranked list without ties—of as many candidates as they wished to order (Hare assumed that there would be some 2,000 to 3,000 candidates for the 650 or so seats in the House of Commons), and had elaborate provisions for votes that were surplus to quota to be transferred to the next available candidate on the voter's list. Thus, like Condorcet's, Hare's scheme paid no attention to the restricted computing capacity of actual voters or election officials. It also had no satisfactory solution to the problem that, after all feasible transfers had been made, there would typically be too few valid votes remaining to give any further candidate a quota of votes. In short, it was far from a satisfactory scheme of proportional representation.

However, it immediately became the best-known scheme of PR in the English-speaking world, to the extent that "the Hare system" has become a synonym for STV in both popular and technical literature, even though a defensible form of STV is due more to Catherine Spence, Carl Andrae, and H. R. Droop (see below) than to Hare. This was due not only to Hare's own inexhaustible efforts but even more to his sponsorship by the most influential writer on democracy of the day, John Stuart Mill. In chapter 7 of his *Considerations on Representative Government,* Mill calls the Hare scheme "among the very greatest improvements yet made in the theory and practice of government" (Mill [1861] 1972, 263). Mill was briefly a Member of Parliament during the debates on the Reform Bills of 1866 and 1867. He moved an amendment to the 1867 Reform Bill incorporating the Hare scheme with one national constituency. It was not taken seriously by other speakers, and Mill withdrew the amendment without a vote. Hart (1992, 52–55) is surely right to say that Mill's "virtual intoxication with Hare's scheme" did the cause of PR more harm than good; it enabled those who had vested interests against it to write it off as impracticable and obscured the real issues from those who had no vested interest.

The first known informed criticism of Hare came from a curious source: Robert Lytton, the newly appointed secretary to the British Embassy in Copenhagen, in 1863. Having intended to write the sort of report expected of an ambassador, on Denmark's trade and tariff policies, Lytton announced that as the Rigsraad, a federal parliament, had unexpectedly voted to reduce Danish tariffs, he would write about the electoral law for the Rigsraad instead. His express purpose was to show that the Danish law, introduced by the mathematician Carl Andrae when he was Finance Minister in 1855, was very similar to the Hare scheme and demonstrably better in some respects. His underlying purpose, to judge from remarks in the report about the U.S. House of Representatives (which "has long been virtually a House of Delegates, wherein the majority of speeches made are addressed, not to the conviction of the House, but to the passions and prejudices of the constituencies who have sent its members to sit in political fetters," *PP* 1864 61, 594), may have been to show that a parliament elected from multimember districts could legislate in the public interest (that is, reduce tariffs) rather than in the district interest (that is, maintain protection). If so, his paper is a remarkable anticipation of themes in modern political economy; however, he does not make any explicit connection between the Rigsraad's electoral law and its vote on the tariff. Where Hare and Mill had argued on chiefly political grounds, Andrae had argued on chiefly mathematical ones. Andrae believed that achieving a quota (defined in the same way as by Hare) was a necessary and sufficient criterion for election. His practical procedure was simpler than Hare's and relied on classical statistics for its validity. Ballots were to be taken in random order from an urn. When a candidate had achieved a quota, further votes giving him first preference were replaced in the urn with his name deleted in favor of the next preference expressed. The electoral law contained more details than Hare's about completing the election given incomplete orderings by the voters, but it was still incomplete.

Lytton not only demonstrated that the Andrae scheme was better specified than the Hare scheme but also added two pertinent criticisms of both schemes, though he went on (wrongly) to belittle the second and more damaging one. The first was that the quota rule as specified by Hare and Andrae meant that in a single-member district, nobody could be elected except by unanimity (for $S = 1$, $V/S = V$). The second was an example constructed by an unnamed Dane in which the transfers of votes from a candidate elected with a surplus over quota could operate under Andrae's rules in such a way that the Borda (and Condorcet) winner among the remaining candidates was not selected. Lytton accepted Andrae's reply to this criticism, which was that the example depended on ballots being selected in a particular order, which was infinitesimally unlikely: he calculated the probability of the outcome as around 10^{-8}, and later revised the figure to 10^{-116} (*PP* 1864 61, 598; Andrae 1926, 72, 95–99). Neither seems to have realized that this criticism goes to the heart of STV and all other elimination-based schemes, which are non-monotonic and violate path independence (see Doron and Kronick 1977, an important part of whose argument is anticipated by the unknown Dane reported by Lytton). One of Andrae's critics, Hother Hage, proposed remedying this defect by inventing (yet again!) the Borda count (Andrae 1926, 97).

Lytton's first criticism of Hare and Andrae was met by H. R. Droop, who in papers of 1868, 1869, and 1871 proposed two amendments that make the Hare scheme workable. The first was to have districts of a manageable size, with "only a limited number of representatives a-piece, say from five to seven or nine" (Droop 1869, 476). The second was to express the quota, where V

votes have been cast in an S-member district not as V/S but as the next integer above $V/(S + 1)$. One rationalization of this is as the smallest number that ensures that not more than S candidates can be elected in the extreme case where all candidates have an equal number of first preferences. This has two consequences: by setting the quota no higher than the smallest number necessary, it reduces the problem of incomplete ballots, and it reconciles STV with simple majority rule in the single-member district. It was the Hare scheme as modified by Droop that was presented to Parliament in the next unsuccessful proposal for PR, by Walter Morrison in 1872, and has become the standard version of STV as advocated by the Proportional Representation Society (later the Electoral Reform Society) and as introduced in Ireland and Malta in 1919–1922 (Hart 1992, 70–72, 200–205).

Two other devices that achieved some proportionality, and with which Dodgson and Nanson were familiar, were the limited vote and the cumulative vote. A limited vote is any rule that features multimember districts and gives each voter fewer votes than there are seats to be filled. Between 1867 and 1885, twelve districts had three seats each, but voters had only two votes each; one (the City of London) had four seats, and voters had three votes. The limited vote is to be found today in Japan, where voters have one vote each in multimember districts. It was designed to avoid the "block vote" effect: if voters have as many, unranked, votes as there are seats to fill, and if they generally vote straight party tickets, then the party with a plurality of support will win every seat. The limited-vote idea was proposed by W. M. Praed in the debates leading to the 1832 Reform Act but not understood. It was revived by the Liberal leader Lord John Russell in a Reform Bill of 1854 but got a poor reception, even from Russell's own colleagues; however, it was written into the Oxford University Act 1854, apparently to prevent the nominees of any one college or faction gaining a majority on the new universitywide governing body it prescribed.

The appearance of the limited vote in the 1867 Reform Act owes nothing to mathematics and very little to political principle. It was inserted into the bill in the House of Lords against the wishes of Disraeli's minority Conservative government. When the bill including the limited vote clause returned to the House of Commons, Disraeli announced that the government would accept it. Disraeli's actions at the time seem to indicate that he was prepared to accept any bill that would carry a majority of the Commons and divide the opposition. The limited vote clause did the latter admirably because its most vociferous Commons support came from the conservative Liberals led by Robert Lowe who thought that widening the franchise would lead to working-class dominance and the politics of expropriation. They saw the limited vote as a bulwark against the propertyless majority's oppression of the propertied minority. The limited vote clause just survived an attempt to repeal it in 1870. In

Birmingham, the Liberal caucus found a way to defeat the intentions of the limited vote. The caucus leaders divided the city into three areas, and in each third advised their supporters to vote for a different pair of the three Liberal candidates; all three were elected. This maneuver doomed the limited vote, which, although not repealed, was in effect abolished by the elimination of all the three-member seats by the 1885 Redistribution of Seats Act.

The cumulative vote, so named by James Garth Marshall in 1853, is a rule that allows voters to give more than one of their votes to the same candidate. It was introduced by a government backbencher to a bill setting up elected school boards in 1870, in the following terms:

At every such election every voter shall be entitled to a number of votes equal to the number of the members of the school Board to be elected, and may give all the votes to one candidate, or may distribute them among the candidates as he thinks fit.

Surprisingly, the clause was accepted by Gladstone on behalf of the government and carried without a division. Hart (1992, 78) believes that the ready acceptance may have been partly due to a simple confusion by Gladstone (and presumably others) with plural voting—that is, a rule that those qualified for the franchise in more than one way (for instance as property holders or university graduates) were entitled to more than one vote. In *A Discussion of the Various Methods of Procedure in Conducting Elections*, the first of Dodgson's three social choice pamphlets of the 1870s, (see chap. 12), he quickly dismisses the cumulative vote, which he calls "The Method of Marks." Dodgson argues that as soon as it became known that one faction intended to cumulate its votes on a favorite candidate, the others would have to do the same, and the cumulative vote would thus degenerate into relative plurality rule. Droop (1869, 472) had already come to the same conclusion.

Until 1884, no party leader took the trouble to understand or analyze the arguments about PR in Britain. While happy to see it introduced in places where they perceived a need for the protection of minority rights (South Australia, Oxford University, and the Cape of Good Hope, where the cumulative vote was introduced for legislative elections in 1850), they met any arguments for PR in the United Kingdom with misunderstanding (willful or otherwise) and inconsistency. Russell, despite having proposed the limited vote in his bill of 1854, wrote in 1865 to extol "good old English notions of representation" against "contrivances altogether unknown to our habits, such as the plan of Mr Hare, though sanctioned by the high authority of so profound a thinker as Mr Mill" (quoted by Hart 1992, 48–49). It would be anachronistic to suppose that PR was a cause for liberals and constitutional reformers; Gladstone opposed it on majoritarian grounds, while John Bright for instance neither understood nor sympathized with it (Hart 1992, 22, 87). Rather, it tended to appeal to thinking conservatives alarmed by the extension of the franchise. In this respect Mill himself was a thinking conservative since, like many mid-Victorians, he was concerned that the working class would use the franchise to transfer wealth from the rich minority to the poor majority. For the same reason Robert Lowe enthusiastically backed the limited vote in 1867.

But the most substantial thinking conservative was the 3d Marquess of Salisbury, leader of the Conservatives from 1884 to 1902. In 1884, the Conservatives used their power in the House of Lords and the fluidity of the House of Commons to block the Liberal government's reform bill, which extended household franchise from borough to county constituencies, until they extracted a promise from Gladstone that the government would introduce a redistricting scheme supported by both parties. The scheme that was introduced in 1885 was the work of a two-party committee, of whom contemporary gossips alleged only Salisbury, Gladstone, and Sir Charles Dilke understood what they were doing (Jones 1972, 82, 205). It abolished the limited vote and introduced single-member districts with boundaries to be drawn in cities "according to the occupations of the people." This has been widely hailed (see, e.g., Cornford 1963) as Salisbury's masterstroke, that enabled him to convert the Tory Party from a rural to a suburban one. So it may have been, but there is some evidence (summarized by Hart 1992, 109–11) that Salisbury was drawn to proportional representation. He certainly ought to have been, given both his party interests and his arguments.

Salisbury saw two grave dangers to the Conservatives. One was the possibility of a narrow (or even negative) Liberal lead in votes translating into a substantial Liberal lead in seats; the other was Ireland. Both of these need some contextual explanation as they are vital to the circumstances in which Dodgson (a friend of Salisbury and a tutor at Salisbury's Oxford college, with which he had close links) wrote his *Principles*.

The General Election of 1880 was the closest since 1841 to a straight two-party contest in England, Scotland, and Wales (Cox 1987, especially tables 9.4 and 9.5; McLean 1992). It was therefore the best illustration for forty years of the exaggerative effect of the relative majority (first-past-the-post) electoral system. For some years since its rediscovery by Kendall and Stuart (1950), this has been known as the cube law, because in the circumstances that obtained in 1880, the ratio of seats won by the two largest parties can be expected to be the cube of the ratio of their votes. (For a more general formula giving estimates to cover a wider range of circumstances, see Taagepera and Shugart, 1989 chaps. 14 and 16). Salisbury (1884) noted this effect for 1880, saw that the Liberal lead in votes had produced an exaggerated lead in seats, and claimed that unless the 1884 extension of the franchise was accompanied by a redistribution of seats, the result could be the destruction of the Conservatives in parliament even if their share of the vote was reduced only slightly or not at all by the franchise extension. He showed that if the electorate of a seventeen-seat legislature with single-member districts was split between Catholics and Liberals in the proportion eight to nine, there were two circumstances in which the Liberals would win all seventeen seats: where the population was exactly evenly mixed and where it was completely segregated (say into a Liberal city surrounded by Catholic countryside), but constituencies were drawn in such a way (in this case, radially from the city center) that each constituency contained the same ratio of Catholics to Liberals as the population. It is no surprise that Salisbury took an active part in the 1885 redistribution conference.

Ireland was even more threatening. Since 1874 and especially since 1880, seats in Catholic Ireland had been falling to militant supporters of Home Rule, who used every procedural means open to them to disrupt Parliament. The franchise reform of 1884 proposed to extend the franchise in Ireland, as in the rest of the country, to rural householders. Would this not mean a great boost to Parnell, the Home Rule leader, with consequent threats to public order and the unity of the UK? The uncomfortable truth was best pointed out by Sir John Lubbock, one of the saner advocates of PR, in the autumn of 1884:

At the general election of 1880, 86 seats were contested. Of these the Home-rulers secured 52, the Liberal[s] and Conservatives together only 34. Yet the Home-rule electors were only 48,000, while the Liberals and Conservatives together were no less than 105,000. . . . we are told . . . that under the new Redistribution Act the Home-Rulers will secure 90 seats out of 100, leaving only a dozen to the Liberals and Conservatives together. . . . out of Ulster it is probable that scarcely a single Liberal or Conservative member will be returned. The result of this system, then, will be that Ireland will be entirely misrepresented, and that we shall have gratuitously created serious and unnecessary difficulties for ourselves. To adopt, indeed, a system of representation by which we shall exclude from the representation of Ireland one-third of the electors, and give almost the whole power to two-thirds, would, under any circumstances, be unjust; but to do so when the one-third comprise those who are moderate and loyal, while the two-thirds are led by men not only opposed to the Union, but in many cases animated by a bitter and extraordinary hatred of this country, seems to be an act of political madness. (Lubbock 1885, 20–21)

Lubbock went on to draw an analogy from the U.S. presidential election of

1860, in which Abraham Lincoln won an absolute majority of the Electoral College on less than 40 percent of the vote. Lubbock's prediction was exactly correct. The Home Rulers won eighty-five seats in the ensuing General Election and continued to do so at every election until 1910. Anglo-Irish war was about to break out in 1914 but was delayed for the First World War to take place. The Irish war lasted from 1919 to 1922, and some would say it has not yet ended. Thus electoral systems have important consequences.

6.3 Dodgson on Proportional Representation

This then is the anxious context in which Dodgson wrote his "Principles." The career and personality of Charles Lutwidge Dodgson (1832–98), alias Lewis Carroll, are so well known that we can be brief. A shy bachelor with a stammer, he became a lecturer in mathematics and a fellow at Christ Church, Oxford in 1856. He gave up the lectureship in 1881 to concentrate on research and writing but continued with the fellowship until his death. He lived all his adult life in Christ Church, with only short seaside holidays. Both in Oxford and on holiday he cultivated the company of little girls, of whom he took beautiful photographs; however, he did not believe that women should be admitted to study at Oxford University; he wished rather to establish a separate "Women's University." *Alice's Adventures in Wonderland* was published in 1865 and *Through the Looking Glass* in 1871; the stories were first told to Alice Liddell, daughter of H. G. Liddell, the Dean of Christ Church. Dodgson's relations with Alice's parents deteriorated in the 1870s when Dodgson criticized Liddell fiercely on various matters of college and university politics. As a mathematician Dodgson was conspicuously solitary; he worked at problems from his own perspective without considering previous writing on the same subject. Until the publication of Duncan Black's *Theory of Committees and Elections* (1958), nobody had ever taken his professional work seriously. Some mathematicians, philosophers and logicians do now take him seriously, a good example being Martin Gardner (1970, 1982), the *Scientific American* columnist.

Dodgson was a political Conservative as well as a temperamental conservative. He met Salisbury and his family in 1870, for once (uncharacteristically) using his fame as the author of *Alice* to obtain an introduction to Salisbury's wife and daughters (Cohen 1979, 211). Despite the gulfs of class and temperament, Dodgson was welcomed by the Salisbury family and spent the New Year at their great house, Hatfield, several times in the 1870s and 1880s. Dodgson seems to have thought about PR for the first time in 1882, in connection with college politics (see his diary entry for 17 May 1882 in Green 1953, 405–6), but it was the reform crisis of 1884 that brought him into print. He wrote several letters on it to the *St James's Gazette*, his ideas evolving continuously. In June he hit on the most distinctive feature of his scheme, "the giving to each candidate the power of transferring to any other candidate the votes given for him" (Diary for 3 June 1884 in Green 1953, 426). In July he sent it to Salisbury saying "How I wish the enclosed could have appeared as *your* scheme. . . . That *some* such scheme is needed, and much more needed than *any* scheme for mere redistribution of electoral districts, I feel sure." Salisbury replied immediately, acknowledging the need for electoral reform but stressing the difficulty of getting a hearing for "anything . . . absolutely new . . . however Conservative." Dodgson replied the next day. After congratulating Salisbury for the speech in the House of Lords in which he had insisted that the Conservatives would not accept franchise reform unless it was linked with redistribution, Dodgson went on "*please* don't call my scheme for Proportionate Representation a 'Conservative' one. . . . *all* I aim at is to secure that, *whatever* be the proportions of opinion among the Electors, the *same* shall exist among the Members" (the three letters are partly quoted and partly paraphrased in Cohen 1979, 544–45).

Like Sir John Lubbock, Dodgson saw that Salisbury had failed to accept the implications of his own argument. No redistribution that retained single-member districts with the plurality voting rule could be guaranteed to save the Conservatives in Britain or either of the British parties in Ireland. As Salisbury (1884) himself pointed out and as Dodgson repeated in *The Principles*, single-member districts combined with an even distribution of supporters of two parties around the country could lead to the larger of the two wiping out the smaller in terms of seats. It seems that Salisbury could not shift his perspective from majoritarian to proportional in order to see the true implications of his own argument.

It is unfortunate that points that Dodgson took for granted and passed over quickly were exactly the ones that mainstream politicians could not accept, even when it was in their own interest. Dodgson takes for granted both that guaranteeing the survival of minorities in parliament requires multimember districts and some form of minority representation (which the politicians should have accepted but did not) and that the number of electors per MP should be equal (which almost no parliamentarian in the 1884 debates did). This was probably enough on its own to blind contemporaries to the more striking features of *The Principles*. Indeed, even Black (1958, 191) dismissed them, although he later changed his mind. (More detailed analysis than is possible here will be found in Black (forthcoming); for a preliminary version of Black's argument see Black 1967).

The Principles is the earliest known work to discuss both the assignment of seats to each of a number of multimember districts (the apportionment problem) and the assignment of seats within each district to the parties (the PR problem). There is no sign that Dodgson had read Jefferson, Hamilton, or

Webster on the first, nor Gilpin or Victor d'Hondt (the reinventor of the Jefferson scheme for PR) on the second. Dodgson's quota is quite different from Hamilton's. Table 1 of *The Principles* shows that a small district would have to have an electorate of 9,000 under Dodgson's apportionment quota before it qualified for even one MP, whereas one of 4,000 would qualify under the Hamilton quota. If he got thus far, Salisbury would have found yet more evidence of Dodgson's impracticality in a proposal that would have favored heavily populated (mostly Liberal) areas against thinly populated (mostly Conservative) ones.

For the assignment of seats to parties, Dodgson recommends the Droop quota, though he naturally does not cite Droop and there is no reason to suppose he read him. He parts company with the Proportional Representation Society, whose literature he does cite, because he makes the same case against Hare as Andrae's unknown Danish critic had against him.[11] Having shown that Hare's rules could lead to the defeat of a candidate who had obtained a Droop quota (indeed, though Dodgson is not at all in a Condorcetian mood in *The Principles*, he could have pointed out that in his example the Hare scheme elects the Condorcet loser among the last three candidates), he briskly concludes that he has "sufficiently proved the fallacy of its method for disposing of surplus votes." But note that here Dodgson shares Hare's notion that the issue is one of surplus votes. This implies that the second preferences of voters whose first preference has counted toward a quota are of no further concern and the issue is only that of the second preferences of voters whose first preferences have not been required to achieve a quota. "Clearly *somebody* must have authority to dispose of them: it cannot be the Elector (as we have proved); it will never do to refer it to a Committee. There remains *the Candidate himself, for whom the votes have been given.*" Some may find this reasoning too much like Lewis Carroll's rather than Charles L. Dodgson's, but if it seems bizarre, note that it flows from an assumption that Dodgson *shared* with Hare and his followers and that precluded Dodgson from seeing the problem in a way in which either the Borda winner or the Condorcet winner would have been relevant. From a social choice perspective, the root problem of STV and all other elimination systems is that they use information about voters' preferences other than their first in an arbitrary way. The $n + 1$th preference of a voter whose nth preference has been eliminated is counted. The $n + 1$th preference of a voter whose nth preference has been elected with a surplus is counted with reduced weight, and the $n + 1$th preference of a voter whose nth preference is elected with nothing to spare is not counted.

---

11. Dodgson had worked out a case in which "the chance of the wrong man coming in on their [Hare's] system . . . exceeds $1/2$" by 15 May 1884 (Dodgson, unpublished diary).

Thus preference orderings are not treated equally. When writing about majority rule, Dodgson had shown himself well aware about this; when writing about PR, he did not consider it.

6.4 Dodgson on Majority Rule

We have discussed Dodgson's work on PR first because it was part, however uncomfortable, of a recognized political discourse in its time. However, his enduring fame in social choice rests more on his totally original pamphlets of ten years earlier, which had neither forebears nor successors. In the following discussion we will abbreviate them to *A Discussion* (1873), *Suggestions* (1874), and *A Method* (1876). Here again we can be brief; most readers will already know the context as described by Black (1958, 192–213), and those who do not should certainly read Black. We wish to add only a few small details not in Black.

In the 1860s Dodgson was a compulsive pamphleteer on university and college matters, but no specialist interest in elections emerges from his writings before December 1873. On 13 December 1873, he "began writing a paper (which occurred to me last night)" (Green 1953, 324) for a meeting to elect two fellows (i.e., college faculty members; known in Christ Church as students) on 18 December. He immediately found the subject "to be much more complicated than I expected" (*A Discussion*, preface). He recommended using the Borda count, treating "no election" as if it were a candidate. The college "partly used my method" in the election (Green 1953, 324): in fact, in one of the elections, the Borda scores of the top two candidates were forty-seven and forty-eight, but in a runoff the first beat the second by eleven votes to nine and was elected.

The two unusual facts here are that Dodgson's method was adopted and that it immediately seems to have thrown up a case where the Borda and the Condorcet principles diverged. By his own admission, Dodgson was rarely influential. For instance, when he first proposed a PR system within the college, "my scheme was not even seconded" (Green 1953, 405–6; diary for 17 May 1882). He repeatedly described himself as "no orator" in his leaflets about University affairs. He parodied himself as the Dodo (a pun on the extinct bird and the stammerer who could not pronounce his own name) in the "Pool of Tears" chapter of *Alice*:

"In that case," said the Dodo solemnly, rising to its feet, "I move that the meeting adjourn, for the immediate adoption of more energetic remedies—"

"Speak English!" said the Eaglet [Alice's younger sister]. "I don't know the meaning of half those long words, and, what's more, I don't believe you do either!" And the Eaglet bent down its head to hide a smile: some of the other birds tittered audibly.

Black (1958) suggests that the emotional drive behind all three pamphlets was Dodgson's growing dislike for Liddell ("L is for . . . . , relentless reformer" Dodgson had written in a mock ABC in 1864).[12] By 1873 Liddell was relentlessly proposing controversial changes to the fabric of Christ Church. Besides,

> by about 1872, when Alice Liddell, a girl of outstanding beauty and charm, reached twenty, surrounded by some of the most eligible young bachelors in England, and Dodgson reached forty without much reputation in Christ Church, he realized that Alice Liddell, who had meant so much to him, was slipping out of his life. (Black 1958, 199)

Nobody else entered Dodgson's private world. But they may have seized on his voting procedure as a way to resolve embarrassing conflicts.

The conflict between the Borda and Condorcet principles (which indeed is latent in *Discussion*, Case β), plus perhaps the experience of having "no election" in a fellowship election (Green 1953, 328; diary for 28 February 1874), encouraged Dodgson to think more deeply about elections. Indeed, on holiday on the Isle of Wight in the summer of 1874, he resolved "to do a good spell of work . . . including my . . . book on *Elections*" (Green 1953, 330; 3 July 1874), but there is no evidence that he made any progress on a book. He rushed out *Suggestions* in time for a college meeting that was to decide on designs for a controversial belfry in the corner of the main quadrangle. Again, the evidence (Black 1958, 206–7) is that the college followed Dodgson's procedure. He had by this time dropped his recommendation of the Borda count in favor of searching for the Condorcet winner.

The occasion for *A Method* may well also have been university politics, Dodgson's hatred of Dean Liddell, or both, but it seems less tied to a specific controversy than the two earlier pamphlets. In March 1876, Dodgson ordered 100 copies, 50 of them to be interleaved with plain paper; he specified that the heading was to be changed from NOT PUBLISHED YET to NOT YET PUBLISHED (Cohen 1979, 244). He circulated some of the interleaved copies with requests for them to be returned by a certain date (the copy at Christ Church has "June 1876," in Dodgson's hand, in the blank on the title page; other copies were (re-)circulated in 1877 with a request for com-

---

12. Oxford, Bodleian Library, Arch. AA d. 157. For the background on the politics of Christ Church at the time, see further Bill and Mason (1970).

ments by 1878). There is evidence from the pamphlet itself that some colleagues at Christ Church understood Dodgson's findings and arguments about cycles and made proposals for breaking cycles that he demolished. There is no evidence that anybody outside the college did, and Dodgson turned to other matters without developing his fundamental insights on cycles any further.

Dodgson made one other, hitherto unrecognized, contribution to social choice. Some time in or before the summer of 1882, a friend complained to him that in a tennis tournament he "had been beaten . . . early in the contest, and . . . had had the mortification of seeing the 2nd prize carried off by a Player whom he knew to be quite inferior to himself" (Woollcott 1939, 1082–91, quoted at 1082). Tennis was a newly fashionable game. Tournaments were arranged in the way in which they still are: players are randomly paired for the first round, and the survivor of each pair goes forward to play in the next round. Dodgson showed that in a thirty-two-player tournament, it was possible that, although the first prize would go to the best player, the second prize might go to the seventeenth-best, the third to the ninth-best, and the fourth to the twenty-fifth-best. Although the Wimbledon authorities seem never to have recognized it, the proof is elementary: it is only necessary to hypothesize that the initial draw pits the players in descending order of ability. Dodgson's real originality is in his solution concept:

A list is kept, and against any name is entered, at the end of each contest, the name of any one who has been superior to him—whether by actually beating him, or by beating someone who has done so (thus, if A beats B, and B beats C, A and B are both "superiors" of C). (Woollcott 1939, 1084)

This is (or could have been) the germ of the idea of *covering*, which has emerged since 1980 as a powerful solution concept for social choice tournaments (see especially Miller 1980). On this as on PR, even Duncan Black failed to see Dodgson's originality, calling the pamphlet on tennis tournaments "quite trivial" (1958, 213).

6.5 Nanson

E. J. Nanson was born in Penrith on the edge of the English Lake District in 1850. He was educated locally and in Ripon, Yorkshire, where he married the daughter of his former headmaster just before emigrating to Australia in 1875. He graduated in mathematics from Cambridge in 1873, where he was Second Wrangler and won the Second Smith's Prize. He was presumably recommended by his tutors for a good teaching position, since he became a fellow of his Cambridge college (Trinity) and professor of applied mathematics at the

Royal Indian Engineering College in Surrey in 1874. At the end of that year, the professor of mathematics at the University of Melbourne died suddenly. Presumably, the authorities there asked colleagues in Cambridge to suggest somebody quickly. Nanson was elected to the chair in January 1875 and arrived in Melbourne in June. He remained there for the rest of his uneventful life, retiring in 1922. He had ten children, five of them by his second wife whom he married in 1913. He died in 1936.

"Nanson did not profess a popular discipline," according to the obituarist in the *Australian Dictionary of Biography*, writing shortly after his death. He evidently did not enjoy teaching compulsory elementary mathematics to students in other subjects with little preparation or motivation. The source continues:

> Kind but reserved in manner, mild in temperament, a field naturalist given to solitary rambles, Nanson received unsympathetic treatment from the reforming royal commission on the University of Melbourne (1902–4) which criticized student absenteeism and lack of tutorial teaching, but affirmed his industry and stature as a mathematician. . . . Intellectually lonely in his theoretical interests he found some companionship in the Mathematics Association of Victoria.

Nanson wrote and campaigned extensively on elections. He got the University of Melbourne and (probably) a number of bodies in the Anglican church in Victoria to adopt his method of elections. A scheme of his was written into electoral bills for Victoria and for the Commonwealth of Australia but was not enacted in either case. "Methods of Election" is the only publication mentioned in the entry for Nanson in *Who's Who in the Commonwealth of Australia* (Johns 1922), in which the entries were compiled by the editor, not the subject.

Nanson's paper takes the Condorcet criterion for granted. His method is explicitly to show that various methods in use are not Condorcet efficient— that is, that they can reject a Condorcet winner. This allows him to reject plurality, the Borda rule, the French runoff system, and what he calls the Ware system (now known in Britain as the Alternative Vote); although he observes correctly that the last two at least cannot choose a Condorcet loser. Borda had shown that, if the number of candidates is at least as great as the number of electors, only a unanimity rule guarantees the choice of the Borda winner. Like Daunou, Nanson remarks that this should have led Borda to question his rule. He also notes the opportunities for strategic voting in the Borda and runoff systems.

Nanson had read our chapters 5, 6, and 8, and some of Condorcet's other writings on voting (for which see Sommerlad and McLean 1989 and 1991;

McLean and Hewitt forthcoming). He was aware of the existence of Lhuilier's paper but seems not to have seen it. Although he had access to an earlier collected edition of Condorcet's works that includes our chapter 7, he probably missed it, because he believes that he is the first person to have proved that the Borda scheme is not Condorcet efficient, something that Condorcet does in our chapter 7 (as do Lhuilier and Daunou).

Todhunter (1865) influenced Nanson's reading of Condorcet (Urken 1991). So it is not surprising that Nanson pays little attention to the philosophy underlying Condorcet's theory of voting. But, unlike Todhunter, Nanson discusses cycles. He argues that in a three-candidate cycle the natural thing to do is reject the candidate with the smallest majority. He does not propose a general method of breaking cycles; although he has read Condorcet's method (see chap. 6 and our discussion above), he believes that in the general case Condorcet's rules "are stated so briefly as to be hardly intelligible. . . . it is not easy to reconcile these rules with the statements made in [Condorcet's informal description of them in 1789], and as no examples are given it is quite hopeless to find out what Condorcet meant" (but see Young 1988).

Nanson's own voting procedure is Condorcet efficient, and in the case of a three-candidate cycle it produces the same result as does the commonsense rule of dropping the candidate with the smallest majority. It is to conduct an iterated Borda count, at each stage dropping the candidate(s) with less than the average Borda score. (Nanson says "not more than," but in the event of an n-way tie in Borda scores, this could lead to all n candidates being eliminated). Borda scores for the remaining candidates are then recalculated, and so on as often as necessary until only one candidate (who must be the Condorcet winner) is left. Voters with weak orderings—whether those who deliver short ballots that do not list every candidate or those who wish to register indifference among sets of candidates—cause considerable practical difficulties for Nanson's method. He therefore has to devote quite a lot of his space to the problem and comes up with a practical solution that he admits is not perfect. Note that his algebraic method for working out the properties of various systems is remarkably close to Lhuilier's.

Ever since Rowland Hill, PR had been actively discussed in Australia, and elsewhere in his writings Nanson comments on it extensively. In "Methods of Election," however, he restricts himself to the curt comment that

> it follows from the principles which have been established in this paper [viz., that Condorcet efficiency is the correct criterion by which to judge electoral systems] that the process of "elimination", which has been adopted by all the exponents of Hare's system, is not satisfactory.

This is quite true, of course. Any elimination-based PR system can reject the

Condorcet winner. However, Nanson's paper appeared in a survey commissioned in 1907 by the British government of methods of PR in use in British colonies and abroad. It is unfortunate that the man best qualified to advise it was represented in the survey by a 20,000-word paper of which just one sentence—the last—dealt with PR. This was not Nanson's fault. But yet another opportunity to bridge the gulf between mathematical discussion of social choice and politicians' discussion of PR was missed. The gulf was never bridged in the nineteenth century and has been bridged with depressing rarity in the twentieth.

7. Discussion

We have shown that many issues in the current literature of social choice were aired between A.D. 105 and 1884, with a peak between 1770 and 1803. Both in modes of reasoning and in substantive concerns, the literature we have reviewed seems remarkably modern. Pliny understood the strategic implications of ternary versus binary procedure. Lull stumbled on the method of pairwise comparison and proposed a matrix notation for it. Cusanus prescribed the Borda count in exact detail. Some reasoning by Condorcet and his contemporaries seems very close to ours. For instance, Condorcet (when in social choice mode) takes it as axiomatic that the majority winner should be chosen and that the choice from a set of options should be independent of irrelevant alternatives. He then proves that the Borda count violates both of these, although the first was implicit in Borda's own statement of the problem. Daunou, who supported Borda in 1796, came to share this opinion by 1803 and uses the same form of reasoning to attack Borda, Morales, and Laplace; the last remarkably bold in that a writer and administrator with a purely literary background was taking on a colleague who was already recognized as one of the greatest mathematicians of his day. Lhuilier turns this axiomatic method against Condorcet himself by proving that his own practical procedure does not satisfy his axioms. Our authors were well aware of the manipulability of the Borda count and sought a nonmanipulable system. Condorcet's practical procedures were diverse; though he was satisfied by none of them, it is of interest that at one point he proposed the Copeland rule supplemented by the Borda count as a tie breaker.

Black's (1958) claim that Condorcet's probabilism was an obstacle to the development of social choice is descriptively correct but need not be analytically correct; the probabilistic theory of voting has merits that are only now being recognized (Urken 1991). The jury theorem is a perfectly valid piece of reasoning that can be applied both to normative political theory (axiomatizing Rousseau's General Will) and to the analysis of voting situations that meet its preconditions. An example of the latter is to set rules for the majority required before a number of computer systems should close down machinery that some of them report to be malfunctioning. Here is an application where, with a known v, it is easy to calculate the threshold value of $h - k$ to achieve the desired balance between avoiding a false positive and a false negative. (For a current review, see Berg 1992.) Another use of probability was exploited particularly by Lhuilier (and to some extent by Laplace and Daunou): calculating the probability of the possible profiles in a set of orderings, given an assumption that any ordering of a pair is as likely as any other (what is now labeled an impartial culture).

We have noted above that neither politicians nor mathematicians understood this work. Dodgson obtained his results entirely from scratch. Nanson knew some, but by no means all, of his predecessors' work. But this is merely to redescribe, not explain. The *mathematics* of social choice is not difficult; it seems that the difficulty for Condorcet, as for his predecessors Lull and Cusanus and his successors Nanson and Dodgson, lay in persuading colleagues that there was a problem or phenomenon that required explanation. Lull, Cusanus, Condorcet, Dodgson, and Nanson were each regarded as lonely thinkers and difficult-to-follow teachers. Lull revealed in his autobiography that nobody understood him when he lectured at the University of Paris. Cusanus wrote bad Latin, by his own admission ("We Germans . . . are able to speak Latin correctly only with great effort, overcoming, as it were, the force of nature," Sigmund 1991, 3). Condorcet's attempts to teach were embarrassing failures. Dodgson was an eccentric, none of whose colleagues shared his mathematical interests. He was not as solitary a mathematician as he has usually been portrayed: for instance, he corresponded with Todhunter about probability. But Todhunter could scarcely have led him to Condorcet, whom Todhunter himself totally misunderstood. Both of them were entirely out of touch with developments in Continental mathematics at a time when Oxford and Cambridge were both backwaters. Dodgson hated teaching ("I gave my first Euclid Lecture . . . on Monday Jan: 28, 1856. It consisted of twelve men, of whom nine attended. This morning I have given what is probably my *last*: the lecture is now reduced to nine . . . this morning only two appeared," diary for 30 November 1881; Green 1953, 402). Nanson was also uninterested in teaching and was reproved by a Royal Commission for the poor state of mathematics teaching at the University of Melbourne. And Lhuilier, although he was a successful teacher, seems to have been personally self-effacing and timid like a number of our other authors. Perhaps there is a lesson for us even today: it is as important to communicate with the outside world as with one another.

But to blame the failure of social choice to spread on the introversion of its originators will not do. They may have failed to speak clearly, but it is more important that the world failed to listen clearly: their listeners did not recognize a problem that could not be handled by established routines. Breakdowns in voting systems are difficult to see because voters are conditioned to accept traditional methods for breaking ties or achieving decisive outcomes. Probably the basic problem faced by our authors is the same as is depressingly familiar to anybody today who tries to explain social choice to politicians or citizens. Lay people do not *expect* the theory of voting to be difficult. The abstract logic can be simple to grasp. Saari (1992) found that a class of fourth-grade school students in Pittsburgh picked up the basic ideas of the Condorcet and Borda principles so quickly that they "expressed the class' growing exasperation with the slow witted mathematics professor who couldn't understand the obvious." But adults can find the abstract logic difficult to relate to voting situations, for even when there is an undeniable crisis, there is usually an ad hoc way round it, so voters remain unaware of the implications of different methods. Although experts can say for sure that different procedures applied to a given set of preferences will lead to different outcomes, they usually lack sufficient data to work back from an outcome to a root set of preferences and therefore cannot usually demonstrate that a different procedure would have led elsewhere (but see Riker 1982). Meanwhile, the (apparently) commonsense notion of majority rule appears to have magical properties that inhibit our contemporaries from visualizing a majority in Condorcetian fashion as a measure of consensus that can and should be gauged as strong or weak according to its size and the existence of any cycles around it. In short, it is often hard to persuade anyone that there can be anything to theorize about. Social choice theorists face a problem that theoretical physicists do not: their subject looks on the face of it like no more than applied common sense. Gouverneur Morris, one of the principal drafters of the U.S. Constitution in 1787, later succeeded Jefferson as American minister in Paris. In March 1791 he met Condorcet:

> Talk with Condorcet after supper on the principles of the *économistes*. I tell him, which is true, that once I adopted those principles from books, but that I have since changed them from better knowledge of human affairs and more mature reflection. (Diary for 17 March 1791 in Morris 1889).

Condorcet's response is not recorded. Let us therefore reply on behalf of him and all our authors. Principles from the books we have excerpted and translated have shown how deep and pervasive are the problems of social choice. As is now, belatedly, realized, the problem is not only what to do when democracy does not produce a consensus but how to choose a voting method and how to decide what information should be collected (and how to collect it) to make a rational choice. The historical study of social choice makes us aware of the problems of social choice engineering. We might now have better knowledge of human affairs and more mature reflection than our forebears, but we still need to design choice rules according to principles from books. Otherwise, we might find ourselves having to believe six impossible things before breakfast.

8. A Note on Sources

In chapters 2 to 14, translators' notes are placed between square brackets []; notes without brackets are original. The algebra in chapter 9, although elementary and correct, is very compressed; we have therefore expanded it in a number of places and marked our expansions by square brackets. These have been left in place and not brought down to the Notes. The mathematics in chapter 6 employs modern notation.

Chapter 2. Latin text, Mynors 1966. Translation based on Radice 1969. Minor amendments by McLean in consultation with Chris Pelling.

Chapter 3. Catalan text of *Blanquerna* from Alcover 1914. Translation by London. Latin text of *De Arte Eleccionis* in Honecker 1937a. Original manuscript in Cusanus's library in Kues; photocopy kindly supplied by Professor R. Haubst. Translation by McLean and Murray.

Chapter 4. Latin text in Kallen 1964. Translation by Murray.

Chapter 5. Original text, *HARS* and *MARS* 1781. Part of Condorcet's manuscript in Condorcet Manuscripts, Bibliothèque de l'Institut de France, Paris. Translation by McLean and Hewitt.

Chapter 6. Original text, Condorcet [1785] 1972. Translation by Urken, with Roger Pinkham and James E. McClellan.

Chapter 7. Source, Arago and O'Connor (1847, vol. 8). Translation by McLean and Hewitt.

Chapter 8. Source, Arago and O'Connor (1847, vol. 12). Translation by McLean and Hewitt.

Chapter 9. Original text, Lhuilier [1794] 1976. Translation by McLean, Hewitt, and Ingram. Algebra checked by McLean and Ingram.

Chapter 10. Original text, Morales 1797, copy kindly supplied by New York Public Library. Translation by Powell, reviewed by McLean with the assistance of Richard Gillespie.

Chapter 11. Original text, Daunou 1803, copy kindly supplied by the British Library. Translation by McLean, Hewitt, and Urken.

Chapter 12. Copies in Bodleian Library and Christ Church Library, Oxford, and in the papers of Duncan Black, now in the Archives, University of Glasgow.

Chapter 13. Copy in Black papers, as above.

Chapter 14. Original text, Nanson [1882] 1907.

Part 1
Precursors

CHAPTER 2

Pliny the Younger

Letter to Titius Aristo, A.D. 105

To Titius Aristo:

As you are such an authority on private and public law, including senatorial procedure, I am particularly anxious to hear whether or not you think I made a mistake at a recent meeting of the Senate. It is too late to be put right about past events, but I should like to know what to do in future should any similar situation arise. You will wonder why I am asking a question I ought to have been able to answer myself. The fact is, we have forgotten our knowledge of senatorial procedure, as of other honest practices, in the servitude of former times; very few people have the patience and willpower to learn what is never likely to be of any practical use, and it is besides difficult to remember what you have learned unless you put it into practice. So now that Liberty is restored, she finds us awkward and inexperienced; carried away by her charms we are compelled to do some things before we know how.

In ancient times it was the recognized custom for us to learn from our elders by watching their behavior as well as listening to their advice, thus acquiring the principles on which to act subsequently ourselves and to hand on in turn to our juniors. Hence young men began their early training with military service, so that they might grow accustomed to command by obeying and learn how to lead by following others; hence as candidates for office they stood at the door of the Senate house and watched the course of State councils before taking part in them. Everyone had a teacher in his own father or, if he was fatherless, in some older man of distinction who took his father's place. Thus men learned by example (the surest method of instruction) the powers of the proposer, the rights of expressing an opinion, the authority of office-holders, and the privileges of ordinary members; they learned when to give way and when to stand firm, how long to speak and when to keep silence, how to distinguish between conflicting proposals and how to introduce an amendment, in short the whole of senatorial procedure. For our own generation it was different. Though our early manhood was spent on military service, it was at a time when merit was under suspicion and apathy an asset, when

67

officers lacked influence and soldiers respect, when there was neither authority nor obedience and the whole system was slack, disorganized, and chaotic,
better forgotten than remembered. We too were spectators in the Senate but in
a Senate which was apprehensive and dumb since it was dangerous to voice a
genuine opinion and pitiable to express a forced one. What could be learned at
that time, what profit could there be in possessing that learning, when the
Senate was summoned to idle away time or to perpetuate some vile crime and
was kept sitting for a joke or its own humiliation, when it could never pass a
serious resolution, though often one with tragic consequences? On becoming
senators we took part in these evils and continued to witness and endure them
for many years, until our spirits were blunted, broken, and destroyed with
lingering effect, so that it is only a short time (the happier the time, the shorter
it seems) since we began to want to know our own powers and put our
knowledge into practice.

   I have then all the more reason to ask you to forgive any mistake I may
have made and then to remedy it with your expert knowledge, for you have
always made a special study of private and public law, ancient and modern,
with reference to exceptional as well as current problems. Personally I think
that the kind of question I am putting to you would be unfamiliar even to
people whose constant dealing with large numbers of cases makes them
conversant with most possibilities; it might be entirely outside their experience. So there will be the more excuse for me if perhaps I was at fault and the
more credit to you if you can instruct me on a point on which you may not
have been informed yourself.

   The case at issue concerned the freedmen[1] of the consul Afranius Dexter,
who had been found dead; it was not known whether he had killed himself or his
servants were responsible and, if the latter, whether they acted criminally or in
obedience to their master. After the proceedings one opinion (whose?—mine,
but that is not important) was that they should go free, another that they should
be banished to an island, and the third that they should be put to death. Such
diversity of sentences meant that they had to be considered singly, for what have
death and banishment in common? Obviously no more than banishment and
acquittal,[2] though a vote for acquittal is nearer banishment than is a vote for
death, for the first two leave a man his life while death removes it. Meanwhile
those who voted for the death penalty and banishment respectively were sitting
together and shelving their differences by a temporary show of unity.

---

   1. [A freedman was a former slave liberated by his master and working as a paid servant.]
   2. ["Acquittal" is not quite right, because it carries overtones of Anglo-Saxon legal procedure which are inappropriate here. The option was rather to let the freedmen "go free," as
translated above, without pronouncing them not guilty of a crime. But we retain "acquittal" from
here to the end of the chapter in deference to the classic treatment (and notation) of Farquharson
(1969).]

I asked for the three sentences to be reckoned as three and that two should not join forces under a momentary truce. Therefore I insisted that the supporters of the death penalty should move away from the proposers of banishment and that the two parties should not combine to oppose those asking for acquittal when they would afterward disagree among themselves, for it mattered little that they were united to oppose the same view when their positive proposals were so different. Another point I found extraordinary was that the member who proposed banishment for the freedmen and death for the slaves should have been obliged to divide his vote, while the one who was for executing the freedmen could be counted as voting for the proposer of banishment. For if one person's vote had to be divided because it covered two distinct sentences, I could not see how the votes of two people making such different proposals could be taken together.

Now, although the case is over let me treat it as still open; let me explain to you, as I did to the Senate, why I held this view; and let me assemble now in my own time the points I had then to make piecemeal amid considerable interruption. Let us suppose that three judges only have been appointed for this case, one of whom has said that the freedmen should die, the second that they should be banished, and the third that they should be acquitted. Is the combined weight of two of these sentences to defeat the third, or is each one to be weighed against the others and the first and second to be combined no more than the second and third? It follows that, in the Senate, all different opinions expressed ought to be counted as conflicting. But if one and the same person proposed both death and banishment, could the prisoners suffer both punishments by one person's proposal alone? Could it be considered as one proposal at all when it combined two such different things? How then, when one person proposes death and another banishment, could these be held to be a single proposal because expressed by two people when they were not a single proposal if expressed by one person?

Well, the law clearly states that sentences of death and banishment should be considered separately in its formula for taking a division: "All who agree go to this side, all who support any other proposal to the side you support." Take the words one by one and consider them. "Who agree" means "Who think the prisoners should be banished"; "to this side" is the side of the House where the proposer of banishment is sitting. It is clear from this that those who want death for the prisoners cannot stay on that side. "Who support any other proposal"—you will observe that the law is not content with saying "other" but has added the word "any." Can it be doubted that those who would put the prisoners to death "support any other proposal" in comparison with those who would banish them? "Go to the side you support": surely the wording of the law seems to summon and even compel those who disagree to take sides. Does not the consul also indicate not only by the established formula but by a movement of the hand where everyone is to remain or to what side to cross?

But it can be argued that if the proposals for death and banishment are taken separately it will result in the acquittal having a majority. That is no concern of the voters, and it certainly ill becomes them to use every weapon and device to defeat a more lenient sentence. Or again, it can be said that those voting for death and banishment should first be matched against those supporting an acquittal and then against each other. In some of the public games, one gladiator draws a lot which entitles him to stand aside and wait to fight the victor; so I suppose there are to be first and second rounds in the Senate too, and the third proposal is to wait and meet the victor of the other two. What about the rule that if the first sentence is approved, all the others are defeated? On what principle can these sentences not start on the same footing, seeing that they may all subsequently cease to count? I will put this again more clearly. As soon as the proposal of banishment is made, unless those in favor of execution immediately cross over to the other side, it will be useless their afterward opposing what they agreed with a short time before.

But I should not be the one to give instruction when I really wanted to learn whether the two sentences should have been subsequently divided or all three voted on separately. I carried my point, but nonetheless I want to know whether I should have made it. How did I manage this? The proposer of the death sentence was convinced by the fairness of my request (whether or not it was legal), dropped his own proposal, and supported that of banishment. He was afraid, no doubt, that if the sentences were taken separately (which seemed likely if he did not act), the acquittal would have a majority, for there were many more people in favor of this than of either of the other two proposals taken singly. Then, when those who had been influenced by him found themselves abandoned by his crossing the floor and the proposal thrown over by its author, they dropped it too and deserted after their leader. So the three proposals became two, and banishment[3] carried the day by the elimination of the death penalty, which could not defeat both of the others and therefore chose to submit to one.

---

3. [Latin *ex duabus altera* (the second out of the two); the penalty that was eliminated is called *tertia* (the third). Pliny has introduced them in the order Acquittal, Banishment, and Condemnation; therefore, there is no doubt that the "second" is banishment and the "third" is execution. As this is a key point for readers interested in this letter from a social choice perspective, we have made our translation of this difficult final sentence more explicit than previous versions.]

CHAPTER 3

Ramon Lull

From *Blanquerna*, Chapter 24, ca. 1283

All the sisters wanted to elect their abbess by their usual electoral method, but Natana said that she had heard of a new electoral method, which consisted in art and figures; this art follows the conditions laid out in *The Book of the Gentile and the Three Wise Men*, which follows *The Art of Finding Truth*. "By this method," said Natana, "truth is found, and by this truth we will be able to find which of us is best and most suitable to be our abbess."

All the sisters asked Natana to reveal the way in which, through art, they could find and elect the sister best suited to be abbess. This was Natana's reply: "I will briefly tell you about the principles of the art of election. This art is divided into two parts: the first part involves electing those who will elect the leader; the second part concerns the way in which they should elect the superior. So I will first tell you about the first part and then the second."

Natana said, "There are twenty of us in this chapter who have the right to vote in the election of our leader. According to the art, we must elect from these twenty sisters an odd number, which should be five or seven, because this number is more appropriate for an election than any other, and the number seven is more appropriate than the number five. All the sisters should first take an oath to tell the truth. Then the first sister should be asked in secret which of the nineteen are most suited to be among the seven who can elect the superior. Afterward, the second sister should be asked, then the third, and so on, in order, until the last. And on each occasion the answer of each sister should be written down. In the end, let it be ascertained which of the sisters have won the most votes, and those who have the most votes will be the seven sisters to elect the abbess.

"The second part of the election concerns how the seven electors elect their leader. Firstly, the seven electors should agree upon a certain number and upon certain names for election, as they best see fit. They should compare them with each other according to four conditions, namely, which of them best loves and knows God, which of them best loves and knows the virtues, which of them knows and hates most strongly the vices, and which is the most suitable person.

"Each of the seven electors can choose one person to be in the total number of those from whom the superior will be elected, and each elector shall herself be among that number. So that you can understand the art more clearly, let us suppose that the given number of people from which our superior is to be elected is nine. Thus, the seven should be divided into two groups: two in one and five in the other. The five should decide which of the two should be elected and write in secret the name of the one who has won more votes. Afterward, the sister who has won more votes should be compared with another of the five; this other sister should replace the one who has been defeated by reason of fewer votes. The defeated sister should be put in the place of the sister who is compared with the first or the second. This procedure should be repeated, in order, with all the others, and the eighth and ninth candidates, who are not among the electors, should be included in this number. Therefore, taking this number as an example, thirty-six compartments[1] will be produced in which the votes of each candidate will appear. The candidate to be elected should be the one with the most votes in the most compartments."

When Natana had explained the art of election, one of the sisters asked her, "If it turns out that some candidates have as many votes as each other in the compartments, what procedure does the art recommend?" Natana replied, "The art recommends that these two or three or more should be judged according to art alone. It should be found out which of these best meets the four aforementioned conditions, for she will be the one who is worthy to be elected."

All the sisters were very pleased with the art and the electoral system. They all said that if they followed this art there could be no error in the election. So they all established a rule according to which they would always carry out their elections according to the way explained by Natana, and they began to find out about the art and learn it. After a few days, they had an election according to the art and discovered that Natana was to be abbess.

Natana was elected abbess. She was very upset by being honored in this way. She blessed God for honoring her above all the other sisters. However, she thought that the sisters might have made a mistake in the art and wanted to see the thirty-six compartments in which the art was arranged, to see if they had made a mistake and that she should not, in fact, be abbess, in which case, they should elect the sister indicated by the working of the art. Natana and the other sisters who had not been among the seven electors checked the method which had been followed according to the art in the election and confirmed

---

1. [The Catalan word is *cambres*. We assume that Lull had in mind the sort of triangular half-matrix he later draws in "De Arte Eleccionis."]

that the art had been followed as was indicated. Then Natana began to think deeply about how she would learn and be able to rule herself and the sisters, and every day she meditated as to how she could manage the convent in right ways.

The Art of Elections, 1299

In the Holy Church, good elections are greatly needed to choose representatives, as the church is to be governed by them and they must fight her enemies—sinners, infidels, and schismatics. These elected representatives cannot do this unless they are good men, well adapted to the service of their Mother, who is good and noble, namely the Holy Catholic Church. For the Church suffers greatly from those who pretend to be her faithful sons but who are in fact evil men who do harm to their Mother and usurp her possessions.

Therefore we wish to propose a method of electing a representative in accordance with the Third Figure of the General System of Knowledge such that by following the stages of this method the electors may publicly choose the better person and that, if they do not choose the best, it will be obvious to everyone in the chapter that they are choosing the worse candidate and perjuring themselves without any color of an excuse. The method of election is as follows:

Let b stand for the first candidate to have entered the Church,[2] c the second candidate, and so on to k, so that the first person to have held church office is called b, the second c, and so on. If there are more than nine candidates in the church, the cells in the figure above are multiplied by adding l; if there are eleven, then m. If there are more candidates than letters in the alphabet, we use numbers, so that one brother is called candidate 1, another 2, and so on in the same way.

First, let all voters take an oath that they will elect the better and more suitable candidate. Next, let the electors sit down, and let b and c stay standing at the side, near enough to hear what the electors say and so that they

---

2. [Latin *quae in ecclesia prius fuit recepta*. This could alternatively mean "the first person to have entered the church," i.e., the first to step into the building, in which case "the first person to have held church office" should rather be translated "the first person to enter the room." The consequences of the distinction between the two meanings are nontrivial. The first person to enter a set of pairwise votes is always at a disadvantage if voters vote sincerely in accordance with their preferences. So if the interpretation in our translation is correct, Lull's proposal biases selection against the most senior. If the interpretation in this note is correct, it biases against the most punctual, or the most pushy. Unfortunately we cannot decide from the Latin which is correct.]

bc	cd	de	ef	fg	gh	hi	ik
bd	ce	df	eg	fh	gi	hk	
be	cf	dg	eh	fi	gk		
bf	cg	dh	ei^a	fk			
bg	ch	di	ek				
bh	ci	dk					
bi	ck						
bk							

Fig. 3.1. Ramon Lull's voting matrix. Cusanus Library, Cod. Cus. 83, 47V. Note that at superscript *a* the manuscript has *el* in this cell.

themselves are visible to all. Then let *d* ask everyone who is sitting down which of *b* and *c* he prefers for abbot, prior, or bishop and go on until he has asked them all. The votes of the several electors are then counted, and if *b* has more than *c* let *c* sit down in his place and *b* remain standing or vice versa. Then let *d* be set against *b*: let *c* stand up and ask everybody which of *b* and *d* he prefers as prelate, and if *b* has more votes, let *d* sit down. Let *e* go with *b*, and let *c* or *d* or another ask each voter, in the presence of all, which of *b* and *e* he prefers for master. Suppose *e* beats *b*; then let *f* go to *e* or vice versa; if *b* is defeated, let *c* ask each which of *e* and *f* he prefers for master; and so on in order to *k*, so that with *k* the election comes to an end whether *k* wins or loses. Likewise if there are ten in the chapel, the last decision comes with *l* in order, as just explained.

This method of election is most useful and safe because it does not involve secret ballots and private pacts, which are more open to fraud than the above method. Those who choose openly are so placed as to be in disgrace with their colleagues if they choose badly. Those who elect in secret are not.

This new method of election is also good in that it is more general than any other method can be because for every candidate in the chapter, a reckoning is made of each elector's wishes in one of the cells of the above figure, and so each elector is happier with the result.

Similarly, by this method of election, any person in the chapter might suggest that it would be a good and honorable thing if this method were to be used in electing prelates, and he would obtain friends in the church, bring about peace, and avoid animosity, so that he might be chosen when the election came, and his colleagues would show mutual love, so that in an election one should stand for another and so the standing of the chapter would be raised through the charity, justice, prudence, and other virtues shown by the brethren toward each other.

If an election of persons not present is to be made, it should be done by the aforesaid method.

This method of election was devised in Paris in the year of the incarnation of our Lord Jesus Christ 1299 on the first of July. Thanks be to God.

CHAPTER 4

Nicolaus Cusanus (Niklaus von Kues)

From *On Catholic Harmony*, Book III, Chapter 37, 1434

535 When the electors of the Holy Roman Empire wish to proceed to the election of a future emperor, let them convene on the day arranged. In all humility and with the utmost devotion to the things of God, let them strip themselves of all sin so that Christ should be as Lord in their midst and the grace of the Holy Spirit whom they have invoked.

After a devout entry to the proceedings, let them establish the names of all those persons conceived as worthy, by dint of both external and internal qualities, to function in so majestic an office. So that the election may be made with unrestricted liberty and secrecy and free of all fear, let the electors then proceed as follows. After first swearing an oath on the Lord's altar to elect the person whom their free conscience shall duly judge best, the electors should get a notary to write, on slips of paper precisely equal in size, the names of the candidates. One name should go on one slip of paper, and after the name a clear digit—1, 2, 3, and so on—until there is a slip for each of the persons whom their previous deliberations have agreed to be worthy of consideration.

536 Let us now suppose that ten persons, found from throughout Germany, have been thus deemed worthy and that it is from among these that the most worthy is to be elected by common resolve. One only of these names is to be written on each slip. Under or beside the name a number is to be written (from one to ten). Ten slips, each with the name of one of the ten candidates, should then be given to each elector. When the electors have got their slips, each of them should go off alone, secretly (with a secretary if he cannot read), and, putting all ten slips in front of him, read the name on each.

537 Let the elector then ponder in his conscience, in God's name, which of all the candidates is least suitable. Let him make in ink a single stroke on the appropriate slip to indicate the number "one." Then let him consider who is the next–least worthy and write with two simple strokes of the pen the number "two" [in Roman characters—translators]. So he should go on, through the others, until he comes to the candidate who is in his judgment the best. On his slip he will write the number ten—or whatever number corresponds to the total of candidates.

538 It is recommended that all electors write with the same ink and with similar pens and similar strokes, long or short, as they shall agree. In this way no one's writing will stand out as recognizable from the others', and the electors will therefore be able to act with greater freedom and general harmony be preserved among them.

539 When the marks have been thus made, let each elector take his own bunch of slips in his hand and throw them, with his own hand, into an empty bag hung up in the midst of the electors. When all the slips are in the bag, the priest who celebrated Mass should be summoned, and a teller with a writing block on which the names of those to be elected—ten in the example—are written in the established order. Sitting in the middle of the electors, the priest should then take the slips out of the bag one by one, in whatever order his hand may find them, and read out the name and the number written on it. Meanwhile, the teller at his side should note down each number as it comes. When they are all recorded, the teller must add up the numbers by each name, and the candidate who has collected the highest total will be emperor.

540 By this method innumerable malpractices can be avoided, and indeed no malpractice is possible. In fact, no method of election can be conceived which is more holy, just, honest, or free. For by this procedure, no other outcome is possible, if the electors act according to conscience, than the choice of that candidate adjudged best by the collective judgment of all present. Nor will any surer method be discovered for reaching so infallible a formulation of collective decision. For this method takes account of all comparisons of candidate to candidate—in whatever groupings or combinations—that any elector can make. I have myself been unable to find a better method than this even after much effort; and you can safely take it that a more perfect method cannot be found.

Part 2
The Golden Age

CHAPTER 5

Jean-Charles de Borda

On Ballot Votes: Commentary by M. J. A. N. de Caritat, Marquis de Condorcet, 1784

In a ballot vote, we generally use one of two methods: either we say that the candidate who gets the most votes is elected, or else we hold repeated elections and elect the first candidate to get more than half or more than two-thirds of the votes.

The second method necessarily means that a certain number of voters end up having to choose the worthiest, not of all the candidates, but of those they think capable of obtaining sufficient votes. So by using this method, we succeed not in choosing the best candidate but in electing a man who is not considered unworthy by the plurality: we seem to be trying not so much to make the best choice as to be certain of not making a bad one.

M. le Chevalier de Borda's paper concerns the first method in particular. First he observes that in elections of this type, the apparent will of the plurality may in fact be the complete opposite of their true will. Suppose three candidates, A, B, and C. If A has eight votes, B seven, and C six, then A obtains the plurality. However with this type of voting, all we know is simply that eight people prefer A to his two opponents; we do not know if they prefer B to C or vice versa. We know that seven people prefer B to both A and C, but we do not know whether they prefer A or C. And finally, we do not know how the six voters who prefer C would rank B and A. Yet, if the eight voters who preferred A had ranked C above B, the seven who preferred B had ranked C above A, and the six who preferred C had ranked B above A, then both B and C would beat A by thirteen votes to eight, in which case A should be excluded. And since C would beat B by fourteen votes to seven, he would be the real favorite. The true wishes of the plurality would in fact have been for C, who got the fewest votes, and would have placed A last, although he got the most.

Having shown the failings of the conventional method, M. de Borda now goes on to propose a solution.

First, he asks each voter to list the candidates in order of merit, or else pronounce on the merit of the candidates, taken two by two. Clearly, once the list of candidates in order of merit has been submitted, we can extract from it each voter's judgment on the relative merits of any two candidates.

M. de Borda represents the degree of merit of the candidate in last place by an undefined value and the degree of merit of the one ranked next to last by this value, plus another to show his superiority; we add the same value once again to get the degree of merit attributed to the third candidate. This means that the merit of someone who has three or four candidates ranked below him is expressed by the value which represents the degree of merit of the one ranked last plus three or four times the constant value, which represents the difference in merit between two candidates ranked one immediately after the other.

In this way, we obtain the degree of merit assigned by each voter to each candidate, and by totalling these up, we obtain a value which represents their general opinion of the merit of each candidate. The candidate for whom this value is the greatest is the one who has plurality support.

Since any candidate can be ranked last by any voter, the value attributed to that place is always the same. The value which is added to it is proportional to the difference in merit between two consecutive candidates ranked one after the other and so cannot affect any comparison we make of the respective merits of candidates after the votes have been cast. We can therefore regard it as representing the unit or degree of merit.

Finally the multiple of this degree of merit for each candidate is exactly the same as the number of times he would have obtained the preference in successive pairwise comparisons; the plurality therefore support the candidate who obtained it most often.

Returning to our earlier example, we find that A, with eight first places and thirteen last, will get sixteen degrees of merit plus the value common to all. B, with seven first places and six second, will get twenty degrees of merit plus the same value; and finally C, with six first places and fifteen second, will get twenty-seven degrees of merit. We can see that each of these numbers is equal to the number of times each candidate was preferred to each of the others.

M. de Borda next examines what plurality is necessary to ensure that the candidate elected by the conventional method is the one who would obtain plurality support in the stricter method he is proposing as a substitute.

To do this he takes the worst possible situation for any candidate who has obtained the plurality: that in which one of his opponents has all the other first place votes and is ranked second by all those who do not rank him first, while the candidate who obtained the plurality, on the other hand, is ranked last by all those who did not rank him first.

From this, it follows that if we are to ensure that an election conducted along conventional lines gives a true expression of the plurality will, then the number of votes obtained by the winning candidate must be greater in relation to the total number of votes than the number of candidates minus one in relation to their total number. If there are three candidates, then the winning one must obtain more than two-thirds of the votes; if there are four, then he must obtain more than three-quarters; and if the number of candidates is equal to or greater than the number of voters, then the winner must have unanimous support.

M. de Borda observes that the laws of Poland require this unanimity for the election of their king, and since any Polish noble can be elected, this is precisely a case of the number of candidates being equal to or even greater than the number of voters. The parallel is striking, but this law could hardly have been determined by such reasoning as ours, or established in an effort to extract the true will of an assembly from that of the plurality.

M. de Borda's observations on the drawbacks of the election method used almost everywhere are very important and totally original. He had already developed these ideas in a paper read to the Academy in 1770.[1]

On Elections by Ballot[2] by M. de Borda

There is a widespread feeling, which I have never heard disputed, that in a ballot vote, the plurality of votes always shows the will of the voters. That is, that the candidate who obtains this plurality is necessarily preferred by the voters to his opponents. But I shall demonstrate that this feeling, while correct when the election is between just two candidates, can lead to error in all other cases.

Suppose an election between three candidates, *A, B,* and *C,* with twenty-one voters. Out of these twenty-one voters, thirteen prefer *B* to *A* and only eight prefer *A* to *B*. The same thirteen voters also prefer *C* to *A*, while the other eight prefer *A* to *C*. In the collective opinion of the voters, then, candidate *A* is decidedly inferior to both *B* and *C*, because when each of these is compared to *A*, he has thirteen votes while *A* has only eight. It follows that the will of the voters demands that candidate *A* be excluded. However, if we use

---

1. [The first page of the manuscript has been lost, and in the collection of Condorcet's manuscripts at the Bibliothèque de l'Institut de France, this paper begins with the second page ("in this way, we obtain the degree of merit . . . "). At the end of the paper, Condorcet has written, and then crossed out, the words "mais elle paraissait si éloignée des idées communes que . . ." ("but it seemed so remote from ordinary ideas that . . .").]

2. The ideas put forward in this note were presented to the Academy fourteen years ago, on 16 June 1770.

the conventional election method, such a candidate might actually obtain the plurality. We need only suppose that out of the thirteen voters who prefer both *B* and *C* to *A*, seven rank *B* above *C* and six rank *C* above *B*. On adding up the votes, this gives us the following result:

> eight votes for *A*,
> seven votes for *B*,
> and six votes for *C*.

Candidate *A* would have the plurality, although, *ex hypothesi*, the plurality of the voters were against him.

On reflection, we see that candidate *A* gains the advantage only because candidates *B* and *C* have more or less equally split the thirteen votes against him. We might compare them to two athletes who, having exhausted themselves competing against one another, are beaten by a third who is weaker than either.

Clearly then, the conventional form of election is highly unsatisfactory, because in this type of election, the voters cannot give a sufficiently complete account of their opinions of the candidates. Suppose that out of several candidates, *A, B, C, D,* etc., someone votes for *B*, and someone else for *C*. The first person simply singles out *B* as better than all of the others and says nothing about the position he would assign to *C* in the unranked group. Similarly, the second person ranks *C* as best overall but says nothing of the position he would assign to *B*. This is by no means inconsequential, as, all other things being equal, we have good reason to prefer the one who is placed higher in the unranked group; and in general, the claim of each candidate to nomination by the voters is a result of the different ranks he occupies in their opinions. If a form of election is to be just, the voters must be able to rank each candidate according to his merits, compared successively to the merits of each of the others.

There are two election methods which allow the voters to do this: in the first, each voter ranks the candidates in order of merit, and in the second, we hold as many elections as there are combinations of candidates taken two by two so that each candidate can be compared to each of the others in turn. It is easy to see that this second method necessarily derives from the first. Each method clearly gives us the most complete expression possible of the voters' opinions on all the candidates. What I am going to examine here is how we can derive a result from the votes cast in these two types of election.

I shall begin with the first, which I shall call *election by order of merit*. Suppose that there are just three candidates and that each voter has written their names on a voting slip, ranking them according to the degree of merit he attributes to each, so that these voting slips read

A	A	B	C
B	C	A	B
C	B	C	A

and so on.

First of all, let us examine just one of these slips, the first one, say, where the voter ranked A first, B second, and C third. Now, we must assume that the degree of superiority which this voter gave A over B is the same as that he gave B over C. As candidate B is no more likely to be ranked in one particular place on the scale between A and C than in any other, we have no reason to say that the voter who ranked the candidates ABC wanted to place B nearer A than C or vice versa; no reason to say, that is, that he accorded the first more superiority over the second than he accorded the second over the third. Furthermore, because of the supposed equality between the voters, each rank must be assumed to have the same value and to represent the same degree of merit as the same rank assigned to another candidate, or even by another voter.

If we take a to be the degree of merit which each voter attributes to last place and $a + b$ the degree of merit attributed to second place, we can represent first place by $a + 2b$. The formulae will be just the same for the ranks assigned by other voters, so that every last place will be represented by a, every second place by $a + b$, and every first place by $a + 2b$.

Now, suppose that there are four candidates. We can prove in just the same way that the superiority of first place over second, of second over third, and of third over fourth must all be considered equal, and that corresponding places assigned by different voters must represent the same degree of merit. So the merit attributed by the voters to fourth, third, second, and first place can be represented by a, $a + b$, $a + 2b$, and $a + 3b$. The method will be just the same when there are more candidates.

Having established this, it will now be easy to compare the value of the votes given to different candidates in any election. To do this, we multiply by a the number of times each candidate is ranked last, by $a + b$ the number of times he is ranked second to last, by $a + 2b$ the number of times he is ranked in next place up, and so on, and the sum of these results is the value of his votes.

Clearly, a and b can represent whatever value we like. Suppose therefore that $a = 1$ and that $b = 1$ and that the value of each candidate's votes can be obtained by multiplying the number of times he is ranked last by 1, the number of times he is ranked second to last by 2, the number of times he is ranked third from last by 3 and so on, up to the number of times he is ranked first, which will be multiplied by the number of candidates.

We shall now give an example of this type of election. Suppose once again that there are twenty-one voters and three candidates, *A*, *B*, and *C*, and that the twenty-one voting slips are as follows:

```
A  A  A  A  A  A  A  A  B  B  B  B  B  B  B  C  C  C  C  C  C
B  C  C  C  C  C  C  C  C  C  C  C  C  C  C  B  B  B  B  B  B
C  B  B  B  B  B  B  B  A  A  A  A  A  A  A  A  A  A  A  A  A
```

By multiplying the first place votes by 3, the second place votes by 2, and the third place votes by 1, we obtain the comparative values of each candidate's votes:

$$
A \left\{ \begin{array}{lll} 8 \text{ first places} & \times\ 3 = 24 \\ \\ 13 \text{ third places} & \times\ 1 = 13 \end{array} \right\} = 37
$$

$$
B \left\{ \begin{array}{lll} 7 \text{ first places} & \times\ 3 = 21 \\ 7 \text{ second places} & \times\ 2 = 14 \\ 7 \text{ third places} & \times\ 1 =\ \ 7 \end{array} \right\} = 42
$$

$$
C \left\{ \begin{array}{lll} 6 \text{ first places} & \times\ 3 = 18 \\ 14 \text{ second places} & \times\ 2 = 28 \\ 1 \text{ third place} & \times\ 1 =\ \ 1 \end{array} \right\} = 47
$$

So candidate *C* wins, with *B* second and *A* last.

Note that if we had used the conventional election method, the result would have been as follows:

eight votes for *A*
seven votes for *B*
six votes for *C*

That is, *A* would have had the plurality although he is actually last in the opinion of the voters, and *C* would have had fewer votes than either of the other two although he is really the favorite.

Let us now examine the method of separate elections, once again with three candidates, *A*, *B*, and *C*. As we can combine these three candidates taken two by two in three different ways, we shall have to hold three separate elections. Suppose that the results of these elections are as follows:

First election between *A* and *B*: $\left. \begin{array}{l} a \text{ votes for } A \\ b \text{ votes for } B \end{array} \right\}$

Second election between A and C: $\left\{ \begin{array}{l} a' \text{ votes for } A \\ c \ \text{ votes for } C \end{array} \right\}$

Third election between B and C: $\left\{ \begin{array}{l} b' \text{ votes for } B \\ c' \text{ votes for } C \end{array} \right\}$

In order to find the comparative values of each candidate's votes, we shall suppose that these elections are the result of an election by order of merit. It is quite possible for this to be the case, as once we know how each voter has ranked the candidates, we can easily calculate the number of votes a candidate would obtain in an election between himself and any other candidate. Let us, then, take y to be the number of first places that candidate A obtained in this election by order of merit, x the number of second places, and z the number of last places. Clearly, the value of the votes obtained by A can be represented by $3y + 2x + z$. But $y + x + z =$ the total number of electors, and we can call this number E. If we eliminate z, we can represent the value of A's votes by $2y + x + E$, or simply by $2y + x$, because E is common to every candidate. Now, for each first place that A has in an election by order of merit, he has two votes in the separate elections, that is, one in the election between A and B and one in the election between A and C. For each second place he has in an election by order of merit, he has just one in the separate elections, and for each third place, he has none. From which it follows that the number of votes he obtains in the separate elections, that is $a + a'$, will be equal to $2y + x$, and we have just seen that this represented the value of the votes in an election by order of merit. $a + a'$ will therefore represent that value for separate elections, that is, the value of the votes given to each candidate will be represented by the total of the votes he had in all the separate elections. Clearly this also applies to elections where there are a greater number of candidates.

If we set the values of a, a', b, b', c, c' according to the supposition that separate elections are the result of the election by order of merit reported above, we shall find that

$$a \ = 8 \quad b \ = 13 \quad c \ = 13$$

$$a' = 8 \quad b' = \ 8^3 \quad c' = 13$$

and that consequently,

A's votes $= a + a' = 16$

---

3. [Borda has 13 here. This is a mistake.]

B's votes $= b + b' = 21$[4]

C's votes $= c + c' = 26$

and that the candidates are ranked in exactly the same order as in the first type of election.

Now, the second type of election would be awkward in practice because if there were a large number of candidates, we would have to hold a great many separate elections. We should therefore prefer the form of election by order of merit, which is far less time-consuming.

I shall end this paper by examining a particular question related to the conventional election method. I have shown that in these elections, the plurality of votes is not always a definite indication of the will of the voters. However, this plurality can sometimes be so big that it would be impossible for the voters actually to support anyone other than the candidate who obtained the plurality. To discover when this is the case, let us call the number of candidates M, the number of voters E, the candidate with the plurality A, the candidate with the next number of votes B, and finally let us say that y is the number of votes obtained by A and z the number of votes obtained by B.

Now, suppose that we conduct an election by order of merit between all the candidates. Clearly, candidate A will have a number of first places equal to y, and candidate B will have a value of first places equal to z. Now, the worst possible result for A would be if all the voters who did not put him first ranked him last and all those who did not put B first ranked him second. Since the number of first places is represented by m, of second places by $m - 1$, and of last places by 1, the value of A's votes is $my + E - y$ and that of B's votes is $mz + [(m - 1) \cdot (E - z)]$; if the result is to come out in favor of A, it must be the case that

$$my + E - y > mz + [(m - 1) \cdot (E - z)], \text{ [5]}$$

or that

$$y > \frac{z + E(m - 2)}{m - 1}$$

If $m = 2$, then we shall have $y > z$, that is, when the election is between just two candidates, the candidate with the plurality can be legitimately elected. In

---

4. [Borda has 12 here. This is a mistake.]

5. [Borda has $my + E - y > (mz - 1) \cdot (E - z)$. This is a mistake.]

this case, and in this case only, the conventional form of election gives the right result.

If candidate B gets all the votes not obtained by candidate A, then we shall get $z = E - y$, and by inserting this into the equation above,

$$y > E \cdot \frac{m - 1}{m}$$

If for this last equation, we take m to be 3, we shall get $y = 2E/3$; that is, when there are three candidates, one of them must get more than two-thirds of the votes to be sure of having plurality support.

Similarly, when there are four candidates, y must be greater than three-quarters of E, and so on.

Finally, if the number of candidates is equal to or greater than the number of voters, the expression above

$$y > \frac{z + E(m - 2)}{m - 1}$$

will become $y > E - 1$. That is, the election can then only be satisfactorily decided by unanimity, and this surprising result justifies the way in which one of the Northern nations elects its kings.

In conclusion, I must stress that everything we have said here about elections also applies to any debate conducted by any company or body of men; these debates are really no more than a type of election between the different opinions put forward and are therefore subject to the same rules.

CHAPTER 6

M. J. A. N. de Caritat, Marquis de Condorcet

From *An Essay on the Application of Analysis to the Probability of Decisions Rendered by a Plurality of Votes*, 1785

[The page references in this chapter are to Condorcet (1785) 1972.]

Fifth Part

Here we give an example of the application of the preceding theory:

1. The constitution of a tribunal in which the tort caused by error is the same regardless of which of the two contradictory propositions, though false, has gained a plurality of votes. This situation occurs, for instance, if two men are disputing a property in a civil case and have an equally favorable case.
2. The constitution of a tribunal in which one of the decisions must not be accepted until truth is proved. For instance, in a criminal judgment, sufficient assurance that the accused is guilty is required in order to decide the sentence.
3. An election method that provides sufficient assurance that the person elected will be the most worthy competitor.
4. And finally, comparison of the probabilities produced by assemblies where the number of voters becomes larger and larger while the probabilities of the new voters become smaller.

First Example

Constitution of a tribunal in which the harm caused by a false decision is the same whatever the decision, particularly in a civil tribunal.

I. In this case, it is sufficient to prefer an opinion if it is more probable than its contradiction. And we have seen above that the probability produced by a decision can never be larger than the actual probability of the adopted proposition; and this probability, not unity, is the limit of the probability of these decisions. This observation leads to a first condition: laws that are sufficiently clear and simple to create M', an assurance that the probability of each person's equity will not fall below a particular limit L, so that $(M' + L)/2$ represents the mean value of the real probability and $M'(1 + L)/2$ describes the same value when favorable probabilities below L or even $M' L$ are not distinguished from contrary probabilities. In general, this probability, P' will be the *minimum* of all the probabilities that can be calculated.

II. Now suppose that the decisions of a tribunal of inquiry indicate that its members have a probability of voting correctly of v and a probability of voting incorrectly of e. If q' is the plurality used to render this decision, then

$$P \frac{v^{q'}}{v^{q'} + e^{q'}} + (1 - P) \frac{e^{q'}}{v^{q'} + e^{q'}}$$

will be the probability of this decision. And if we exclude the terms that describe incorrect decisions that result from voter mistakes in accepting an opinion as most probable when it is least probable but true, the probability of the truth is reduced to only

$$P \frac{v^{q'}}{v^{q'} + e^{q'}},$$

and the probability of selecting the most probable opinion will be

$$\frac{v^{q'}}{v^{q'} + e^{q'}}.$$

III. Now if q is the number of voters, and

$$\frac{V'_q}{V'_q + E'_q}$$

is the probability of having a plurality of q', expressed by M^*, and if $M^\#$ represents

$$\frac{v^{q'}}{v^{q'} + e^{q'}}$$

then M', M^*, and $M^\#$ must equal M', where M is the required reliability that the decision will favor the opinion whose probability is above L. This probability describes the decision before it has been rendered.

IV. At one, when the plurality is smallest, the probability $M'Lv$ that the decision is true can be obtained by removing all the cases in which truth is not produced by counterbalancing errors. Therefore if, as on page 232 of part three, $M = 23,999/24,000$, or $35,999/36,000$, then $M'_\cdot M^*M^\# = 23,999/24,000$, or $35,999/36,000$; and $M'L'v > 1/2$ will be a necessary condition for this type of tribunal. Consequently, any tribunal that does not fulfill these conditions should be regarded as defective.

V. Here three positions can be taken.

1. Always use an odd-numbered tribunal with plurality rule even if the margin is one vote.
2. Require a larger plurality, and if it does not occur, have a second tribunal make the decision.
3. Make a plurality decision but require the same tribunal to judge equity to reduce the severity of the judgment.

Since it is limited to selecting the most probable of two opinions, the first position has the drawback of relying on a very small probability of choosing correctly to decide an important point. The third position partially eliminates this limitation by allowing compensation that can be regulated by law. In addition, this small plurality obviously makes it credible that the real probability of the opinions that make up the decision of the voters is very small. Part three of Problem V gives the probability that it is below the given limit as well as the limit above which it is very unlikely to rise. In this case, we can suppose that the right of one of the two competitors is not much more probable than that of the other. So the person whose right is less probable can be compensated without injustice. The second position has the drawback of greatly prolonging decisions. Also, this position is liable to produce a minority opinion if the sufficiency of the first decisions is not scrutinized (see above pages 80–81). However, scrutinizing first decisions forces a choice between the injustice of rejecting new information and the uncertainty of the influence created by this information. Moreover, this position necessarily introduces uncertainty in decisions that cannot be removed without calling for a second judgment from the judges who voted in the first decision and allowing them the liberty of changing their opinions. As we have seen above, this would diminish the probability even more!

For instance, consider an odd-numbered tribunal where three votes are required. If the laws are clear and well formulated, we can assume that in most questions, L, or the limit of the real probability, equals $999/1,000$, and that M' is very large so that without much error, it can be assumed to equal unity. Then if $v/e = 4$, the probability of a judgment in the most unfavorable case occurs and equals $999/1,000(64/65) = 63,936/65,000$, or only $3,996/5,000$ or even much less, for it is reasonable that L can be much smaller when the same tribunal forms a court of equity to decide on compensation according to limits and substance fixed by law.

In the same hypothetical situation, if $v/e = 9$, the smallest probability when there is a decision equals 728,271/730,000, where the risk of error is less than 1/365, and, if there is compensation, it would be smaller than 8,991/10,000 since L would very probably be below 999/1,000. Now this probability ought to be quite small so that compensation or some type of apportionment of rights can be required without injustice.

If $q = 25$, $q' = 5$, and $v/e = 9$, it satisfies the condition $M'M*M^\# = M = 35,999/36,000$. In other words, 25 voters will suffice.

The assumption that $v/e = 9$ may seem very small for tribunals that judge on the basis of laws that are simple and very clear, but to increase reliability, it is not necessary to take the average probability for v but the limit of the probability below which there is an assurance $M^\wedge$ that the probability will not fall for any of the members of the tribunal. Consequently, if v' is this limit, the previous value of

$$\frac{v^{q'}}{v^{q'} + e^{q'}}$$

actually represents

$$M^\wedge \frac{v'^q}{v'^q + e'^q}$$

and in $M'Lv$, v carries the value of $M^\# v'$. In this hypothetical situation, the assumption that $v/e = 9$ is not much below the truth even for judges who are very well informed.

In the same hypothetical situation, suppose that the number of judges is always greater than 25 and is even- or odd-numbered. When the number of voters is even, compensation can be accepted in case of a tie or when the plurality is only two votes. In the latter case, the insufficient probability is approximately 80,719/82,000, and the risk is nearly 1/82, but a little larger, around 1/10, but a little smaller, as there is only a plurality of one vote. Therefore here we find simultaneously a risk that is too small to accept compensation and that is too large to ignore it. Consequently, the number of judges must always be uneven.

Second Example

Constitution of a tribunal that chooses only one of two opinions when the probability of the truth of the decision is very large, particularly for a criminal trial.

In the fourth part, page 273, we demonstrated that the assurance necessary for not acquitting a guilty person and not convicting an innocent person can only be obtained in a tribunal in which a choice for or against the accused is made after all votes have coalesced for the same opinion. We also showed that this structure will not prevent acquitting a guilty person even if the truth of his crime is sufficiently proved, and it will also convict an innocent person with a probability that is less than justice requires.

Moreover, we observe

1. That whenever possible, any type of influence on voters' choices should carefully be avoided. In fact, as we saw on page 79, avoidable uncertainty cannot be introduced by the form of judgment without harming justice. We cannot condone convicting a man on the basis of a probability, however large, solely because certainty is impossible. Requiring unanimity can introduce voluntary uncertainty because weariness, excessive constraints, and hunger can lead eleven out of twelve judges to adopt the opinion of the twelfth judge. In regard to this latter point, it is quite just to reproach English law because it gives a strong, roguish jury many advantages over a jury that is weak but honest.

2. Let us consider the risk of convicting an innocent person. If there are twelve judges and v is the probability that each one will vote correctly, then

$$\frac{v^{12}}{v^{12} + e^{12}}$$

is the probability that the convicted defendant is guilty where v is what each voter's probability becomes in this form of voting. Now if another tribunal decides with a plurality of only eight votes and has a probability of v', the two cases can produce an equal assurance only if

$$\frac{v'^8}{v'^8 + e'^8} = \frac{v^{12}}{v^{12} + e^{12}} \quad \text{or} \quad \frac{v'}{e'} = \left(\frac{v}{e}\right)^{3/2}.$$

In other words, to have a tribunal of learned jurists using a plurality of eight votes match the reliability of an English jury, it would be sufficient that the unanimous opinion of two men accustomed to discussing an issue be as good as the opinion of three decision makers selected by chance. This comparison can be recognized without making an overly favorable assumption about the first set of jurors, but it leads us to suppose that a plurality of eight votes will be required.

Here the first condition will be

$$PM^\wedge \frac{v'^{q'}}{v'^{q'} + e'^{q'}} = \frac{144,767}{144,768},$$

where P is the real probability of a fact regarded as rigorously proved and v' is the limit below which there is a probability $M^$ that the truth of none of the votes will fall. Now it is easy to see that this first condition will be satisfied if $v = 9/10$ and if P and $M^$, similar quantities, are on the order of

$$\left(\frac{144,767}{144,768} \right)^{1/3}.$$

Now consider the second condition—the reliability that a legislator or any wielder of public power needs not to convict an innocent person within a generation. This condition can be represented (see page 239) by $M^V'/(V' + E')$ or

$$M^ \frac{v'^{q'}}{v'^{q'} + e'^{q'}} = \left(\frac{1,899}{1,900} \right)^{1/1,000},$$

which makes it necessary to have $M^'V'/(V' + E')$ or

$$\frac{v'^{q'}}{v'^{q'} + e'^{q'}}$$

on the order of $(1,899/1,900)^{1/2,000}$. The last two quantities of this condition can also be satisfied by making $q' = 8$ and $v'/e' = 9$. The value of $M^$ will depend on the care taken to comprehend each voter's degree of probability.

In order to make $PM^V'/(V' + E')$ or

$$PM^ \frac{v'^{q'}}{v'^{q'} + e'^{q'}}$$

equal to $(1,899/1,900)^{1/1,000}$, the three factors must be on the order of $(1,899/1,900)^{1/3,000}$. This condition is also fulfilled by the hypothesis that $q' = 8$ and $v'/e' = 9$. In fact, it is only necessary that $M^$ increase and that P be of the order of $(1,899/1,900)^{1/3,000}$. But here P represents the real probability of the event being decided, so it seems useless to include it in the second condition. And it also seems sufficient that a legislator's fear of convicting an innocent person in a generation should not be less than a man's own indifference about mistakes in necessary precautions so that the judgment is as certain as human wisdom and the nature of the proposed questions permit.

The third condition, not allowing the guilty to go unpunished, is described by $V' = 99,999/100,000$ and $1 - V' - E' = 1/144,768$. The quantity P should not be included at all in these estimates. Here, in fact, $1 - P$

expresses the probability of judging badly in deciding that a man is or is not guilty despite the strength of the evidence for the opposing opinion. This expression also includes the example of encouraging crime by allowing a guilty person to escape with impunity when it is as probable that he is guilty as it is that the crime is not proved. This latter condition will be satisfied if we assume that $q' = 8$ and $v'/e' = 9$ and that there are thirty judges. Since this number of judges must always be provided, a rather large tribunal must be formed, especially if, as justice seems to require, some challenges without cause are allowed and if, except in very rare cases, the use of unknown members is to be avoided.

Third Example

The Form of Election

First we determine if it is appropriate that electors using plurality rule decide the eligibility of all candidates who nominate themselves or who are nominated by the body that is charged with that duty.

This first precaution makes the following election simpler and, at first glance, does not involve any drawback. For if more than half of the voters admit an unworthy candidate, it is evident that they would have elected him under any form of election. In contrast, if more than half of the voters exclude a man of merit with the intention of facilitating the success of an inferior candidate, the first deliberation would not make any difference. In the same case, if aversion to the first candidate leads to his exclusion, this form of election would be better because it leaves open the possibility of choosing among the remaining candidates. Without this option, excluding the first candidate can produce intrigue and lead to a worse choice. The only drawback of this first deliberation occurs when two parties, divided between two subjects, unite to exclude a third candidate. But it is easy to see that these parties would achieve the same objective anyway by distributing their votes to rank the third candidate last in merit. Thus in the form of election that was proved to be most preferred in the first part, it will be useful to deliberate first to set the number of candidates.

Then when each elector submits a list of these candidates in order of merit, we can deduce the $n(n - 1)/2$ propositions accepted by a plurality for a number, n, of candidates. And if V and E are constant, we can deduce the probability that the plurality opinion will not be based on inconsistent propositions. In general, this expression will be

$$(V + E)(v^2 + VE + E^2)(V^3 + V^2E + VE^2 + E^3) \ldots$$

$$(V^{n-1} + V^{n-2}E + V^{n-3}E^2 + \ldots + E^{n-1}).$$

This formula states that the plurality opinion favors one of the $n!(n - 1!$
$\ldots 2!1!)$ possible combinations. If $V = 1$, it becomes 1, as it should. If
$V = E$, it becomes

$$\frac{1!2! \ldots . n!}{2^{\frac{n!(n - 1)}{2}}},$$

as it also should because when all combinations become equally likely, the
probabilities must be the same as the number of combinations.

As long as there is a sequence of $n - 1$ propositions $(A > B, A > C,$
$A > D$, etc.) for a candidate, A, it does not matter if the other propositions that
only affect the rankings of the $n - 1$ other candidates form a true or false
system. Thus instead of considering the $n(n - 1) \ldots 2 \cdot 1$ possible combinations, there are

$$n \cdot 2^{(n-1)} {(n-2)/2}$$

possible combinations that give a true result. Here the probability of having a
true system becomes

$$V^{n-1} + V^{n-2}E + \ldots + E^{n-1}.$$

In other words it is still 1 when $V = 1$ and

$$\frac{n}{2^{n-1}},$$

or the same number of combinations as when $V = E$. In the first case, the
probability of the truth of the entire judgment is $V^{n(n - 1)/2}$, and in the second
case it is V^{n-2}.

It is worth noting here that these probability estimates presuppose that
combinations that give results and those that do not and systems that are
possible and those that are absurd can have all the possible pluralities. This
point is true only for possible systems. Thus the probabilities assigned above
are the same as those that would be produced if we took successive votes on
$n(n - 1)/2$ propositions about n candidates by allowing each voter the liberty
of choosing a contradictory system. So these values of the probability are too
small, but since more exact values would be very difficult to assign and are
unfavorable for the proposed method, we will use them here.

Suppose that a plurality of a certain number of votes is desired instead of a simple plurality. If V and E are the probability that this plurality will decide in favor of truth or error, the probability will be described by the same formulas.

This reasoning suggests that

1. When V and E are constant, the probability of having a decision and the probability of having a true decision diminish as the number of candidates increases.

2. V^{n-1} must be a very large number in order to have sufficient reliability. For instance, if the desired probability of having a true decision is $1,899/1,900$, see page 239, and if there are ten candidates, then it is necessary that $V = (1,899/1,900)^{1/9} = 9,995/10,000$, so that the risk of having a plurality in favor of a false proposition will only be $1/20,000$.

3. Since

$$V^{n-2} + V^{n-2}E + \ldots + E^{n-1} = V^{n-1}\left(1 + \frac{E}{V} + \ldots + \frac{E^{n-1}}{V^{n-1}}\right)$$

$$= V^{n-1}\frac{1 - \dfrac{E^n}{V^n}}{1 - \dfrac{E}{V}}.$$

And since a false decision should be avoided above all, E^n/V^n, which can generally be ignored, must be large enough so that $1/[1 - (E/V)] = V/(2V - 1)$ approaches unity very closely. For instance, if there is a decision and if the desired probability of all constituent propositions is $1,899/1,900$, then it is necessary that it is necessary that $V/(2V - 1) - 1 = 1/1,900$, or $V = 1,901/1,902$. This condition does not require a very great probability of each voter's vote.

4. As V becomes larger, and n stays the same, then as

$$V^{m-1}\frac{1 - \dfrac{E^n}{V^n}}{1 - \dfrac{E}{V}}$$

approaches unity, the larger V^{n-1} becomes in relation to the remainder of the term. From this it follows that if a true decision cannot be derived from a vote and other voters are therefore designated to help the first set of voters, the more frequently these voters are called, the larger the probabilities of having a decision and having a true decision.

If a single election orders all candidates among each other, the first formulas above must be used. The probability of having a true decision will be $V^{n(n-1)/2}$, the probability of having a decision will be

$$V^{n(n-1)/2} \frac{\left(1 - \dfrac{E^2}{V^2}\right)\left(1 - \dfrac{E^3}{V^3}\right)\left(1 - \dfrac{E^4}{V^4}\right) \ldots \left(1 - \dfrac{E^n}{V^n}\right)}{\left(1 - \dfrac{E^n}{V^n}\right)^{n-1}},$$

and the probability that the decision rendered will be true will be

$$\frac{\left(1 - \dfrac{E}{V}\right)^{n-1}}{\left(1 - \dfrac{E^2}{V^2}\right)\left(1 - \dfrac{E^3}{V^3}\right)\left(1 - \dfrac{E^4}{V^4}\right) \ldots \left(1 - \dfrac{E^n}{V^n}\right)}.$$

From this we conclude that

1. As soon as n becomes large, it will be difficult to make V very large. In fact, for 1,899/1,900, we find that even for $n = 5$, V is 99,997/100,000 and the risk of not having a true decision must become less than 3/100,000. And for ten candidates, V must be 99,991/100,000, and the risk is then 1/100,000,000.

2. The formula

$$\frac{\left(1 - \dfrac{E}{V}\right)^{n-1}}{\left(1 - \dfrac{E^2}{V^2}\right)\left(1 - \dfrac{E^3}{V^3}\right)\left(1 - \dfrac{E^4}{V^4}\right) \ldots \left(1 - \dfrac{E^n}{V^n}\right)}$$

can be represented without noticeable error by

$$\frac{\left(1 - \dfrac{E}{V}\right)^{n-1}}{2 - \dfrac{1}{1 - \dfrac{E}{V}}}.$$

or

$$\frac{\left(1 - \dfrac{E}{V}\right)^{n}}{1 - \dfrac{2E}{V}}.$$

By calling this formula a, we derive

$$1 - E/V = a^{1/n}\left[1 - \frac{2}{n-2}(1 - a^{1/n})\right].^{1}$$

If, as above, it is desired that $a = 1,899/1,900$, then, $n = 10$, and $1 - E/V = (999,973/100,000) \times (999,993/1,000,000) = 999,966/1,000,000$, which implies that $E/V = 34/1,000,000$. In other words, $V = 1,000,000/1,000,034$ and $E = 34/1,000,034$. The latter value is not hard to obtain since we previously saw that quite natural hypothetical situations yield E below $1/2,000,000$ for a rather small number of voters. Thus here, as in the previous case, the fear of having no decision should be of greater concern than the fear of a false decision.

3. That when n is constant, the probability of having a decision, the probability of a correct decision, and the probability that the decision obtained will be true increase as the number of voters grows. It follows that if some voters have the same degree of probability as the first group and their votes can be collected when the first group does not reach a decision, then there will always be increasing probabilities of arriving at a decision and of rendering one that is true.

If a plurality of a single vote is acceptable, the least favorable case occurs when the $(n-1)$ or the

$$\frac{[n(n-1)]}{2}$$

propositions only have this probability, so the probability of having a true decision will be v^{n-1} or $v^{n(n-1)/2}$. If q' is the required plurality, it will be

$$\left(\frac{v^{q'}}{v^{q'} + e^{q'}}\right)^{n-1}$$

or

$$\left(\frac{v^{q'}}{v^{q'} + e^{q'}}\right)^{n(n-1)/2}.$$

This requires that v or

$$\frac{v^{q'}}{v^{q'} + e^{q'}}$$

---

1. [The original text for the last term in this expression is "$(1 - a^{/n})$."]

equal

$$a^{1/n-1}$$

or

$$a^{2/[n(n-1)]}$$

to have a probability of a in the most unfavorable case. For instance, suppose that $a = 99/100$, which seems sufficient. If $n = 10$ and $v = 9/10$, then it is necessary that

$$q' = \frac{\frac{1}{9}\ln\frac{99}{100} - \ln\left(1 - \frac{99^{2/9}}{100}\right)}{\ln 9},$$

or

$$\frac{\frac{1}{45}\ln\frac{99}{100} - \ln\left(1 - \frac{99^{1/45}}{100}\right)}{\ln 9}.^2$$

In other words, when the plurality is 4, $q' = 4$ in both cases. And it will be sufficient to take a number of voters so that $V'/(V' + E') = 999,991/1,000,000$ in the second case and $V'/(V' + E') = 1,901/1,902$ in the first case. This result can be obtained without making the number of voters very large.

Therefore we can create an advantageous form of election with the sole stipulation that if an electoral choice is absolutely necessary, but not produced, other voters can be called until their votes produce a veritable election. If an election is necessary and an election does not occur even though all possible votes have been exhausted, the method proposed in the first part, pages 124 and 125 can be followed.

But here we must observe that

1. The probability of preferring the best candidate may be below half even though it will be more probable that the candidate elected is the best.
2. Where n is the number of voters, there can be an equivocal electoral outcome only for the top three, four, or more candidates. Conse-

---

2. [In the original text, the denominator is 9 without the log notation.]

quently, in this case there can be a very large probability of choosing the best one of the three, four, or more best candidates. And if the electors are of good faith and their probability of voting correctly is above half, it is very probable that they will make one good choice, a good one if not the best one, unless all of the candidates except one are bad.

Since each voter ordered candidates A, B, and C and this order is $A > B > C$, up to this point the three propositions $A > B$, $A > C$, and $B > C$ were assumed to be equiprobable. However, here it might seem that the proposition $A > C$ must be more probable. In fact, it may be proved by comparing A and C, A and B, and B and C. Moreover, since the difference articulated between A and C is larger than the stated difference between B and C, we ought to be less mistaken.

But it could be argued that

1. In many cases, two propositions can be regarded as equiprobable even though they do not agree about the difference between two objects.
2. If the comparison is based only on a single quality, the first reason advanced is just the same as in the second proposition, and the probability would not be increased because the comparison of A with B and B with C does not furnish any proof about the superiority of A over C that cannot be provided by the immediate comparison of A with C.
3. The same observation can still be made if the comparison is based on two or several qualities. For instance, suppose that A prevails over B for one of these qualities and over C for the other. Then, comparing B and C, if one is advantageous for the first quality and the other for the second quality, my preference for B would only be my preference for the first of these qualities. And the probability that this preference is just makes it probable that the larger difference between A and C is correct, but it does not affect the existence of this difference in favor of A in this way.
4. Finally, if the propositions $A > B$ and $A > C$ are taken separately without comparing B to C, they are not necessarily more probable whatever the comparison of B and C.

Therefore, in general, it is better to interpret all of these propositions as equiprobable with equal plurality because the often null or very small differences in their probability can only be evaluated in a very arbitrary way.

As above, we might take[3] each voter's decision as an ordering of the

3. [The original text term *prendre* is translated literally here, although Black (1958) and others have suggested "interpret" as a translation. The more literal translation takes account of

candidates. Next the value of their vote for the first candidate can be assumed to be 1, the value for the second candidate would be $b < 1$, and the value of the vote for the third candidate would be $c < b$. This ingenious idea was proposed by a celebrated geometrician[4] but should not be adopted for the following reason. Suppose that there are three competitors, A, B, and C, and six alternatives, $A > B > C, A > C > B, C > A > B, B > A > C, B > C > A$, and $C > B > A$, that correspond to combinations 1, 2, 4, 5, 7, and 8 from those on page 120. If thirty voters choose combination 1, one voter chooses combination 2, ten voters select combination 4, twenty-nine choose combination 5, ten select combination 7, and one voter selects combination 8, we will have

for the proposition $A > B$: 41 against 40 votes
for the proposition $A > C$: 60 against 21 votes
for the proposition $B > C$: 69 against 12 votes

or a decision in favor of A. Now according to the other method, if the decision is to favor A, it is necessary that $31 + 39b + 11c > 39 + 31b + 11c$, which makes $b > 1$, a result that is contrary to the hypothesis.

If the method discussed on page 122 were used, then we would have

for $A > B$: 41 against 40 votes
for $A > C$: 60 against 21 votes
for $B > A$: 40 against 41 votes
for $B > C$: 69 against 12 votes

But as long as the probability of each vote is above three quarters, the decision will obviously favor A because the probability that the propositions that make up this decision are true simultaneously is above half. Thus in order to have the illustrated method produce the same result in this example, it would still be necessary that $b > 1$, which is contrary to the hypothesis.

Fourth Example

Investigation of the probability of decisions of assemblies in which the number of members grows but the probability decreases in proportion to the growth of membership and examination of the most reliable form of decision making appropriate for these assemblies.

Condorcet's ambivalence. But this passage is the closest Condorcet comes to describing voting as a process that can filter information about voter preferences through plurality or Borda voting.]
    4. [Borda, in chapter 5.]

To begin, assume that all voters' probabilities range from one to half and that their number is inversely related to their probabilities. Therefore we will have

$$\int_{1/2}^{1} \frac{1}{x} \, dx = \ln 2,$$

and the mean probability will be

$$\frac{\int_{1/2}^{1} \frac{1}{x} x \, dx}{\int_{1/2}^{1} \frac{1}{x} \, dx} = \frac{\frac{1}{2}}{\ln 2} = \frac{1}{2 \ln 2},$$

where the logarithms are hyperbolic. Then the number of voters whose probability is between 1 and $a > 1/2$ is $-\ln a / \ln 2$, and their mean probability is $(1 - a)/ -\ln a$. For instance, if $a = 9/10$, the number of voters will be $(\ln 10 - \ln 9)/\ln 2$, and the mean probability will be $1/[10(\ln 10 - \ln 9)]$. Thus the mean probability of all voters will be nearly $1,000/1,386$, the ratio of the number of voters whose probability exceeds $8/10$ to the total number of voters will be $105/697$, and their mean probability will be $1,000/1,005$. But since one voter has a probability of 1 and two voters have probabilities of $1/2$, the hypothesis is too favorable for the voters' probabilities and should be rejected.

Instead, if we suppose that the number of voters is proportional to $1 - x$, that the number of voters who never make mistakes will be zero, and that half the voters make a mistake 50 percent of the time, the hypothesis would be more consistent with nature.

So here, the number of voters will be

$$\int_{1/2}^{1} (1 - x) \, dx = \frac{1}{8}$$

and the mean probability will be

$$\frac{\int_{1/2}^{1} x(1 - x) \, dx}{\int_{1/2}^{1} (1 - x) \, dx} = \frac{\frac{2}{3} \times \frac{1}{8}}{\frac{1}{8}} = \frac{2}{3}.$$

In other words, the number of voters will be $1/8$, and the mean probability will be 2/3. For a probability of $a > 1/2$, the ratio of the number of voters will be $8(1/2 - a + a^2/2)$ and the mean probability will be

$$\frac{1/6 - a^2/2 + a^3/3}{1/2 - a + a^2/2}.$$

If $a = 9/10$, the first number becomes $1/25$, and the mean probability $14/15$. We stop with the following hypothesis: if there are 2,500 voters, 100 of them will have a probability of voting above $9/10$. Let us suppose that a plurality of five votes is sufficient and that the mean probability is $14/15$. Then to seek the number of voters required to have the same reliability derived from a mean probability of $2/3$, the equations $2^{q'} = 14^5$ or $q' = 5(\ln 14)/\ln 2$ must be used. In other words, we must have $q' > 19$ or $q' = 20$ unless $q' = 19$, which very closely approaches the true value, is not acceptable. Whence clearly if only a plurality of 20 out of 2,500 votes is required, we have

1. the same reliability as in the case with the smallest plurality, and
2. quite sufficient probabilities of having a decision and having a correct one obtained by only considering the mean probability.

These formulas are sufficient to show that increasing the number of voters so that they become less enlightened decreases the mean probability of making a correct decision quite rapidly. But this way of evaluating the probability is only exact if the number of voters is assumed to be infinite, as it was assumed in determining the law. In other words, for example, suppose that 100 out of 2,500 voters have a mean probability of $14/15$ and that the other 2,400 have a mean probability of $236/360$. So when one voter is picked as one of the first 100, there is always a probability of $1/25$, not $99/2,500$, that the second is selected from the smaller group. But this occurs only if we assume that the law is established for everyone for a very long time.

Suppose that we do not accept this hypothesis and seek the probability, for instance, when S voters are added to this law, but so that if n voters have a particular mean probability, then n/S is the probability that a voter will be picked for this group, and $[n(n - 1)]/[S(S - 1)]$ is the probability that two voters will be picked. In this case, the expression n^2/S^2, derived from the first hypothesis, is replaced, so investigating the probability becomes more difficult. Here we describe ways of finding it.

To do this, suppose that the probabilities are divided into u classes and that the mean probability of each class is N so that the first class has one voter, the second two voters, . . . and the nth, n voters, which gives $S = [n'(n' + 1)]/2$, where n' is the last value of n. Clearly

1. The mean probability of a single vote will be $\Sigma(nN)/S$, where the finite constant difference is 1 and the integral is taken from 1 to n'. In the same case, the probability of error will be $[\Sigma n(1 - N)]/S$ and their sum will be $\Sigma n/S = 1$, as it should be.

2. To obtain the probability of the second vote, we find that if the first one belongs to the class n, the probability of the second will be $[\Sigma(nN) - N]/(S - 1)$, so the total probability will be $\{\Sigma[nN(\Sigma nN - N)]\}/[S(S - 1)]$. The probability of a true decision and a false one will be

$$\frac{\Sigma\{nN[\Sigma[n\,(1 - N)] - (1 - N)]\} + \Sigma[n\,(1 - n)\,(\Sigma nN - N)]}{S\,(S - 1)},$$

and for two false decisions, the probability will be

$$\frac{\Sigma\{n\,(1 - N)[n\,(1 - n) - (1 - N)]\}}{S\,(S - 1)}.$$

The sum of these values is 1, as it should be.

3. For a third voter, the probability that all three will be true is

$$\frac{\Sigma[nN(\Sigma nN - N)\,(\Sigma nN - 2N)]}{S\,(S - 1)\,(s - 2)\,(S - 3)},$$

and in the same case, the probability for four voters is

$$\frac{\Sigma[nN(\Sigma nN - N)\,(\Sigma nN - 2N)\,(\Sigma nN - 3N)]}{S\,(S - 1)\,(s - 2)\,(S - 3)}.$$

And for any number, q, of voters, the probability is

$$\frac{\Sigma[nN(\Sigma nN - N)\,(\Sigma nN - 2N)\ldots[\Sigma N - (q - 1)\,N]\}}{S\,(S - 1)\,(s - 2)\,(S - 3)\ldots(S - q + 1)}.$$

Here it should be noted that each integral sign includes all the terms that multiply nN under this sign. If $N = 1$, this quantity becomes 1, as it should be; if $N = v$, where v is constant, it becomes v^q, as it also should be in this case.

4. If the value of the probability for a number q is sought according to this formula, the equation

$$P_q = AP_{q-1} + BP_{q-2} + CP_{q-3} + DP_{q-4} + \ldots + \text{etc.},$$

can be formed where the P_q's, P_{q-1}'s, etc. designate probabilities pertaining to the numbers q, $q - 1$, etc., and where we have the following values:

$$A = \frac{\Sigma nN}{S - q + 1}$$

$$B = \frac{-(q - 1)\Sigma nN^2}{(S - q + 2)(S - q + 1)}$$

$$C = \frac{(q - 1)(q - 2)(q - 3)\Sigma nN^2}{(S - q + 3)(S - q + 2)(S - q + 1)}$$

$$D = \frac{-(q - 1)(q - 2)(q - 3)\Sigma nN^4}{(S - q + 4)(S - q + 3)(S - q + 2)(S - q + 1)}^5$$

5. If the probability of a false vote can be obtained by replacing N with $1 - N$ in each term of the first formula in the preceding statement; and if P' designates this probability, the equation is

$$P'_q = A'P_{q-1} + 2B'P_{q-2} + 3C'P_{q-3} + \ldots + AP'_{q-2}$$

$$+ BP'_{q-2} + CP'_{q-3} \ldots A', B', \text{etc.}$$

where A, B, etc. are transformed by replacing one of the N's with $1 - N$. For two false votes, the probability is obtained by taking of the n's from the first formula (number 3) created by replacing N with $1 - N$ in each of its combination of terms taken two at a time. And calling this term P^*, we have

$$P^*_q = B^*P_{q-2} + 3C^*P_{q-3} + 6D^*P_{q-4} + \ldots + A'P'_{q-1}$$

$$+ 2BP'_{q-2} + 3C'P'_{q-3} + \ldots + AP^*_{q-1} + BP^*_{q-2}$$

$$+ CP^*_{q-3} \ldots .$$

The law derived from these formulas is evident.

6. P_q can also be represented in the following form:

$$\frac{\Sigma nN_q - Q'\Sigma nN_{q-2}\,\Sigma nN_2 + Q^*\Sigma nN_{q-3}\,\Sigma nN_3 + Q^\#\Sigma nN_{q-4}\Sigma nN_4 \ldots}{S(S - 1)(S - 2)\ldots(S - q + 1)}$$

---

5. [The original text for the last two terms in the denominator of D is $(S - q + 2) \cdot (S - q + 1)$.]

where Q' is the sum of the numbers $1, 2, 3, \ldots, q$, Q^* is the sum of the products of these numbers taken two at a time, and $Q^\#$ is the sum of these numbers taken three at a time.

Similarly, we have

$$P'_q = q\Sigma nN_{q-1} \ \Sigma n \ (1 - N) - Q' \left\{ \begin{array}{l} (q - 2) \ \Sigma nN_{q-3} \ \Sigma n \ (1 - N) \ \Sigma nN^2 \\ + 2\Sigma nN_{q-2} \ \Sigma nN \ (1 - N) \end{array} \right\}$$

$$Q^* \left\{ \begin{array}{l} (q - 3) \ \Sigma nN_{q-4} \ \Sigma n \ (1 + N) \ \Sigma nN^3 \\ + 3 \ \Sigma nN_{q-3} \ \Sigma nN^2 \ (1 - N) \end{array} \right\} \ \ldots$$

and so forth. Moreover,

$$P^*_q = \frac{q \ (q - 1)}{2} \ \Sigma nN_{q-2} \ \Sigma n \ (1 - N)^2$$

$$-Q' \left\{ \begin{array}{l} \dfrac{(q - 2) \ (q - 3)}{2} \ \Sigma nN_{q-4} \ \Sigma n! \ (1 - N)\Sigma nN^2 \\ + 2 \ (q - 2) \ \Sigma nN_{q-3} \ \Sigma n \ (1 - N) \ \Sigma n!N! \ (1 - N) \\ + \Sigma nN_{q-2} \ \Sigma n^2!(1 - N)^2 \end{array} \right\}$$

$$-Q^* \left\{ \begin{array}{l} \dfrac{(q - 3) \ (q - 4)}{2} \ \Sigma nN_{q-5} \ \Sigma n! \ (1 - N)^2\Sigma nN^3 \\ + 3 \ (q - 3) \ \Sigma nN_{q-4} \ \Sigma n \ (1 - N) \ \Sigma nN^2! \ (1 - N) \\ + 3 \ \Sigma nN_{q-3} \ \Sigma nN! \ (1 - N)^2 \end{array} \right\} \ldots,$$

a pattern that is easily grasped.

We will not push these formulas any further, for they would be of little use to us here. Actually, we have already mentioned several times that one must not be satisfied with taking account of the mean probability but that the necessary reliability must be sought, even in case of the smallest probability. Where the probability can decline to $1/2$, we must at least be assured a very large likelihood that the probability of a plurality decision will not fall below a particular limit. For this to happen, let q' be the plurality that occurs and let m be the limit below which $v^{q'}$ should not fall. Then we have

1. A probability of $(1/6) - (x^2/2) + (x^3/3)$ in this hypothetical situation and

$$\int \left[((1/6) - (x^2/2)) + (x^3/3) \frac{m^2 \, dx}{x^3} - \frac{m^3 \, dx}{x^4} \right]$$

is integrated from $x = 1$ to $x = m$ if $m > 1/2$, and from $x = 1$ to $x = 1/2$ if

$m < 1/2$. Integrating this formula with A evaluated from 1 to x yields the same conditions, and the process continues by repeating these integrations $q' - 1$ times.

2. The formula

$$\int \left[\left(\frac{1}{2} - x + \frac{x^2}{2} \right) \frac{m\,dx}{x^2} - \frac{m^2\,dx}{x^3} \right]$$

can be evaluated as above and the same integration can be repeated $q' - 1$ times. That said, if P is the first formula and P the second one, the probability that $v^{q'}$ will be above m will be $p/p'(3/2)^{q'}$. But without going into the details of this calculation, it is easy to see that if this value is to be very large and equal to $144{,}767/144{,}768$, for instance, m must be assumed to be too small for

$$\frac{v^{q'}}{v^{q'} + e^q}$$

to give sufficient assurance, at least of making q' very large. So the reliability required for decisions on important matters cannot be straightforwardly obtained. But this shortcoming can be overcome. In fact, for example, although many men vote with very little probability when they make instant decisions on a matter that requires learning and argument, it is very possible that these same men will judge with much more probability by selecting a more enlightened subset of the assembly to decide. Thus by entrusting them with this election, there is a probability of making a correct decision of $M' > 144{,}767/144{,}768$, or any other designated limit, so that the probability of each person selected will not be below m', and $M'm'$ will be 9/10. At that point, the new assembly would be reliable enough if it satisfies the sufficient conditions which, as described above, are very easy to satisfy. And since (cf. page 297) the probability of 100 out of the 2,500 voters picked in this hypothetical situation is above 9/10, it is easy to see that the number of voters necessary to have this probability can be expected.

If a hypothetical situation is chosen with some voters having a probability below 1/2, precisely the same consequences are derived even if this only means that the probability declines more rapidly in proportion to an increase in the number of voters. But it must be noted that in the last case, it might be more difficult to have a sufficient probability with those charged with rendering the decision by a plurality of votes, even if each voter had a probability of $M'm'$ or 9/10. Because prejudices generally make the probability fall below 1/2, it seems natural that voters making the choice would place their confidence in those who share their prejudices. Consequently, there may be no way out as long as those regarded by a country's public opinion as educated are not above prejudice.

This suggests that there are many ways of forming an assembly whose decisions have the necessary reliability by limiting the right of choice to selecting those who will decide matters, even with a large number of poorly enlightened voters. But even this option will not work when prejudice combines with lack of enlightenment.

Similarly, it must be noted that in this case, any precautions that are taken would only increase the certainty of producing a false decision about all matters affected by prejudice. Consequently there would be greater hope of avoiding error if, by chance, the decision were entrusted to one person or a very small number of men from a class of those who can be counted on to seek knowledge.

Therefore we can see that it is not only important that men be enlightened, but that it is also crucial that public leaders be free of prejudice. This latter condition itself is the most essential one since nothing can remedy the drawbacks it entails.

We will end this essay here. The difficulty of obtaining data reliable enough to apply calculations has forced us to limit ourselves to general insights and hypothetical results. But it is sufficient to have established some principles and demonstrated their applications so that they can be used to discuss these questions or apply the theory usefully.

Mathematical Notation

The following notation is used in Condorcet's argument

q	The number of voters in a voting body
q'	The marginal size of the plurality
q^*	The threshold for the limit of q'
E_q	The group probability of making an incorrect choice
V_q	The group probability of making a correct choice
$1 - V_q$	The probability of rejecting truth
M	The minimum acceptable probability of making a correct choice
v	The average individual probability of making a correct choice
e	The average individual probability of making an incorrect choice
i	The average individual probability of voting for uncertainty
V'	The maximum group probability of making a correct choice

$1 - V_q - E_q$	The probability of an indecisive collective choice
W	The group probability of making a decision
*	The second derivative of a function
#	The third derivative of a function
^	The fourth derivative of a function

CHAPTER 7

Condorcet

On the Constitution and the Functions
of Provincial Assemblies, 1788

All enlightened men agree that establishing assemblies in every province
which had neither an Estates General nor a new provincial administration was
the beginning of a new era, an era which would have an enormous effect on
the nation. We certainly cannot doubt the good they will do the present
generation, but any good they can do future generations depends on the
constitution they are given and the way in which they exercise the functions
conferred upon them.

They may be run in the interests of the public or the aristocracy; they may
become isolated within the State or continue to represent the citizens. Everything depends. upon how they are formed.

The truth of an Assembly's decisions depends as much on the form by
which they are reached as on the enlightenment of its members. Its functions
and the unity of its actions are also dependent on this form. If the form is
faulty, then a body with the purest of intentions may itself become, through its
lengthy, incoherent methods, a greater obstacle to the destruction of abuse
than the corruption and the ignorance of a single administrator. Finally, if the
actions of this body are not carried out according to certain principles, its
errors may cause more harm to the nation it represents than the abuse of power
in the hands of a single man. . . .

Section V: On the Form of Elections

The commonest form of election is that in which each voter is asked to say
which of the given candidates he prefers and where the candidate who obtains
the most votes is considered to be preferred and therefore elected by the
plurality. However, if there are more than two candidates and none of them
obtains more than half of the votes, this method can in fact lead to error.

What exactly do we mean by being elected? Is it not the fact of having
been judged preferable to your opponents? This judgment is made dependent
on the opinion of the plurality because we consider a proposition asserted by

fifteen people, say, more probable than its contradictory asserted by only ten. So, the person who really obtains the plurality in an election must be the one whose superiority over his opponents is most probable and consequently the one judged by the plurality to be superior to all of the others. Now, even when there are just three candidates, it is quite possible for one of them to obtain more votes than either of the others and yet for one of these other two, perhaps even the one with the fewest votes, to be the one that the plurality really considers the best.

This assertion seems paradoxical, but we can see that it is not if we consider that when someone votes for one particular candidate, he simply asserts that he considers that candidate better than the others and makes no assertion whatsoever about the respective merits of these other candidates. His judgment is therefore incomplete and must be completed if we are ever to arrive at a true idea of his will.

Suppose that there are three candidates and twenty-five voters. The first candidate gets ten votes, the second eight, and the third seven. Clearly, those who voted for the first have expressed no preference between the second and the third, and had they done so, they might have preferred the third to the second. Similarly, those who voted for the second have made no distinction between the first and the third, and they too might have preferred the third. And, finally, those who voted for the third have not distinguished between the second and the first, and they might all have preferred the second. Let us suppose this to be the case. Then, the third candidate would beat the first by fifteen votes to ten and the second by seventeen votes to eight, while the second would beat the first by fifteen votes to ten. Had the voting been complete, therefore, the third candidate would have obtained the plurality and the second candidate would have been ranked above the first. Yet the first candidate had the most votes, and the third candidate the least. Clearly, then, the voting in the conventional form of election is incomplete, and such an election can in fact express the complete opposite of the plurality will.

People instinctively recognized this problem long before it was brought into the open. Perhaps they sensed that it was ridiculous to claim that if one of several candidates obtained a small number of votes, then this was an expression of the general will. Granted, that will is expressed even less in favor of each of the other candidates, yet at the same time there is a sense in which it goes directly against the candidate who is said to have obtained the plurality, since more than half, and maybe even more than three-quarters, of the voters have not only not voted for him but have actually ranked him below one of his opponents. The problem was quite evident to the intelligent observer, and various methods of remedying it were suggested or adopted.

In several countries, it was overcome by saying that for a candidate to be elected, he had to get more than half, or in some countries two-thirds, of the votes cast; if no one obtained this majority, then the election was held again and again until one of the candidates finally did obtain the required majority.

This method depends on voters changing their vote, and since it is unlikely that they will also have changed their views, it necessarily forces them to vote against their own opinions.

Furthermore, it could be such a long-winded process that the voters often had to be forced to unite. Sometimes they would be kept locked up without food, sometimes in unhealthy and uncomfortable conditions, and at times they would even be deprived of their right to vote so that this right could be given to others. Such measures hardly encourage voters to follow the dictates of their reason and conscience but rather make them liable to intrigue and to all kinds of corruption.

Moreover, this method does not by any means give us the true will of the voters. It simply shows that the candidate it favors is not detested by half or a third of those who have been allowed to vote. It does not prove that the voters prefer the one who is chosen but simply that they can put up with him. The voters are not exercising their right of election but rather their right of exclusion, for when the choice is limited by the refusal of half or a third of the voters to accept a given candidate, the election is really no more than a matter of chance.

Another method is to make elections more complicated, either by having a second group of voters confirm the initial vote or by getting one group of voters to propose a limited number of candidates and a second group to choose between them. The combinations are clearly endless, and yet not one of these methods can fulfill our aim of discovering the true will of the voters and obtaining a judgment on the merit of the candidates which can be regarded as dictated by reason alone.

Examining the other two forms of election, only one of which can lead to the correct result, would involve too lengthy a discussion not to exhaust the reader. (See appendix 1 [the next section of this chapter]).

Besides, the only method that I consider accurate is also very complicated and would, in practice, be dishearteningly time-consuming. So rather than suggest that we immediately try it out on elections as important as those for provincial assemblies, I would prefer to illustrate a simpler version of it which, while it does not actually determine the worthiest candidate, at least ensures the choice of a man that the greatest plurality considers capable of filling the post. Indeed, this is exactly what we should aim for when a great many candidates are eligible for a limited number of places, as this necessarily implies that the post does not require any particular talents and could be filled by more than one man. This being the case, it is better to be certain of finding a candidate capable of filling the post than to vainly search for the one who would fill it best.

We suggest that each voter makes a list of the twenty candidates he considers most worthy of the post.

If just one name is present on more than half of the lists, then that candidate is elected. If several names are present on more than half of the lists, then the candidate whose name is on the most lists is chosen. If two or more names are on the same number of lists, then the candidate whose name appears most often in the top nineteen (or the top eighteen . . .) is chosen. Should there be a complete draw, the election would have to be decided by lots.

This method would enable us to choose the candidate whom the greatest number considered worthy of the post, and when two or more candidates were equally worthy, we would choose the one whom the plurality would have placed on a shorter list. An equal plurality would show that a candidate was considered worthy of the post, and a greater plurality would show that he was considered worthier than the others, since he would have been nominated even had the list been shorter.

This method has several other advantages besides that of being very simple. First, everyone can nominate his friends and favorites and still have plenty of room on the list to include the names of truly worthy men. Partiality favors a system with just one vote and could not have much effect on a list of twenty names. Our method would generally lead to a just result, and it is highly unlikely that a deserving man would be passed over just because he had no party behind him. Second, a faction made up of less than half of the voters would have no means of electing a candidate opposed by the others, who would easily be able to prevent him from winning, without having to sacrifice their views and all vote for the same person.

Admittedly, in any election which requires more than one vote to be given, a voter can improve the chances of his preferred candidate by filling the rest of the list with what we call straw men, an expression which already exists for this kind of deceitfulness. However, this should not pose a serious problem, as a voter will only use this technique to remove a few candidates who threaten the man he wants to win. For it to really pose a problem, all the voters, or at least a great many of them, would have to be conspiracy-minded enough to vote in this way; they would have to be divided between the candidates so that none of them obtained a majority and to support their candidate to such an extent that they wanted no one but him to win. Clearly then, we need not worry about partisan groups: they would hardly go to such lengths to elect their candidate to a relatively unimportant post, which would neither fulfill one of his ambitions nor be a way of making his fortune. Partisan politics is only to be feared where it is not a certain man that voters wish to elect but a man of a certain party. In such a situation the largest party would necessarily have the advantage if the others did not join forces against them.

However, in our method, this joining of forces is far from unlikely, since no one needs to sacrifice his principles in order to exclude the candidates of an overinfluential party. And in any case, as long as the voters are well chosen and have limited duties and no possibility of promotion to a higher office, there is no real threat of parties being formed.

An assembly formed along these lines would not be rowdy; the voters could accomplish all their duties in just one day and then go their separate ways, thus making corruption and intrigue almost impossible.

Or we might go further and abolish these assemblies altogether.

Suppose that on a given day, each voter had to submit his signed and sealed vote, declaring whether he rejected or retained the members whose term had come to an end. The number of seats to be filled could be quickly calculated, and on another given day each voter would send, signed and sealed in the same way, a list of twenty names, if there was just one place to fill, of twenty-one names if there were two, or of twenty-two if there were three, and so on; it would be easy to find the candidate or candidates named in the most lists and therefore considered worthy of the seats by the greatest plurality.

Even when the voters do hold an assembly, I consider this method preferable to that in which a new vote is taken for each seat. In fact, it is most important that the votes are collected only once in an election, to avoid as far as possible the voters changing their minds. While this may sometimes be a result of a deeper awareness or a closer examination of the situation, it usually has some less honorable cause. Any method where more than one vote is taken encourages factions and opens the way for intrigue, offering voters the chance to sound out opinions and take steps to ensure a certain result.

These lists would be sent to the clerk of the district or provincial assembly, and it would be his responsibility to check the votes, along with the president of the middle committee and four citizens picked at random from those resident in the capital. The lists would then be placed in a sealed envelope so that they could be checked after the result was announced if two, or even just one, of the voters protested against it. If, after a fixed period, no protests had been made, the envelope would be burnt in the presence of the scrutineers.

If it was felt necessary to hold very short assemblies to conduct elections, then three or five of the voters, chosen at random, could act as scrutineers.

In my opinion, however, the first method is preferable: it avoids expense and is effective at combatting corruption, for people would need to go to quite ridiculous lengths to exert any influence upon men scattered all over the country. Moreover, voters are much more likely to express their true feelings if they draw up their lists at home, where it is difficult for them to confer with one another before submitting them or to influence one another with the powers of rhetoric which are so worthy of eloquence and so dangerous for reason.

The preceding method is not new, at least as regards collecting votes from voters scattered about the country: it has been adopted in Italy by a recently formed association of intellectuals from the different states which make up this part of Europe, and it has just been suggested by the Philadelphia Convention [of July–November 1787] for use in the election of the president of Congress.

It has only been for the purposes of illustration that we have suggested having a list of twenty names. The number of names on the list should in fact be assessed for each separate election, according to the proportion of all the candidates put forward who might truly be considered worthy of the post. It should not be made too small, to give a good chance that one of the candidates will obtain a majority and to give the voters scope to be partial without affecting the justice of the election. It should not be made too big, to guarantee that even once they have rejected some deserving candidates because of personal animosity, the voters can still complete the list without having to nominate candidates they consider unworthy.

It would be perfectly possible for no name to appear on more than half of the lists. This should only happen very rarely if the number of names to be listed has been fixed in the way we outlined above, but it could occur and we should therefore be prepared for it. In this situation, the lists should be given or sent back to the voters for them to add a certain number of names—a third or a quarter again of what was on the first list—and so on, until one candidate has obtained the plurality.

We suggested that in the event of a complete draw, the election should be decided by lots and that when two or more names occurred with the same frequency, we should base our choice on their order in the lists.

Alternatively, in either of these cases, we could use the method suggested in the Appendix, which is highly practicable when the number of candidates is very small, as it must necessarily be in these situations, or the method of adding names to the list that we described above.

In both cases, the lists would need to be returned to the voter before he wrote down his new vote, to ensure that this new vote did not contradict the first. Anyone who has seen how most election choices are made will immediately appreciate the importance of this condition, and it needs only a little thought on the part of those who have not to understand its necessity. But since we ought only very rarely resort to a method involving a second vote, let us limit its use to cases in which there is a complete draw, to prevent the election from being decided by lots. In fact, when the candidates draw simply in the number of times their names appear on the lists, we can be certain of electing one of the men considered by the plurality to be among the twenty most capable candidates and indeed the one considered most capable among the top nineteen or top eighteen and so on. To a certain extent, this follows from the very principles on which this method of election is based.

We have already fixed the legal conditions for eligibility,[1] but there is another condition as well—the consent of the man who is elected or retained. In our opinion, this consent should precede the voting, for if someone refused to accept a seat once the votes had been cast, it would either prolong the election assemblies or increase the number of votes requested from the scattered voters. Furthermore, voters would be inhibited in their choice if they were unsure whether a certain candidate would accept, and by hinting that he would not, unscrupulous men could prevent those who would otherwise have nominated him from doing so. There are, however, no drawbacks to insisting that each candidate's promise to accept the seat should precede the election. Making such a promise would not be a sign of conceit, nor would there be any need for a candidate to feel ashamed of having made such a declaration if he were not in fact elected. However, if this was felt to be a problem in a country where men are oversensitive to other people's opinions, especially when vanity is at stake, steps could be taken to safeguard against it. We might, for instance, state that in order to be eligible, a candidate must be nominated by three or four voters, one of whom vouches for his acceptance. Vanity would be no more at stake here than when a candidate himself tries to obtain a seat, for nothing would show whether a candidate had wanted to be nominated or had simply given in to the will of the voters. This method would have the advantage of making elections more certain, by decreasing the number of candidates and thus the number of wasted votes without at the same time limiting freedom of choice, since a candidate who was not nominated by at least three or four voters would in any case not have been elected.

To put this method into practice, the municipal assembly of each community would need, each year at election time, to print a list of all the men who were legally eligible, having first presented such a list to the general assembly of the same community. It is on these lists that the voters would base their votes.

Everything we have outlined so far can only apply to representatives who have already been chosen to vote. The election of these representatives should be undertaken by the general assembly of each community and, since the members of the assembly are close at hand in the community, there is nothing to stop the assembly from being convened; the members who make up the assembly may be chosen as voters. At the general assembly, the list of eligible citizens drawn up by the municipal assembly should be read out and, once

---

1. [Not translated here. For the French, see Arago and O'Connor (1847, vol. 8, 127–43 and 150–78).]

approved, reread so that all those who do not consent to being nominated can be excluded. The voters can then use the method outlined above to choose between all those who consent.

Although we have limited our discussion of ballot voting to elections, we consider it the best means of deciding any sort of debate. However, several thinkers have criticized this method, claiming that it is both weak and hypocritical. A virtuous man, they say, does not try to hide his opinions or his choice. No man whose intentions are pure and honest can be afraid of speaking his thoughts, and anyone who is afraid to speak the truth in the service of his country is refusing to commit himself for her. But by condemning this method, they have failed to realize that good laws are the ones which require only limited knowledge and common integrity and that any law which requires great talents or heroic virtues is dangerous and cannot be useful for any length of time.

The form of ballot vote that we are suggesting might seem less secret than an ordinary ballot, but no ballot in any form of election can be truly secret, and in any case, we have many reasons other than secrecy for favoring the ballot vote. First, in every country where men can write, it is absurd not to insist upon written votes, however few voters there are and however unimportant the question upon which they are voting. The only exception is when the question is very simple, requiring only an answer of yes or no, and when unanimity is required. When the voters need only reply yes or no, but a plurality is sufficient, it is no quicker, and far less exact, to do as they do in some countries and organize the voters into different corners of the room, make them pass between two pikes, or hand over white or black beans, than it is to ask them to write yes or no on a slip of paper.

Furthermore, whenever the votes do not come out as a comprehensive yes or no, they can only be assessed with any degree of accuracy if they are written down. Ballot votes have another advantage: men vote calmly, in silence, and are therefore less liable to be influenced by other voters; individual votes are not announced and so cannot hurt people's feelings; their fears are only confirmed later, and less certainly.

So this method is best because it ensures clear opinions and accuracy in the way the votes are counted at the same time as making allowances for human failings without compromising truth.

We have even suggested that it is not necessary to convene an assembly to hold an election, because public discussions about candidates can be more dangerous than useful, leading to factions being formed, and because such discussions favor slander and impudence rather than justice and merit, since it is impossible to keep the assembly in session until after any criticism of a candidate has been confirmed or disproved.

Our opinion on ballot voting is the same as that of the author of *Histor-*

ical and Political Studies on the United States of Northern America[2]—one of the wisest, most enthusiastic, and most enlightened defenders of freedom and the rights of mankind; and if he considers that this method should be adopted in a country where all men are equal, where those in power call themselves and even consider themselves simply the officers of the people, where the humblest and poorest citizen can have nothing to fear from the richest and most respected, then surely it must be all the more important to adopt it in a country where there are powerful citizens and privileged castes, with powers that do not come directly from the nation and a sovereign who is singled out by it.

It is not necessary for every voter to have given or sent in his votes in order for an election to be valid, but it is vital to fix a minimum number of voters whose participation is necessary. This should be a general rule for all types of debate; it is already current in France for judicial sentences and in America for all the business conducted by the various assemblies which make up the Constitution. As each community is represented by the voters for each district, we shall first insist that each community has at least two voters and then we shall require the participation both of three-quarters of the voters and of voters from five-sixths of the communities. We could use the same principle for voters from the provinces.

As for elections carried out within a community, we can only require the fulfillment of one of these conditions, but in this case it would be wise to require the participation of a larger percentage than just three-quarters of the voters.

We should stress that since we are only requiring voters to draw up a list of the candidates they consider most worthy, health problems or alternative commitments would be unlikely to push the number of voters below the minimum. After all, what possible motive could make recently elected or retained men refuse to carry out their only duty, which they have just freely accepted? So we are not really in any danger of making the formation of assemblies more complicated when we say that if the minimum number were not attained then we should need to ask communities and districts to nominate other voters to replace those who had failed to carry out their duties. Rather, by foreseeing this eventuality, we have simply prepared a remedy for extraordinary circumstances and a kind of punishment by public opinion for those voters who neglected their duties.

---

2. [*Recherches historiques et politiques sur les Etats-Unis de l'Amerique septentrionale, par un citoyen de Virginie,* written anonymously by Philip Mazzei (or Mazzey) with help from Condorcet and Jefferson, and published by Jefferson's Paris bookseller in 1788. It also included Condorcet's anonymous *Lettres d'un Bourgeois de Newhaven*—the New Haven Letters discussed in the Introduction. For Mazzei, see Marchione (1983). For his role as a transmission belt between Condorcet and the American revolutionaries, see McLean and Urken (1992).]

Finally, in elections carried out by the general assembly of each community, it would be sufficient for two-thirds, or even for simply more than half, of the voters to be present. Such voters are really exercising a right rather than fulfilling a duty; they vote mainly for themselves so that the laws can relate more closely to their own interests. Moreover, since there are more of them and they are not all elected, some citizens already having the right to vote, they more often have reasons to be absent.

If the number of voters in one of these assemblies falls below the minimum, then a new assembly should be convened for one week later. Small groups of landowners, or the individual cantons whose voter had been absent, would be allowed to choose another for this second assembly. But however few voters were present at this next assembly, it would be legal, for by then the citizens of each area would have been given the chance to be properly represented, or even to take part in the assembly themselves. If they did not make use of this chance, then we could reasonably conclude that they were content for their interests to be left in the hands of the small group who form the assembly.

APPENDIX 1: ON DISCOVERING THE PLURALITY WILL IN AN ELECTION

This Appendix is simply an extract of my discussions on the same topic in *An Essay on the Application of Analysis to the Probability of Decisions Rendered by a Plurality of Votes*.

As we have already seen, in the conventional form of election each voter names the candidate he considers best, and the one with the most votes is elected and considered to have plurality support. But we have also seen that when there are more than two candidates and no individual gets more than half the votes, then the election result can often bear no relation whatsoever to the will of the plurality. We have explained this by saying that in the conventional form of election, the votes given are incomplete.

1)[3] Suppose three candidates, Peter, Paul, and James. Someone who votes for Peter expresses a preference for Peter over and above the other two but says nothing as to the respective merits of James and Paul. Similarly, someone voting for Paul expresses no preference between Peter and James, and someone voting for James expresses no preference between Peter and Paul.

If the votes had been complete, things would have been clearer. Suppose that the first voter ranked Paul above James, that the second ranked James above Peter, and that the third ranked Paul above Peter. Paul would then beat

---

3. [This and later examples have been set out in modern notation at the end of the section.]

both Peter and James by two votes to one, and despite the fact that with an incomplete vote the candidates had seemed to draw, there would really be a plurality preference for Paul.

2) Now, suppose that there are 60 voters for our three candidates. Suppose that Peter gets twenty-three votes, Paul gets nineteen, and James eighteen and that Peter is therefore elected. Those who voted for Peter said nothing about the other two, so let us say that eighteen of them preferred James. Let us suppose that sixteen of the nineteen who voted for Paul without ranking the other two also preferred James and that thirteen of the eighteen who voted for James would have preferred Paul to Peter. If these preferences had been expressed in the vote, James would have beaten Peter by thirty-four votes to twenty-six and Paul by thirty-six votes to twenty-four, while Paul would have beaten Peter by thirty-two votes to twenty-eight. So there would actually have been a large plurality in favor of James, although in the conventional election method he received the fewest votes. Furthermore, the plurality would have considered Peter to be the worst even though he received the most votes in the conventional election method.

We gave a similar example in the text. The problem is as follows: Peter gets the most votes when compared to both of the others at once, while at the same time being judged worse than either of them taken individually. This is because most of the voters who are split between Paul and James consider Peter to be worse than either.

So whenever no candidate obtains more than half of the votes, the conventional form of election can lead to error, making it seem as though someone is elected by the plurality when the plurality is in fact against him. The greater the number of candidates, the more prone to error this method becomes, but the greater the number of voters, the more likely it is to be correct.

Where there are three candidates, it might be proposed to eliminate the one with the fewest votes and choose between the remaining two or in general to eliminate the candidate with the fewest votes and then choose between the others. However, this method is also prone to error. In our last example, we would have eliminated the very candidate that the plurality would have elected if the voting system had allowed them to express their true preferences. Moreover, if James were eliminated and a vote was taken between Peter and Paul, then Paul would win by thirty-two votes to twenty-eight. Paul would be elected instead of Peter, who won on the conventional method, or James, who in fact had plurality support.

Nor can we hope to resolve these injustices by holding an election again and again until one of the candidates obtains a majority, for this method forces the voters to change their minds, or at least their votes, and so cannot give us a true expression of the plurality will. One advantage of this method, however, is that when an election is reheld you can still vote for a candidate who got no votes in the first round. And, whenever there are more than two candidates, it is quite possible for the plurality to in fact prefer such a candidate.

(2b) We shall use the same example but this time with a fourth candidate called John, who gets no votes. Suppose that the twenty-three people who voted for Peter ranked the others John, Paul, James; that the nineteen who voted for Paul ranked them John, Peter, James; and that the eighteen who voted for James ranked them John, Peter, Paul. John would therefore beat Peter by thirty-seven votes to twenty-three, Paul by forty-one votes to nineteen, and James by forty-two votes to eighteen. So the plurality really considered John as better than each of the others, although no one ranked him as best overall.

A famous mathematician [Borda] has suggested another method in which each voter ranks the candidates in order of merit, with a certain value being attached to first place, a lower one to second, and so on. Each candidate can then be given a score, according to the number of times he has been ranked first, or second, and so on, and the candidate with the highest score is elected.

We can illustrate this using our two earlier examples. In the first, we had three candidates and three voters. Let us give three points for first place, two for second, and one for third. One voter ranked the candidates Peter, Paul, James; another Paul, James, Peter; and the third James, Paul, Peter. Peter would therefore score five points with one first place and two third, Paul would score seven with one first place and two second, and James would score six with one first place, one second and one third. Paul would therefore be the winner, with James second and Peter last, which is exactly the same result as we obtained by our method.

In the second example, eighteen people ranked the candidates Peter, James, Paul, and five ranked them Peter, Paul, James. Sixteen people ranked them Paul, James, Peter, and three ranked them Paul, Peter, James. Thirteen ranked them James, Paul, Peter, and five James, Peter, Paul. Peter, with twenty-three first places, eight second places, and twenty-nine third places, would therefore score 114. Paul, with nineteen first places, eighteen second places, and twenty-three third places, would score 116; and James, with eighteen first places, thirty-four second places, and eight third places, would score 130. James would therefore be the overall winner, with Paul second and Peter last, which is once again the same result as we obtained by our method.

3) But this method will not always give us the same result. Suppose that out of eighty-one voters, thirty rank the candidates Peter, Paul, James; and one ranks them Peter, James, Paul. Twenty-nine rank them Paul, Peter, James; and ten rank them Paul, James, Peter; ten rank them James, Peter, Paul; and one ranks them James, Paul, Peter.

Peter thus has thirty-one first places, thirty-nine second places, eleven third places and a score of 182. Paul, with thirty-nine first places, thirty-one second places, and eleven third places, scores 190. And James, with eleven first places, eleven second places and fifty-nine third places, scores 114. Paul thus beats Peter and James, and Peter beats James. But if we examine the voting more closely, we find that Peter beats Paul by forty-one votes to forty and James by sixty votes to twenty-one, while Paul beats James by sixty-nine votes to twelve.

The plurality therefore supports Peter, not Paul, and the above method is erroneous, as is the ordinary one.

4) Suppose another example, this time with thirty voters for the same three candidates, Peter, Paul, and James. Nine voters rank the candidates Peter, Paul, James; and three rank them Peter, James, Paul; four rank them Paul, Peter, James; and six rank them Paul, James, Peter; four rank them James, Peter, Paul; and four rank them James, Paul, Peter. Here, Peter has twelve first places while Paul has ten and James eight. So by the conventional method, Peter would win and would be considered to have plurality support. On the method suggested above, Peter would score sixty-two with twelve first places, eight second places, and ten third places; Paul sixty-three with ten first places, thirteen second places, and seven third places; and James fifty-five with eight first places, nine second places, and thirteen third places.

Paul therefore wins by the new method, whereas Peter would have won by the conventional one. On studying the votes, however, we find that Peter beats both Paul and James by sixteen votes to fourteen while Paul beats James by nineteen votes to eleven. It is therefore Peter who has plurality support. In this case the conventional method gives the correct result while the new one leads to error.

We do not even need to study the votes to see that the new method can sometimes be inaccurate when the conventional method would have given the right result, because it can even give the wrong result when one candidate has more than half of the votes and is clearly preferred by the plurality.

5) Suppose once again that there are thirty voters and three candidates. Nineteen voters rank the candidates Peter, Paul, James; and the other eleven rank them Paul, James, Peter. Peter therefore beats both Paul and James by a plurality of nineteen to eleven, that is, by a very large plurality of eight out of the thirty voters. Yet, if we followed the new method, Peter would score sixty-eight, Paul seventy-one, and James forty-one; and Paul would be elected.

This new method is not only no better than the conventional one, it is actually worse. At least in the conventional method, it is just a possibility that the result was wrong and that we are going against the true will of the plurality. With the new method we can be sure that it was wrong and that we are having to act in accordance with totally erroneous results.

We might argue that the results are wrong because of the particular values, 3, 2, and 1, that we have assigned to each place and claim that with different values the result would have been correct. We could claim that it is not the method itself which is erroneous but rather the arbitrary assignment of a value equal to the number of candidates to first place and the subtraction of one point to get the value for each place below that. We could claim that if the values were assigned differently, perhaps not in arithmetical progression, then we would always get the right result.

Suppose that in our last example (number 5), we had instead assigned a value of four to first place, two to second place, and one to third. Peter would then have scored eighty-seven, Paul eighty-two, and James forty-one, and not only would we have obtained the same result as on the conventional method, but also this result would be the correct one.

However, there are some situations in which, whatever revisions we introduce, this method will always give the wrong result. Example 3 is one of them. In fact, the problem here is nothing to do with assigning values; as both Peter and Paul are ranked last eleven times, altering the values could make no difference. Since Peter has thirty-one first places and Paul thirty-nine, Peter must necessarily score eight × (whatever value we give first place) less than Paul. And since Peter has thirty-nine second places and Paul has only thirty-one, Peter must score eight × (whatever value we give the second place) more than Paul. To give an accurate expression of the plurality will, Peter's total would have to be greater than Paul's, and we would therefore need to assign values such that eight × (the value of second place) was greater than eight × (the value of first place); we would need, that is, to give second place a higher value than first place, which is not only illogical, but also totally contradicts the basic principles of the method.

But how is it that Paul is not the clear winner when the only difference between himself and Peter is that Peter got thirty-one first places and thirty-nine second, while Paul got thirty-nine first and thirty-one second? Well, out of the thirty-nine voters who put Peter second, ten preferred him to Paul, whereas only one of the thirty-one voters who put Paul second preferred him to Peter. The points method confuses votes comparing Peter and Paul with those comparing either Peter or Paul to James and uses them to judge the relative merits of Peter and Paul. As long as it relies on irrelevant factors to form its judgments, it is bound to lead to error, and that is the real reason why this method is defective for a great many voting patterns, regardless of the particular values assigned to each place. The conventional method is flawed because it ignores elements which should be taken into account and the new one because it takes into account elements which should be ignored.

Thus, the only method remaining to be examined is that by which we have been judging the others. Each voter ranks the candidates in order of merit. From his ranking, we can easily extract his opinion of the relative merits of each candidate, and by collating all the individual opinions we can discover the candidate considered best by the plurality. That is, we need only do precisely what we have been doing in our examples in order to find the plurality will.

But on a closer examination, we find that even with just three candidates, this method can apparently give a totally absurd result, which in practice means it gives no immediate result at all.

6) Suppose the same three candidates, this time with sixty voters. Twenty-three voters rank the candidates Peter, Paul, James while no one ranks them Peter, James, Paul. Two rank them Paul, Peter, James; and seventeen rank them Paul, James, Peter; ten rank them James, Peter, Paul; and eight rank them James, Paul, Peter. The proposition "Peter is preferable to Paul" therefore has a plurality of thirty-three to twenty-seven. "James is preferable to Peter" has plurality of thirty-five to twenty-five; and "Paul is preferable to James" a plurality of forty-two to eighteen. So the three propositions asserted by the plurality are

> Peter is preferable to Paul,
> James is preferable to Peter, and
> Paul is preferable to James.

Clearly, these cannot all be true at the same time because the first two taken together, or indeed any two taken together, entail a proposition which is incompatible with the third. Suppose, therefore, that we adopt just two of the propositions: from the first two we would conclude that James is the best, from the first and the third that Peter is the best, and from the second and third that Paul is the best.

This method seems to give an absurd result, or rather no result at all, whereas by the conventional method, Peter would have won with twenty-three votes, compared to Paul with nineteen and James with eighteen. And by the points method, Paul would have won, with a score of 129 (nineteen first, thirty-one second, and ten third places), compared to Peter with 118 (twenty-three first, twelve second, and twenty-five third places) and James with 113 (eighteen first, seventeen second, and twenty-five third places).

If we use the conventional method and Peter wins, then we are rejecting the proposition "James is preferable to Peter," which had a plurality of thirty-five to twenty-five, and accepting in its place the proposition "Peter is preferable to Paul," which had a plurality of just thirty-three to twenty-seven. If we use the points method, we would reject this last proposition, which in fact is the one with the smallest plurality. As it happens, the points method this time gives the same result as we shall get if we pursue with our method. Clearly, if we have to reject one of the propositions asserted by the plurality, then we should reject the one with the smallest plurality, which in this case is the first one. This would mean that Paul was the winner. How far this result is an expression of the plurality will depends on the truth of the two propositions "Paul is preferable to James," which has a plurality of forty-two votes to eighteen, and "Paul is preferable to Peter," which has a plurality against it of twenty-seven votes to thirty-three. Similarly, the accuracy of a result in favor of James would depend on the truth of the two propositions "James is preferable to Peter," which has a plurality of thirty-five votes to twenty-five, and "James is preferable to Paul," which has a plurality against it of eighteen to forty-two. And the accuracy of a result in favor of Peter would depend on the truth of the two propositions "Peter is preferable to Paul," which has a plurality of thirty-three to twenty-seven, and "Peter is preferable to James," which has a plurality against it of twenty-five votes to thirty-five. The first result is therefore the most probably correct and should be adopted if a choice has to be made. This result, which is different to the one obtained by the conventional method, conforms quite coincidentally to the one obtained by the points method, which can in other cases make us reject a more probable proposition in favor of one which is less probable.

The method we have been examining is the only one which can reveal the plurality will whenever it exists and which, when it does not, at least shows us the choice which has the lowest probability of being wrong. It should therefore be preferred. However, it does have some drawbacks. If there are a lot of voters and several candidates, it can be very long-winded, demanding complicated checks which can become quicker and simpler only with experience.

If there are three candidates and we compare them two by two, we finish up with three propositions. But if there are four candidates, the number of propositions increases to six, because the new candidate must be compared to each of the old ones. So for a fifth candidate, who must be compared to each of the other four, the number of propositions jumps to ten. A sixth candidate would have to be compared to the other five, so we would end up with fifteen propositions, with twenty-one for seven candidates, and so on. For twenty candidates, there would be 190 propositions, and for 100 candidates, there would be 4,950. This method is quite impracticable unless the number of candidates is limited.

Now, when an election is open to any citizen from a whole district, or even province, there is nothing wrong in limiting the number of candidates by stipulating that they must be nominated by at least three or four voters who can vouch for their acceptance. This is not really a restriction, since clearly any candidate who cannot even find three or four people to nominate him would not in any case have been elected. This method would also avoid having to rehold elections because of candidates turning down a seat to which they are elected.

After reducing the numbers in this way, there could be a yes/no vote on whether each remaining candidate should go forward; once again it is clear that anyone the plurality declared inadmissible would not in any case have been elected.

The method of limiting the number of candidates by an initial vote as to their worth, while perfectly just and not restrictive in itself, might still prevent some worthy men from standing. However, this drawback cannot be judged in isolation but only in relation to the individual views and personalities of the candidates. Good laws will never encourage vanity, which is the most degrading of all passions, involving, as it does, a return to the pettiness of childhood. If we attach importance to a ribbon or a new trinket, we risk degrading the spirit of the nation, but protecting vanity is not the same as encouraging it. Since it is a childish vice, we should treat it as such and combat it with reason rather than antagonism and constraint.

There is another way to simplify our method. As soon as one candidate's name has appeared above, say, the twenty-first place on more than half of the lists, we can eliminate anyone who is not ranked in the top twenty, because they would always have a plurality against them who favored the other candidate; someone who was only ever ranked below the person whose name was on more than half of the lists could never be elected.

And as soon as a name was found on more than two-thirds of the lists, it would exclude first all those who had not yet appeared on a sixth of the lists[4] and second all those who had appeared on a maximum of a sixth but ranked below the candidate whose name was on two-thirds of the lists. It would be easy to multiply these principles and find ways of applying them to ballot votes.

It would not be difficult to find other ways of making the process shorter and easier to put into practice. But while these methods of exclusion would certainly speed things up, the procedure is still very complicated and would only really be practical in a country where vanity did not react violently against the suggestion of a public judgment of each candidate's worth prior to the actual election; where men were concerned only with the importance of making good choices; where the duties of each successful candidate were important enough to make everyone participate in their election; where public-spiritedness was strong enough to compensate the limitations and long-windedness; and finally, where, despite the complications, the voters would still be enlightened enough to distinguish the big issues from the mass of detail.

Unless we accept the modifications that a candidate could only stand if nominated by at least three or four voters, one of whom vouched for his acceptance, and if more than half of the voters accepted his candidacy in a yes/no vote, then this method is totally impracticable for the election of provincial assemblies. However, it does have some advantages. There would be

---

4. [Condorcet must mean one-sixth of all the lists, not one-sixth of the two-thirds counted so far.]

no threat of factions in the initial vote to see whether a candidate could stand, as no candidate who was rejected by more than half of the voters could ever have been elected by a plurality, and in the same way, factions would have little influence in the election itself. We are not referring to factions made up of more than half of the voters: no form of election could prevent them, since they do actually express the will of the plurality, however corrupt. A good form of election aims only to reveal this will; its conformity with truth depends on the enlightenment and integrity of the voters. We are referring only to factions made up of less than half of the voters, which in the conventional form of election, for example, control the result because the other voters are split. It is a problem which causes the still greater problem of the voters having to then form into just two parties. This would never need to happen with the method we have been outlining here.

Suppose that out of thirty voters, thirteen form a party supporting Peter, and the remaining seventeen are split between Paul and James. In the conventional method of election, the first party would control the result unless the others agreed to join forces against them. In our method, however, the seventeen who do not support Peter need only rank him last for him to have no chance of winning and for his faction to be thwarted. Since the majority of the votes would then be split between Paul and James, one of them would win without anyone having had to compromise themselves by voting against their views. If the remaining seventeen voters do not consider that a party has been formed to back Peter, then they can rank him second or third as they wish and he may then be elected. If he is, it will not be because of a party formed by less than half of the voters having an unfair advantage but simply a true expression of the plurality will.

[The examples in appendix 1 are set out below in modern notation.]

Peter: *A*
Paul: *B*
James: *C*
John: *D*

1) | *A* | *B* | *C* |
    | *B* | *C* | *B* |
    | *C* | *A* | *A* |

2) | 18 | 5 | 16 | 3 | 13 | 5 |
    |----|----|----|----|----|----|
    | *A* | *A* | *B* | *B* | *C* | *C* |
    | *C* | *B* | *C* | *A* | *B* | *A* |
    | *B* | *C* | *A* | *C* | *A* | *B* |

2B) 23 19 18
    A   B   C
    D   D   D
    B   A   A
    C   C   B

3) 30   1 29 10 10   1
   A A B B C C
   B C A C A B
   C B C A B A

4)   9   3   4   6   4   4
   A A B B C C
   B C A C A B
   C B C A B A

5) 19 11
   A B
   B C
   C A

6) 23   2 17 10   8
   A B B C C
   B A C A B
   C C A B A

APPENDIX 2: ON THE FORM OF DECISIONS MADE BY A PLURALITY VOTE

First, let us examine the custom which some assemblies have of reducing the subject for debate to the most widely supported opinions about it and, if possible, to just two of them.

As soon as there are more than two possible opinions and none of them has a plurality, then clearly we need to find and then support the one which the plurality considers the best. This is just like choosing the best out of a similar number of candidates, after excluding anyone who obtained no votes, and we proved in appendix 1 that this exclusion was unjust, because the plurality might in fact favor a candidate who obtained no votes in a first election conducted according to the ordinary method. In just the same way, the true opinion of the plurality might not be catered for by the opinions to which the debate has been reduced. If we try to break the debate down to just two opinions, by a series of votes whereby those who support the opinions with the least votes are obliged to give their support to some other opinion instead, then we shall find that just as the candidate who obtained the fewest votes when compared to all the others at once might very well have had a plurality if the voting system had allowed the true will of the plurality to be expressed, so the least popular opinion, which we have quite happily excluded, might also be the real opinion of the plurality.

It is not far-fetched to compare the process of decision making with that of elections. As soon as a voter lends his support to a different opinion to the one he initially supported, we can conclude one of three things: either that, having been forced to combine with others, he has changed his mind; or that any opinion he is forced to support against his better judgment carries just the same weight as his initial one; or that in supporting a different opinion, he is simply saying that having preferred his first opinion to all of the others, he now prefers this new one to all of the others (except his first one). Clearly the last conclusion is the only justifiable one. This form of decision making is precisely a way of electing an opinion, and we have already proved that this method of election is inherently unjust (see Appendix One).

Moreover, there is a drawback to this method of reduction which does not exist for an election conducted on the same lines. Once a voter has stated a preference for a certain candidate, he can rank anyone he likes in second place without contradiction. But once he has favored a certain opinion, there are some opinions amongst which he is then asked to choose that he cannot adopt without contradiction. It is even possible that each of the other opinions involves at least one proposition which directly contradicts some aspect of his original one. And what is more, if his first opinion is made up of, say, five basic propositions, then the voter would contradict himself more by adopting an opinion made up of five contradictory propositions than he would by adopting one which involved just one contradictory proposition. If, when a voter is forced to alter his opinions, his new choice is somehow dependent on his old one, then not only is his choice not free, but also this method requires him to make a complete and accurate analysis of all the opinions, thus opening itself up to all kinds of error and to giving results that totally contradict the plurality will.

The system in the House of Commons in England is as follows: one of the members proposes a bill, which is examined and discussed. Often the member who proposed it makes amendments, and finally they debate whether it should be passed or rejected. As it stands, this method would be unbearably time-consuming; if a bill could only be passed or rejected, then it might be rejected because of just one clause, which would then have to be altered before the bill could be put forward again. If it was rejected again, it would have to be realtered and the bill put forward a third time, as long as it was clear that it was only certain clauses which did not have plurality support and not the very essence of the bill itself. To avoid such a long, drawn out process, the voters would either have to reject a bill they considered essentially just or pass one which still had clauses of which they did not approve. To remedy this, the voters are asked to vote on the amendments at the same time as they vote on the bill and so they debate three questions all at once: whether to pass the proposed bill, whether to pass the amended bill, or whether to pass neither. Should they first debate whether to adopt one of them or reject them both and then, if necessary, which one to adopt? Here votes for the bill and votes for the amendment are grouped together, even though there is no doubt that when either the bill or the amendment is passed, some of the people who voted against it would have preferred neither to be passed, although they would have preferred most of all the one which did not gain plurality support and which was the one they were voting for when they voted to pass one of them rather than to reject them both. In this case, something would be passed which the voters were actually in favor of rejecting.

Perhaps the voters should therefore vote first on the bill itself and then, if that is rejected, on the amendment. Here, voters who support the amendment are grouped with the negative votes while those who vote for the bill itself are able to vote for or against the amendment if it is rejected. Once again, we have the same problem: those who voted against the bill itself because they preferred the amendment might very well have preferred the original bill to nothing at all. So maybe they should vote on all three options at once, reject the one with the fewest votes, and make its supporters vote for one of the other two instead. But then if it is the option of rejecting them both which has minority support, we are back at the first problem outlined above, and if it is one of the bills, we are back at the second.

The situation is just the same as an election between three candidates: someone who votes for the first bill expresses no preference between the amendment and the rejection of both bills, and the other votes are all incomplete in the same way. But adopting the same remedy as we used for elections would not bring us much nearer a form of decision making which could give a true expression of the collective will of the members of an assembly when the question for debate was not a simple one but involved several propositions, either connected or separate. When someone rejects a bill that is put forward, does he reject it all or just some aspects of it? When someone accepts it as a whole, has he disentangled all the propositions it involves, and if so, would he not have rejected some of them if he had been able to do so without causing the whole act to be defeated? Surely it is obvious that your average man makes fewer mistakes if he is asked to vote on a series of simple propositions rather than on the system which involves them all at once. We often come to false conclusions because of not having analysed the question properly. In fact, this is one of the commonest causes of error, even for a philosopher who thinks slowly and in silence, so it is not hard to imagine its impact when voters have to make instant decisions amid the hubbub of an assembly.

We must therefore establish a form of decision making in which voters need only ever pronounce on simple propositions, expressing their opinions only with a yes or a no.

When an assembly is to debate a given subject, they should entrust a group of people with the job of analyzing it and reducing all the different opinions about it to a series of basic propositions and their contradictories.

These series of propositions can be of two different types. First, the propositions can be separate, so that the voters can assent or dissent to any of them without contradicting themselves. Second, they can be linked, so that once someone has assented or dissented to the first few, he has to then continue voting in a certain way if he is not to contradict himself. To analyze a subject of debate is therefore to reduce it to a series of basic, separate propositions or to a series of separate groups of interdependent basic propositions. So really, an election is just a type of debate, where the options are reduced to a single group of interdependent propositions.

Suppose that the analysis has been completed and that, instead of being asked to debate the issues, the assembly is presented with a table of basic unrelated propositions, or of the various groups of interdependent propositions, and asked to come to a decision about each of them. Clearly, each voter has only to answer *yes* or *no* to each proposition. If the subject has been reduced to a series of unrelated propositions, then bringing together all those which obtained plurality support will *ex hypothesi* give us a noncontradictory combination which will express the plurality will. Out of all the possible combinations, it will be the only one made up of propositions which are all more probable than their contradictories and the one which is most probable as a whole. When the subject is reduced to separate groups of interdependent propositions, we would adopt the method described for elections in the preceding appendix. That is, each voter would vote for or against each proposition in a group but without contradicting himself. He would therefore have to choose some combination of the various groups which did not involve contradiction, just as in an election each voter has to choose a possible combination such as "Peter is better than Paul," "Peter is better than James," and "Paul is better than James" and not just reply arbitrarily to the three questions "is Peter better than Paul?" "is Peter better than James?" and "is Paul better than James?" which might result in a contradictory combination like "Peter is better than Paul," "James is better than Peter," and "Paul is better than James."

Clearly, if anyone's vote was self-contradictory, it would have to be discounted, and we should therefore establish a form of voting which makes such absurdities impossible.

Decisions about groups of propositions are liable to the same problems as we encountered in our examination of elections. It could well be that a combination of all the propositions with plurality support did in fact involve some contradiction. When this happens we should postpone making a decision unless it is absolutely necessary to do so at once, in which case we should choose the noncontradictory system which contains the proposition or propositions rejected by the lowest plurality. This system will not be made up entirely of propositions which are more probable than their contradictories, or which are really probable when taken as a whole, but it will be the most probable of the possible combinations and the one in which we are forced to accept only the least improbable propositions.

This method, which we are suggesting as a means of analyzing a subject of debate, would be just as useful in any type of discussion and is perhaps the only one which can conclusively demonstrate the justice of one of the various solutions or even reveal that solution whenever this depends not on discovering but simply on recognizing a truth.

We should stress that the table embodying the exact analysis of a subject of debate should not be drawn up in the same way as we would draw one up for ourselves, to help us examine a question. For a proposition to be considered simple, it is enough that it can only be accepted or rejected. It is on propositions like these that the voters should be asked their opinions and not on the reasons which make them accept or reject the various propositions. The analysis should stop there. If it did not, not only would the method become impracticable, but also we could claim that voting was useless, except on questions of fact, since once the analysis was complete, the justice of the decision could be proven, and if the analysis was accurate, it would be impossible not to have total unanimity. But to ensure that it is opinions which are being voted upon and not the grounds for them, we shall often need to present these opinions in the form of candidates at an election and to ask the voters to rank them in order of preference.

Even the most complicated subject of debate can be reduced to a table like the ones we have outlined above. Anyone can judge the accuracy of the table by judging whether or not each proposition can be answered by a *yes* or a *no* and whether, by answering *yes* or *no* to each, he can arrive at a true expression of his own opinion.

We do not necessarily need to go to the trouble of drawing up a complete table before the debate takes place. There can of course be another kind of relationship between the propositions. Suppose for example that we have a choice of two options. Once one of them has been adopted, we still have to decide how it should be enforced, and it would not be at all contradictory for those who voted for the option that was rejected to still have an opinion as to how the option they voted against should be enforced. So to represent the whole of the subject in a table, we would need to make all the propositions about putting the accepted option into practice conditional upon its acceptance. We would have to say, "if we accept this option, then such and such a thing should be done," and "if we accept this other one, then such and such a thing should be done instead." Including all the conditional propositions would not only make the table extremely complicated but is also quite unnecessary, since we only ever need to debate on the consequences of one of the options. We should therefore divide the subject of debate into several parts and make one table for absolute propositions, whether separate or interdependent, and another for each of the series of conditional propositions which might become absolute once the initial decisions had been taken.

We shall now demonstrate the method we have described, using a question which we discussed earlier, namely the composition of provincial assemblies.[5] To begin with, there are three main questions. Who should be a member? How many members should there be? And how long should membership last? It is sometimes considered best to have representatives of different orders in an assembly, and since this can influence the number of members or the way in which they are replaced, we need to examine first of all the question, who should be a member? and then progress to the others, which are necessarily conditional upon it. For example, if we want our assembly to be made up of representatives from three orders in equal proportions, then we obviously need to set a total number of members which is divisible by three. But if we want one of the three orders to have the same number of representatives as the other two put together, then the total number must be divisible by four. But we should not link decisions about the total number of members and about the composition of the assembly, because someone who voted for an equal ratio between the three orders can still without contradicting himself, vote for a total number which is divisible by four if the plurality voted for an unequal ratio, which makes such a number necessary. All propositions about number should therefore be conditional, and we need only debate those which apply once the decision upon which they were conditional has been taken. There is no point in debating the others.

The question of renewing the members should be dealt with before that of their number. If we decided that the members should be renewed, say, over a three-year period, then the total number of members would have to be a multiple of three and therefore a multiple of nine or twelve depending on whether the ratio of members from the different orders had required a total number divisible by three or four.

So, let us examine the first question. The conditions which we demand of each member are general or relative to his order and, above all, need not always be identical; they can depend on whether the assembly is in some way

5. [Not translated here. For the French, see Arago and O'Connor (1847, vol. 8, 178–93).]

to be divided into different orders. So before anything else, we need to decide if there will be any distinction between the orders, deciding everything else afterward, just as in the example of setting the number of the members. If we decided first of all what we expected of each representative, we would be dealing with conditionals, and it is quite unnecessary to debate these until we have discovered which ones apply.

First, then, we need to make a decision about distinctions between the orders. There are three options. First, to make no distinction at all. Second, to admit a set number of members of each order; and third, to divide the assembly into as many chambers as there are different orders.

Initially, we seem to be able to reduce this question to two basic propositions. Should there be a distinction between the orders or not? And if so, then which of the two distinctions should we prefer? Or instead of this reduction, we might ask each voter to rank the three options in order of preference.

Suppose that out of sixty voters, twenty-five are in favor of there being no distinction at all, while the other thirty-five feel there should be one of some kind. On a second vote, thirty-five are in favor of each order having a separate chamber, while the remaining twenty-five feel that they should all be mixed up. Apparently then, the plurality is in favor of separating the three orders. But this might in fact not be the case. Using the second method, where the voters are asked to rank the options in order of preference, might lead to a different result. [The options are A: to make no distinction at all, B: to admit a set number of members from each order, and C: to divide the assembly into as many chambers as there are orders.] Suppose that eighteen voters rank the options ABC, while seven rank them ACB; seven voters rank them BAC, ten rank them CAB, and eighteen rank them CBA. The first option therefore has a plurality of thirty-five to twenty-five compared to the second and of thirty-two to twenty-eight compared to the third. So when we used the first method and voted on each of the two questions separately, the result we obtained was in fact against the will of the plurality, who, as we now see, favor the first option.

In this example, if we had asked the voters to choose between all three options at once, there would have been twenty-five votes for option A, seven for B, and twenty-eight for C; and if we had then asked the seven who voted for the option with the fewest votes (B) to choose between the two others, then we would have obtained the same result of thirty-two votes to twenty-eight in favor of option A.

However, this last method of decision making might have been erroneous with a different disposition of votes. Suppose that fifteen voters rank the options ABC and three, while still preferring A overall, prefer C to B. Seventeen voters rank them BAC, and three rank them BCA. Fourteen rank them CAB, and eight rank them CBA. Clearly, by this method, option A has a plurality of thirty-two to twenty-eight compared to option B and of thirty-five to twenty-five compared to option C. Had we begun by asking, should we make some distinction between the orders? there would have been a plurality of forty-two votes to eighteen in favor of such a distinction; there would then have been thirty-five votes to twenty-five in favor of the type of distinction described in option B, and the method would have led to error. Finally, if we had asked the voters to choose between the three options at once, A would have had eighteen votes, B twenty, and C twenty-two; and when we asked the eighteen who had supported option A to now choose between options B and C, there would be a plurality of thirty-five to twenty-five in favor of option B, which once again is against the true will of the plurality.

But how can asking two simple questions like, should there be a distinction? and if so, then should it be of the first or second kind? give us the wrong result? Because it is not the simple putting into practice of our method of analysis that it appears to be. The proposition, we should have some sort of distinction between the members of an assembly, is not really a basic one at all, because while someone who rejects it certainly rejects the need for any type of distinction, someone who accepts it may be asserting two very different things: either that there should be some distinction, no matter what kind, or else that there should be a certain type of distinction and that if this cannot be effected, then it would be better to have no distinction at all than to have any other type. The analysis was therefore incomplete. We laid ourselves open to misjudging the true will of the plurality by assuming that everyone who said that there should be a distinction was actually saying the same thing, by assuming that they preferred both forms of distinction to the option of no distinction at all, and this assumption is totally unfounded.

Some people might feel that the advantages of having a distinction between the members of an assembly were outweighed by the disadvantages of segregating them, and others, whatever their reasons for supporting a distinction, might be able to see nothing good in a system whereby a distinction was made but the orders were mixed up. We clearly need to link the three options together and use the same form as we did for elections (See appendix 1).

Going back to our example, suppose that option B had plurality support. We would then need to debate how many orders we wished to admit; evidently, there can only be two, three, or four different ones (assuming we have already decided that a benefice as such can properly be counted as a piece of property). We can therefore divide the assembly into privileged and non-privileged; into nobility, clergy, and third estate; or into nobility, clergy, town and country dwellers. At the same time, we need to decide whether each order should be entitled to the same number of members, whether we should allot the privileged orders a certain number of seats and also allow them to stand for the others, as representatives of the unprivileged, or alternatively allot a certain number of seats to the unprivileged and allow them to stand for the others as well.

Before we can answer these questions, we need to debate the following interrelated ones. Should we allot a set number of seats to both the privileged and the unprivileged, or just to one or the other? Suppose that using the method we described above, the plurality come out in favor of the first option. We would then go on to ask whether the privileged and unprivileged should be allotted an equal number of seats; this proposition could be answered by a simple *yes* or *no*, and if the majority answered *yes*, then the question would be resolved. If they answered *no*, then we would need to set the proportions. To do this, we could ask whether the proportions should be fixed in relation to, say, the ratio of members of each order, or the income from property for the particular province, or for the kingdom as a whole, or else in relation to other reasons the voters might have for considering candidates suitable.

So we have three separate questions, each of which can be answered with a *yes* or a *no*. "Should the proportions be fixed according to some principle?" "If so, should that principle be the ratio of the various orders or their revenues?" and "should we use the ratios from each separate province so that the number of members is different for each assembly, or from the country as a whole so that the number of members is always the same?" We might be criticized for not asking the voters to choose among the two ways of establishing the ratio of the members and the option of establishing it arbitrarily, since we seem to have just the same situation here as when we debated the distinction between the members. Indeed, we would have to approach the question in the same way if anyone favored the third option, preferring to establish the ratio arbitrarily over using a particular one of the suggested ways, while at the same time preferring overall the other way of doing so. But since it is hardly conceivable that this could happen, we suggest that the question be debated using our first method, unless one of the voters protests that he cannot truly express his opinion by answering *yes* or *no* to the two questions with which he is presented and demands that the stricter method be used.

If the voters do not wish to establish the ratios according to some principle, then we can proceed as follows: first of all we must decide which of the two orders will have the most seats. Second whether there will be more than twice as many members of that order as members of the other, and third if there are not more than twice as many, then whether the ratio between the orders will be somewhere between 2:1 and 3:2, between 3:2 and 1:1, and so on until we arrive at a very precise ratio. Then, we will ask whether the privileged should be split into two orders, each with a fixed number of members, and we will establish the ratio between these two groups in just the same way. And finally, we will debate any divisions which could be made between the unprivileged orders.

Having decided how the assembly will be made up, it simply remains for us to decide what shall be the conditions of membership for each order of candidate. These conditions fall into two types. First, there are good reasons why certain people should be excluded, and second, there are certain qualities which are useful for the common good and which we have a right to demand. We should draw up a complete list of the first type and consult the assembly about each one.

The second type can only be considerations about the type and amount of income, or about tax rating. So, first of all, we should decide which of these two is to apply to each order. We would look at the privileged orders and decide whether the type of property for the nobles, or benefices for the ecclesiastics, should be taken into account, and if we decide that it should, then we would grade all the different types of property and benefice. Then, we would decide whether this condition was sufficient, or whether we also needed to have some condition about minimum revenue. If so, we would fix one using the same method as we used to fix the ratio of privileged and unprivileged members; that is, we would work out the limits between which it fell by debating questions which could only be answered by a *yes* or a *no*.

It only remains for us to decide whether or not each district should have its own representatives and to then decide on the number of representatives and the rules for their reelection. This should not lead to complications, unless the number of districts and of divisions between the members takes the total number of representatives above certain limits, thus making assemblies too rowdy. Questions about limiting both the number of representatives and the number of districts could be linked with the others, and perhaps even with the very first question about whether any distinction should be made.

We can end our example here; it has amply shown that no question is so complicated that it cannot be decided by an assembly, as long as the members are only asked to give their views on basic propositions, whether isolated or interdependent.

The only real problem is that of properly distinguishing isolated conditional propositions from interdependent ones, but we can solve this by observing that confusion only occurs in situations where those who support a certain condition might prefer to reject it altogether than accept one of the two possible consequences on which they would have to vote if that condition was passed. Using this general rule, we will always be able to tell where it is best to isolate propositions, and where it is best to group them together.

Forming a committee to analyze a subject so that the decision at which an assembly arrives will truly express the will of the plurality must not be confused with giving any group of men, or even any individual, the right to suggest a subject for debate. Even if precautions were taken to prevent this right from becoming an actual legislative power, limiting the powers of the debating body to simple negation, it would always give those who had it a dangerous advantage. However, the members of the committee do not have a special right, but merely a function; they are simply offered the mental challenge of creating something. The committee is not a senate separately exercising legislative power; it is a commission asked by the body of representatives to make an accurate analysis of the subject they have decided to debate. Men employed in public office tend to regard it as giving them some power or special right; they imagine that it confers some special authority on their wills, not that they are simply being asked to use their reason to decide questions, establish principles, and draw conclusions. And yet that is how any man who believes in the rights of his peers should react, whatever the office in question. When one man elects another to an assembly, he is not giving that man or that assembly of men any power over himself; he is simply giving them the job of deciding certain questions on his behalf, and on behalf of those who share his interest, and undertaking with or without restrictions to accept and abide by this decision.

And when someone elects a committee, he is not asking others to judge for him; as we have already noted, the accuracy or inaccuracy of the analysis can easily be proven. The committee set up to analyze the question could not abuse its power without risking public condemnation for dishonesty or for lack of enlightenment.

The committee would need to present the assembly with the whole subject of debate and a table of all the propositions on which they had to vote. Each voter could then easily judge whether his opinion was catered for by voting *yes* or *no* to the propositions in the table; if it was not, then that would show the analysis to be faulty, and it would have to be corrected. Each member would thus get a graphic illustration of what overall opinion he should hold according to his particular ones, and this would compensate for the lack of wisdom and enlightenment which we can expect in the voters. At the same time, an inaccurate table could be easily remedied as long as just one of the voters noticed that there was a possible opinion for which it did not cater—a simple observation which could be easily verified against bogus claims.

As we noted above, when the propositions are interdependent, this method can have the same disadvantages when applied to decision making as we earlier discovered it had for elections. That is, it can give a seemingly contradictory result. However, this drawback is inherent in any form of decision making which seeks to find the plurality will from a series of interdependent propositions, and this method tells us as much as the examination of votes ever will. We may not have the perfect result; its probability may in fact be very small; we cannot even be certain that the decision is correct; it is just the most probable of all the possible solutions.

Whenever possible, if the result is contradictory, another vote should not be taken, but the decision should quite simply be postponed. We are attempting not to find the collective will of an assembly but a result that we can regard as conforming with the truth because it is favored by the plurality of the voters, who, it is supposed, favor truth rather than error. Before debating the question again, we should therefore wait long enough for any change in opinion to be brought about by a better understanding of the question and not just by personal motives.

We referred to debates in which the representatives express not their own will but that of the district they represent. Clearly, the tables of basic propositions would then have to be presented first of all to the district assemblies so they could come to a decision on the subject.

However, we might object that the will of the plurality of districts would sometimes be opposed to the will of the plurality of the voters in the district assemblies. Suppose that there are twelve districts, with twenty-four members in each assembly. A proposition is supported by eight out of the twelve districts, but in these eight districts the members were fourteen to ten in favor of supporting it, whereas the members in the four other districts were twenty to four against. The proposition supported by the eight districts would therefore have just 128 votes in its favor, while the opposite proposition supported by just four districts would have 160.

However, this is not a reason to reject our distinction between decisions supported by a plurality of representatives and decisions supported by a plurality of districts. In any debate where we ask each member of an assembly to vote according to his own opinions, we are simply trying to obtain a decision which conforms with truth, and any method which leads us to follow the opinion of a minority is inherently flawed. But in debates about matters which relate to the rights or common interests of the citizens, the members should attempt to find out exactly what the citizens consider to be their rights, or in their interests, and only they can be the judges of that. The particular will of a district can be shown far less equivocally by a plurality vote in its district assembly than by the vote of just one representative of that district, and the plurality of votes from the districts indicates their common will. So, whenever it is simply a question of finding out what is true, we should use the first method, and whenever we want our decision to be an expression of the general will, we should use the second.

Besides, whenever such a debate occurs, as it should not often do, we can avoid contradictions between the plurality of the votes and the plurality of the districts by stipulating a minimum plurality which would ensure both a plurality of members and a plurality of districts. This would be done by ensuring that the plurality of the districts required by law is large enough for a proposition accepted by the smallest possible plurality and unanimously rejected in the districts which rejected it to still have a plurality in favor of it. So, with twelve districts and twenty-four members, we would need to stipulate a plurality of two districts and eighteen votes in each, or of four districts and twelve votes, or of six districts and eight votes.[6]

We would also sometimes need to make districts conform to the will of communities. However, there is no point in prolonging this discussion, as from now on it will be nothing more than very simple applications of the same basic principles.

---

6. [The arithmetic of this example works as follows. Twelve districts with 24 members each equals 288 members. On worst case assumptions, if each of seven districts splits 21 to 3 in favor of a proposition, there will be 147 votes for it. If each of eight districts splits 18 to 6 in favor of a proposition, there will be 144 votes for it; and if each of nine districts splits 16 to 8 for a proposition, there will again be 144 votes for it. Note that in the last two cases, the worst case would lead to a tie, not, as Condorcet claims, a majority for a proposition.]

CHAPTER 8

Condorcet

From *A Survey of the Principles Underlying the Draft Constitution*, 1792

[For the full voting rules in Condorcet's Constitution of February 1793 see McLean and Hewitt forthcoming.]

An examination of all the different forms of election shows that they can only reveal which candidates a majority of the voters consider as worthy of a place if there is an initial majority declaration to limit the number of candidates put forward which states that the voters are restricting themselves to choosing only between candidates that they consider capable of exercising the functions of the post to be filled. So, at the very least, each voter will have to nominate as many candidates as he considers worthy of the place. Everyone will then have to pronounce on the merits of each candidate, even if they have only been nominated by one person. We could not dispense with this stage without having to accept as candidates even those who are nominated by only one voter. Each voter would then express his complete will, by making a comparative judgment between all the candidates taken two by two, and from the majority will on each comparison, we could deduce its general will. However, this method will often give an unsatisfactory result and will not always reveal which candidate the majority prefers, since there may sometimes be no such thing as a majority preference.

Now, it is both awkward and time-consuming to form an initial judgment about the merits of the candidates and difficult to rank a large number of candidates in order of merit. Moreover, to extract from these lists each voter's opinion on all the candidates taken two by two and to use this to deduce a general result would be an immense and lengthy task. Clearly then, this method, which may in any case only reveal the preferences of a relative plurality, and not a majority, is totally impractical for an electoral assembly, even if it is made up almost entirely of enlightened and nonpartisan men.

Now, since we cannot use the only method which usually reveals the candidates considered most worthy by a majority, and since the other methods can only reveal which candidates a greater majority considers very worthy of the post, we have had to choose the simplest and most practical one, the one that is least susceptible to factions and intrigue and most certain to fulfil the only possible requirements for any election method.

In our preferred method, the will of each primary assembly is conveyed to the main town of each department, to form the general will of the citizens of that department. This general will is then conveyed to the place where the legislative body sits, in order to form the general will of all the citizens of the republic.

Regardless of the number of places to be filled for the same office, each voter will only have to express his will twice: first, to list a set number of candidates, and second, to complete the election.

In this initial vote, each voter will nominate a set number of candidates.

For example, if a department is electing representatives to the National Assembly then each citizen will list as many names as there are representatives. Three times as many candidates will be put forward as there are places to be filled, and the list of candidates to whom the choice will be restricted will therefore be formed of the names of those who obtain the most votes. For example, if there are ten representatives, then the thirty citizens who obtain the most votes in this first round will make up the list of candidates.

In the second vote, each citizen will judge which candidates he considers most worthy of the place, and list as many of them as there are places to be filled and then the same number of those he considers the next most worthy.

So, if there are ten places to be filled, each citizen will select first the ten most worthy of the thirty candidates and then the ten next most worthy of the twenty remaining ones.

The first votes will then be assessed and any candidates who have obtained an absolute majority will be elected. If there are more candidates with an absolute majority than there are places to be filled, then the candidates with the greatest majority will be elected.

If the election is not completed by the first vote, then the second votes will be assessed, and the candidates with the greatest majorities will be elected.

When the two lists are brought together, there are necessarily at least as many candidates with an absolute majority as there are places to be filled. Imagine once again that there are ten places and 1,000 voters. Ten thousand names will therefore be listed in the first 10 votes. It is therefore possible for nineteen candidates to obtain more than 501 votes and for the election to be completed using only the first vote. We may even have to select the candidates with the most votes out of all those who obtained a majority.

However, it is also possible that no candidate obtains a majority, since some of the thirty candidates may obtain 334 votes and all the others 333.

We would then consider the second votes, on the subsidiary list. Each voter has then named 20 candidates, so (with the same number of places and voters as before) there will be 20,000 names. Imagine that 9 candidates obtain unanimous support and that they therefore obtain a total of 9,000 votes. The remaining 11,000 votes can only be divided between the remaining 21 candidates if at least one of them obtains more than 500 votes, which is an absolute majority.

The tasks which this election method requires of the citizens are very short and simple and can be made simpler still by removing everything which might make them difficult for the simplest man.

The method is only time-consuming for the men who have to interpret the will of the individuals or of the separate assemblies, in order to form a general will, and this too can be made quicker and easier.

Let us now examine the method in itself. First, we note that requiring the list of candidates to have only three times as many names as there are places to be filled does not really restrict the election. It is only rarely that someone who could have had the people's support will be excluded.

It is theoretically possible that the citizens will sometimes concentrate their support on a small number of individuals and that the list of candidates will therefore not include enough names. However, this will never actually occur in practice. If it did, it would be easy to find some means of completing the election which did not contradict the spirit of the method.

The system of giving election votes allows each voter to give a natural, clear, and complete expression of his will. Indeed, it is quite absurd to hold successive votes in order to elect men to completely equal posts. This method, while claiming to reveal the candidate who is preferred by a majority to all the others—which in this case is of no use at all—fails to do even that. It is counterproductive and fails to select the men who, in the opinion of the majority, should be called to fill these places. Moreover, not only does it offer no resistance to factions, but to some extent it actually renders them necessary and, on the occasions when it does not submit the elections to partisan influences, makes them dependent on pure chance.

In our suggested method, however, anyone who is elected after the first vote is necessarily judged by the majority to be more worthy than the other candidates.

And we will still be dealing with the preferences of the majority even when we have to refer to the subsidiary list. It is true that the candidates then elected will not have such strong majority support, but they will have more support than the remaining ones. Moreover, we shall have obtained an accurate expression of the majority will; we can gain nothing by trying to make it stronger than it actually is and by seeming to obtain a will which does not exist.

Substitutes would be chosen first from those who obtained a majority in the first votes but were excluded by a greater majority and then, if necessary, by referring to the subsidiary list and electing them by a simple plurality.

However, this would only occur very rarely, and its occasional drawbacks for the last substitutes are more than outweighed by being able to complete the election by a single vote, using a method that is as quick as it is simple.

If this method is used for elections in separate assemblies, they will be far less exposed to intrigue. It would be virtually impossible to prevent a man of real merit from being included on the list of candidates, if the votes were such that he deserved to be there. It would be equally difficult for a faction to prevent the majority from uniting in favor of a better man or to win them over to a truly unworthy one.

Now, imagine that the citizens are divided into two parties. No election method which is defective in this situation could form part of a good constitution, for although we can suppress political parties, we cannot prevent the formation of groups of people with the same opinions.

However, our proposed method is actually very good at coping with this situation. The largest party has to list at least as many acceptable candidates as the opposing one could but will find it hard to take over the whole list, which will not therefore present another distressing spectacle of the power of one party. Then, it is only necessary for there to be as many names on the list that are approved by the largest party as there are places to be filled for them to win in the actual election. The largest party will therefore necessarily have the advantage, without having to resort to any of the corrupt means which threaten public tranquillity and which, when used over a long period, eventually corrupt the public spirit and threaten the freedom of the people.

The most that may happen is that some of the places will be given to men supported by both the parties, who are tolerated or respected by each because of their character or their wisdom. Men, that is, who can preserve a balance and prevent the quarrels of the party from degenerating into harmful feuds.

In a word, this election method deprives the smaller party of the hope of succeeding through intrigue or rumor and gives the opposing party an assurance of success which means that it does not need to use force. The election will therefore be peaceful, even when the citizens are divided. It will illustrate the power of the parties but will not be at their mercy.

The representatives who form the legislative body are to be elected in each department, and their number will be determined by the size of the population alone. This is another tribute to equality. The system of giving each department three representatives, while a third of the total number of places were distributed in proportion to tax proceeds, undoubtedly corrected the advantage which allocation purely by revenue gave to rich departments.

However, we would prefer not to include any inequalities than to include one which must be counterbalanced.

This election method would also enable the National Council to be chosen by all the citizens. We would need only to make the slight modifications of having a proportionally larger list of candidates when the election is to fill just one place and of being able to nominate several substitutes at once for each place.

We consider it very important that the men in whose hands the national powers will reside are chosen by the citizens themselves, that they are chosen by repute and not intrigue, and finally that these posts are no longer given almost exclusively to the inhabitants of just one city, as would be the case if the election were conducted by the assembly of the people's representatives or any single body. It is right that men who have as one of their primary duties the task of intimately uniting all parts of the Republic belong equally to everyone, and right that the men who are negotiating for our country with foreign nations should be seen to have the direct confidence of the majority of the citizens.

Voting aloud in primary assemblies only causes disorder and confusion. Besides, this method can be rejected purely on the grounds of the influence it gives those who vote first over the votes of those who vote after them. It also supposes a permanent assembly which lasts for the duration of the voting, and this would make things unnecessarily awkward for the citizens. Besides, a written ballot is not necessarily a secret one: each citizen can include his name with his written vote and the names could be read out as the votes were being counted.

We suggest that the voters include their names with the vote which serves to form the list of candidates; there can be no drawback in each voter being answerable for his choice. However, we feel that the names should not be present in the election votes. In the initial indication, there will be no danger to the state if voters list some names for personal reasons. Since the names are only read after all the votes have been cast, the election cannot be influenced by rumors or by the signs of disapproval that some names may cause; if this vote is made public, it can benefit the nation without disturbing the peace of individuals or opening the way to intrigue.

Besides, since this initial vote reveals the citizens' opinions about the best choices to make, it may serve some purpose if the names of the men who have merited such confidence are made known: voters who do not have sufficient personal knowledge of these worthy men can then act in accordance with the clear public judgment of citizens whose probity and enlightenment they admire. This is yet another reason to prefer a written, signed ballot to a spoken one, in which each citizen only knows the will of other members of the same assembly.

The second vote, on the other hand, is a preference vote and should therefore be protected from any kind of influence and kept independent of public opinion and from commitments that may have been made in a moment of weakness. We should try to ensure that the voters can express their will as freely as possible.

CHAPTER 9

S. Lhuilier

An Examination of the Election Method Proposed to the National Convention of France in February 1793, and Adopted in Geneva; Presented to the Legislative Committee by Simon Lhuilier and Printed by Order of the Committee, 1794

To the President and other members of the Legislative Committee

7 July 1794

Citizens,

The examination of the new election method which I present here is taken from a more extensive and more abstract work on this subject. It is a subject which could not fail to interest me, because of the many different combinations of possibilities it involves and its close links with the sciences to which I have devoted myself. And while as a mathematician I would have been content with the remarkable results of my examination, I did not feel that as a citizen I could be satisfied with theoretical speculation. I felt it my duty to present you with some of the results I obtained and to explain them by applying them to elections conducted according to this new method. I have done my utmost to rid my work of anything which might make it look too imposing or scientific.

Since this election method was suggested by a mathematician who was adept at this kind of speculation, I would not have hesitated to show him my work before presenting it to you, if I had been able to do so.[1] I have no doubt whatsoever that when he saw the certainty of the principle on which my examination is based and the necessary link between this principle and the results I have obtained, Condorcet would have rejected his own work. In discussions of this subject with some of my fellow citizens I have convinced

---

1. [This means not that Lhuilier knew that Condorcet was dead, because this was not generally known until the end of the year, but that the conditions in Paris under the Terror were such that it was impossible to contact anybody.]

even those originally most favorable to this method of its drawbacks, and I am certain that this paper will produce the same conviction in each of you. This being the case, I shall end with the hope that, as soon as your other occupations allow, you will suggest to the sovereign council some other election method which, unlike the current one, does not run the risk of giving a result in contradiction with the true decision of the assembly.

Brotherly greetings,

Simon Lhuilier

Examination of the Election Method Proposed to the National Convention of France in February 1793, and Adopted in Geneva

(1) Description of the election method which is the subject of this examination.

Three times as many candidates are presented to the assembly as there are places to fill. Each ballot paper is made up of two columns, headed the *Election Column* and the *Supplementary Column*. Each column contains the names of all the candidates.

Each voter gives as many election votes as there are places to be filled. He also gives the same number of supplementary votes, but to different candidates from the ones he has elected.

A procedure for dealing with invalid ballot papers has been established, and measures have been taken for the case of a tie (which becomes less likely as the numbers of voters and of candidates increase).

A candidate is said to have the *absolute majority* in the election column when the total number of his election votes is greater than half the valid election papers.

If the number of candidates with an absolute majority in the election column is not less than the number of places to be filled, then these candidates are elected in descending order of the number of election votes they obtained.

If the number of candidates with an absolute majority in the election column is less than the number of places to be filled, then the election is completed using the supplementary column. This is done by taking the sum of each remaining candidate's election and supplementary votes and candidates are elected following the order of the size of these totals.

The same procedure is used whenever substitutes have to be elected.

(2) This election method was presented to the National Convention of France in February 1793, in the Constitutional Plan which appeared to be chiefly the work of the academician Condorcet. It is not surprising that since this method carried so much weight with him, a great many of the members of our National Assembly, and following them, a considerable number of my fellow citizens, were biased in its favor, and regarded it as the method most likely to

give an accurate expression of the general will at the same time as removing the need to reconvene sovereign assemblies, which are always costly to the state and often to individuals as well.

Amongst the many fields to which Condorcet applied mathematics, he found the subject of elections of particular interest. He wrote a profound book, called *An Essay on the Application of Analysis to the Probability of Decisions Rendered by a Plurality of Votes*, which proves both his ability to use calculus and the difficulties involved in a close examination of this subject. It seemed extremely probable that an election method which was at least partly produced by a mathematician who had specialized in this subject could be generally approved without having to pass the test of experience.

This election method is not discussed in the book I have just cited. The methods which he examines there would be difficult for large assemblies to apply and are only really practicable for assemblies of elected voters who are precise, free from prejudice, and responsible to themselves for the accuracy of the way in which they rank the candidates according to an assessment of their respective degrees of merit. Indeed, his whole examination is based on this principle.

When it became necessary to make the jump from theoretical speculations to practical applications, the author must have realized the problems involved in applying his abstract considerations to real life, and consequently, there is no discussion in his Constitutional Plan of the various election methods he examines in his book.

Since the proposed constitution did not meet with public approval, the election method suggested in it has not been put into effect in France. It has, however, been adopted in Geneva (with a few slight improvements mainly regarding cases in which there is only one place to be filled) and has been used in the many recent elections of the Sovereign Assembly.

(3) The main advantage that is claimed for this election method is that it requires at least an absolute majority before a candidate can be elected. There are also other subsidiary advantages. For example, the election is conducted in one round, and the voters' choice is wider than if the number of candidates was limited to the number of places to be filled. This method also prevents factions.

It is my main aim to examine the first of these advantages. It is most open to close mathematical scrutiny, and the supporters of the new method seem to consider it the most important advantage and regard the others as subsidiary. However, I also intend to say a word about these.

(4) As this subject falls almost entirely within the field of calculus, some of my fellow citizens may be deterred from reading this paper just by looking at it, and I shall try to prevent this.

Since this subject is of immediate interest and usefulness both to society as a whole and to many of the individuals of which society is formed, I would have failed in my aim if I had not tried to make this examination as basic and easily understood as possible. This was by no means the easiest part of my work. A familiarity with abstract speculations may prevent us from appreciating the difficulty of our reasoning and our calculations, which, while simple for those who are used to this kind of thought, may seem difficult to those who are not. I could therefore only avoid uncertainty as to whether I had fulfilled my main aim in presenting this paper (which is public utility and the agreement of my fellow citizens) by asking the advice of people who were capable of appreciating it and of improving the obscure or inaccurate sections.

Amongst the men of letters who have carefully examined this paper, I should like to make especial mention of our fellow citizen Necker (Germagny), who is well known for his mathematical knowledge. It is to him that I owe both the brilliant idea upon which this paper is based and some of the calculations which apply to the simplest cases. I agreed with his observations, and carefully using them as a foundation, I developed their consequences and told him of my work. We felt it would be useful to bring this important subject to the attention of our fellow citizens, and I took it upon myself to do so.

Although both the general and conclusive examination of this election method fall within the realm of algebra, I have limited myself to simple and purely arithmetical calculations and to expanding only certain examples. Fearing that a scientific format would deter many of my fellow citizens, I have limited myself to presenting some of the general theorems at which I arrived. As my use of algebra is throughout purely elementary (unlike the calculations which Condorcet scattered liberally throughout his work), they can be understood by anyone who has the most superficial knowledge of basic mathematics, and any of my fellow citizens who can follow them will always find me ready to discuss them.

(5) The candidates who have an absolute majority in the election column are elected in the order of this majority.

This rule is so natural and so conformable to the will of the assembly that I would prejudice my work if I began by examining it. I shall therefore regard it as fully established. However, I shall permit myself to make a few remarks about it, partly in order to make my examination complete but primarily to show that whenever other aspects of the new election method contradict this rule, then they become at once defective, even if there is no reason to regard them as defective in themselves.

(6) If the election cannot be completed by the first column, then the supplementary column must be taken into account. The election must be completed

by taking the sum of the election and supplementary votes of the remaining candidates, and electing them in order of the size of these totals.

This forms the main subject of my examination. I shall show that the way in which the votes from the two columns are brought together often changes the nature of the overall vote. I shall prove that this can be the case using hypothetical examples, with no reference to elections that have already taken place. I shall then examine the voting schemes of elections which have already been conducted in this way, and I shall show that in some of them, the will of the assembly may in fact have been different to the result that was announced.[2]

Basic Principle

(7) Any voter who has given one candidate an election vote and another candidate a supplementary vote, prefers the first candidate to the second.

We need do no more than express this principle to see that it has to be true. Everyone with whom I have discussed this subject has considered it indisputable. When the National Assembly proposed this method to the Sovereign, it made a big distinction between these two types of votes; in the explanations which were published at the time and which it ordered to be distributed, an election vote is called *principal* and a supplementary vote *secondary*, and this distinction is repeated in these explanations. As long as a candidate has obtained an absolute majority in these first votes, the distinction is not violated; the last votes are disregarded, whatever their number. They obtain some value only when the first column is not enough, however small the deficit.

Consequence

Having accepted this principle, we cannot reject its immediate consequence. When, in order to complete the election, we resort to the supplementary votes, *a candidate's election votes must not be opposed by the supplementary votes which other candidates have obtained on the same paper.*

This brilliant idea, first thought out by our fellow citizen, Necker, is the basis of this whole paper; the calculations presented are simply applications of it.

In order to show the importance of this principle and its consequences, let us examine the system which was once used in the elections of the Conseil General, when the list of candidates ended with a line called *new election*.

---

2. This second set of examples has been omitted at the request of the Legislative Committee.

A voter who gave fewer election votes than there were places to fill was automatically voting for the line *new election* (treated as a candidate). When it came to interpreting the votes, a vote for *new election* was compared indiscriminately to all of the other candidates, whereas it should only have affected candidates not elected by that voter. This defect was brought to light and remedied in 1768.

A very similar error is made in the current method when we refer to the second column. The supplementary votes are indiscriminately opposed to all the candidates who are still in the running; no account is taken of the way in which the supplementary votes were given, and no distinction is made between candidates who were preferred to him on the same paper by an election vote and those who were not named on the same paper at all, whether as elected or as substitutes. The process should only have any effect on the latter. *The supplementary line has taken the place of the old line of new election,* which had been recognized as defective.

(8) The case in which there is only one place to be filled, and consequently only three candidates, is distinct from all the others because of its simplicity, the smaller number of combinations it presents, and the generality of its results. I feel I should therefore begin with examples involving just three candidates, none of whom have the absolute majority. I shall then show how this case differs from others in which there are more candidates and how the results obtained in this case enable us to confidently draw conclusions about the more complicated cases.

Suppose that there are two candidates. One of them is considered preferable to the other when the number of voters who prefer the first candidate to the second is greater than the number of voters who prefer the second candidate to the first.

Let us examine all the kinds of conflict which have emerged or may emerge between the result pronounced according to the current method and the true will of the assembly.

Candidates who, on the present assessment, are represented as of unequal merit may in fact be considered of equal merit by the assembly; and similarly, candidates who now appear to be of equal merit may in fact be considered of unequal merit.

The candidate who now emerges as preferable may actually be the one the assembly likes least, and vice versa.

The candidate who now emerges as the least favorite may actually be preferred by the assembly, while at the same time the candidate who is shown as the favorite may in fact be the least favorite.

The election may be undecided between two or even three candidates, and yet the current method of assessment always presents it as decided.

Initially, I supported each of these assertions with two different kinds of example; in the first, the conflict was as great or almost as great as possible, and in the second, the conflict was an average one. But since these details gave my work too broad a scope, I have limited myself to just a few examples, and concentrated on showing the fallibility of deducing the will of the assembly simply from a knowledge of the election and supplementary votes.

(9) For brevity, I shall call the three candidates by the first three letters of the alphabet, *A*, *B*, and *C* (which can be taken to represent the initial letters of their names.)

Once candidate *A* has received an election vote, the corresponding supplementary vote can be given to either of the remaining candidates *B* and *C*, resulting in two kinds of ballot paper. In the table below, I shall call them 1 and 2. Similarly, an election vote for *B* gives us the two types of ballot paper 3 and 4, and an election vote for *C* types 5 and 6.

To make things clearer still, I shall present this table in the same form as the ballot papers distributed to the voters in the sovereign assembly [table 9.1].

A voter whose election paper is of the first kind prefers candidate *A* to all

TABLE 9.1.

Type of Paper	Election Vote For	Supplemnnentary Vote For	Election Column	Supplementary Column
1	*A*	*B*	*A* - | -------- *B* ------------ *C* ------------	*A* ------------ *B* - | -------- *C* ------------
2	*A*	*C*	*A* - | -------- *B* ------------ *C* ------------	*A* ------------ *B* ------------ *C* - | --------
3	*B*	*A*	*A* ------------ *B* - | -------- *C* ------------	*A* - | -------- *B* ------------ *C* ------------
4	*B*	*C*	*A* ------------ *B* - | -------- *C* ------------	*A* ------------ *B* ------------ *C* - | --------
5	*C*	*A*	*A* ------------ *B* ------------ *C* - | --------	*A* - | -------- *B* ------------ *C* ------------
6	*C*	*B*	*A* ------------ *B* ------------ *C* ------------	*A* ------------ *B* - | -------- *C* ------------

the others, and more specifically, to candidate B, while preferring candidate B to candidate C. Consequently, when we interpret the votes, the supplementary vote in favor of B should count only against candidate C, who is considered worse than B, and not at all against candidate A, who is preferred to candidate B. We can apply this principle to each of the five other types simply by amending the references to the candidates accordingly.

A is preferred to B by the voters whose ballot papers are of types 1, 2, and 5; B to A by ballots of types 3, 4, and 6; A to C by ballots of types 1, 2, and 3; C to A by ballots of types 4, 5, and 6; B to C by ballots of types 1, 3, and 4; and C to B by ballots of types 2, 5, and 6. In general, *one candidate is preferred to another by all the voters who give him an election vote and by those who give him a supplementary vote while giving their election vote to a third candidate.*

Note: In all of the following examples, I shall suppose that the assembly consists of 2,400 voters.

(10) Before entering into detailed examples, I shall set out some propositions which I am not actually going to prove here, although I am ready to do so if asked.

If a candidate is preferable to either one of the other two, then the sum of the first candidate's election and supplementary votes is greater than the sum of the other two candidates' election votes. Similarly, if the sum of one candidate's election and supplementary votes is less than the sum of the other two candidates' election votes, the first candidate cannot be the favorite.

If the sum of one candidate's election and supplementary votes is greater than the sum of the other two candidates' election votes, then the first candidate cannot be the least favorite.

If we take the number of election and supplementary votes received by two candidates as given, then the amount by which one of these candidates is preferred to the other increases as the number of people who voted for the first and gave their supplementary vote to the second increases.

There can be no doubt that a candidate is the least preferable of the three when the sum of his election votes and of half the number of voters is smaller than the sum of the election and supplementary votes of any one of the other candidates.

(11) *Example One* Suppose that the election results are as follows [table 9.2]: Since no candidate has an absolute majority, this election method pronounces C to be the favorite. However, since C's total of 2,160 is less than the total of A and B's election votes (2,240), he cannot be the favorite (section 10).

The situation which is most favorable for candidate C when compared with candidate A is that in which the 160 people who vote for C give their supplementary vote to A (section 10).

TABLE 9.2.

Candidate	Election Votes	Supplementary Votes	Total
A	1,160	220	1,380
B	1,080	180	1,260
C	160	2,000	2,160
[Total]	2,400	2,400	4,800

This supposition allows us to determine the distribution of election and supplementary votes between the three candidates. Since the 160 people who voted for *C* gave their supplementary vote to *A* and since *A* had 220 supplementary votes, he must have received the remaining 60 supplementary votes from the 1,080 people who voted for *B*. One thousand twenty of these voters must therefore have given their supplementary votes to *C*. *C* obtained 2,000 supplementary votes, so 980 of them must have come from people who voted for *A*. There were 1,160 people who voted for *A*, so 180 of them must have given their supplementary vote to *B*.

The election is therefore as follows [table 9.3]:

TABLE 9.3.

Voters		Election Vote	Supplementary Vote	Voters Who Prefer	
180		A	B	A to B 1,160 160	} 1,320
	1,160				
980		A	C	B to A 1,080 0	} 1,080
60		B	A	A to C 1,160 60	} 1,220
	1,080				
1,020		B	C	C to A 160 1,020	} 1,180
160		C	A	B to C 1,080 180	} 1,260
	160				
0		C	B	C to B 160 980	} 1,140

I shall explain this table so that the reader is not forced to give up, and my explanation will also apply to later examples.

Out of the 1,160 people who voted for A, 180 gave their supplementary vote to B, and the remaining 980 gave their supplementary vote to C.

Out of the 1,080 people who voted for B, 60 gave their supplementary vote to A, and 1,020 to C.

The 160 people who voted for C all gave their supplementary votes to A.

A is preferred to B by the 1,160 people who voted for A and by the 160 people who voted for C and gave their supplementary votes to A, giving a total of 1,320 votes.

A is preferred to C by the 1,160 people who voted for A and by the 60 people who voted for B and gave their supplementary votes to A, giving a total of 1,220 votes.

B is preferred to A only by the 1,080 people who voted for B.

B is preferred to C by the 1,080 people who voted for B and by the 180 people who voted for A and gave their supplementary votes to B, giving a total of 1,260 voters.

C is preferred to A by the 160 people who voted for C and by the 1,020 people who voted for B and gave their supplementary vote to C, giving a total of 1,180 voters.

Although by the current method, C emerges with 780 votes more than A, and 900 more than B, in fact, even in the most favorable comparison of C with A, there are 40 more voters who prefer A to C than who prefer C to A, and similarly there are 40 more voters who prefer B to C than who prefer C to B.

Similarly, in the most favorable comparison of C with B the 160 people who vote for C give their supplementary vote to B. So the election is as follows [table 9.4]:

In this, the most favorable case for C, he is indeed preferred to B by 200 votes, but still loses to A by 360 votes.

In the first case, where the 160 people who vote for C give their supplementary votes to A, the will of the assembly is pronounced as being in favor of A, who is the favorite of the three candidates, and against C, who is the least favorite.

In the second case, where the 160 people who vote for C give their supplementary votes to B, the will of the assembly is not pronounced between the three candidates.

In fact, since B is preferred to A and A is preferred to C, A is neither the favorite nor the least favorite of the three candidates. Similarly, since C is preferred to B and A is preferred to C, C is neither the favorite nor the least favorite of the three candidates. Finally, since B is preferred to A but C is preferred to B, B is neither the favorite nor the least favorite of the three.

We have here an example of an undecided election, or rather of a case in

TABLE 9.4.

Voters		Election Vote	Supplementary Vote	Voters Who Prefer	
20		*A*	*B*	A to B 1,160 0	} 1,160
	1,160				
1,140		*A*	*C*	B to A 1,080 160	} 1,240
220		*B*	*A*	A to C 1,160 220	} 1,380
	1,080				
860		*B*	*C*	C to A 160 860	} 1,020
0		*C*	*A*	B to C 1,080 20	} 1,100
	160				
160		*C*	*B*	C to B 160 1,140	} 1,300

which the will of the assembly cannot be explained. From it, we can conclude that the current method is not only defective in its interpretation but also in its very nature and that even if we went right back to the original votes, we would sometimes be unable to interpret the will of the assembly.

(12) Example designed to show the great indeterminacy of the result pronounced [table 9.5].

    C is declared the favorite and *A* the least favorite. However, it is my claim that the order of preference assigned to these three candidates could be quite different.

    1. [Table 9.6]

TABLE 9.5.

Candidate	Election Votes	Supplementary Votes	Total
A	1,000	480	1,480
B	840	740	1,580
C	560	1,180	1,740
[Total]	2,400	2,400	4,800

TABLE 9.6.

Voters		Election Vote	Supplementary Vote	Voters Who Prefer	
180	⎫	A	B	A to B 1,000	⎫ 1,000
				0	⎭
	⎬ 1,000				
820	⎭	A	C	B to A 840	⎫ 1,400
				560	⎭
480	⎫	B	A	A to C 1,000	⎫ 1,480
				480	⎭
	⎬ 840				
360	⎭	B	C	C to A 560	⎫ 920
				360	⎭
0	⎫	C	A	B to C 840	⎫ 1,020
				180	⎭
	⎬ 560				
560	⎭	C	B	C to B 560	⎫ 1,380
				820	⎭

The election is undecided; but a comparison between A and C gives A a superiority of 560 votes.

2. [Table 9.7]

The election is once again undecided, but a comparison of B and C gives B a superiority of 600 votes.

3. [Table 9.8]

A is the favorite of the three candidates, and C is the least favorite; they are therefore ranked in the order ABC, whereas this current method gives us the ranking CBA. So, the candidate pronounced as the least favorite can in fact be the favorite at the same time as the candidate pronounced to be the favorite may in fact be the least favorite.

In this example, as long as the number of people who vote for A and give their supplementary votes to B is greater than 380 but less than 460, A is the favorite and C the least favorite.

If the number of people who vote for A and give their supplementary votes to B is greater than 460 but smaller than 660, the election is undecided.

Whenever the election is decided, A emerges as preferable to C, which is contrary to the result obtained by the current method.

These results are sufficient to show the defects of the election method that has been adopted, and in accordance with the wishes of the committee, I

TABLE 9.7.

Voters		Election Vote	Supplementary Vote	Voters Who Prefer	
660	} 1,000	A	B	A to B 1,000 / 480	} 1,480
340		A	C	B to A 840 / 80	} 920
0	} 840	B	A	A to C 1,000 / 0	} 1,000
840		B	C	C to A 560 / 840	} 1,400
480	} 560	C	A	B to C 840 / 660	} 1,500
80		C	B	C to B 560 / 340	} 900

TABLE 9.8.

Voters		Election Vote	Supplementary Vote	Voters Who Perfer	
420	} 1,000	A	B	A to B 1,000 / 240	} 1,240
580		A	C	B to A 840 / 320	} 1,160
240	} 840	B	A	A to C 1,000 / 240	} 1,240
600		B	C	C to A 560 / 600	} 1,160
240	} 560	C	A	B to C 840 / 420	} 1,260
320		C	B	C to B 560 / 580	} 1,140

shall not include any discussion of elections which have already been conducted along these lines.

(13) If the sovereign was only ever required to hold elections to fill just one place, it would usually be easy to check the result of a doubtful assessment by returning to the original votes.

In order to compare two candidates, A and B, say, let us take all the ballot papers for C and divide these papers into two groups depending on which of A and B is in the supplementary column. Let us add to A's election votes the supplementary votes he received from the people who voted for C and to B's election votes the supplementary votes he received from the people who voted for C. Whichever of the two candidates A and B then has the greater total will be the favorite.

Whenever the sum of each candidate's election and supplementary votes is equal to the sum of the election votes of the other two candidates, the election remains completely undecided between the three candidates.

In the other cases, this indeterminacy is removed by other considerations. If the sum of one candidate's election and supplementary votes is bigger than the sum of the other two candidates' election votes, then at least one of the remaining candidates has a total of election and supplementary votes which is less than the sum of the election votes of the other two and this candidate cannot be the favorite. But as the number of places to be filled increases, any such verification becomes at once impractical, and more necessary.

As we saw, an election between three candidates gives rise to 6 different types of ballot paper. When there are two places to be filled, or six candidates, this becomes 90. For three places, or nine candidates, there are 1,680, and for four places, 34,650. It increases so rapidly as the number of places to be filled increases that in the election of the thirty-five judges for the Final Appeal Court, the number of possible different ballot papers was greater than one followed by forty-eight zeros:

$$1,000,000,000,000,000,000,000,000,000,000,000,000,000,000,000,000$$

So, whenever there is more than one place to be filled, it would be impractical to assess the votes according to the same easy method we use when the election is to fill just one place. Moreover, since our examination of the simple case of an election to fill just one place revealed complications we would not have expected and since we have proved that there is likely to be conflict between the true will of the assembly and the will pronounced by the current method, there can be no doubt that the causes for such conflict become even more numerous and more powerful when the election is a more complicated one. Clearly, if it was necessary to assess the votes in the first, simple case, then it is even more so in the cases to which this method of assessment cannot be applied.

To make this clearer still, I have made a detailed examination of an arbitrary case of an election between six candidates, and I have proved that there may be conflict between the pronounced result and the real one and that cases of indeterminacy between the candidates may be even more frequent. However, it would give this paper too broad a scope if I set out these calculations here, and I consider that I shall be able to persuade the reader more clearly by concentrating on comparing the candidates two by two. This will make our examination easier, without having any effect on the consequences I intend to draw.

(14) If we compare just two candidates, *A* and *B*, we find that there can be nine different types of ballot paper [table 9.9]:

1. Where both *A* and *B* have an election vote
2. *A* has an election vote and *B* a supplementary vote
3. *A* has an election vote and *B* has no vote
4. *B* has an election vote and *A* a supplementary vote
5. *B* has an election vote and *A* has no vote
6. Both *A* and *B* have a supplementary vote
7. *A* has a supplementary vote and *B* has no vote
8. *B* has a supplementary vote and *A* has no vote
9. Neither *A* nor *B* has any vote at all

Types 1, 6, and 9 do not affect the comparison between the two candidates, with respect to their difference in votes.

Candidate *A* is preferred to candidate *B* by the voters whose papers are of types 2, 3, and 7, and candidate *B* is preferred to candidate *A* by the voters whose papers are of types 4, 5, and 8. If we also give each of these candidates

TABLE 9.9.

Type	Election Vote	Supplementary Vote
1	A B	—
2	A	B
3	A	—
4	B	A
5	B	—
6	—	A B
7	—	A
8	—	B
9	—	—

the first type of ballot paper, which is common to them both, we shall find that (as in the case where there is a single place to be filled—section 9), one candidate is preferred to the other by all those who give him an election vote and by those who give him a supplementary vote and do not vote for the other candidate.

When we are dealing with three candidates, we know the total number of supplementary votes received by two candidates from the voters who only voted for one of them, this total being the number of people who voted for the third candidate. This fully determines the conjectures we can make about three candidates. But the same is not true for a greater number of candidates because of the great many ways in which the people who voted for the remaining candidates may have distributed their supplementary votes.

(15) Suppose an election held to fill several places in which an assembly of 2,400 voters is asked to choose from a number of candidates divisible by three. Suppose that A and B's votes are as follows:

A	800	720	1,520
B	600	1,200	1,800

Difference in favor of B	280

The most favorable situation for A is that in which the 800 people who vote for A give B a supplementary vote, whereas none of the people who vote for B give A a supplementary vote. As far as the difference between the votes of these two candidates is concerned, it is as if the election were as follows:

A	800	720	1,520
B	600	400	1,000

Difference in favor of A	520

It is therefore possible that A is preferred to B by a margin of 520, whereas we were claiming that B was preferred to A by a margin of 280.

The most favorable situation for B is that in which the 600 people who vote for B give A a supplementary vote, whereas none of the people who vote for A give B a supplementary vote. The results are then as follows.

A	800	120	920
B	600	1,200	1,800

Difference in favor of B	980

Between these two extreme cases, which give us a difference of 1,500 between the two candidates, there lie a great many probable intermediate cases, and this illustrates the great lack of determinacy which results from this election method.

When there are 280 more people who vote for *A* and give their supplementary vote to *B* than there are people who vote for *B* and give their supplementary vote to *A*, the two candidates are equally preferable. As far as the difference in their votes is concerned, it is as if the election votes were as follows (whether or not these candidates were also named on other ballot papers).

A	800	720	1,520
B	600	920	1,520

If the number of people who vote for *A* and give their supplementary vote to *B* is more than 280 greater than the number of people who vote for *B* and give their supplementary vote to *A*, then candidate *A* is preferable to candidate *B*. Similarly, if the number of people who vote for *B* and give their supplementary vote to *A* is greater than the number of people who vote for *A* and give their supplementary vote to *B*, or if *A* has less than 280 votes more than *B*, then candidate *B* is preferable to candidate *A*.

Since I have not concerned myself here with whether the number of election votes is less than half of the number of voters, it may happen that the candidate with the absolute majority in the election column is liked less than the candidate with the absolute minority or than a candidate with a smaller absolute majority. This cannot occur in an election between three candidates.

Example [table 9.10]

When 100 more people vote for *A* and give their supplementary vote to *B* than vote for *B* and give their supplementary vote to *A*, the two candidates have equal support. When the difference between these two numbers is more than 100, *A* is preferred to *B*, and when it is less than 100 or when the number of people who vote for *A* and give their supplementary vote to *B* is less than the number of people who vote for *B* and give their supplementary vote to *A*, then candidate *B* is preferred to candidate *A*.

TABLE 9.10.

Candidate	Election Votes	Supplementary Votes	Total
A	1,400	1,900	3,300
B	1,000	1,000	2,000

I shall restrict myself to one example [table 9.11], to show the enormous scope for indeterminacy, even in elections between just three candidates.

When over 80 more people vote for A and give their supplementary vote to B than vote for B and give their supplementary vote to A, candidate A is preferred to candidate B.

When over 100 more people vote for B and give their supplementary vote to C than vote for C and give their supplementary vote to B, candidate B is preferred to candidate C.

And when over 180 more people vote for C and give their supplementary vote to A than vote for A and give their supplementary vote to C, candidate C is preferred to candidate A.

And since all these inequalities may happen at the same time, in a very broad spectrum, we can see that the will of the assembly which is pronounced as decided by the current election method is in fact frequently quite undecided.

(16) The advantages of a large number of candidates being presented to the elective assembly seems, I think, to be outweighed by its disadvantages.

Indeed, several of the proposed candidates have such a small chance of being elected that any votes they are given are effectively lost. Experience of past elections confirms this. Moreover, these valueless votes prevent a true manifestation of the will of the assembly with regard to the candidates who are actually in the running, who are being deprived of votes at a time when it is important to obtain a decision on their respective merits.

The important thing is not so much to propose a great many candidates to the assembly as to propose only candidates who can be given preference votes. The current method of indicating candidates prior to the election is not enough to reassure the voters. Experience shows that a candidate can be put forward for election with so few votes that they could hardly constitute a sign of approval. However, since the voters are forced to complete their voting or have their papers disallowed, they prefer, though perhaps against their better judgment, to prejudice their main will than to make no contribution whatsoever to the functions of the assembly.

For simple convenience, we should undertake to make the operations of

TABLE 9.11.

Candidate	Election Votes	Supplementary Votes	Total
A	800	720	1,520
B	600	1,000	1,600
C	450	1,250	1,700

a large assembly as simple as possible. No one imagined that when the new method was introduced, it would result in the voters making so many mistakes that a great many voting papers were disallowed. There has never been a sovereign assembly in which these discrepancies were greater. For the election of the grand jury, there were 96 void papers out of 964, which is about 1/10. For the election of the administrative council there were 258 out of 2,010, about 1/8. For the election of the legislative council there were 511 out of 2,040, about 1/4. The election of the magistrates of law and order also produced several void papers, even though the candidates were only presented three by three. However, the virtual equality between some of them made it important to have a more precise manifestation of the general will. Errors occur not only in the voters' actions but also in the analysis of their votes. The two columns never present the equality of votes which they should. In fact, the discrepancy has sometimes been considerable, as was the case in the election of the procurer general. And even when it is only small, this discrepancy can have a very great effect, as was the case in the elections of magistrates of law and order. And finally, there was one case in which the discrepancy was so big in some parts of the analysis that its results could not be accepted without the consent of the sovereign council.

(17) While I attach great importance to decreasing the number of elective assemblies, we should not sacrifice the will of the assembly in doing so.

If I did not believe that people would completely reject a method as subject to error as the one we are examining here, I would insist upon various means of limiting its faults. For instance, we could consider anyone who obtained an absolute majority in the initial selection as elected. This would already have spared us several General Councils, for example, because the general treasurer and the ambassador to the French Republic would have been elected after the first stage. In other cases, we would have decreased the number of places to be filled, the number of candidates standing, and the complexity of the final election. Two of the elected Receivers and fourteen of the members of the Legislative Committee obtained a majority in the first round. A modification of this kind would have enabled the will of the voters to be pronounced more clearly on the remaining candidates.

(18) Since the majority we appear to obtain may be, and often is, deceptive, is it not our duty to find another method which is less likely to violate the true will of the sovereign in calculating this majority, to which we attach so much importance?

The following method has the approval of several of my fellow citizens. Instead of indiscriminately referring to the supplementary column when the first column is not sufficient, we should refer to it in the order of the election votes. For example, taking the candidate who, after those actually elected in the first column, has the most election votes, we would add the votes he obtained in the second column to his votes from the first. If this total is greater than half the number of voters, he would be elected. If not, he would be excluded, and the next candidate taken in the same way, always following the order of the first column. In this way, the election votes would continue to have more value, as is proper, and it is very probable (although not certain) that we would stray far less often from the will of the assembly than we do in the current method.

To the reasons I have already put forward for returning, whenever possible, to the origin of each kind of vote for each candidate, I shall add the following: the more election votes a candidate has, the fewer voters remain to give him a supplementary vote and, in particular, the less likely it is that he will receive supplementary votes from the voters who elected his rival, if this latter has fewer election votes than him. However, the fewer election votes this second candidate has, the more voters remain to give him supplementary votes and, in particular, the more probable it is that he will receive several of the supplementary votes distributed by the many people who voted for the first candidate. Clearly, such considerations make our preference of the first candidate over the second more probable.

(19) All the calculations which I have developed so far are based on the fact that a voter's preferences when he elects a candidate are the same relative to all the candidates he does not elect. That is, I am assuming that a second candidate can be placed on the same line whether he only received a supplementary vote in common with the candidate chosen by the same voter, or whether he received no vote at all. The difficulty of appreciating these degrees of preference, especially when dealing with the votes given by a large assembly, when this assembly has to pronounce on several candidates, make this an acceptable supposition; in any case, it conforms with the procedure adopted so far in our elective assemblies.

Advocate Devegobre, a member of the national assembly, suggested that we give supplementary votes a smaller value than that given to election votes and, more specifically, that we regard each of the former as worth just half of the latter. This remedy was rejected, perhaps because it sometimes (though rarely) did not reveal the absolute majority, which is so often deceptive and to which too much importance was attached. However, this solution seems quite natural, at least when there are just three candidates. When none of them is clearly disliked, it is probable that a candidate who has received a supplementary vote falls halfway between the other two candidates when one of them has received an election vote and the other no vote at all.

When this method of estimation is applied to three candidates, it gives

TABLE 9.12.

Candidate	Election Votes	Supplementary Votes	Total	Total Counting Each Supplementary Vote as 1/2
A	1,000	480	1,480	1,240
B	840	740	1,580	1,210
C	560	1,180	1,740	1,150

remarkably similar results to the hypothesis of absolute preference which I have developed. According to both of the methods of assessing the supplementary votes in relation to the election votes, when the sum of each candidate's election and supplementary votes is equal to the sum of the other two candidates' election votes, then these three candidates are equally preferable. (See supplement, section 12.)

This new method also has the advantage of preventing the other cases of indeterminacy which I discussed and illustrated in sections 11 and 12, and so, if we insist on the flawed method of presenting the candidates in groups of three, it should be preferred to the hypothesis I expounded above.

As well as removing this indeterminacy, this method of assessing the supplementary votes seems to place the candidates in an order of preference which corresponds both with common sense and the intention of the voters.

I shall use the case outlined in section 12 as my example [table 9.12].

With the new assessment, the candidates are ranked in the order *ABC*, which is also the order of their election votes, whereas the current method of assessment ranks them in the order *CBA*.

If we apply the same thing to the real cases developed in section 13, we shall see how probable it is that its results will be conformable with the will of the assembly.

Thus, since the votes in section 13 are as follows [table 9.13], the suggested method of assessment gives us [table 9.14]: and the candidates are ranked in the order *ABC*.

This method also has the advantage of not obliging us to return to the origin of each candidate's votes, in so far as it is the difference in their votes,

TABLE 9.13.

Candidate	Election Votes	Supplementary Votes
A	822	273
B	758	315
C	68	1,060

TABLE 9.14.

Candidate	[First Places]	[Second Places]	Total
A	822	136	958
B	758	157	915
C	68	530	598

and not the number of times that one candidate's vote contains the vote of another, that reveals the extent of the assembly's support for him. The development of this remarkable property depends too much on algebra for me to linger on it here.

This method of analysis therefore seems to me very suitable for the case of three candidates, but it appears too arbitrary for elections in which a great many places are to be filled at once. Indeed, it is especially in cases such as these that the candidate who obtains the first of a voter's election votes is in that voter's opinion of far greater merit than the candidates to whom he gives only supplementary votes. Is it practicable in such large assemblies as our sovereign councils to place the candidates in the order of merit attributed to them by each voter, and to use this order to estimate the value of the votes they receive?

(20) It was hoped that the suggested method would prevent factions.[3] Experience has shown the opposite to be the case. What some clever men predicted has occurred, and the true will of the assembly has on occasion been distorted by the effects of factions.

Suppose that there are three candidates, and that two of them have many supporters, whereas the third does not really seem to be in the running. The people who support each of the first two, not wanting to prejudice the chances of their first choice by giving their supplementary vote to the second candidate, give it instead to the third. However few election votes he has, it is still possible that neither of the other two will have an absolute majority in the first column and that because of all his supplementary votes, the third candidate will seem to have almost unanimous support, although as I have shown, he was in fact the least favorite. And while we may consider the voters immoral for behaving in such a way, we should also criticize a method which tempts them to do so.

Even when one of the first candidates is elected by an absolute majority of election votes, people who do not examine the nature of the large number

---

3. I use this expression outside its usual meaning to mean the behavior of each individual voter who does not give his votes in accordance with his knowledge of the merits of the candidates.

of votes given to the third candidate in sufficient detail may still be mistakenly led to regard him as preferable to the elected candidate. And if they consider the latter a usurper, they will not give him the confidence deserved by every public official who has the seal of public approbation.

As my aim is only to discover and expose the truth, I shall not hide the fact that the method which involves giving different values to election votes and supplementary votes also seems likely to encourage factions.

With the current method, intriguers can harm their own interests, and voters who can learn from experience should correct themselves. But by reducing each supplementary vote to a value of 1/2, the intriguers thus run less risk of increasing the chances of the candidate they like least and will not remedy their conduct with regard to the greatest rival of their favorite because of this new knowledge.

(21) So as not to expose myself to the charge of having been wholly destructive, I propose the following method:

Only a few places should be filled at one time.

The initial vote should be carried out by a small body in whom the public has total confidence.

The legislative council, required by the Constitution to present to the sovereign the subjects about which it is required to legislate, could also be given the task of holding an initial vote to select the candidates for its various elections.

The table of suitable candidates should comprise:

1. All those who desire the post which is to be filled and who have placed their names on the relevant list held by the secretary of the council.
2. All those nominated to the secretary by any citizen.
3. All those who are considered acceptable by each of the members of the committee.

No one can propose more candidates than there are places to fill.

The legislative council would check that each proposed candidate was eligible and prepared to accept if elected.

If a table drawn up in this way did not contain at least twice as many candidates as there were places to be filled, the legislative council would take a plurality vote on new candidates, until it succeeded in forming a list of candidates of the required size.

This list of candidates would be presented to the sovereign council and each voter would give as many votes as there were places to be filled.

When the votes were assessed, the candidates who obtained an absolute majority would be elected.

If no candidate had an absolute majority, or fewer candidates obtained such a majority than there were places to be filled, then the names of exactly twice as many of the candidates with the most votes as there were places to be filled would be sent back to the sovereign so that the election could be completed. Then a simple plurality of votes would be enough for a candidate to be elected.[4]

N.B. The places of substitutes are always included in the number of places to be filled, if there is any need for them to be elected.

Whatever the opinion of my fellow citizens on the method I have suggested here, I have at least proved that the drawbacks of the current method are too serious for it to remain unchanged.

Extract from the Registers of the Legislative Committee of 7 July 1794

A letter from citizen Simon Lhuilier was read, explaining that having made a detailed study of the way in which public officers are elected, various drawbacks have come to his attention which he has set out in a paper and presented to the committee. This paper was sent to citizen Louis Odier for him to make an immediate report on the subject.

15 July 1794

Citizen Louis Odier read his report on citizen Lhuilier's paper. The reporter concluded that, in accordance with the Constitution, the Sovereign should be asked whether it wishes to authorize the committee to present a plan to change the election method and, if so, whether it wishes them to propose a new method. This report is followed by two plans which correspond to these propositions. The committee admitted them for discussion, voted to have them printed and having decided that it could authorize the printing of a paper presented by a citizen when such a paper might help it do its duty by shedding light on matters entrusted to it by the Sovereign, it also decreed that citizen Simon Lhuilier's report should be printed, along with the extract from the registers which requests him to reduce the number of examples, to make those which are necessary more general, and to insert proofs of some of the propositions contained in his paper.

---

4. It has been objected that the second elective assembly would probably be small, and experience has proved that this has indeed been the case when an assembly has been convened simply in order to complete an election. But to counteract this, we could in some way, which remains to be established, take into account the votes each candidate obtained in the first assembly.

Supplement to the Previous Paper

Containing the algebraic development of various propositions, at the invitation of the Legislative Committee.

§ I.

In the following development of some general propositions to which this *Examination of the Election Method* has led me, I begin with the case of just three candidates.

For convenience, I propose the following notation.

Candidates are designated throughout as	$A, B, C.$
Their first votes as	$a, b, c.$
Their supplementary votes as	$a', b', c'.$

To designate the number of voters for one candidate who have given their supplementary votes to one other, I introduce a two-letter symbol, where the first letter (in capitals) designates the first candidate and the second letter the second candidate.

Thus, Ab denotes the number of voters for A who have given supplementary votes to B. The following five symbols are explained analogously: Ac, Ba, Bc, Ca, Cb.

One candidate is preferred to another, firstly by all the voters for the first and secondly by those voters for the third candidate who have given their supplementary votes to the first.

Thus, A is preferred to B by the number of votes $a + Ca$.
And B is preferred to A by the number of votes $b + Cb$.

Hence the comparison of A and B with each other is reduced to the comparison of the two quantities $a + Ca$ and $b + Cb$. That is to say, A is preferred to B, indifferent to him, or ranked below him, according as $a + Ca$ is greater than, equal to, or less than $b + Cb$.

[Translators' note. From the above, it follows that the following substitutions are admissible:

$$a + b + c \equiv a' + b' + c' = \text{number of votes cast}$$

$$a \equiv Ab + Ac$$

$$a' \equiv Ba + Ca, \text{ etc.}$$

These may be helpful in interpreting the manipulations in the theorems.]

§ II

THEOREM 1. *If a candidate (say* A*) has an absolute majority in the Election column, he is the most acceptable of the three.*
  Required to prove. If

$$a > (a + b + c)/2, \text{ then } a + Ca > b + Cb \text{ and } a + Ba > c + Bc.$$

Proof. By supposition $a > (a + b + c)/2$, therefore $2a > a + b + c$, and $a > b + c$. Therefore *a fortiori* $a + Ca > b + c - Ca$. But $c - Ca = Cb$, therefore $a + Ca > b + Cb$. In the same way it can be shown that $a + Ba > c + Bc$.

§ III

THEOREM 2. *If the sum of a candidate's (say* A*'s) first and supplementary votes is less than an absolute majority, he is the least acceptable of the three.*
  Required to prove. If $a + a' < (a + b + c)/2$, then $a + Ca < b + Cb$ and $a + Ba < c + Bc$.
  Proof. By supposition $a + a' < (a + b + c)/2$. Therefore $2a + 2a' < a + b + c$ and $a + 2a' < b + c$ or $a + 2Ba + 2Ca < b + Ca + Cb$. Therefore $a + 2Ba + Ca < b + Cb$ and *a fortiori* $a + Ca < b + Cb$. In the same way it can be shown that $a + Ba < c + Bc$.

§ IV

THEOREM 3. *If the votes for two candidates (say* A *and* B*) are such that for each the sum of first and supplementary votes is greater than the sum of first votes of the two others, then the sum of first and supplementary votes for the third candidate is smaller than the sum of first votes for the other two.*
  Required to prove. If $a + a' > b + c$ and $b + b' > a + c$, then $c + c' < a + b$.
  Proof. Since $a + a' > b + c$ and $b + b' > a + c$, $a + b + a' + b' > a + b + 2c$. Therefore $a' + b' > 2c$. Therefore $a' + b' + c' > 2c + c'$, or $a + b + c > 2c + c'$. Therefore $a + b > c + c'$, or $c + c' < a + b$.
  Remark. For brevity, I have stated this proposition in terms of the relationship $>$ in the supposition, but it may be stated in terms of the relationships $=$ or $<$ by substituting in the conclusion the relationship $=$ or $>$ for $<$.

§ V

Theorem 4. *If the sum of first and supplementary votes for a candidate (say
A) is greater than the sum of first votes for the other two, then double the first
votes of this candidate exceeds the sum of the supplementary votes of the other
two.*

Required to prove. If $a + a' > b + c$, then $2a > b' + c'$.

Proof. Since $a + a' > b + c$, $2a + a' > a + b + c$ or equivalently $2a +
a' > a' + b' + c'$. Therefore $2a > b' + c'$.

§ VI

Theorem 5. The reciprocal of Theorem 4. *If double the first votes of a
candidate (say A) exceeds the sum of the supplementary votes of the other
two, then the sum of first and supplementary votes for this candidate is greater
than the sum of first votes for the other two.*

Required to prove. If $2a > b' + c$, then $a + a' > b + c$.

Proof. Since $2a > b' + c'$, $2a + a' > a' + b' + c'$, or equivalently $2a +
a' > a + b + c$. Therefore $a + a' > b + c$.

The *Remark* at the end of Theorem 3 also applies to Theorems 4 and 5.

§ VII

Theorem 6. *If the votes for two candidates (say A and B) are such that
double the first votes for each of them exceed the sum of the supplementary
votes for the other two, then double the first votes for the third candidate is
smaller than the sum of the supplementary votes for the other two.*

Required to prove. If $2a > b' + c'$ and $2b > a' + c'$, then $2c < a' + b'$.

Proof. By supposition $2a > b' + c'$ and $2b > a' + c'$. Therefore

$$2a + 2b > a' + b' + 2c'$$
$$> a + b + c + c'$$
$$a + b > c + c'$$
$$a + b + c > 2c + c'$$
$$a' + b' + c' > 2c + c'$$
$$a' + b' > 2c, \quad \text{or} \quad 2c < a' + b'$$

The *Remark* at the end of Theorem 3 also applies to Theorem 6.

§ VIII

THEOREM 7. *If a candidate (say A) is more acceptable than each of the other two, then the sum of the first and supplementary votes for this candidate is greater than the sum of the first votes for the other two.*

Required to prove. If $a + Ca > b + Cb$ and $a + Ba > c + Bc$, then $a + a' > b + c$.

Proof. By supposition $a + Ca > b + Cb$ and $a + Ba > c + Bc$. Therefore $2a + a' > b + c + Cb + Bc$. But $Cb = c - Ca$ and $Bc = b - Ba$. Therefore $Cb + Bc = b + c - a'$. Therefore

$$2a + a' > 2b + 2c - a'$$

$$2a + 2a' > 2b + 2c$$

$$a + a' > b + c$$

COROLLARY I. *If a candidate (say A) is more acceptable than each of the other two, then double the first votes of this candidate exceeds the sum of the supplementary votes of the other two.* (See Theorem 4).

COROLLARY II. *If the sum of the first and supplementary votes for a candidate is smaller than the sum of the first votes of the other two, this candidate cannot be the most acceptable of the three. And if double the first votes of a candidate is smaller than the sum of the supplementary votes of the other two, this candidate cannot be the most acceptable of the three.*

The *Remark* at the end of Theorem 3 also applies here.

[Translators' note: Corollary II is the reciprocal of Theorem 7 and Corollary I].

COROLLARY III. *If the three candidates are equally acceptable, the sum of the first and supplementary votes for each of them is equal to the sum of the first votes for the other two; and double the first votes of each of them equals the sum of the supplementary votes for the other two.*

§ IX

THEOREM 8. *If a candidate (say A) is more acceptable than one other (say B), then the sum of the first votes for A and of those of his supplementary votes which he has received from the supporters of C is greater than half the number of voters.*

Required to prove. If $a + Ca > b + Cb$, then $a + Ca > (a + b + c)/2$.

Proof. Since $a + Ca > b + Cb$, $a + Ca > (a + Ca + b + Cb)/2$. But $a + Ca + b + Cb = a + b + c$. Therefore $a + Ca > (a + b + c)/2$.

The *Remark* at the end of Theorem 3 also applies here.

COROLLARY. *If two candidates are equally acceptable, the number of voters is even.* In this case, the number of voters who prefer one of these candidates to the other is half of the total number of voters.

[Translators' note. The Corollary follows by substituting $=$ for $>$ in Theorem 8. $a + Ca$ must be an integer; therefore by Theorem 8, $a + b + c$ must be even. The second sentence of the Corollary follows immediately.]

§ X

THEOREM 9. *If the sum of first and supplementary votes for each candidate equals the sum of first votes for the other two, then, compared two by two, they may be pronounced equally acceptable.*

Required to prove. If we have the three equations $a + a' = b + c$, $b + b' = a + c$, and $c + c' = a + b$, then we may [*sic*] have at the same time the three equations $a + Ca = b + Cb$, $a + Ba = c + Bc$, and $b + Ab = c + Ac$.

Proof. To satisfy the equation $a + Ca = b + Cb$ write

$$a + Ca = (a + b + c)/2 \text{ and } Ca = (a + b + c)/2 - a$$

$$b + Cb = (a + b + c)/2 \text{ and } Cb = (a + b + c)/2 - b$$

[From the Corollary to Theorem 8.] Hence

$$Ba \ (= a' - Ca) = a + a' - (a + b + c)/2$$

$$= b + c - (a + b + c)/2$$

$$= (a + b + c)/2 - a$$

$$Ab \ (= b' - Cb) = b + b' - (a + b + c)/2$$

$$= a + c - (a + b + c)/2$$

$$= (a + b + c)/2 - b$$

$$Bc \ (= b - Ba) = a + b - (a + b + c)/2$$

$$= (a + b = c)/2 - c$$

$$Ac \ (= a - Ab) = a + b - (a + b + c)/2$$

$$= (a + b + c)/2 - c$$

$a + Ba = (a + b + c)/2$; $c + Bc = (a + b + c)/2$; therefore $a + Ba = c + Bc$.

$b + Ab = (a + b + c)/2$; $c + Ac = (a + b + c)/2$; therefore $b + Ab = c + Ac$.

Remark. The present procedure may show candidates who are truly equal to be unequal. In symbols: The equalities $a + a' = b + c$, $b + b' = a + c$, and $c + c' = a + b$ are consistent with the inequality of the three quantities $a + a'$, $b + b'$, and $c + c'$.

Example. Let $a + a' > b + b'$. But $a + a' = b + c$, therefore $c > b'$. Likewise, let $b + b' > c + c'$. But $b + b' = a + c$, therefore $a > c'$. Therefore, if we have $a > c'$ and $c > b'$, we will have $a + a' > b + b' > c + c'$.

§ XI

THEOREM 10. *If the sum of first and supplementary votes for each candidate equals the sum of first votes for the other two, then, compared two by two, the superiority (if any) of the first candidate over the second is the same as that of the second candidate over the third, and again the same as that of the third over the first; so that nothing can be said about one of the candidates which cannot equally be said of each of the others.*

Required to prove. If we have the three equations $a + a' = b + c$, $b + b' = a + c$, and $c + c' = a + b$ and the equation $a + Ca = b + Cb + d$, then we also have $b + Ab = c + Ac + d$ and $c + Bc = a + Ba + d$.

[d, not defined here, is the superiority of a over b, b over c, and c over a. In other words it represents the symmetrical component of a cycle.]

Proof. Since $a + Ca = b + Cb + d$, $Ca = (a + b + c)/2 - a + \frac{1}{2}d$ [from Theorem 8]. Hence

$$Cb \; (= c - Ca) = a + c - (a + b + c)/2 - \frac{1}{2}d$$

$$= (a + b + c)/2 - b - \frac{1}{2}d$$

$$Ba \; (= a' - Ca) = a + a' - (a + b + c)/2 - \frac{1}{2}d$$

$$= b + c - (a + b + c)/2 - \frac{1}{2}d$$

$$= (a + b + c)/2 - a - \frac{1}{2}d$$

$$Bc \; (= b - Ba) = a + b - (a + b + c)/2 + \frac{1}{2}d$$

$$= (a + b + c)/2 - c + \frac{1}{2}d$$

$$Ab \ (= b' - Cb) = b + b' - (a + b + c)/2 + \frac{1}{2}d$$

$$= a + c - (a + b + c)/2 + \frac{1}{2}d$$

$$= (a + b + c)/2 - b + \frac{1}{2}d$$

$$Ac \ (= a - Ab) = a + b - (a + b + c)/2 - \frac{1}{2}d$$

$$= (a + b + c)/2 - c - \frac{1}{2}d$$

$$a + Ca = (a + b + c)/2 + \frac{1}{2}d$$

$$b + Cb = (a + b + c)/2 - \frac{1}{2}d$$

Therefore $a + Ca - (b + Cb) = d$ or $a + Ca = b + Cb + d$.

$$b + Ab = (a + b + c)/2 + \frac{1}{2}d$$

$$c + Ac = (a + b + c)/2 - \frac{1}{2}d$$

Therefore $b + Ab - (c + Ac) = d$ or $b + Ab = c + Ac + d$.

$$c + Bc = (a + b + c)/2 + \frac{1}{2}d$$

$$a + Ba = (a + b + c)/2 - \frac{1}{2}d$$

Therefore $c + Bc - (a + Ba) = d$ or $c + Bc = a + Ba + d$. These three candidates are thus equal, in the following sense: that there is nothing to be said about one which cannot equally be said of each of the other two.

§ XII

THEOREM 11. *If the sum of the first and supplementary votes for a candidate exceeds the sum of the first votes for the other two and if each supplementary vote is counted at half the value of a first vote, then such a candidate is regarded as having more than an absolute majority in his favor.*

Required to prove. If $a + a' > b + c$, then $a + \frac{1}{2}a > (a + b + c)/2$.
Proof. By supposition $a + a' > b + c$. Therefore

$$2a + a' > a + b + c$$

$$a + \frac{1}{2}a' > (a + b + c)/2$$

The *Remark* at the end of Theorem 3 also applies here.

COROLLARY. In particular, *if three candidates are equally acceptable, they are still regarded as equally acceptable if each supplementary vote is counted as half a first vote.*

§ XIII

THEOREM 12. *If a candidate (say A) is more acceptable than another candidate such as B, then half of the excess of voters preferring A to B over those preferring B to A equals the excess of the number of voters for A who gave their supplementary votes to B plus half of the total number of voters over the total of first and supplementary votes for B.*

Required to prove. If $a + Ca > b + Cb$, then $[(a + Ca) - (b + Cb)]/2 = Ab + (a + b + c)/2 - (b + b')$.

Proof. $a + Ca = a + c - Cb$. Therefore

$$(a + Ca) - (b + Cb) = a - b + c - 2Cb$$

$$= (a + b + c) - 2(b + Cb)$$

Therefore

$$[(a + Ca) - (b + Cb)]/2 = (a + b + c)/2 - (b + Cb)$$

$$= (a + b + c)/2 - (b + b' - Ab)$$

$$= Ab + (a + b + c)/2 - (b + b')$$

COROLLARY. *If A may be more acceptable than B, he beats him by a larger margin the more of his supporters have given their supplementary vote to B. If A cannot be more acceptable than B, the latter beats him by a smaller margin the more of his supporters have given their supplementary vote to B.*

In particular, if one or other of the following cases occurs, viz., that all A's voters give their supplementary votes to B, or that all B's voters give their supplementary vote to A, the resulting distributions of votes are the most favorable to A. [The Corollary is intended to show the perverse consequences of Condorcet's 1793 method.]

§ XIV

THEOREM 13. *If the votes of the three candidates have the following properties,*

1. A *has more supplementary votes than* C *has first votes,*

2. A *has more first votes than* B *has supplementary votes,*

3. *The sum of* B*'s and* C*'s first votes exceeds* A*'s supplementary votes,*

4. *The sum of* A*'s first and supplementary votes exceeds the sum of* C*'s first votes plus half of the total number of voters,*

then A *is more acceptable than* C.

Required to prove. Let $a' > c$, $a > b'$, $b + c > a'$, and $a + a' > c + (a + b + c)/2$. Then $a + Ba > c + Bc$.

Proof. The most favorable case for C in comparison with A is that in which all his voters give their supplementary vote to A [from corollary to Theorem 13]. Then the election is as follows:

$$Ca = c. \qquad Ab = b'. \qquad\qquad Ba = a' - c.$$

$$Cb = 0. \qquad Ac = a - b'. \qquad Bc = b - a' + c.$$

By the first three suppositions all these quantities are positive [*sic*—they are nonnegative], and the hypothesized distribution of votes is possible.

We thus have

$$a + Ba = a + a' - c$$

$$c + Bc = b - a' + 2c$$

By supposition $a + a' > (a + b + c)/2 + c$. Therefore $a + a' - c > (a + b + c)/2$ or

$$a + Ba > (a + b + c)/2$$

$$> (a + Ba + c + Bc)/2$$

Therefore $(a + Ba)/2 > (c + Bc)/2$ and $a + Ba > c + Bc$. Thus, in the least favorable case for A in his comparison with C, he is nevertheless more acceptable than C. Therefore A is always more acceptable than C.

COROLLARY I. *In this case* a + Ca = a + c *and* b + Cb = b. *Thus, if* a + c > b *(that is, if* B *does not have an absolute majority of first votes),* A *is also more acceptable than* B. *Hence* A *may be the most acceptable of the three.*

COROLLARY II. *If the above suppositions hold between* A *and* B *with the latter taking the place of* C *in the previous analysis,* A *is the most acceptable of the three candidates.*

COROLLARY III. *If the same suppositions are made between* B *and* C, *such that* B *takes the place of* A *above,* C *is the least acceptable of the three candidates.*

Remark I. Given the assumptions of Corollary III (viz., *C* being the least acceptable of the three candidates), if neither *A* nor *B* obtains an absolute majority of first votes, either may be preferable to the other. Hence the present mode of counting declares the election determined when it is in fact undetermined, if one candidate is determined to be the least acceptable of the three.

Remark II. The inequalities $a' > c$, $b' > c$, $a > b'$, $b > a'$, $b + c > a'$, $a + c > b'$, $a + a' > (a + b + c)/2 + c$, and $b + b' > (a + b + c)/2 + c$ may coexist with the inequalities $c + c' > a + a'$ and $c + c' > b + b'$. Hence the candidate who is truly the least acceptable to the Assembly may be pronounced, according to the present method of counting, the most acceptable.

§ XV

THEOREM 14. *Let there be three candidates, none of whom has an absolute majority of first votes. Let their first and supplementary votes conform to the following pattern:*

1. *The sum of the first and supplementary votes for one candidate (say* A*) exceeds the sum of the first votes for the other two.*
2. *The sum of* A*'s first votes and half the number of voters exceeds each of the sums of first and supplementary votes for the other two candidates.*

Then A *may be the most acceptable of the three.*

Required to prove. The conjunction of $a + a' > b + c$, $a + (a + b + c)/2 > b + b'$, and $a + (a + b + c)/2 > c + c'$ is consistent with the conjunction of $a + Ca > b + Cb$ and $a + Ba > c + Bc$.

Proof. To satisfy the inequality $a + Ca > b + Cb$, let $Ca > (a + b + c)/2 - a$, and to satisfy the inequality $a + Ba > c + Bc$, let $Ba > (a + b + c)/2 - a$ [hence $-Ba < a - (a + b + c)/2$, therefore $a' - Ba < a + a' - (a + b + c)/2$]. Hence $Ca < a + a' - (a + b + c)/2$. Since Ca is constrained within the limits $(a + b + c)/2 - a$ and $a + a' - (a + b + c)/2$, the [hypothesized?] distribution of votes is possible [because

$$(a + b + c)/2 - a < Ca < a + a' - (a + b + c)/2,$$

$$(a + b + c)/2 - a < (a + a + a')/2 - a$$

$$< a'/2$$

while

$$a + a' - (a + b + c)/2 > a + a' - (a + a + a')/2$$

$$> a'/2 \ ].$$

We therefore have

$$Ca \qquad\qquad > (a + b + c)/2 - a$$

$$< a + a' - (a + b + c)/2$$

$$Cb \ (= c - Ca) < (a + b + c)/2 - b$$

[change of inequality sign from line 1 because $-Ca < a - (a + b + c)/2$; adding c to both sides produces line 3]

$$> (a + b + c)/2 + c - (a + a') \quad \text{[analogously]}$$

$$Ba \ (= a' - Ca) < a + a' - (a + b + c)/2$$

$$> (a + b + c)/2 - a$$

$$Bc \ (= b - Ba) \ > (a + b + c)/2 + b - (a + a')$$

$$< (a + b + c)/2 - c$$

$$Ab \ (= b' - Cb) > b + b' - (a + b + c)/2$$

$$< (a + b + c)/2 + a - (c + c')$$

$$Ac \ (= a - Ab) \ < (a + b + c)/2 + a - (b + b')$$

$$> c + c' - (a + b + c)/2$$

By supposition $a + a' > b + c$; therefore

$$a + a' - (a + b + c)/2 > b + c - (a + b + c)/2$$

$$> (a + b + c)/2 - a$$

[i.e., Ca by supposition; therefore $Ca > 0$]. Thus

$$c - \{a + a' - (a + b + c)/2\} < c - \{(a + b + c)/2 - a\}$$

or

$$(a + b + c)/2 + c - (a + a') < (a + b + c)/2 - b \ [Cb > 0]$$

$$a' - \{(a + b + c)/2 - a\} > a' - \{a + a' - (a + b + c)/2\}$$

or

$$a + a' + (a + b + c)/2 > (a + b + c)/2 - a \ [Ba > 0]$$

$$b - \{a + a' - (a + b + c)/2\} < b - \{(a + b + c)/2 - a\}$$

or

$$(a + b + c)/2 + b - (a + a') < (a + b + c)/2 - c \ [Bc > 0]$$

$$b' - \{(a + b + c)/2 - b\} < b' - \{(a + b + c)/2 + c' - (a + a')\}$$

or

$$b + b' - (a + b + c)/2 < (a + b + c)/2 + a - (c + c') \ [Ab > 0]$$

$$a - \{b + b' - (a + b + c)/2\} > a - \{(a + b + c)/2 + a - (c + c')\}$$

or

$$(a + b + c)/2 + a - (b + b') > c + c' - (a + b + c)/2 \ [Ac > 0]$$

[*Examination of* Ca.] By supposition $a + c > b$; therefore

$$2a + 2c > a + b + c$$

$$a + c > (a + b + c)/2$$

$$c > (a + b + c)/2 - a$$

By supposition $[b + c > (a + b + c)/2$, so a fortiori] $a + a' > (a + b + c)/2$; therefore $a' > (a + b + c)/2 - a$. Hence, Ca may well have a value between $(a + b + c)/2 - a$ and $a + a' - (a + b + c)/2$.

Examination of Cb. By supposition $(a + b + c)/2 > b$ and $a + a' > (a + b + c)/2$; therefore $(a + b + c)/2 + c < a + a' + c$; thus $(a + b + c)/2 + c - (a + a') < c$. By supposition $(a + b + c)/2 + a > c + c'$ and $(a + b + c)/2 + a + a' + b' > c + a + b + c$ and $b' > (a + b + c)/2 + c - (a + a')$.

Examination of Ba. By supposition $a + a' > (a + b + c)/2$. By supposition $(a + b + c)/2 > c$; $a + b > c$; $2a + 2b > a + b + c$; and $a + b > (a + b + c)/2$; $(a + b + c)/2 - a < b$. By supposition $a + a' > (a + b + c)/2$; $(a + b + c)/2 - a < a'$.

Examination of Bc: By supposition $(a + b + c)/2 > c$. By supposition $a + a' > (a + b + c)/2$; therefore $(a + b + c)/2 + b - (a + a') < b$. By supposition $(a + b + c)/2 + a > b + b'$; therefore $b + b' - a < (a + b + c)/2$ and

$$(a + b + c)/2 + b + b' - a < a + b + c$$

$$< a' + b' + c'$$

$$(a + b + c)/2 + b - a < a' + c'$$

$$(a + b + c)/2 + b - (a + a') < c'$$

Examination of Ab: By supposition $(a + b + c)/2 + a > c + c'$. By supposition $(a + b + c)/2 + a > b + b'$; therefore $a > b + b' - (a + b + c)/2$. By supposition $(a + b + c)/2 > b$; therefore $b' + (a + b + c)/2 > b + b'$; $b' > b + b' - (a + b + c)/2$.

Examination of Ac: By supposition $(a + b + c)/2 + a > b + b'$. By supposition $(a + b + c)/2 + a > c + c'$; therefore $a > c + c' - (a + b + c)/2$. By supposition $(a + b + c)/2 > c$; therefore $c' + (a + b + c)/2 > c + c'$ and $c' > c + c' + (a + b + c)/2$.

Hence, taking $(a + b + c)/2 - a < Ca < a + a' - (a + b + c)/2$, we may make all of Ca, Cb, Ba, Bc, Ab and Ac[5] positive and satisfy the inequalities $a + Ca > b + Cb$ and $a + Ba > c + Bc$.

---

5. [In the original, Ca and Cb appear in error for Ac and Ab here.]

§ XVI

THEOREM 15. *If the votes for three candidates are as follows,*

1. *the number of first votes for one of them (say* C) *is smaller than an absolute majority,*
2. *the sum of first and supplementary votes for* C *is smaller than the sum of first votes for the other two,*
3. *the sum of first and supplementary votes for each of the others is greater than an absolute majority,*
4. *The sums of the first votes for each of the other candidates with half of the total number of voters exceeds the sum of first and supplementary votes for* C,

then C *may be the least acceptable of the three.*

Required to prove. The conjunction of $(a + b + c)/2 > c; a + b > c + c'; a + a' > (a + b + c)/2; b + b' > (a + b + c)/2; (a + b + c)/2 + a > c + c'$; and $(a + b + c)/2 + b > c + c'$ is consistent with the conjunction of $a + Ba > c + Bc$ and $b + Ab > c + Ac$.

Proof. We obtain the two inequalities $a + Ba > c + Bc$ and $b + Ab > c + Ac$ by making $[a + Ba > c + b - Ba$, thus $2Ba > c + b - a$, thus] $Ba > (a + b + c)/2 - a$ and [analogously] $Ab > (a + b + c)/2 - b$; from which we deduce that $Ba < (a + b + c)/2 + b - (c + c')$.[6]

We thus obtain

$$Ba > (a + b + c)/2 - a$$

$$< (a + b + c)/2 + b - (c + c')$$

$$Bc < (a + b + c)/2 - c$$

[$Bc = b - Ba$, then from line 1 add b to both sides and multiply rest by -1]

$$> c + c' - (a + b + c)/2$$

$$Ca < a + a' - (a + b + c)/2 \ [Ca = a' - Ba]$$

$$> (a + b + c)/2 + c - (b + b')$$

---

6. [This deduction, although valid, requires seven intermediate steps for a full solution. In view of the length of this chapter, we have not inserted the steps. They are all elementary and similar to those Lhuilier makes elsewhere in this section.]

$Cb > (a + b + c)/2 + c - (a + a') [Cb = c - Ca]$

$< (b + b' - (a + b + c)/2$

$Ab < (a + b + c)/2 + a - (c + c') [Ab = b' - Cb]$

$> (a + b + c)/2 - b$

$Ac > c + c' - (a + b + c)/2 [Ac = a - Ab]$

$< (a + b + c)/2 - c$

[Each odd-numbered line derives from an earlier odd line, and each even line from an earlier even line.] Since $a + b > c + c'$ (by supposition), therefore $(a + b + c)/2 + a + b > (a + b + c)/2 + c + c'$ and $(a + b + c)/2 + b - (c + c') > (a + b + c)/2 - a$ [therefore the limits for *Ba* satisfy their requirements] and we may take *Ba* as intermediate between $(a + b + c)/2 - a$ and $(a + b + c)/2 + b - (c + c')$. Hence we may show that the remaining quantities *Bc*, *Ca*, *Cb*, *Ab*, and *Ac* lie between their upper and lower limits, and (as in § XV) that in accordance with our suppositions, they are then all positive.

§ XVII

THEOREM 16. *If the votes for the three candidates are as follows,*

1. *neither* B *nor* C *has an absolute majority of first votes,*
2. *for each of* A *and* B *the sum of first and supplementary votes exceeds half of the number of voters,*
3. *the sum of* A*'s first votes and half the number of voters exceeds the sum of* B*'s first and supplementary votes,*
4. *the sum of* B*'s first votes and half the number of voters exceeds the sum of* C*'s first and supplementary votes,*

then A *may be more acceptable than* B *and* B *more acceptable than* C.

Required to prove. The conjunction of $(a + b + c)/2 > b$; $(a + b + c)/2 > c$; $a + a' > (a + b + c)/2$; $b + b' > (a + b + c)/2$; $(a + b + c)/2 + a > b + b'$; and $(a + b + c)/2 + b > c + c'$ is consistent with the conjunction of $a + Ca > b + Cb$ and $b + Ab > c + Ac$.

Proof. We obtain the two inequalities $a + Ca > b + Cb$ and $b + Ab > c + Ac$ by making $Ca > (a + b + c)/2 - a$ and $Ab > (a + b + c)/2 - b$; from which we deduce that

$$Ca > (a + b + c)/2 - a$$

$$> (a + b + c)/2 + c - (b + b')$$

$$Cb < (a + b + c)/2 - b$$

$$< b + b' - (a + b + c)/2$$

$$Ba < a + a' - (a + b + c)/2$$

$$< (a + b + c)/2 + b - (c + c')$$

$$Bc > (a + b + c)/2 + b - (a + a')$$

$$> c + c' - (a + b + c)/2$$

$$Ab > b + b' - (a + b + c)/2$$

$$> (a + b + c)/2 - b$$

$$Ac < (a + b + c)/2 + a - (b + b')$$

$$< (a + b + c)/2 - c$$

It may be shown as above [analogously to Theorem 15] that, according to these suppositions, all these quantities may be positive.

§ XVIII

THEOREM 17. *If the votes for the three candidates are as follows,*

1. *none of them has an absolute majority of first votes,*
2. *the sum of first and supplementary votes for each of them exceeds an absolute majority,*
3. *the sum of A's first votes and half the total number of voters exceeds the sum of B's first and supplementary votes,*
4. *the sum of B's first votes and half the total number of voters exceeds the sum of C's first and supplementary votes,*
5. *the sum of C's first votes and half the total number of voters exceeds the sum of A's first and supplementary votes,*

then the following may occur simultaneously: A *is more acceptable than* B, B *is more acceptable than* C, *and* C *is more acceptable than* A.

Required to prove. If $(a + b + c)/2 > a$; $(a + b + c)/2 > b$; $(a + b + c)/2 > c$; $a + a' > (a + b + c)/2$; $b + b' > (a + b + c)/2$; $c + c' > (a + b + c)/2$; $(a + b + c)/2 + a > b + b'$; $(a + b + c)/2 + b > c + c'$; $(a + b + c)/2 + c > a + a'$; then the following may coexist: $a + Ca > b + Cb$; $b + Ab > c + Ac$; $c + Bc > a + Ba$.

Proof. We satisfy the inequalities $a + Ca > b + Cb$; $b + Ab > c + Ac$; $c + Bc > a + Ba$ by setting $Ca > (a + b + c)/2 - a$ [$Cb = c - Ca$, so $a + Ca > b + c - Ca$]; $Ab > (a + b + c)/2 - b$ [analogously]; and $Bc > (a + b + c)/2 - c$. From this we obtain

$$Ca > (a + b + c)/2 - a$$

$$> (a + b + c)/2 + c - (b + b')$$

$$> a + a' - (a + b + c)/2$$

$$Cb < (a + b + c)/2 - b \ [Cb = c - Ca]$$

$$< b + b' - (a + b + c)/2$$

$$< (a + b + c)/2 + c - (a + a')$$

$$Ba < a + a' - (a + b + c)/2 \ [Ba = a' - Ca]$$

$$< (a + b + c)/2 + b - (c + c')$$

$$< (a + b + c)/2 - a$$

$$Bc > (a + b + c)/2 + b - (a + a') \ [Bc = b - Ba]$$

$$> c + c' - (a + b + c)/2$$

$$> (a + b + c)/2 - c$$

$$Ab > b + b' - (a + b + c)/2 \ [AB = b' - Cb]$$

$$> (a + b + c)/2 - b$$

$$> (a + b + c)/2 + a - (c + c')$$

$$Ac < (a + b + c)/2 + a - (b + b') \ [Ac = a - Ab]$$

$$< (a + b + c)/2 - c$$

$$< c + c' - (a + b + c)/2$$

[Lines 1–3 each derive from the corresponding line in the previous block; the rest from lines 1–3 as shown.]

By supposition, all the quantities Ab, Ac, Ba, Bc, Ca, Cb are positive if any of them is positive [assuming Ca positive, the other quantities are; but if Ca is not positive, then there can have been no votes] and contained within the given limits.

Hence in these conditions the decision of the Assembly is undetermined, as none of the candidates can be said to be either the most or the least acceptable of the three.

Having dealt so extensively with the case of three candidates, I pass to the more complicated elections in which there is more than one place to fill and where the number of candidates is three times as great as the number of places.

§ XIX

When there are three candidates, the pattern of first and supplementary votes gives information which is in part missing in more complicated cases.

In particular, when there are three candidates the sum of supplementary votes which two of the candidates have got from the supporters of the third candidate is known and equals the sum of his first votes, but this does not hold for a larger number of candidates.

For brevity, let us introduce the following notation:

Ballot papers:	where A has a first vote and B a first vote:	AB
	where A has a first vote and B a supplementary vote:	Ab
	where A has a first vote and B no vote:	a
	where A has a supplementary vote and B a first vote:	Ba
	where A has a supplementary vote and B a supplementary vote:	ab
	where A has a supplementary vote and B no vote:	a'
	where A has no vote and B a first vote:	b
	where A has no vote and B a supplementary vote:	b'

Ballot papers which name neither A nor B in no way affect the comparison between them.

Ballot papers of the forms AB and ab also make no impact on the difference between their vote totals.

A is preferred to B by the voters whose ballots are of the forms Ab, a, a'.

B is preferred to A by the voters whose ballots are of the forms Ba, b, b'.

Thus the first candidate is more, equally, or less acceptable than the second according as $Ab + a + a'$ is greater than, equal to, or less than $Ba + b + b'$, and the difference of their appeal is the difference between these sums.

Adding to each the quantity AB, the difference of their appeal is the difference between $AB + Ab + a + a'$ and $AB + Ba + b + b'$. Denoting by A and B the first votes of A and B, we have $AB + Ab + a = A$ and $AB + Ba + b = B$. Thus A is more or less acceptable than B according as $A + a'$ is greater or less than $B + b'$.

Postscript

One area of the research which is being conducted in the subject I have just discussed is of particular interest to mathematicians and would deserve to be carefully developed, if any practical good could come of it. I am referring to the application of the calculus of probabilities to ballot votes in order to find out, without going back to the origin of the votes, which candidate has the greatest chance in the election.

I shall limit myself to one example with just a small assembly. This will be enough to show, if not the complexity, then at least the time-consuming nature of this method and the impossibility of shedding any light on the will of a large assembly. Suppose that the assembly is made up of twenty-four voters and that the votes obtained by the three candidates A, B, and C are as follows:

A	B	C
$a = 11$	$b = 9$	$c = 4$
$a' = 5$	$b' = 7$	$c' = 12$

We can make only five possible suppositions about the compositions of the papers:

Ab	Ac	Ba	Bc	Ca	Cb
7	4	1	8	4	0
6	5	2	7	3	1
5	6	3	6	2	2
4	7	4	5	1	3
3	8	5	4	0	4

In the first three suppositions, A is preferred to B; in the fourth, they are equally preferable, and in the fifth, B is preferred to A.

In the first supposition, A and C are equally preferable, and in the remaining four, A is preferred to C.

In the first four suppositions, B is preferred to C, and in the fifth, they are equally preferable.

From this alone it would seem that A is likely to be elected and that C is so lacking in merit that there is no situation in which he is preferred to either of the candidates.

But it is not sufficient to present these suppositions; we must also assess the probability of each one of them or, in other words, the number of cases in which these suppositions could occur.

The number of cases in which the first supposition could occur is expressed by the continual product of the following factors:

1. The number of ways in which A's eleven election votes can be taken four by four, that is

$$\frac{11 \cdot 10 \cdot 9 \cdot 8}{1 \cdot 2 \cdot 3 \cdot 4} = 330$$

2. The number of ways in which B's nine election votes can be taken one by one, that is, nine.
3. The number of ways in which C's four election votes can be taken four by four, that is, one.
4. The number of ways in which A's five supplementary votes can be taken one by one, that is, five.
5. The number of ways in which B's seven supplementary votes can be taken seven by seven, that is, one.
6. The number of ways in which C's twelve supplementary votes can be taken four by four, that is

$$\frac{12 \cdot 11 \cdot 10 \cdot 9}{1 \cdot 2 \cdot 3 \cdot 4} = 495$$

Hence, the number of ways in which the election could conform to the first supposition is $330 \cdot 9 \cdot 5 \cdot 495 = 7{,}350{,}750$.

Similarly, the number of cases in which the second supposition could occur is the product of the following numbers:

$$\frac{11 \cdot 10 \cdot 9 \cdot 8 \cdot 7}{1 \cdot 2 \cdot 3 \cdot 4 \cdot 5} = 462$$

$$\frac{9 \cdot 8}{1 \cdot 2} = 36$$

$$\frac{4}{1} = 4$$

$$\frac{5 \cdot 4}{1 \cdot 2} = 10$$

$$\frac{7}{1} = 7$$

$$\frac{12 \cdot 11 \cdot 10 \cdot 9 \cdot 8}{1 \cdot 2 \cdot 3 \cdot 4 \cdot 5} = 792$$

which comes out as 368,831,232.

Similarly, the number of cases in which the third supposition could occur is 4,518,182,592; the fourth supposition could occur is 2,305,195,200; the fifth supposition could occur is 60,031,125.

For example, comparing A and B, we find that the number of cases in which A is preferred to B is in the same relation to the number of cases in which B is preferred to A, as the number 4,894,364,574 is to 60,031,125. And consequently, although the method which we are examining here pronounces the three candidates to be equally preferable, the number of cases favorable to A's being elected is more than 80 times greater than the number favorable to the election of B.

If we wanted to make our analysis of the voters' judgment on the candidates more accurate still, we would have to take into account the number of votes by which one candidate is preferred to another in each of the preceding suppositions, take the difference between the number of votes by which the first candidate is preferred to the second and the number of votes by which the second is preferred to the first, and multiply these differences by the number of ways in which the election may conform to these suppositions. Assessing the will of the voters on candidates A and B in this way, we would find that A's chances when compared to B emerge as considerably greater than when we did not take these differences into account. However, I must stress that in a large assembly, it is impractical to proceed according to the rules of the calculus of probabilities.

In fact, if this subject did not serve the purpose of illustrating the complexity and uncertainty of the will pronounced by a large assembly, it would have to be relegated to the class of mathematical speculations which have no application in real life.

CHAPTER 10

Joseph Isidoro Morales

Mathematical Memoir on the Calculation of Opinion in Elections, 1797

By order of His Majesty: Madrid, Royal Press, 1797

To His Excellency Prince de la Paz:

Your Excellency,

The invention of differential calculus had a thunderous impact on all the physical sciences. But as soon as it was realized that the same calculus could be applied with equal exactitude to any other subject capable of human valuation, it became possible to recreate and refound the political and moral sciences. The importance which all savants, and even some governments, have accorded this invention is today so broadly recognized in all countries that even the most illustrious cannot be offered a more welcome and acceptable gift than a new application of this analysis, even in the form of an essay.

The theory of opinion, and of the methods of calculating it in an election, is such a case. If only for this reason, the present analytical study should always attract the attention of philosophers. It should equally be of general interest, through the connection between its subject and public happiness. Everything points to the conclusion that the attention of intelligent individuals and professional bodies will be drawn to this memoir not only in Spain but elsewhere.

The warm welcome which Your Excellency had the goodness to show when I had the honor of presenting this to you, and your mandate to have it printed by Royal order, is not the first nor will it be the last indication which the Nation will see of Your Excellency's wish to educate the public on any subject which contributes to its happiness. I am the first to say that I have no wish, by putting this memoir under your protection, to intimidate the censor or avoid the honest judgment of my readers. Hence the homage I pay Your Excellency is all the more pure and dignified: it is founded only in your high qualities, in my respect, and in the prior rights of Your Excellency to my recognition.

Joseph Isidoro Morales   Madrid, 1 March 1797

Prologue

In the French newspaper *La Décade Philosophique*, number 83, of 20 Thermidor, Year IV (7 August 1796), there appeared an article which read thus, p.306:

> The National Institute has just announced appointments to fill five vacancies. The election procedure is simple and easy and should therefore be known and followed in elections involving numerous candidates. Each member produces a list with the three names of those proposed for the category for which there is a vacancy. A 3 is placed next to the name of the favorite, a 2 next to the second in order of preference, and a 1 against the name which is thought to be least appropriate. The numbers for each candidate are added and the highest sum decides the election.
>
> For instance, those eligible to fill the vacancy in Mechanics were Carnot (a member of the Directory), Breguet, and Janvier. Every voter wrote the number 3, 2, or 1 beside each name. Carnot was elected because he had 250 units or votes, while Breguet had 182 and Janvier 114.
>
> Borie, a member of the old Academy of Sciences, was elected to the Astronomy vacancy, having had 225 votes. The other candidates had 196 (Jeurat) and 147 (Lacroix).
>
> Larcher, elected to the Classics branch, had 248 votes, Sainte-Croix 171, and Chardon 115.
>
> For the Architecture vacancy, Leon Dufourny was elected with 204 votes, Chalgrain had 192, and Antoine 132.
>
> Gandmesnil obtained 211 votes for the chair in Oratory, Caillot obtained 173, and Talma 114.

This is all the above-mentioned newspaper mentioned, and it was this which has led to the present memoir.

Every thinking person knows that with the current methods of election from a plurality of absolute votes, there is more routine than accuracy or rigor. But this is known only in general terms, because in order to advance beyond that and determine with accuracy the extent to which the existing methods are faulty, it is first necessary to analyze opinion, and once the nature of this moral entity is better understood, a proper way of enunciating it has to be deduced and subsequently evaluated. Once all the elements which enter into the calculation have been determined and represented with adequate symbols, they may be subjected to the necessary comparisons by means of analysis, and their results may be presented in general formulae, thereby revealing the conditions which are lacking in current methods of election; and finally, we will be able to deduce the safe rule for voting and electing, independently of circumstances which currently make it more or less mistaken according to the case.

This is the plan I will follow in this study. I know not whether any of the wise men of the National Institute have preceded me in their investigations. It is clear that this wise body of men is rightly persuaded of the accuracy of the method it has adopted for its elections, given the importance they attribute to it, and given that it is prescribed in its new statutes, which is all the news that has reached me.[1] But the public have not yet seen this theory submitted to analysis and calculation to demonstrate the exactitude of the method, and the flaws of the others now in use. Finally I intend to resolve the different issues arising from this research, deducing from the general formulae the character and conditions of the rules that one must follow in this matter, which have been suggested to me by the above-mentioned *Décade* article. The originality of this research, which is unrelated to its intrinsic merit, is of no consequence unless it proves useful. Its usefulness will be judged by the reader when he compares the conclusion to the study with the newspaper article which inspired it.

It is understood that this study is of general interest, but it is especially interesting for the courts, councils, universities, and other institutions and bodies, whether secular or religious, where elections are decided by votes.

Since different electoral systems are nothing but methods whereby each voter may express his opinion of each candidate, which is then calculated to discover who has most support, it will be analytically shown that the methods used hitherto are mistaken and flawed, because they are based on the assumption that to *elect* (that is, to determine which candidate has most support) is the same as to decide in favor of or against a certain statement, as happens in decisions and sentences. The method of the absolute majority of the suffrage is as just in the latter as it is unjust in the case of elections, whose very nature differs fundamentally from the assumptions on which the electoral methods currently in use are based. Once this is clear, calculus[2] is applied to show how

---

1. Loi contenant la Règlement pour l'Institut National des Sciences et des Arts: du 15 Germinal an IV [3 April 1796]. [This law was probably written by Daunou, who was an active member of the Council of 500, referred to by Morales especially in his note at the end of chapter 10.]

2. [*Cálculo* for Morales, like *calcul* for Condorcet, means something more than calculus

the current methods are far from truthful and accurate (on which the fairness of the process depends), and analysis is used to demonstrate the rigor and accuracy that are inherent in the electoral method that we must adopt, which is as simple as any of those now in use but free of their mistakes, for it presents as many obstacles to abuse as can be attributed to an electoral system.

Mathematical Memoir on the Calculation of Opinion in Elections

I. Elections in which the sum of two-thirds of the votes are required encounter the difficulty that one candidate has to attract two-thirds of the votes. Sometimes this is impeded by the balanced merit of the candidates, which does not allow voters to reach an opinion clearly in favor of one of them. Alternatively, it may be impeded by the passion of the electorate, who may easily frustrate the election of a candidate if they so wish. This is something which is generally accepted. The same is not true of the fact that elections decided by two-thirds of the votes may be unjust and may exclude from the election a candidate who has a better claim than the person actually elected by this method.

II. Elections that are determined by the rigorous and absolute majority of voters (that is, half plus one) have the same shortcomings as the previous method. And although it is easier to obtain this majority, it is precisely this which makes it unfair. Neither one nor the other plurality have by themselves any connection with the majority of the opinion, and neither can guarantee the fairness of the election, as we shall see later. In neither case has it been possible to know and combine the conditions in which a certain number of votes, whatever this may be, may or may not determine an election, in order to deduce from this finding the simple though exact and secure method of knowing which candidate has most support. However, both types of election are known as "canonical," which means that they conform to the rules laid down by law in the early thirteenth century, in order to prevent the arbitrary nature and other abuses present in elections until then. Both electoral systems were adopted on the grounds that they seemed fair at first sight, and the practice became generalized throughout Europe in courts, colleges, universities, councils, and other institutions, both religious and secular.

III. There is another type of election, which is even more unfair, namely that which is carried out according to relative majority, that is to say, that in which the candidate who has relatively more votes is elected, as happens in many corporations and courts. In this type of election a candidate who would

(because it includes calculus but is not restricted to it) but less than calculation (because the connotation is of precise algebraic methods). *Analysis* in a technical sense might be a better translation, but none is entirely satisfactory.]

have been deemed least worthy according to the majority system is often elected. For instance, if out of sixteen voters, five vote for *A*, five for *B*, and six for *C*, the latter would be elected, on the grounds of relative majority, even though ten of those who voted regarded him as the most inferior candidate. In a word, none of the electoral methods used until now have considered anything other than the absolute vote[3] and the single judgment awarded by each voter to the candidate of his choice, without taking into account his order of preference in relation to the candidates for whom he does not vote.

IV. Only a method which meets these requirements, by allowing us to discover the true nature of majority opinion, can be described as fair, as we shall demonstrate with the accuracy of our calculations.

V. The method that the National Institute of Arts and Science of France (the former Paris Academy of Sciences) adopted in their elections for the first time is precisely such a method. My aim is first to analyse this electoral method, to prove by analysis that it is the only one which conforms with the theory of opinion, and to compare the analytical results with the ones obtained by the electoral methods now in use, to make us realize the extent to which they have divorced themselves from accuracy and justice.

VI. We will begin to explain this method by means of some easy examples, before exploring the general implications of this theory, which we will be able to examine later, independently of the examples.

VII. Let us suppose that *A*, *B*, and *C* are three candidates standing for election. Since the numbers 1, 2, and 3 can only be combined in six possible ways, there are not more than six ways of classifying the relative merit of the candidates. If there are six voters and no two of them fully coincided in their opinions of the candidates, there would be a perfect balance of opinion, and each candidate would obtain the same sum of votes. The voting would be as follows:[4]

EXAMPLE I.

$$\left.\begin{array}{ccccccc} A & 1 & 1 & 2 & 2 & 3 & 3 = 12 \\ B & 2 & 3 & 1 & 3 & 1 & 2 = 12 \\ C & 3 & 2 & 3 & 1 & 1 & 2 = 12 \end{array}\right\} = 36$$

VIII. This tie, which is very frequent in other electoral methods, is very rare in this one due to the precise circumstances that it requires. Thus if there

---

3. [By *absolute vote* Morales means *first preference*.]

4. In this and the following examples each column of numbers denotes the grades of opinion which one elector has assigned to each candidate. If we then add up each row of numbers, we obtain the respective sum of points obtained by each candidate. The logic of this is very straightforward, if one accepts the simple idea and description of this method outlined in the Prologue.

were not three candidates, or not six voters, or if at least two of the sequences were the same, there would be a predominant opinion. In the other electoral methods, based on absolute votes, there is almost always a tie, even though there is no real balance of opinion but rather a considerable imbalance, which is difficult to determine on the basis of absolute votes, as we shall see.

IX. The other methods are also unfair in that they may deprive a candidate of election even if he enjoyed the greatest support, merely because he fails to obtain the number of votes which has been deemed to express the preponderance of opinion. Take as an example the following:

EXAMPLE II.

$$\left. \begin{array}{ccccccc} A & 3 & 3 & 3 & 2 & 2 & 2 = 15 \\ B & 1 & 2 & 2 & 1 & 1 & 3 = 10 \\ C & 2 & 1 & 1 & 3 & 3 & 1 = 11 \end{array} \right\} = 36$$

Who has any doubt that it would be unfair to deprive candidate A of the election if the six electors had voted in this order? A would have obtained fifteen votes against ten and eleven in the case of the other two candidates. But if we judge this election by the first two methods described, A would not be elected because the sum of the three highest marks obtained was still lower than the half or two-thirds required.

X. This injustice becomes more evident as the number of voters increases. If for instance we take sixteen voters, of whom seven favor A, five select B, and four prefer C, without expressing what they think about the candidates for whom they have not voted, when we came to calculate the weight of opinion behind each candidate it would be impossible to choose, because the seven votes accumulated by A represent less than half and less than two-thirds of the number of voters. But if the vote was taken in the manner we propose, we would have known how voters valued the candidates for whom they were not voting, and the choice could have been made without any doubt. This is clear from the following:

EXAMPLE III.

$$\left. \begin{array}{cccccccccccccccccc} A & 3 & 3 & 3 & 3 & 3 & 3 & 3 & 2 & 2 & 2 & 2 & 2 & 2 & 2 & 2 & 2 = 39 \\ B & 1 & 2 & 1 & 2 & 1 & 2 & 1 & 3 & 1 & 3 & 1 & 3 & 1 & 3 & 1 & 3 = 29 \\ C & 2 & 1 & 2 & 1 & 2 & 1 & 2 & 1 & 3 & 1 & 3 & 1 & 3 & 1 & 3 & 1 = 28 \end{array} \right\} = 96$$

In this election it would be unfair if A is not elected, since he has accumulated thirty-nine points as opposed to twenty-eight and twenty-nine, even though he does not have half the total number of votes. In elections where there are fifty voters or more, this type of injustice, which we could describe as *negative*, is even more striking: it can result in a failure to elect anyone, while penalizing the candidate with the best claim.

XI. The third electoral system is even more unfair and absurd, for it results in a positive injustice, not only by depriving the best candidate of election but also by resulting in the election of the candidate who has been deemed least worthy by a majority of the voters. For example, if we have seven voters, of whom three vote for A, two for B, and two for C, following this electoral method A would be elected because he obtained more votes than the others, even though he may be the least attractive candidate for the voters in question. Indeed, assuming that the four voters who did not favor A considered him the least worthy candidate, is it not true that A would have been excluded by a majority of votes in the same election, if the question asked had been "Who is the least worthy candidate?" If we add the votes according to the new method of voting, it becomes clear that even though he enjoyed a relative majority, A was regarded as the worst candidate overall, as we can see from the following:

EXAMPLE IV.

A	1	1	1	1	3	3	3 = 13	
B	2	2	3	3	2	1	1 = 14	= 42
C	3	3	2	2	1	2	2 = 15	

XII. In this method of election by relative majority, there is more place for injustice the larger the number of voters, due to a vice inherent in the system. Let us assume there are sixteen voters, six of whom vote for A, five for B and five for C. If A were elected, we would not be taking into account the fact that, as often happens, the ten voters who did not vote for A may have thought him the worst candidate. In this case, in all justice, A would be eliminated following the same rigorous majority rule if the question posed was, which is the worst candidate of the three presented? In this example the vote would have the following result:

EXAMPLE V.

A	3	3	3	3	3	3	1	1	1	1	1	1	1	1	1	1 = 28	
B	2	2	2	2	2	2	3	3	3	3	3	2	2	2	2	2 = 37	= 96
C	1	1	1	1	1	1	2	2	2	2	2	3	3	3	3	3 = 31	

XIII. From the above it is possible to infer that the three methods commonly used to select candidates are faulty and incorrect and may lead to grave injustice. They not only deprive the rightful candidates of election but also result in the selection of the candidate least favored by those same electors.

XIV. Wherever there is obscurity or error, there are also vague or ill-defined ideas. This was surely the case when we came to adopt the current electoral methods as supposedly fair ways of discovering majority opinion. To vote is to express one's opinion of all the candidates. Once this has been done, votes are counted in such a way as to evaluate the weight of opinion behind each candidate, and to elect is to announce which of the candidates has most. There is thus only one accurate and fair method of election, which is that of *compensation*. This method compares and weighs the degrees of opinion in the same way that a scale compares different weights in order to discover even the slightest difference that may exist between them. Indeed, if it had been realized that opinion is not something that can be quantified but rather something which has to be weighed, people would not have decided upon a certain number of votes so unjustly without previously examining whether that particular figure really expressed majority opinion. In this respect it can be said that the three electoral methods discussed so far are like rough and coarse scales which are by definition inaccurate. But the method of added compensation is so accurate that it is capable of detecting the slightest difference in merit (merit of opinion), as we will see by looking at the theory and principles on which it is based.

A Theory of Elections and General Formulae of This Method

This theory is based on the theory of permutations, and on that of arithmetic progressions. It can be stated that:

XV. In order to judge the merit of the candidates, each voter can use as many votes or units of opinion as are expressed in the sum of a progression of the natural numbers 1, 2, 3, 4, 5, etc., whose total number will be the same as the number of candidates. These progressions are illustrated in the vertical columns of the previous examples. Thus, when there are three candidates, each voter can make use of six points of opinion; when there are four, ten; when there are five, fifteen; etc.

XVI. The total sum of votes or units of opinion distributed among all candidates is equal to the sum of the said progression multiplied by the number of voters.

XVII. These units of opinion must be distributed by the voter among the candidates in arithmetic progression, 1, 2, 3, 4, 5, etc., selecting the order in which they appear according to his opinion of the comparative merits of each candidate.

XVIII. This freedom of voting can be extended and varied (mathematically speaking) to the different permutations that those numbers allow, which are the same as the number of candidates permits.

XIX. In all cases, the number of permutations is limited, as is the absolute discrepancy between the votes awarded.

XX. Since the number of permutations may rise very rapidly (three candidates can produce 6 different votes; six candidates can lead to 720; and seven candidates to 5,040, etc.), a small number of candidates can be the subject of a considerable number of different judgments or possible ways of voting.

XXI. However much discrepancy there may be over the candidates, this will hardly ever be expressed in as many different ways as there are possible results. This is due to the fact that such a disagreement will be based on other principles and will be based on other elements, namely the moral circumstances which surround every election and which limit it to a small number of opinions or entirely different ways of voting. Thus it is morally impossible that seven candidatures, for example, when submitted to the opinion of 5,040 voters, will produce 5,040 entirely different views, even though, mathematically speaking, 5,040 permutations are possible. In each election, we will see that in fact only a small number of options are used up, while other possible options are left unused.

XXII. In view of the above, the number of voters will almost always be larger [*sic*] than the number of options which are mathematically possible, when there are no more than six of these, which will happen whenever there are more [*sic*] than three candidates. When there are more than three candidates, the number of voters generally exceeds the number of morally acceptable opinions.[5]

XXIII. Since the number of permutations and votes does not depend on the number of voters but rather on the number of candidates, when there are more voters than there are morally and mathematically possible permutations (as generally happens, as we saw above), many voters will emit the same vote, which will be repeated often.

XXIV. As a result of these repetitions, in any real or imagined examples, the horizontal rows of numbers (which represent the respective sum of opinion obtained by each candidate) will become increasingly differentiated as votes are repeated.

XXV. The repetition of a favorable vote will gradually tilt the scale in favor of the best candidate to the detriment of the worst.

XXVI. The repetitions of negative votes will gradually compensate and restore the balance of opinion, tilting it toward another candidate.

XXVII. The movement of this scale will correspond exactly to the differences of opinion that each permutation—or vote—adds to each candidate. The result of these differences will be found in the sum of each horizontal line.

XXVIII. The compensations discussed in XXVI will sometimes balance opinion. This will happen when (other than when certain unusual circumstances arise) these compensations take place in inverse order from one another.

XXIX. Since this case depends on such rare conditions, when these are

---

5. [The mistakes in this paragraph seem to arise from Morales's having forgotten a "not," or substituted a "more" for "fewer."]

not met it is not only difficult but actually impossible to have a tie, and there will therefore always be a majority of opinion in favor of one candidate.

XXX. Even if one should wish to lay down that a small majority (say of one, two, or three votes) is not enough to win an election, this could be decided rationally, without affecting the accuracy of the method used, which constitutes the main weakness of other voting methods.

XXXI. Finally, this method of determining the sum or weight of opinion which each candidate has won is as accurate as any calculation can be.

XXXII. Let e be the number of voters; let c be the number of candidates, and finally let $1, 2, 3, 4, \ldots, c$ be the progression of numbers destined to gauge and determine the merit of the candidates. The sum of the said progression $c\,(c + 1)/2$ will equal the total number of votes that each voter can award the different candidates in arithmetic progression (XV). Hence $ce\,(c + 1)/2$ will be the sum total of votes cast by all voters, to be distributed among all candidates (XVI).

XXXIII. It is clear that if that sum is divided by the number of candidates c, the quotient $e\,(c + 1)/2$ will represent the case of a true balance of opinion between the candidates, or that each has the same weight of opinion in his favor (see example 1). There can be other cases of such a balance, but it would be partial or relative among two, three, or more candidates, which would differ from all the rest, as can be easily demonstrated.

XXXIV. Call the quotient $e\,(c + 1)/2 = q$. Since it would be absurd and impossible for the weight of opinion obtained by a candidate (which is the product of the addition of whole numbers) to be a mixture of a whole number and a fraction, it is clear that in order for q to be a whole number, it will suffice that e or $c + 1$ are even numbers. And given the assumption that if $c + 1$ is even, c must be an odd number, we may conclude that in order to prevent a case of generalized balance of opinion, it is necessary to have an odd number of voters and an even number of candidates, because in that case neither of the two factors $e/2$ or $(c + 1)$ are even.

XXXV. The expression $q = e\,(c + 1)/2$ implies that the candidate who does not reach that number of votes cannot be elected fairly, because he will always be beaten by another candidate, as we will see later. This injustice is the most frequent in practice because the voting methods generally used are incapable of preventing it.

XXXVI. This same formula may be used to discover the number of voters and candidates in an election, and the number of votes that the chosen candidate must obtain. We can thus discover the number of officials who voted in order to fill the five vacancies in the National Institute mentioned in the Prologue, even though this was not mentioned in the article published in the *Décade*. Assuming that $e = 2q/\,(c + 1)$, we learn that in Carnot's election for the Mechanics post (by 250 votes to 182 and 114), there were ninety-one voters. In the third vote, by which Larcher obtained the Classics chair (by 248 points to 171 and 115), there were eighty-nine voters. In the fourth election, where Leon Dufourny won the chair in Architecture (by 204 votes to 192 and 132), there were eighty-eight voters. In the fifth, in which Grandmesnil stood for the chair in Rhetoric (winning 211 points against 173 and 114), there were eighty-three voters. And finally, Borie obtained the Astronomy chair by 225 votes to 196 and 147, from which we may deduce that there were ninety-four and two-thirds voters. Given that this result is absurd, either a mistake was made when adding the votes or there is a misprint in the *Décade*.

XXXVII. If (as we said in XXXII) $ce(c + 1)/2$ is equal to the total sum of opinion distributed among all candidates, we will demonstrate how mistaken it is to assume that it is the same for a candidate to obtain half of the favorable votes as it is for him to enjoy half the support of the voters. Let us suppose that half the voters have given A the best mark but that the other half have taken him to be the worst candidate. We will take n/m as being the total support that A can obtain. Let $1, 2, 3, 4, \ldots, c$ be the progression of numbers with which an opinion can be expressed, c being the best and 1 the worst. At the same time, half the number of voters is $e/2$. Thus $ec/2 + e/2$ will be the total amount of support that A can obtain. This will give us the following equation,

$$\frac{ec}{2} + \frac{c}{2} = \frac{n}{m} \cdot \frac{ec(c + 1)}{2},$$

which expresses the situation. Dividing by $e/2$, we have $c + 1 = nc(c + 1)/m$; and further dividing by $c + 1$, we have $1 = nc/m$. And finally, $n/m = 1/c$. This means that the amount of support A has in the proposed case is equal to 1 divided by the number of candidates.

XXXVIII. When a candidate has obtained a majority vote from half the voters, far from being the same as having obtained half the weight of opinion, it merely means that he has one-third of the support, if there are three candidates; one-fifth if there are five, one-twentieth if there are twenty, etc. This will happen every time that the candidate obtains the support of half the voters and is judged to be the worst candidate by the other half. This happens regardless of the number of voters taking part in the election.

XXXIX. This also means that (following what was said in XXXV), if the amount of support A can obtain in this case does not exceed $1/c$ of the total opinion, he cannot in justice be elected (despite having half the support), because he is always surpassed by one of his rivals or equalled by the rest. For instance, if there are five candidates, in the case quoted above A cannot have more than one-fifth of the total support. The remaining four-fifths will be evenly or unevenly distributed among his rivals. If it is evenly distributed, A

will have as many votes as the rest. If the votes are distributed unevenly, and one of the candidates has less than one-fifth of the votes, it will mean that there is another candidate who has more than one-fifth and who will therefore beat A. In other words, A can never be elected with justice. There is no more frequent injustice than that committed by most voting systems, which ignore this compensation and therefore only take into account the maximum, absolute number of votes obtained by each candidate, as if they expressed the true weight of opinion obtained in the vote, without considering the weight of contrary opinion.

XL. It therefore follows that elections determined according to the relative majority principle are even more unfair. Such a majority can in fact be obtained by the candidate with least support, as examples IV and V have shown. This has already been explained and will become clearer in later examples.

XLI. We will now explore whether a candidate who obtains a rigorous majority (half plus one) of preferences actually enjoys the support of majority opinion. In order to do this we will imagine two cases (and there are only two) in which this is indeed true. We will thereby see that it is not an analytical examination of the principles in question but rather an illusion which has been the origin and cause of the faulty rules which currently regulate elections.

XLII. Imagine an election involving two candidates and any number of voters, and another involving three candidates and four voters, conducted in the following ways:

$$A \quad 2 \quad 2 \quad 2 \quad 2 \quad 1 \quad 1 \quad 1 \quad 1 = 12 \atop B \quad 1 \quad 1 \quad 1 \quad 1 \quad 2 \quad 2 \quad 2 \quad 2 = 12 \Bigg\} = 24$$

$$A \quad 3 \quad 3 \quad 2 \quad 2 = 10 \atop B \quad 2 \quad 2 \quad 3 \quad 3 = 10 \atop C \quad 1 \quad 1 \quad 1 \quad 1 = \ 4 \Bigg\} = 24$$

In both cases A is challenged by B, due to the fact that both have the same number of votes. But notice that if only one of the latter vertical columns was altered to give A one more preference than he already has, A would have the highest number of votes (half plus one), and thus the majority of opinion behind him. This would appear to be a general truth. However, it is nothing but an illusion based on examples which happen to be the only two exceptions to the rule. We are going to show, firstly, that only when there are two candidates is it true to say that he who has a majority of preferences (half plus one) is the candidate favored by a majority of opinion, whatever the number of voters.

XLIII. Let $(e/2) + 1$ be the number of top preferences that a candidate has obtained in an election. And let us suppose that the rest of the voters (numbering $[e/2] - 1$) give him the lowest score. If c is the highest score and 1 is the lowest, the sum of his support will be $c [(e/2 + 1] + (e/2) - 1$. Compare this with the best possible result that his rival may obtain, which is to be the most favored candidate in the eyes of half the voters minus one. Assume that the rest of the voters (who regard the first candidate as their favorite) regard this other candidate as second best (scoring $c - 1$). This second candidate will have a score of $c [(e/2) - 1] + (c - 1)[(e/2) + 1]$. Now compare the two results in order to find the two conditions that will allow the first to be better than the second.

XLIV. We will have $c [(e/2) + 1] + (e/2) - 1 > c [(e/2) - 1] + (c - 1)[(e/2) + 1]$. Multiplying out, we obtain $(ec/2) + c + (e/2) - 1 > (ec/2) - c + (ec/2) + c - (e/2) - 1$. Eliminating the quantities common to both sides and reducing them, we will have $e > (ec/2) - c$, or alternatively $c/(c - 2) > e/2$. In other words, half plus one of the votes will reflect majority opinion if the number of candidates divided by itself minus two is larger than the number of voters.

XLV. This formula $c/(c - 2) > e/2$ indicates that only when there are two candidates (in which case $c - 2 = 0$) can it be said that the first member of this comparison is larger than any finite number of voters that can be assumed in the other member. Thus, only when there are two candidates can the absolute majority of votes be regarded as a true indicator of the majority of opinion, independently of the number of voters. And that is why it worked out thus in the first proposed example (XLII).

XLVI. If there are more than two candidates, he who has half plus one of the votes may or may not have the support of the majority, depending on the number of candidates and voters who take part in the election. This is limited to so few cases that in fact there is only one that needs discussion.

XLVII. In order to demonstrate this, before applying the formula $c/(c - 2) > e/2$, it is necessary to understand, first, that when the number of voters is even, when one has more than half the votes, the assumption that one has half plus one the number of votes is correct. But when the number of voters is odd, to have more than half the votes is not the same as having half the number of votes plus one. For example, if there are nine voters, the candidate who has five votes has more than half the number of votes but does not have half the number of votes plus one. Only he who, on being deprived of a vote, is left with half the votes, can be said to have half the number of votes plus one.[6]

---

6. If anyone should suggest that when the number of voters is odd, a majority exceeding half the votes, even if not by half plus one, can in fairness be considered an absolute majority, they should note that such a (minimal) majority is not, in itself, an indicator of majority opinion.

Second, it must also be noted that any number of votes or absolute preferences that a candidate obtains in an election is always a whole number. Given the nature of the object that is being calculated, it is impossible that the number of votes a candidate obtains can be a mixture of whole and fractional numbers. Thus half the votes plus one, that is $(e/2) + 1$, must be a whole number, even if it is smaller than a unit. Thus when applying the formula it is necessary to meet the condition that $e/2$ must be a whole number or, what is the same, that e is an even number. This is a condition that reduces the cases to just one, as we said earlier (XLVI), as we will see using the formula described earlier.

XLVIII. Let us apply the formula if there are more than two candidates. If $c/(c - 2) > e/2$ and $c = 3$, then $6 > e$. But since e must be an even number smaller than six, when there are three candidates, the number of voters should not exceed four in order to remain compatible with the general rule.

XLIX. If we continue with the substitutions, and in the same formula $c/(c - 2) > e/2$, we make $c = 4$, we will then have $2 > e/2$ or $4 > e$. But since e must be even and smaller than four (XLVII), when there are four candidates, the number of voters can be only two. And this same number of voters will result if we replace c with any number of candidates larger than four. But since it is obvious that when there are only two voters, to have half the number of voters plus one is to have them all, every case which goes beyond $c = 3$ must be excluded. Thus there is only one case—and it depends on the number of voters—in which the rigorous majority of votes (half plus one) is truly indicative that a candidate has obtained more support than any of his competitors. And this single case is that in which there are three candidates and four voters.[7]

L. The general rule which determines elections by rigorous majority, or by half the number of votes plus one, is a rule that should be enunciated in exactly the reverse way to that in which it is generally applied. If we take it inversely, it would only have, as we have seen, two exceptions. One is independent of the number of voters when there are only two candidates, and another is when there are exactly three candidates and four voters (assuming the latter case can be counted as an exception, as we saw in the footnote).

That majority is represented by $(e + 1)/2$; and if we establish a comparison with the conditions that affect the case under discussion (XLIII), this would result in $(c/2)(e + 1) + \frac{1}{2}(e - 1) > c(e - 1)/2 + (c - 1)(e - 1)/2$. This gives $c/(c - 2) > e$ where c cannot be larger than 2 without producing an illusory result. Because if $c = 3$, $3 > e$. And since e must be odd and smaller than 3, this would mean that, if there are three candidates, such a majority is a fair guide only when there is just one voter. And we would have the same reasoning if c were any number larger than 3.

7. This is the only exception to the general rule, which many will rightly refuse to accept as such, because in fact, when there are four voters, to have half plus one of the votes is to have more than two-thirds, that is three-quarters of the electorate; thus this example does not belong to the case we started examining in XLI.

LI. Thus we can see that the exceptions have until now been accepted as the general rule for a fair election. It goes without saying that this has been the case even in the most important elections, because all elections are important when justice is to be done. As far as I know, until now calculus has not been applied to the theory of elections, and so I may be forgiven for saying that for centuries we have been acting as blindly in electoral matters as we were in Physics or Mechanics before the invention of analysis. The old methods are still present with all the errors which characterize the middle ages, the period during which they were adopted and established in Europe. Are we not allowed to denounce the fact that even in this age of enlightenment methods adopted in the dark ages still survive? Not a single day goes by without the courts, communities, universities, municipalities, and public establishments carrying out an unjust election against their own wishes. Your elections may have been carried out with just intent but without a fair electoral method. I am accusing not men but methods. Examine! Examine! That must be the clamor behind all reform of such abuses.

LII. But let us return to our examination of the matter. And I would like to say that not even in the two cases in which half plus one of the number of preferences is accompanied by the majority of opinion is it true to say that the candidate enjoys half the total weight of opinion. This is an error which allows no exception, and it should be clarified because it will shed light on the preceding and subsequent cases and it will add accuracy and precision to a matter which is not often discussed.

LIII. If we want to know what number of votes or highest preferences will clearly indicate that a candidate enjoys half the support, let x be that number of highest votes, and let $e - x$ be the number of lowest votes, both of them obtained by the same candidate. Taking into account what has been said (XXXII), that the total support distributed among all the candidates is $ec\,(c + 1)/2$, we will obtain the following balance based on the terms in which the question has been posed: $cx + e - x = ec\,(c + 1)/4$. Solving for x we have

$$x = \frac{c(c + 1) - 4}{4\,(c - 1)}e$$

LIV. If in this formula we make $c = 2$, we obtain $x = e/2$, and therefore $e - x = e/2$. So, if there are two candidates (which is the smallest possible number in an election), one would need half the highest votes to obtain half the total opinion, since the other candidate has the other half and in the same circumstances there would be an equal amount of support and neither can be elected.

LV. But if $c = 3$, we will have $x = e$. In other words, if there are three candidates, it is necessary to obtain the highest votes of all of those voting (whatever their number) in order to obtain, independently of any circumstance, half the total support. If we continue with the substitutions in the formula we will find out that if there are more than three candidates it would be necessary to have more votes than there are voters in order to obtain the same result.

LVI. We may deduce from this that it would be a mistake to believe that in order to have the right to be elected it is necessary to have at least half the total amount of support. This would be the same as saying that in no circumstances would a candidate have this right. This right is not based on a certain amount of support (for it is impossible to fix a level, since it is different in every case) but in having a greater level of support than any other of the candidates. And this relative majority is in no way linked to, nor dependent on, the number of absolute preferences that a candidate obtains in one vote; because none of these, whatever they may be, are (by themselves, independently of other circumstances) a definitive indication of majority preference in relation to other candidates. This relative majority is precisely that which decides which candidate has merited the highest level of esteem, appreciation, and support in the judgment of the voters and thus who is considered the best candidate and therefore has the right to be elected. In a word, to elect is to compare, or rather, the former is a necessary consequence of the latter. Whoever emerges from that comparison with an excess of support in his favor has the right to be elected, whatever the size of his advantage, unless an agreement has been reached to the contrary. This is what justice demands; anything else is a purely arbitrary measure which can only be justified by ignorance.

LVII. This arbitrariness could introduce, and can still maintain, the useless practice of demanding that the most deserving candidate obtain two-thirds of the votes or one more than half the number of votes. Ignorant of the method whereby they could discover which candidate had most support, they were happy to demand either a two-thirds or a simple majority. They were pleased to think that the most appropriate candidate had been chosen and that no injustice had been committed.

LVIII. We will now demonstrate that neither half, nor two-thirds, nor three-quarters, nor four-fifths, nor nineteen-twentieths, nor in general $e(c - 1)/c$ of the votes or highest preferences guarantees that one has a greater level of support behind one than any other candidate.

Let x be the number of voters who have chosen A as their favorite; and let us assume that the rest of the voters, $e - x$, have given him their lowest mark. Even if this situation were not as frequent as it is, it would be enough that it could happen at all for us to include this case in the general result or solution that we are looking for. The amount of support that A would have in this case is $cx + e - x$.

Let B be another candidate, whom x voters (who chose A as the best candidate) regard as second best; and let the rest of the voters $e - x$ consider him the best candidate. The amount of support that B would have in this case is $x(c - 1) + c(e - x)$.

LIX. Let us compare these two levels of support with a view to knowing how many top scores A needs to obtain so that the level of support for him is higher than for B, who is his closest rival, thereby allowing him to be elected. If $cx + e - x > x(c - 1) + c(e - x)$, then $cx + e - x > ce - x$. And finally $x > e(c - 1)/c$. This means that the minimum number of top scores that A must obtain in order to be elected may be learnt by dividing the number of candidates minus one by the total number of candidates. And this condition is independent of the number of voters.

LX. Thus, if in our formula we make $c = 2$, then $x > e/2$. In other words, when there are only two candidates, A must have more than half the highest scores. If we make $c = 3$, then $x > 2e/3$. Thus, if there are three candidates, A must obtain more than two-thirds of the votes or highest scores. If we continue with the substitutions, we will find that when there are four candidates, A must obtain more than three-quarters of the highest scores. If there are five, A must have more than four-fifths. And finally, if there are twenty, fifty candidates, etc., A must obtain more than nineteen-twentieths, forty-nine fiftieths, etc., of highest scores, so that in themselves they may provide a clear indication that the candidate has in his favor a greater weight of opinion than any of his competitors.

LXI. The number of votes (however many they may be) is thus a false and misleading indication when trying to determine who enjoys most support or has the greatest right to be elected. This depends on, and must be combined with, other conditions and circumstances, namely those which are present in the formula, so that we can be sure that there have not been compensations which could undermine A's majority. Since these conditions and circumstances have never been taken into account in practice, because they were unknown and have remained unspecified, the methods currently used in elections are the falsest guide that could be used to obtain the desired end.

LXII. But there is more. Given the conditions in the situation already discussed, candidate A can obtain two-thirds, four-fifths, nineteen-twentieths, forty-nine fiftieths, etc., of highest scores and yet be exceeded in weight of opinion by a candidate B, who therefore will have a positive right to be elected instead of A.

LXIII. To prove it, it is only necessary to take the same comparison as before (LVIII and LIX), which produced $cx + e - x > x(c - 1) + c(e - x)$, and develop it here as we did there, only with a view to finding out when the first member, or sum of opinion, is smaller than the second. And since the procedure is the same, the result will be identical except for the direction of the inequality. That is, $x < e(c - 1)/c$.

LXIV. In other words: the maximum score that A can obtain and still be beaten by B, will be found by dividing the number of candidates minus one by the total number of candidates irrespective of the number of voters.

LXV. And thus if we substitute c as in LX, we will discover that A can be beaten if, when there are three candidates, he obtains fewer than two-thirds of the votes; if, when there are four candidates, he gets fewer than three-quarters of the votes; if, when there are five candidates, he gets fewer than four-fifths; if, when there are twenty or fifty, etc., candidates, A does not obtain at least nineteen-twentieths, forty-nine fiftieths, etc., of the top scores. And all of this is unrelated to the number of voters.

LXVI. We have thus clearly and rigorously shown that no fixed quota of votes, whatever it may be, represents majority opinion, because the quota is different in each case, depending on the number of candidates, whatever the number of voters. And it is as absurd to expect the elected candidate to obtain half plus one the number of votes, or two-thirds, as it is to demand three-quarters, four-fifths, eight-ninths, nineteen-twentieths, etc., or any other quota indicated by the general formula $(c - 1)/c$. Because majority opinion (that is, that which distinguishes the chosen candidate and which denotes the esteem in which he is held) is something which is independent of any fixed number of votes or, what is the same, it has a varying relationship with this figure, according to the circumstances. No single number of votes can be chosen which might not be associated with minority opinion, unless it is directly in relation to the relevant number of candidates, circumstances which are taken into account in the above-mentioned formula. If this happens with the electoral methods generally thought to be the most reliable, what can we expect of elections carried out by simple majority rule? Nothing can be more absurd and unfair than this method.

LXVII. All methods of election by absolute unqualified vote, in which each voter expresses only his opinion of the candidate for whom he votes, are thus unfair. To count these votes and allow them (whatever their number) is to use the worst and least subtle scale by which to measure a quality or a moral entity such as opinion, and it amounts to attempting to value it when it is only half expressed.

LXVIII. It is repugnant that justice has been compromised by an indicator as unreliable as a fixed number of absolute votes. It is also repugnant that merit should be subordinated to a circumstance which is rarely met and which, when met, proves useless in an attempt to discover the true weight of opinion. And it is also odd that this circumstance should in itself lead not only to injustice but also to the most surprising absurdity. Because what can be sillier than to exclude from the purpose of an election the candidate who has met (after compensation) the highest level of support? And what could be more unfair than to elect another candidate who (after compensation) turns out to have received less support and is in fact judged inferior to another candidate who is excluded?

LXIX. For instance, who would hesitate to elect a candidate, if he were told that, in competition with another four, he had obtained fifty-three votes against the forty of his strongest competitor? This would be the case for *A* in the following example in which twelve voters have taken part:

A	4	5	4	5	4	5	4	5	4	5	4	4 = 53
B	5	1	5	1	5	1	5	1	5	1	5	5 = 40
C	2	3	3	3	2	4	3	4	3	4	3	3 = 37
D	3	4	2	4	3	3	2	3	2	2	2	2 = 32
E	1	2	1	2	1	2	1	2	1	3	1	1 = 18

$= 180$

Here we see that *B* has seven of the highest scores, that is half plus one of the number of voters; but he is nevertheless inferior to *A* in the voters' opinion. And indeed so it must be. We can see that the highest scores obtained by *B* alternate with the lowest awarded by the rest of the voters and this compensates the quantity or total weight of opinion. On the other hand *A* is superior to *B* in the opinion of the voters. *A* obtained five top scores and the seven other voters gave him the second-best marks. This logically and morally guarantees *A*'s election, as is demonstrated by the excess of opinion in his favor.

LXX. With the methods generally used in elections, *B* would have been elected by simple majority of top scores, which would have been a grave injustice, because using only absolute votes it is impossible to discover the general opinion of the voters; and this cannot be discerned without compensating by means of a method as simple as that which we have proposed.

LXXI. The same injustice would still be possible even if *B* had two-thirds of the top scores. There are as many examples as one can imagine, taking into account the conditions and circumstances of the general formula described above. I would save you further examples, if it were not for the fact that I wish to place some fully in view of those who, due to their lack of familiarity with calculus, may not have appreciated the rigor of the formulae.

· LXXII. The following example is that of an election conducted, like the previous one, among five candidates and twelve voters, in which *B*, in spite of obtaining two-thirds of the top scores, is awarded no more than forty-four votes, as opposed to *A*'s fifty-two.

A	4	4	5	4	4	5	4	4	5	4	4	5 = 52
B	5	5	1	5	5	1	5	5	1	5	5	1 = 44
C	2	3	3	2	3	4	3	3	4	3	3	4 = 37
D	3	2	4	3	2	3	2	2	3	2	2	2 = 30
E	1	1	2	1	1	2	1	1	2	1	1	3 = 17[8]

$= 180$

---

8. [Morales has 18 here. This is a mistake.]

LXXIII. We have said in general (LX), that no fixed proportion of the vote can be specified as being necessary to win an election and that the lowest limit which can be assigned to this is that no candidate may win over others in terms of number of votes unless his votes exceed more than one-third of the total, given that there are three candidates; one-fifth if there are five; one-ninth if there are nine, etc. (XXXV and XXXIX). It must be stressed, of course, that exceeding the proportion of the votes mentioned is not a sufficient condition for winning but that any candidate not exceeding it will always be beaten by another, or, put another way, that to exceed this proportion is a necessary condition in order to compete against or beat other candidates. The winner, who will qualify for the right to be elected, will be he who exceeds this quota by the largest number of votes; for it is he who, at that point, will have a higher relative proportion of the opinion than any other candidate.

LXXIV. This relative majority of votes (and here lies the absurdity of these methods) has been thought to depend only on the absolute number of votes or higher qualifications. We have already shown in the preceding sections how inaccurate an indication this is on its own, when not in combination with other criteria, different in each case, to which no importance has so far ever been attached. Their lack is what renders the system incorrect, and this error is then built into the method, going completely against the weight of opinion (majority), had this opinion been wholly expressed by the electors, that is, if each had, by means of some sign, expressed their opinion on each candidate. Thus accounted for, the overall opinion would inevitably favor the election of the most worthy candidate, and this decision would thus be one made by Justice herself. If there is a place for her in the decisions of governments, then she asks to be placed where error and ignorance have pained her for centuries and where merit and virtue have always been defeated. All those whose sacred duty it is to administer her stand only to gain from this, from the Monarch himself down to the last person in charge of applying her.

LXXV. Once the relative majority of the opinion becomes the only criterion which affords the right to be elected, and this majority is independent of the absolute number of votes of higher qualification, it will follow that the totals or amounts of opinion obtained by each candidate will be maintained and remain unaltered, even when the number of the said votes becomes altered by different combinations. In this way—and if the objective of the statutes and legal orders which proposed a fixed number of votes was to ensure that the elected candidate had in fact the majority or most of the opinion in his favor—in agreement with the just purpose and will of the law, we will achieve what Justice herself was unable to achieve, if by having the means to measure this majority directly, we make use of it exclusively in order to determine the outcome of the elections, since this majority or excess remains unaltered, even when the number of votes changes. There are infinite examples of this since the situation we describe is always possible. We will give one example to illustrate this property and then move on to describe it in more general terms.

LXXVI. Let us suppose that in a vote cast by six electors between three candidates, *A*, *B*, and *C*, *A* obtained fourteen points of opinion in his favor against eleven obtained by each of his competitors. What further information is necessary in order for *A* to be elected other than that he has beaten his competitors in quantity of opinion? Similar quantities of opinion can arise from different voting patterns (in terms of number of votes). For example, it could have arisen as follows, with *A* gaining two-thirds of the top voting scores:

A	3	3	3	3	1	1 = 14	
B	2	2	2	1	2	2 = 11	(total = 36)
C	1	1	1	2	3	3 = 11	

But the same totals of fourteen versus eleven may also arise, even if *A* obtained only one-half of the top scores as follows:

A	3	3	3	2	2	1 = 14	
B	2	2	2	1	1	3 = 11	(total = 36)
C	1	1	1	3	3	2 = 11	

Yet another (different) voting pattern could have given rise to the same result of *A* winning by fourteen against eleven; and in this case *A* may have obtained but one-third of the top voting scores, as is shown below:

A	3	3	2	2	2	2 = 14	
B	2	1	3	3	1	1 = 11	(total = 36)
C	1	2	1	1	3	3 = 11	

In all three cases the totals of the added voting scores are the same (fourteen against eleven), and thus so must the outcome of the election be the same in leading to the election of the same candidate in each case. The election is similar in each case, although each result arises from a different combination of votes, a combination which is so contingent that to decide by it the outcome of the election would be to turn the application of the law into a most ridiculous game.

LXXVII. Despite this, if such an election were judged according to the methods currently in use, it would be proclaimed fair (in favor of *A*) in the first instance because the combination results in two-thirds of the voting score in his favor, unfair in the second because there exists no clear majority of top voting scores, and a draw in the third because all candidates have received an equal number of top voting scores. And yet in all three instances the electors have divided their opinion equally, that is to say, given that opinion is the criterion for election, they have made the same choice in each case.

LXXVIII. This number of different combinations, leading to the same result, could be increased at will if instead of taking this previous example, which can only be altered in the three ways shown, we had chosen one with more candidates or electors. Such an example would then allow a considerable number of solutions, or different ways of obtaining the same result of opinion, with very many possible variations in the number of votes.

LXXIX. It is unnecessary to add more tangible examples to prove that one-half, two-thirds, three-quarters, four-fifths, etc., of top voting scores not only fails to carry the majority of opinion but may even carry only a minority unless these results are combined with other factors, as we have shown (LVIII–LXVI).

LXXX. It thus becomes clear that the error intrinsic to all the usual methods of election is that they all involve a single type of absolute vote (equivalent to the highest score above), and the number of such votes will decide the outcome of the election. Each elector votes for the candidate he considers most worthy in his opinion, but he cannot express any opinion on all the other candidates for whom he does not vote. In this way, each and every elector remains unable to express his opinion on any candidate save one. As a result there is no possibility of accounting for the differing levels of support that each candidate may deserve from each elector; nor can the amount of accumulated support for each candidate be assessed, since the electors have been unable to express it. Which is equivalent to each elector assigning absolutely no worth to every single candidate except one, thereby expressing his opinion on the latter by the highest voting value and his opinion on the rest (which some or many electors may consider worthy of some voting value) with a zero. I do not know whether anyone may pretend that this constitutes a vote. But if anyone does, I beg them to use some argument to support it other than "we have always voted thus."

LXXXI. The truth is that by assessing opinion by such inaccurate indicators, and by rules that scarcely deserve the name of exceptions, so far it has not been the true majority of opinion which has so far dictated elections but the silent approval of methods whose injustice had not been suspected, or had not been successfully avoided.

Because if we have shown (LX) that even with only three candidates (irrespective of the number of electors) it is necessary for one of them to attain *more* than two-thirds of the top voting scores in order for these on their own, without having to take any other factors into consideration, to serve as absolute guarantee that he has attained a higher amount of opinion in his favor than any other, what sort of election would it be if there were fewer than three candidates? Has there ever been one in which more than two-thirds of the vote has been required by a candidate to be elected?

LXXXII. If this is the case when there are only three candidates, if with four candidates three-quarters are not sufficient; with five, four-fifths are not enough; with nine, eight-ninths do not suffice, etc., what could be more ridiculous than to decide elections on this quantity alone, which on the one hand is so difficult and morally impossible to determine, especially in bigger elections, and on the other hand if the amount of votes required in each case is not attained, any other majority of votes might be linked to the minority of opinion? In this way that person whom the electorate had favored with the majority of opinion (had this opinion been properly evaluated) will fail to be elected, and justice itself will be wronged.

LXXXIII. Why then will we not abandon such methods which, while they persist, will inevitably lead to so much injustice? Why not adopt the only one which can accurately select the candidate who holds the majority of opinion in his favor in such a way, and so finely balanced, that it highlights the slightest difference in the opinion, without the need to resort to erroneous criteria so difficult to obtain and so inaccurate once obtained?

LXXXIV. Give to each elector a list with the names of all the candidates, and let the elector place by each name a number which corresponds to the amount of support which that candidate deserves, in his opinion, with respect to the rest. For example, if there are eight candidates, he must put an 8 by the candidate who merits the most support, a 7 by the candidate after this who deserves the most support, and in this way assign a value to each candidate in decreasing order of support until assigning a 1 to the candidate least worthy of support. If there are three candidates (as is the case when three are proposed) the scoring will start with a 3 as the maximum, followed by a 2, and then a 1. Assessing thus the merit of each candidate, it remains only to add the numbers obtained by each candidate on the lists, and the highest score (which represents absolutely the greatest proportion of the opinion, with all factors taken into account) is what decides the outcome of the election. Were two candidates to attain equal scores, only they would be subject to a second voting.

LXXXV. If the vote is to be taken secretly, give to each elector the numbers representing the scores in the form of small balls, wedges, or strips of paper. Then, each elector can place his ball or strip into a jar or vase (according to custom) each marked with the name of one of the candidates, the votes in each jar can then be counted by adding the scores as shown. Alternatively, a single jar may be used to collect separately the scores for each candidate, repeating the process as many times as there are candidates. No matter how simple the methods currently in use for elections, I doubt the method we propose to be any less so; nor do I believe that it might cause any embarrassment to the less·experienced communities being, as it is, such an easy procedure.

LXXXVI. Perhaps some may think that the practice used in certain professional bodies and tribunals (for proposals, not elections) of voting for first, second, and third place, has something in common with the method we are describing; they are entirely wrong and will become aware of this by realizing that these numbers mean nothing, as they are not used with the intent of adding their values up later and deciding the election or the proposal in favor of the *lowest* total. I say *lowest* as it is customary in such professional bodies to assign a 1 to the highest voting qualification, a 2 to the second highest, etc., and thus the strongest support would be indicated by the lowest score of all. The idea is essentially the same and is as correct as carrying out the procedure in the reverse order.

LXXXVII. I have said in passing, but will now dwell on it, that the method we are describing can be used successfully, not only in elections but also in proposals, which currently are dealt with by similar and even more erroneous methods than those by which elections are decided, when they can be run with as much correctness and justice as we would wish for in elections. Apply what has been suggested for the method of elections (LXXXIV); let each voter place next to each candidate on the list the numbers which represent the level of support which he is to give to each, by adding these numbers, the three *highest* scores, or the three *lowest* (depending on the order in which the numbers were given), will give the three which are justly deserving to be elected and must be chosen in the same order as their respective quantities of opinion suggest, although he who obtained the highest value of opinion would have the legitimate right to be elected, had this been an election; I have considered this scenario simply as a proposal, as I have assumed that the proposers are not able to nominate nor do they have the right to elect.

LXXXVIII. A further property arises from the advantages of this method we have outlined in which election is a result of the balance of opinion as determined by the electors: to encourage merit to instill in electors who are just more serenity and resolution and to discourage the unjust.

LXXXIX. In the methods for election currently in use, apart from the intrinsic injustice present which we have highlighted (even if the electors were all as fair-minded as Aristeides[9]), an area lies open to private or personal injustice by the electors, as, depending on the situation, one, two, three, or more of them can prevent the election of the most deserving candidate if they thus wish to contravene the course of justice. This system is so well known

---

9. [Arist[e]ides "the Just," ca. 530–468 b.c., an Athenian politician who was ostracized (banished from Athens as the result of a popular vote) ca. 488, probably as the result of a campaign by his rival Themistocles. He became legendary for his fair-mindedness and tolerance.]

and occurs so often that an explanation of it is redundant. What is important is to determine and show how difficult it would be to prevent the just and fair outcome of an election, when the method followed is that of compensation and addition which we propose.

XC. In such an election, merit and justice are safeguarded by censorship of the other electors in the case of a public election, and pangs of conscience if it is secret. Even if men's passions cause them to lean toward injustice, their pride will lead them to conceal it. And even if one cannot assume all electors to be lovers of justice, one can assume most of them at least not to be indifferent. I appeal to my readers' experience: tell me if ever they have known an unjust elector or judge who did not speak as the fairest of men and to whom the thought of even being suspected of committing an injustice was not totally abhorrent. All other passions, for the sake of which virtues had been sacrificed, are themselves sacrificed for pride: and the latter acts as a substitute for the former in men who lack them.

XCI. In all elections carried out by absolute votes, each elector gives his vote to the candidate he judges to be more deserving of it or whom he wants to be elected, without assigning any qualification to the rest of the candidates who will in turn have been voted for by other electors. As every elector acts in the same way, this method of election conceals the comparative judgment that the elector has undertaken and simply announces the final result. This in itself cannot reveal whether behind such an analysis lay an unjust man intent on excluding the fairest candidate or a man who has made a small mistake—a problem which may arise and indeed arises often when trying to make the right decision. In any case this exclusion has taken place already to its full extent, and the deserving candidate thus excluded will be unable to ascertain how far he might be from being elected. Or put another way, by this silence of votes he is as far from being elected as the least deserving of all the candidates. In a word, if each candidate has the right to be judged by all the electors and that they express their opinion of him, can there be a system which more directly responds to passions than one in which a candidate is only considered in terms of those electors who vote for him? Can there be anything more ridiculous than a practice and method which allows weak or easily influenced electors to make entirely wrong decisions without giving them the possibility of at least partly avoiding them?

XCII. None of this would arise were elections to be carried out as suggested (LXXXIV). Each candidate is evaluated by each and every elector, depending on the amount of support they wish to give him. The sum of these scores (and not the absolute number of votes) is the score that each candidate carries and compares against those of other candidates, the candidate with the highest score being the one who is elected. The majority which this candidate holds cannot have been destroyed in one blow by the possible tactical voting of a few unjust electors, since these, in failing to give him the highest score, would be ashamed to give him the lowest; the fear of censure would hold them back. Even if this were to happen in the case of one elector, it would be very difficult to convince others to follow the same extreme route. This is to say that, given that a condescending or influenced elector were to give a higher score to a less worthy candidate, the matter would end there and the elector would be satisfied. Injustice would reach only a certain level and stop there even if it were only for fear of the injustice becoming too obvious. He would give the highest score to a less worthy candidate but would not dare deny the candidate which he judged most worthy the second or third highest score; each of these degrees only reduces the total score that the latter candidate would obtain by one. Therefore the difficulty which many electors might experience in manipulating every single one of the scores is clearly a characteristic of this method, which not only makes extreme injustices very unlikely to occur but also prevents them from having their full effect even if some are committed.

XCIII. Unfortunately, this welcome difficulty in falsifying a just election will obviously be limited, and a certain number of unfairly placed scores from the highest to the second highest on to the third highest, etc., down to the lowest, will eventually bring the total score of the most worthy candidate down to that of the least worthy. But *what are these limits*? They can only be loosely determined by reason. Analysis will allow us to interpret them accurately; and if I still insist in applying it to this latest problem, it is because certain results would appear incredible unless proven by analysis.

XCIV. Let us begin by analyzing one example, and we will then go on to give a general solution to the problem which is applicable to all cases. Within this work, we have, in the preface, a list of some elections carried out by this means. Let us choose any of these, for example the one in which Leon Dufourny was elected as a member of the National Institute in the discipline of architecture by a score of 204 in favor versus 192 and 132 against. Applying the formula $e = 2q/(c + 1)$ to this vote, we find (XXXVI) that eighty-eight electors had taken part. Let us expand on these data.

XCV. Let A, B, and C be the three candidates, and let us find out in how many ways could the voting take place in order to give A always the same voting score and majority of opinion of 204 versus 192 and 132? This question is indeterminate and has many possible solutions. Let us consider these solutions in two extreme cases in order to determine the limits within which a fair election is assured and how much injustice is intrinsic to elections determined by absolute majority, or by any fixed number of absolute votes of only one type.

XCVI. As there are only three candidates, the uppermost score will be 3, the middle 2, and the lowest 1. Let m be the number of top scores obtained by

A; n the number of middle scores that he obtained. Therefore (with eighty-eight electors) $88 - m - n$ will give the number of lowest scores obtained. By multiplying each factor by the corresponding score, we obtain the sum total or score of opinion of A. This will be $3m + 2n + 88 - m - n = 204$, i.e., $2m + n = 116$.

XCVII. Let us now consider one of the extreme cases. Let us try to determine in all the possible ways in which A's voting score could have been obtained—which combination has the lowest number of highest scores in order to give a total score of 204?

XCVIII. It is obvious that not all of the eighty-eight electors gave A the highest voting score (if this had been the case, the sum of the voting scores would have been 88 multiplied by 3, which equals more than 204). It is also obvious that the lower the number of highest scores that are needed to make up such a total, the higher the number of higher grade scores are needed by the rest of the electors. And as we can assume that the remaining electors assigned to him the second score, therefore the lowest number of highest scores which the total score of A can have occurs in the case where the number of lowest scores, i.e., 1, is none. Thus in this case $88 - m - n = 0$. We also infer from this that $m + n = 88$. Therefore we now have the following equations:

$$2m + n = 116.$$

$$m + n = 88.$$

By subtracting the second from the first equation, we obtain $m = 28$ and therefore $n = 60$.

XCIX. Thus 28 is the lowest number of maximum scores which A's vote may have contained (among the 60 remaining second-grade votes) in order to obtain a score of 204. In this way B will have always been beaten by 204 against 192, even if B had obtained 52 votes of highest qualification (which is virtually twice as many as A's 28) and which is the highest number of top scores which B's total score can possibly have had, as we will now demonstrate.

C. The higher the number of top scores present in the total of 192, the lower the score given to B by the remaining electors who did not give him a top score—the reason for this being equally obvious to, and the reverse of that explained above (XCVIII). And since we can assume that the remaining electors assigned to him the lowest score, i.e., 1, then the highest number of top scores with which the total of 192 can have been arrived at is in the situation in which there were no second-grade votes. In this case $n = 0$,; and the first equation (XCVI) which in B's case would be $3m + 2n + 88 - m - n$

= 192, becomes $m = 52$ (as $n = 0$). The remaining 36 votes (making up the total of eighty-eight electors) will be of the lowest score, 1. With such a distribution of votes, B will always have obtained the same total of opinion of 192. This will inevitably be lower than that of A, who by virtue of having 204 in his favor, will always win the election.

CI. Let us now ponder briefly over these latest results. If this election had been carried out by absolute votes of one qualification, a grave injustice would appear to have been committed in not electing B or at least preventing A from being elected: B would have had fifty-two absolute votes against only twenty-eight in favor of A who would remain excluded with all the good will in the world but against justice's will. This is because justice demands that each elector expresses his support for, or opinion on, each candidate and that all the levels of support be taken into consideration; and nowadays, an elector only expresses his opinion on the candidate to whom he gives his absolute support. The opinion which is not assessed in any way cannot be evaluated or influence the election in any way. Thus it is not represented in the voting results, and its only purpose is to build up false illusions and lead to the gravest errors in this most serious and delicate matter.

CII. However, if it is true (as we have just shown) that A's total of opinion (204) against B's of 192, may have arisen from a vote in which A had only 28 top votes against 52 in favor of B, it is also true that the same totals of opinion may have arisen from a vote in which A had 58 top votes and B 16, which represents the other extreme defining the limits within which we can verify the vote in different ways in the example we have just explained, as we will now show.

CIII. We are thus attempting to answer the following question: which is the highest number of top votes with which A's total of opinion of 204 may have arisen? Going back to what we have said (C), the larger the number of highest scores which such a total can have, the lower the grade of the remaining qualifications. And, because we are at liberty to assume that these remaining scores were all 1 (i.e., the minimum), the situation we are searching for is that in which there are no qualifications of medium value, that is to say, when $n = 0$. Therefore the main equation (XCVI), which was $3m + 2n + 88 - m - n = 204$, becomes simply $m = 58$. Thus 58 is the highest number of top scores that A can have in his total as the 30 remaining are minimum scores. With this his total of opinion will remain as always 204.

CIV. However, what in this same case is the lowest number of top scores that B can have obtained? There is no doubt (by what was said in XCVIII) that the higher the scores assigned by the remaining electors, the lower the number of top scores that B's score of 192 can accommodate. And if we assume that all the remaining electors assigned to B the second score, this leaves no room for minimum scores. Thus on the one hand we have the main equation (C) which is $3m + 2n + 88 - m - n = 192$, which becomes $2m + n = 104$; on the other hand the assumption that $88 - m - n = 0$ will give us another equation: $m + n = 88$. Thus the answer required will be determined by these two equations:

$$2m + n = 104.$$

$$m + n = 88.$$

Subtracting the second from the first we have:

$$m = 16.$$

$$n = 72.$$

Therefore, 16 is the lowest number of top scores with which *B*'s total of 192 can be obtained—with the remaining 72 scores having therefore a value of 2.

CV. We have seen the limits within which the number of highest scores obtained by *A* and *B* can vary in an example chosen by chance, using always the same totals of opinion of 204 versus 192. And that these same totals and scores can be obtained in 31 different ways, as there lie within the limits we have found another 29—these limits being twenty-eight top scores for *A* against 52 for *B* on the one hand and 58 top scores for *A* versus sixteen for *B* on the other. While maintaining always the same majority of opinion in his favor, the number of top scores that *A* can obtain varies within these very disparate limits. This makes it absolutely evident how false and equivocal an indicator of the majority of opinion is that system in which only the majority of absolute votes of one qualification (or type) is considered—a method which on an endless number of occasions elects someone to whom the electors have not given the majority of their support, were this support to be declared in its entirety and justly evaluated. Ultimately the reader will find that when the success of an election is not dependent on the number of absolute or top votes but on the addition and consideration of all qualifications, the election cannot be invalidated by the desertion of a few unfair electors. Achieving this purpose was the the intent with which we began this investigation, even though it has only been applied to one example.

CVI. All that remains now is to find a general solution to the problem posed by deducing the formula which can be used to find these answers in every case. In finding this solution we will have completed the examinations which we undertook to make on such an important and delicate matter as are elections.

CVII. Before so doing, I must warn that I define a *just* election as one which is thus defined in this matter, and which should more accurately be defined as *justified*: that is, one in which each elector has assigned to each candidate the level of support which in his judgment he deserves in comparison to the rest.

CVIII. I define *desertion* as the exchange of the score which an elector would fairly give to a candidate whom he considers as the most deserving for a lower one which he would give to a less worthy candidate with intent to exalt the latter and abase the former. If we consider carefully the effect which these desertions should have on an election we will see the following:

CIX. That because their purpose is to reduce the quantity of opinion in favor of the worthiest candidate, an increasing number of desertions (of whatever grade) will be required the larger the difference between his score and that of the less worthy candidate whom the desertions favor, i.e., the less worthy the candidate who is to be exalted to the abasement of the worthiest.

CX. That the higher the difference in grade with which the desertion is being made, from the highest grade to 1, the more unjust and hard to commit the desertion becomes.

CXI. That a small number of desertions of the category just described have the same effect as a large number of desertions of other categories, as in the former case, the highest score which the most worthy candidate deserves, is exchanged for the lowest, which should have been assigned to the least worthy candidate.

CXII. That even though, for this reason, fewer desertions are required in this case, there is another factor that counteracts this (which stems from what was said in CIX): that the difference of opinion which one is trying to diminish and indeed abolish represents the highest differential since it is that between the score obtained by the most worthy candidate and that obtained by the least worthy.

CXIII. That desertions made in favor of scores nearer to the higher or intended score are that much easier and more discrete to carry out.

CXIV. That in this case, this ease is counteracted by the larger number of such desertions required in order to negate the majority obtained by the most worthy candidate—since the score is replaced only by a narrowly inferior one.

CXV. That fewer desertions are necessary in order to invalidate a just election if they all favor the same (inferior) candidate—as in this case the points lost by the most worthy candidate all benefit a single opponent whose score increases directly and more rapidly reaches that of the first. The opposite is also true: a larger number of desertions are also needed in order to invalidate the elections when a number of different candidates are favored—in this case, all their respective scores increase more slowly.

CXVI. That (from what was said in CXIV) the lower the original grade assigned to the worthiest candidate by an elector committing a desertion, the larger the number of desertions required to diminish his majority. Thus, more are needed if they are made from the second grade than if they are made from the first, more from the third than from the second. It is understood that, by first grade, I mean the highest score and with reference to it I refer to the rest as second, third, etc. Thus, in an example with seven candidates, seven is the first grade, six the second, five the third, and one the lowest.

CXVII. All these observations are establishing how safe from invalidation is a just election when carried out by the simple method we propose and how difficult it would be to negate it by the actions of a few electors voting unjustly. In addition, all these attributes which are becoming apparent will become yet more so when incorporated into and defined by the general formula which will now be derived.

CXVIII. Let m, n, h, etc., [*sic*] be the number of votes of first grade, second grade, third grade, etc., respectively, from which the total sum of opinion in favor of a candidate, A, has been derived, which sum we will call s. By multiplying each factor by its corresponding value or grade, we obtain the following voting total: $cm + n(c - 1) + h(c - 2)$ etc. $+ e - m - n - h = s$.

CXIX. Let p, q, r, etc., be likewise the number of votes of first grade, second grade, third grade etc., respectively, from which the total sum of opinion in favor of a second candidate, B, has been derived, this total being less than A's by a certain amount, which we will call d. We shall use the same symbols as in earlier calculations in this report. By multiplying each factor by its corresponding value or grade, we obtain the B's corresponding voting total: $pc + q(c - 1) + r(c - 2)$ etc. $+ e - p - q - r = s - d$.

CXX. Simplifying both equations, we have:

(A) . . . $m(c - 1) + n(c - 2) + h(c - 3) +$ etc. $= s - e$

(B) . . . $p(c - 1) + q(c - 2) + r(c - 3) +$ etc. $= s - e - d$.

CXXI. With these assumptions, the object is to ascertain *the number of desertions necessary for* B's *total or score to reach or equal that of* A, assuming at this stage that the desertions occur from the highest qualification, c, to any other grade, which we shall call g, and that in such desertions the higher scores given to A are exchanged for the lower ones, of whatever grade (g) which corresponded to B.

CXXII. Let x be the number of such desertions. The effect of these is to reduce the number of top scores in A's total to $m - x$. In their stead, A's score must be incremented by a number x of scores of value or grade g. Accounting for these desertions alters the first term of the main equation (CXVIII), which now represents A's revised total of opinion, to the following, $c(m - x) +$

$n(c - 1) + h(c - 2)$ etc. $+ e - m - n - h + gx$, which can be simplified to: $m(c - 1) + n(c - 2) + h(c - 3)$ etc. $+ e - x(c - g)$.

CXXIII. By applying the same reasoning to the equation (CXIX) representing B's total of opinion—which process involves adding the top scores subtracted from A and in turn removing x number of inferior qualifications of value g (for which the former were exchanged) from that same total, we observe that the first term of that equation then changes as follows, leading to the following equation representing B's new vote and total of opinion after the desertions: $c(p + x) + q(c - 1) + r(c - 2)$ etc. $+ e - p - q - r - gx$, which simplifies to $p(c - 1) + q(c - 2) + r(c - 3)$ etc. $+ e + x(c - g)$.

CXXIV. This term representing the opinion of B and the one representing that of A (CXXII) must be equivalent, as they both represent their respective totals of opinion having accounted for the desertions. In this instance of the two expressions being equal, x represents the exact number of desertions required in order to bring B to at least draw with A in the election. The equation is thus $m(c - 1) + n(c - 2) + h(c - 3)$ etc. $+ e - x(c - g) = p(c - 1) + q(c - 2) + r(c - 3)$ etc. $+ e + x(c - g)$.

CXXV. If we now go back to No. CXX, in which the values of the two following series were found, $m(c - 1) + n(c - 2) + h(c - 3)$ etc. $= s - e$ and $p(c - 1) + q(c - 2) + r(c - 3)$ etc. $= s - e - d$, by substituting the values for these series into the equation obtained in the previous section, we have $s - e + e - x(c - g) = s - e - d + e + x(c - g)$, which reduces to $2x(c - g) = d$. From this equation we obtain finally the following general formula: $x = d/[2(c - g)]$.

CXXVI. Had we assumed the desertions to be taking place not from the highest level or score, c, but from the next one down, i.e., $(c - 1)$, to a lower grade, d, then n would become $n - x$, and applying the same reasoning as before, the formula now becomes $x = d/[2(c - 1 - g)]$, which differs from the original only in the factor which we have chosen to alter, since in this case, the qualification from which the desertion is made (c) becomes $c - 1$, and g is the grade to which the desertion is made.

CXXVII. The general rule in all cases as derived from the formula is as follows: that in order to at least equal the score of the most worthy candidate, the number of desertions necessary is equal to half the difference or majority of opinion between that of the most worthy candidate and any other candidate (whose score might reach the former's) divided by the difference between the two scores exchanged—given that both these scores can take any values and that all desertions favor a single candidate.

CXXVIII. For example, take six candidates among whom A has a score forty points higher than B (B being his closest competitor or the worthiest candidate after him). In order for B to be chosen instead of A, *more than four desertions in which a 6 is exchanged for a 1 are needed; more than five* from a 6 to a 2 or from a 5 to a 1; more than seven from a 6 to a 3 or from a 4 to a 1, etc. All this is necessary for the smallest of injustices possible to occur—since we have assumed that *B* is the most worthy candidate after *A*, or the one whose score is nearest to his. It is evident that many more desertions are needed in order for *A* to be beaten by one of the candidates of lowest worth.

CXXIX. As the denominator in the expression $d/[2(c - g)]$ is the difference between the qualifications exchanged, the value of the fraction (and therefore that of *x*) will increase as this denominator decreases, i.e., as the difference between the qualifications decreases—this property has been stated previously (CXIV). Also the higher the value of the numerator *d*, i.e., the larger the difference between *A* and his competitor, the more desertions will be required, as has been explained (CIX).

CXXX. In this way, every single property mentioned between Nos. CIX and CXVI could be described in detail, since all of these properties are contained in this very simple formula. However, as we have been unable to avoid other repetitions, we would wish to avoid this one.

CXXXI. However, it is worth pointing out that the same differences (of ten, twenty, thirty units) indicate a higher majority of opinion when there are fewer electors, other conditions remaining the same. This knowledge may be useful in cases in which a "consolation prize" were required for the runner-up: the difference in the score required for this could be increased or decreased depending on the larger or smaller number of electors or censors.

CXXXII. The calculations which we have applied to the theory of elections are totally unnecessary for the purpose of using and carrying them out, provided the method we suggest is followed, by reducing it to the very simple operation we described (LXXXIV). However, these calculations were necessary in order to prove its accuracy and the favorable properties by which this method assures fair elections by preventing the abuse of the system—as it is the only fair way of assessing opinion in order to decide the outcome of elections by the majority of it. These calculations were also necessary in order to demonstrate how incorrect, unjust, and ridiculous are the methods of election currently used, all of which involve absolute votes of one qualification the majority of which is generally assumed to represent the majority of opinion. Thus a grave injustice is committed in this very crucial matter.

CXXXIII. The last question remaining to be examined is *whether there are any elections in which absolute majority may be considered sufficient without the need to resort to the rigor and accuracy of this method of compensation and addition.* Of course we agree that there are. However, without intending to answer the very delicate political question of which are precisely these elections, let us deduce the rules to be applied by examining the differing nature of elections. Firstly, as we said in the preface, absolute majority suffices in all "deliberations." Not only because these are not elections properly speaking but also because they imply doing or not doing, approving or not approving of something, they are equivalent to a decision in an election between only two candidates, in which the absolute majority of votes corresponds inevitably to the majority of opinion, independently of the number of electors (XLV). In what concerns elections properly speaking, the results sought after in many cases do not depend on the levels of support which the electors' judgment assigns to each candidate on the list. In such elections one seeks more directly the result of the *general will* of the electors, as is the case in elections by exclusion, reduction, and generally in all elections by elimination. And even if the expression of the will of each elector is preceded by a more or less deliberate act of comparison, will itself is not expressed by grades as is opinion. For that same reason, absolute majority is sufficient not only in popular elections where these are performing a sovereign role but also in any others (although these will be fewer in number) the object of which is to represent the free will of the electors—since also, in this case, the result sought after is the expression of the general will. Absolute majority represents and expresses the general will whenever possible; or, put a better way, amongst opposite wills which do not reach a balance due to unequal competition, absolute majority becomes law, as close as possible to the principles of natural justice and as analogous to the conditions which serve as a basis for social order. However, outside the scope of the elections we have just described and those similar to them, there is an endless number of elections in very frequent and daily use within political organizations in which the result sought after is purely in terms of opinion. These have been the main aims of the Legislature and also of this work. The method of compensation and addition must be applied to all of these if one is to obtain a true and therefore fair result—since preponderance of opinion is independent of the number of absolute votes of one qualification, that is, it bears a different relationship to that number in each case. And any majority of such votes is a false and inaccurate indicator of the fairness of the election unless it is considered jointly with other conditions which are never taken into account. It is these conditions which lead to the analytical equations derived in this report. Finally, in what concerns relative majority, we have already said (LXVI) that it is in all cases the most absurd and unjust of all methods. Elections determined by relative majority are more transactions than elections, in which justice is left aside, and it is not permissible to ignore justice except in situations where the possibility of violating it does not apply since justice itself is not being administered.

CXXXIV. If good order demands compliance with statutes and laws while they are in use, then the same good order will demand their reform whenever it becomes apparent that they are no longer based on equality and justice. We know what means authority can employ to bring this about; but the only means available to reason is to examine, enlighten, and convince before bringing change about. Indeed, a large number of human institutions have already been improved and perfected by the use of observation and analysis. Any improvement brought about by this means should not displease the less passionate lovers of change if, on the other hand, they are, as they should be, greater lovers of justice and truth. Analysis, the tool which in this century our and other nations have used in order to shed light upon and rectify different areas of their legislation, is the same tool which now, although tardily, reveals the elements of opinion and determines in elections the results of a theory as rigorous as that applied to the most precisely defined object. And finally it succeeds in demonstrating on the one hand that a method seemingly so obvious and simple can be subjected to less facile and less obvious investigations, on the other hand, that a practice used so frequently in society, and so important to it, as elections can be based if we so wish on clear and precise principles of equality and justice.

Conclusion

Finally, without wishing to congratulate myself in having, for the first time, subjected to calculation a matter which had not been treated thus before, my only wish is to have carried out a useful task.

Lately, treatises on elections have been written which, if not many in number nor great in quality, are at least very good. The effect that elections have on the well-being of the public means that never before has so much attention been paid to this subject as now, as methods to discover the truth are coming so close to perfection. Those philosophers who have recently dealt with this matter, have treated it more as politicians than mathematicians, though they are both to the highest degree. Assuming opinion to be expressed always by absolute votes and its majority indicated by their majority, they then turned their attention to other political and governmental issues relating to the right to choose and be chosen, to the legitimacy of representation, and to the means of determining the result or expression of general will in the formulation of laws, etc. However, the different circumstances which give rise to an investigation affect its objective in such a way that they change completely its relationship to other things. The crucial political issues which these wise men proposed to resolve, have nothing in common with those problems which we have analysed and solved herein, by considering opinion from a different point of view to which no attention had been paid before. In a word, these wise men considered opinion always independently to the method of assessing and expressing it; or, better put, they assumed it to be assessed and expressed by the means currently in use.[10]

In the analytical examination which I have carried out of this matter, I have limited myself to the solution of such problems and questions which were better able to illustrate it, without delving into others whose object would have merely been to satisfy curiosity. Rather than undertaking a vain display of arithmetical skills, I have preferred to be understood by all: thus I have used examples at the beginning which I have gone on to repeat more often than those who are used to expressing everything in terms of algebraic expressions and formulae might have wished. I have done this, therefore, in order to guide the common reader along the path of this investigation from first principles and to relieve them of the difficulty of having to understand all the interrelationships in the method which multiply as the investigation proceeds. I hope that by taking into account these difficulties, those readers among the wise will be indulgent toward the essay presented on this theory for which I have, on occasions, had to define a new nomenclature, which I have tried to make as clear and precise as possible by attempting to derive it from its only true source, which is analogy.

Some readers may notice the lack of erudition in this work, for the sake of which I should have referred the origin of the electoral methods in practice and make inclusion of the civil and canonical dispositions on this matter. I have omitted to do this in order not to burden this report with matters that bear no relation to the main aim of any work designed to prove the existence of an error and abuse and its negative consequences. Quotations have no place in what attempts to prove and to convince. If as it stands, this work (which contains no more than relates to the display and the use of reason) is of no use or merit in order to portray the opinion of government and of the public, then it would be no more useful if I added to it what is most easy, which is that relating to erudition and the use of books.

Note

I have reserved for this note an observation concerning the article in which the learned editors of the *Décade Philosophique* publish and describe the method for elections adopted by the National Institute of France.

I note therefore that the article in the aforesaid periodical, which we have used as a preface, refers to this method only as simple and convenient. This is

---

10. [It is clear that this paragraph cannot refer to Condorcet, Laplace, or any of their contemporaries translated in this book, as Morales believes himself to be the first mathematical theorist of voting. Perhaps the reference is to earlier Enlightenment writers such as Diderot or d'Alembert; or conceivably to Madison, Hamilton, or Jefferson.]

a very weak description and, speaking frankly, the least truthful which this method deserves if we compare it to other methods in use. It leaves me with no doubt that this description was not borne out of the analytical examination which has been carried out or published of their theory in comparison with others by subjecting to calculation the questions which it poses, indeed, I believe that their method is more accurate and rigorous than any other, even without having to consider analytically its accuracy and its limits. For if that were the case, even if nothing was mentioned of the principles on which this theory was based or of the problems and questions which it poses, its results would at least be presented with the just acclaim and desire for reform which they inspire. In such an instance, this method would not be so half-heartedly recommended for large elections—as we have shown (CXXXIII) that the differing nature of elections is not dependent on their size. The nature of elections (a criterion which should be used in order to decide in favor of one method or another) depends on other principles and considerations, and in addition, we have proved in various instances in this memoir that most of the basic disadvantages of modern-day elections are independent of the number of electors. At the very least, the *Décade* should have suggested what the only just reason is for choosing this method—that other methods are false and unfair. And this would be more truthful than the other characteristics hinted at, that they are less simple or less convenient.

Had the theory of opinion been analysed and its elements written down, the current methods of election would have been rebuked in Europe some considerable time ago. This would be especially true in a nation which has been singled out as exemplary in which the last problem remaining to be solved is that of elections. As proof of the fact that no treatise or book has been published to date relating to this matter from the point of view from which we have considered it, we shall relate a recent happening which, having taken place after the printing of this paper, forces us to extend this note.

The law of 25 Fructidor, an III (11 September 1795), according to which the National Convention dictated the election for certain offices by absolute majority, and the example of the National Institute which a year ago adopted the method of compensation and addition described herein for its elections had not had any effect in improving the most viciously unjust electoral procedures which have been used until now by the Legislative Body, where elections to the offices of the highest importance and even to the chief magistracy of the Republic have been determined by relative majority.

In the sessions of the Council of 500 of the 21st and 22nd of May of this year (as can be seen in all articles which contain or summarize them), a motion by Boissy has been put forward and discussed, the summary of which is as follows:

Boissy points out the disadvantages of elections by relative majority. He referred to the statements with which Representative Daunou had criticized this method when in September 1795, the Convention attempted to resolve the format of certain elections. Boissy expresses his surprise at the fact that despite the forceful reasons that were given for this at the time, we are still victim to the errors and absurdities resulting from elections by absolute majority. By its use, two- or three-tenths of the electorate can place in the highest offices subjects who hold against them a considerable majority of opinion. Elections by exclusion could indeed diminish the effects of such a drawback. However, this type of election is not employed for candidates presented by the Council of 500 to the Council of Elders for the posts of Director or commissioner for the National Treasury. The practice currently in use is to present a list of ten candidates chosen by us by relative majority, for each of these posts, to the Elders. This same erroneous majority is then used by the Elders in order to elect one of the ten candidates on each list.

Why then are elections to the most important and delicate offices in the Republic left to the chance of obtaining a single casting vote? No matter how honorable the electors, this cannot be a sufficient reason when the object of the election is so important. If the representatives are men and, like all other men, liable to prejudice and error, then they will be even more vulnerable than the rest to passions and the influence of party political philosophies. The one-third of each of the two Councils which is reelected every year can easily be tricked and deceived in the elections by the other two-thirds with the need for just a little cooperation between them. For the same reason that in such a vast Republic there is such an abundance of worthy subjects, the inevitable clashes of well-intended opinions can more easily favor obscure or men of dubious repute. Seventy votes out of the five hundred can suffice to give a mere manipulative victory over a Colbert. And this victory is easier and better assured the larger the number of meritorious subjects who are in competition with each other. In such a case, where sensible electors driven only by the spirit of justice and worthiness would be divided among a L'Hôpital, a d'Aguesseau, a Sully, and a Turena, other intriguers would take advantage of this division, unite, and replace these great talents by the mediocre qualities of men more within the grasp of their sinister projects.[11]

---

11. [The people mentioned in these paragraphs are

 Colbert, J. B. (1619–1683), famous administrator and reformer of the public finances of France, reshaped the navy and tried to plan the entire economy; founder of the Academy of Science; tireless and ruthless;

 L'Hôpital, M. de (ca.1505–1573), French politician, Chancellor of France 1560–1568, tried to protect Protestants from religious persecution;

 d'Aguesseau, H. F. (1668–1751), chancellor of France 1717–1718, 1720–1722, and 1727–1737; noted legal reformer;

 Sully, duc de (1560–1641), French Protestant politician, leading statesman un-

Boissy concludes by proposing the repeal of articles 1 and 2 of the fourth volume of the aforementioned law of 11 September 1795 and that the Legislative Body determine the results of its future elections by means of absolute majority. (Taken principally from *La Clef du Cabinet des Souverains* No. 124.)

Such is the summary of the speech delivered by Boissy during the session of May 21st of this year. The following day, having heard the report by a commission, drawn up by Camille-Jourdan, Boissy's motion or proposal was decreed and adopted by the Council of 500.

From this we infer (1) that the least reliable of all methods of election, that of relative majority, has until now been used by the Legislative Body of France, even in the most crucial and important elections. (2) That since there is no mention in any of the speeches which gave rise to this discussion of any work or printed treatise on this matter, one can safely assume that none exists. For if one were in existence in which the theory of elections had been subjected to calculations, analytical results would have been produced in support of such sensible arguments, or instead of them.

---

der the Protestant King Henri IV, Superintendent of Finance 1598–1611, economic and military reformer; and

Turena, which is probably a Spanish version of the name of Turenne, H., vicomte de (1611–1675), French military officer; Marshal of France 1643; briefly joined the Fronde insurrection 1648–1650 but rejoined the royal army 1651; many campaigns, most of them successful, in various wars from then until his death in battle.]

CHAPTER 11

P. C. F. Daunou

A Paper on Elections by Ballot, 1803

Extract from the minutes of the Moral Science and Politics division, 12 thermidor, an VIII [31 July 1800]

The division decrees that citizen Daunou's paper on elections by ballot be printed at its expense and distributed to the members of the Institute.

Signed in the record book, Levesque, secretary

Certified true extract: Joachim Lebreton, secretary

We can, and should, set ourselves two aims in any election method: to obtain good choices and to establish correctly the real will of the voters. On the one hand, we must ensure that the general will is enlightened, honest, and equitable and on the other that it is accurately and faithfully expressed. Not only must the candidate elected be worthy of the votes, he must actually have obtained them. The election result must, that is, be more than intrinsically good; it must also be demonstrably true.

A variety of more or less effective measures can be taken to fulfill our first aim of obtaining good choices: we set conditions about the number and qualifications of the voters, their equal or unequal influence, and their joint or separate functions; about the number and qualifications of candidates and the way in which they are nominated, whether individual votes are secret or public and the extent to which chance is allowed to affect each stage of the election.

And in order to fulfill our second aim of discovering the candidate who is truly elected, we regulate the way in which the votes are given, collected, and assessed.

So, on the one hand, we organize the electoral body in such a way that it both can and wants to make good choices in as many cases as possible. We exclude candidates whose suitability cannot be assumed and try to guarantee the liberty and morality of votes and to prevent or control intrigue and ambition.

And on the other, we concentrate on obtaining a precise statement of the questions to be answered about the candidates; we ensure that each voter gives his answers clearly, accurately, and completely and that when the votes have been carefully collected and compared, there can be no question about the true result.

The first of these aims is undoubtedly the more important, bearing as it does on more political viewpoints and moral observations. In this paper, however, I shall deal only with the second. My discussion of the methods of obtaining intrinsically good choices will relate only to the way in which these methods can affect the verification of the general will.

These two matters are so distinct that confusing them can lead only to problems. I have chosen to begin with the one which, while doubtless drier and less appealing, is also further removed from political controversy and seems likely to have more accurate or more immediately verifiable solutions.

However intelligent and efficient the rules designed to maximize the inner goodness of the individual wills of a corporate body, it can only ever be made very probable. While we can certainly take enough precautions to render absolutely bad choices impossible, it is far more difficult to ensure that the candidate elected is always the best of all those who were eligible. It is indeed possible that no method could produce this goal that is reconcilable with the liberty of the voters and consequently with any errors in their ideas or partiality in their affections.

The second goal seems more attainable, since it is simply a question of recognizing the facts. I am aware that it is not always easy to check a fact, but here we can at least enlist the help of mathematics. The work involved may be long, awkward, and tiring, but it does seem to promise sufficiently rigorous results.

In this paper, then, the words *election method* will be used solely to mean the measures which help to verify the positive results of an election. My examination will be divided into three sections; first, the conditions an election method must satisfy; second, to what extent the methods implemented or suggested so far have satisfied these conditions; and third, what improvements could be made to these methods.

Part One

Conditions Which an Election Method Must Satisfy

It would clearly be inconsistent if we aimed through an election method, as I have just defined it, both to obtain intrinsically good choices and to check the positive will, if we tried to use it not simply to recognize the results but also to correct them. Either the rules relating to the right to elect and to be elected are well devised, in which case we can assume that the actual choice will also be the best, or else these rules are bad and it is they which must be corrected. The way to remedy the defects of these particular rules is not to fundamentally corrupt the others.

If everything is devised so that the truest result must also be the most worthy, we need simply concentrate on checking carefully. If on the other hand, we think that the actual result is not a good one, we must try, if we can, to find a better system of voters and eligible candidates. Now, if we consider the best choice and the actual choice to be two distinct things, it would be unreasonable to attempt to fulfill two diverse aims at once, and to intend either to improve things by checking or to check things by trying to improve them. As we shall see, these ideas have often been confused, but to do so is to have no clear intentions, to take the least decisive course, and to have no real idea of what we want.

First Maxim

I therefore feel able to take as my first maxim that the two parts of a law on elections—relating to their intrinsic goodness and to their simple verification —must be so closely linked that they never interfere with one another. The measures we take to obtain good results must never compromise truth. As soon as we depart from this maxim, our elections are reduced to uncertainty, inconsistency, randomness, and confusion.

Since an election method aims to discover the general will, we need to know what this will comprises.

Except in the case of unanimity, which presents no problem, we have generally taken the general will to be the will of the greatest number. But what is the greatest number?

If we had never debated anything but simple questions which could be answered in just two ways, *the greatest number* would never have meant anything but an absolute majority, that is, more than half of the people debating.

But complex questions which can be resolved in more than two ways can divide an assembly into more than two groups. When one of these is weaker than all of the others taken together, but stronger than each taken individually, it is called a *relative plurality.*

Since the voters are assumed to have equal rights, we need to know, in ordinary debates or in elections, to whom we should attribute the character and authority of the general will, whether to the relative plurality, to a strictly absolute majority, or to a majority in some way greater than absolute—that is, increased to two-thirds or three-quarters or indeed to any fraction greater than half. We must distinguish between cases in which there are just two opinions and those in which there are more than two.

The first case can be subdivided. Either one of the two opinions is positive and the other negative—that is, a simple rejection of the first—or else they are both positive, in which case either it is essential to select one of them or possible to reject both.

When one of two positive opinions has to be chosen, the character and authority of the general will has been given to half of the voters, plus one. It was clearly felt that giving the smaller number an active influence over the greater would contradict the hypothesis of equal rights.

But when we can reject both opinions, it is of course reasonable to demand more than simple majority support before an opinion is adopted. For this rule to be legitimate, it must simply have been agreed before the debate it affects.

Precisely the same is true for the case in which one opinion is positive and the other negative. It can be declared in advance that for particular subjects and in particular circumstances, a positive opinion would be passed only by a majority of two-thirds or three-quarters.

These two exceptions to the natural power of a strictly absolute majority can have beneficial effects, or at least prevent hurried or harmful debates. They have sometimes been effective in legislative debates, and especially in criminal judgments. They are, however, simply free conventions, whereas the authority of the absolute majority, which never changes, would be a necessary and immediate rule in any primitive association of debaters with equal rights.

When the voters must choose between three opinions, or a larger number of positive opinions, our first aim should be to ascertain that no absolute majority has given a preference to one opinion over all of the others. A preference of this kind would obviously make this opinion prevail.

The only case in which a positive opinion can be accepted with a plurality of less than half is when none of the opinions between which a choice must be made obtains an absolute majority of votes.

From this it follows that we should not consider all the various pluralities between one and unanimity from the same point of view and that we must take great care in our calculations not to treat them all as quantities of the same moral kind. The crucial difference is that pluralities of less than half only accidentally, by virtue of special conventions, represent the voters as a whole, whereas pluralities of more than half naturally represent them in all cases and necessarily represent them whenever they express a negative will or one of the positive opinions between which a choice must be made.

Second Maxim

Since these points apply directly to elections, I shall take as my second general maxim for rules on elections that if one of the candidates for a place is preferred by half of the voters plus one, then it is he who will be elected, if it is essential that someone is.

But this absolute majority in favor of one of the candidates does not always exist, or is not always evident. It is here that the problems begin.

It would be very strange if our attempts to resolve these problems extended them to cases they do not affect. Uncertainty between the candidates who have obtained less than half of the votes does not mean that we should disregard and jeopardize the rights of a candidate who has actually been elected by more than half of the voters. Why confuse what is obvious in an attempt to explain what is not?

While it often happens that an individual ballot between several candidates produces no absolute majority, we should not conclude from this that none of the candidates has majority support. Even if out of a total of ninety-nine votes, thirty-three are initially given to each out of A, B, and C, it is quite possible that another vote between the same three candidates taken two by two will show that A is successively preferred by a majority, perhaps even of two-thirds, to each of the other two. This requires only that the thirty-three who voted for C prefer A to B and that those who voted for B prefer A to C.

It seems therefore that we simply need to divide the question and to successively put forward each of its component parts, that is, to ask which of A and B is better, then which of A and C, and finally, if necessary, which of B and C. This is indeed sufficient, and the first two questions alone suffice in the situation we are imagining, that is, when most of the voters who do not rank candidate A in first place would rank him second.

But what if we divide the question and then find that A beats B and that C beats A. Should we conclude from this that C should indeed be elected? This seems quite logical at first glance; how could C, who is better than A, not also be better than B, who has just been judged worse than A?

This logic is quite acceptable as long as it is applied to the successive judgments of a single person. Any man who agreed to these two propositions and then accepted the contradictory of their necessary conclusion would be behaving unreasonably. But as we shall soon see, an electoral body can support a third proposition which contradicts the first two without the slightest inconsistency on the part of any individual voter.

Do you believe that just because a debating body accepts the premises when we successively put to the vote each of the three component propositions of the most conclusive syllogism, it must necessarily accept the conclusion? Suppose that there are 100 voters and that their opinions are of three types: 49 vote in favor of the major premise and against the minor one, 49 support the minor and not the major, and 2 support both. This gives the major premise 51 votes—that is, the 49 first ones and the 2 which support everything. The minor premise also obtains a total of 51, with the 2 votes in support of everything plus the 49 second votes, so both the major and the minor are adopted. If we do not stop there but risk debating the conclusion, it could be rejected by a majority of 98, for only 2 members are strictly obliged to accept it. The 49 who rejected the major and the 49 who rejected the minor have no further responsibilities as regards the conclusion than their desire in such a case to sacrifice their personal opinions.

Of course, if the syllogism was purely speculative and would have no affect on anyone's personal circumstances, we could be quite content with voting on the premises and proclaiming the conclusion by a sort of victor's right. It might, however, be better to debate only the conclusion, and the result would be very different depending on which of these two methods we followed. For if we debate only the premises, the conclusion is passed; whereas if we debate only the conclusion, it is not passed, which seems if not more just in itself, then at least more in conformity with the opinion of the body we consulted. In any case, if each voter is told to express a clear opinion on each of the three propositions on the same ballot paper, the major would obtain 51 votes, and the minor the same number, but the conclusion would be rejected by 98 votes.

But when the debate is an election and involves the determination of personal rights, there would be no equity in limiting ourselves to the first two questions, and in wanting to conclude from these the solution to the third. For the voters' preferences may be such that they result in the election of C, A, or B, depending on whether the pairwise comparisons began with A and B, or B and C, or C and A. Everything depends on the order we follow. If this order is arbitrary, the election will be too; if it is left to chance, so will the election be, and if we use some procedure to determine it, it would be better to apply that procedure directly to the election itself.

So that no doubt is left about the points I have just made, which were clarified but not proved by the example of the syllogism, we must examine some actual elections.

Suppose that there are 100 voters and three candidates, A, B, and C, and that the first ballot is held between A and B. A obtains 70 votes and B just 30. B is rejected, and we now consider it simply a matter of comparing A and C. C obtains 70 votes and A just 30. My claim is that if we infer from this that C is elected, this seemingly legitimate conclusion will not only be hasty but also false. For when we compare C and B, we may still find an absolute majority of 60 votes against C and in favor of candidate B, who had been rejected. To illustrate this point, suppose that the number 100 is divided into three parts of 40, 30, and 30. There may be 40 voters who prefer A to B and then C to A and who conclude from this that C is better than B. But there may also be 30 voters who, having been part of the majority in support of A and against B, then formed the minority for A against C, and 30 others who, before becoming part of the majority for C against A, had been part of the minority for B against A;

and these last two distinct and separate groups of voters may easily form a majority of 60 votes in favor of B against C. Note that if we had begun with a ballot between C and B and then between B and A, B would have obtained 60 votes in the first ballot and A 70 in the second, and we would have felt able to conclude that A was elected. Similarly, if the ballots had been first between A and C and then between C and B, 70 votes for C in the first ballot and 60 for B in the second would have seemed to determine B's election. Conclusions can only be drawn from pairwise comparisons between the candidates when the same candidate beats one opponent in the first ballot and the other in the second.

Obtaining a third result which contradicts the natural conclusion of the first two is by no means a rare occurrence. All that is required is that the two minorities for the premises form a distinct and separate sum of voters, greater than half of the electoral body. This may often be the case.

With 100 voters, there are 48 chances which may lead to a conclusion which contradicts the premises, that is, those in which the sum of the two minorities is between 51 and 98. While with a total of just 51, the two minorities would have to have no common members for the contradictory conclusion to remain possible. As this total increases from 52 to 98, the composition of the minorities becomes less rigid, and the probability of obtaining a third result which contradicts the first two increases appreciably.

Examining Borda counts to see the manner in which the pairwise comparisons between the candidates are made, we often find contradictory propositions supported by majorities that are more than just absolute. Suppose 100 ballot papers, where the six possible combinations of A, B, and C are distributed more or less as follows; 30 with $A3$, $B2$, $C1$; 4 with $A3$, $C2$, $B1$; 3 with $B3$, $A2$, $C1$; 26 with $B3$, $C2$, $A1$; 36 with $C3$, $A2$, $B1$; and just 1 with $C3$, $B2$, $A1$. This would give 70 voters who prefer A to B, 63 who prefer C to A, and finally 59 who prefer B to C, which contradicts the consequence of the first two.[1]

An electoral body choosing among three candidates may often be so placed that an absolute majority prefers each candidate to one of his opponents and not to the other, so that no candidate is preferred to both of the others. Whenever this is the case, it produces three irreconcilable propositions, all of which have the support of different absolute majorities.

It is important to recognize this fact because it is the only real case of

---

1. [In modern notation this would be

30	4	3	26	36	1
A	A	B	B	C	C
B	C	A	C	A	B
C	B	C	A	B	A]

serious problems in elections. It highlights the truly difficult cases and sepa-rates them from those which only appear to be difficult and from those which are not difficult at all.

If there is an absolute majority which ranks one of the candidates in first place, then that candidate is elected and there is no problem.

If there is an absolute majority which, while not directly ranking one of the candidates in first place, prefers him positively—and not just as an indi-rect consequence—to each of the others taken individually, then this candi-date must be considered elected. The difficulty here was only apparent.

But when no candidate is preferred by an absolute majority, either to all of the other candidates together, or to each of them individually, nothing can then be reasonably decided either for or against any one of them. This is the biggest problem we can come across in an election.

In the last case, if it is not absolutely necessary to elect someone, the best solution is to abstain and to adjourn the election for a very long time. But if a result has to be obtained when there is no form of absolute majority, only a relative plurality can represent the general will.

This relative plurality can artificially be given the name and appearance of an absolute majority, either by forcing some of the voters to reject their first votes or by making the number of votes double, three times, or many times the number of debaters. But we are trying to find the real result, and in this example that could never be more than a relative plurality, since we have checked that there is no absolute majority.

These methods should aim simply to discover the relative plurality and the candidate who obtains it. They will be inaccurate if they divert the election to any other aim. They would be faultier still if, when applied to cases in which an absolute majority exists, they could frustrate its will and make that of the minority prevail.

Summary

These are the general points which should be made about the nature of elections. It is from them that I have deduced the maxims which I shall briefly summarize.

To make the rules relating to the accuracy of choices compatible with those relating to checking the results; never to consider anything which could be used to render the result false as a method of obtaining good choices.

To guarantee the rights of the absolute majority of voters and to ensure first that any candidate expressly rejected by this majority can never be elected, and second that no one can be elected in preference to a candidate preferred by this majority to all others, whether collectively or one at a time.

To recognize and clearly distinguish cases in which there is no absolute majority, whether evident or hidden, and not to extend methods designed to find the relative plurality when there is no absolute majority to cases in which an absolute majority exists.

All these rules derive from the premises that I have taken as facts: the equality of the voters, the representation of the universal will by the will of the greatest section, and the determination of the general will by simply counting individual wills, with no regard to their greater or lesser probability of accuracy or to their various intensities.

However, as we shall see in part two of this paper, some election methods take into account two very different elements in order to calculate the general will, that is, the number of votes and their intensity. This system, which runs counter to the hypotheses I have been using so far, needs special examination. I will have achieved nothing if I do not prove what I assumed in the first place, that, except in cases of unanimity, only the will of the greatest number of voters, without regard to the intensity of the votes, can be taken as an expression of the general will. I would have begun with this, but felt that it might confuse the issue if I examined it first.

Personal affection certainly has some power, of which it could not be completely deprived. A voter who wants something more strongly than another is more active, more devoted, and more inflexible; he is better able to reject the arguments against his will, and it is more difficult to resist his. It is in the very nature of things that his influence is increased by the strength of his will, but I consider it neither useful nor in the interests of society to give more value to votes which are more intense.

Intensity of Preference

A strong will is already too powerful on its own. While society may owe some outstanding benefits to strong-willed men, it also owes them a greater number of infamous disasters and above all, an infinite number of smaller problems. Just, enlightened, and healthy affection is often cold and diffident, and, sadly, uncontrolled feelings are usually the most intense. I am inclined to believe that human debates were established mainly to reduce the power of strong feelings to the level of calmer ones. The first condition in any debate should therefore be that all votes will have equal value, whatever their consistency, scope, and strength.

We noted above that anything which is to be debated accurately should be presented in the simplest terms and should therefore, if it is complex, be carefully divided. We saw that all elections between several candidates can be broken down into as many simple questions as there are comparisons to be made between the candidates taken two by two; so that everything was reduced each time to deciding which of A or B should win. Having posed the question in this way, how could the 30 voters who vote for B possibly say to the 70 who vote for A, "True, there are only 30 of us, but each of us prefers B to A four times more than each of you prefers A to B. Our vote for B can therefore be expressed by 120, while your vote for A is just 70. A is more often voted for, but B is elected because he is wanted more." This way of talking and the system it represents, seems to me simply the destruction of all deliberative institutions, since it places society under the control of the strongest wills and even enslaves it to the will of the man who can say "I alone want something more than all of you put together."

These criticisms will become clear if we examine the theory I am attacking.

To carry out this method properly, or at least in a way which is not totally fantastic, each individual voter must have a fairly exact measure of the intensity of his own votes. He must always want to express this intensity truthfully, and must be able to express it accurately.

Our first problem is to find a voter who, when asked to pronounce on ten candidates, can conceive of such fixed and clear relationships between them that he can say to himself, "Out of all the possible numbers, these are the ten which precisely, or at least very nearly, represent the various degrees of my respect for the candidates." But even if this voter has a fixed opinion on the order of the candidates, the reasons which determine this order today may be so ephemeral that he could not reproduce them in four days' time, or even tomorrow, if he has not noted them down. But it is not just a question of the order, but of measuring the intensity of preferences. It is not enough for the voter to know which candidate he prefers; out of an indefinite number of ways of preferring one candidate to another, he must give a precise account of the preference for each candidate compared to each of the others; he must perceive a clear relationship between the first and the second, which of course may well not be the same as that between the second and the third, or indeed between any two of the others. To ask this of him would in fact be to require him to express opinions he has not usually formed.

Besides, even if he does have an opinion on these delicate questions, how can we be certain that he will want to express it sincerely? Although we try to ask his whole conscience, it may be just one particular part of his affection which replies. His most dominating concern is to ensure that one particular candidate beats his most dangerous opponents. This may be the only will which he expresses with all its possible intensity and the sole aim to which he subjects all the combinations about which we ask him. To make his will stronger and more effective, he will want just one thing; he will only, so to speak, put one weight in the balance, but he will choose the heaviest of all those you make available.

Even if this voter intended to express clear and positive opinions with religious integrity, what clear and accurate signs could he use to represent the degrees of intensity of his votes? We dare not allow him to use any number, integer, or fraction, positive or negative, because of the great inequality this would give the value of votes. And yet if we restrict him to the terms of any fixed series, we deprive him of the means to give an exact expression of the relationships he perceives between the candidates. If I can use only the numbers 3, 2, and 1 to vote on A, B and C, then while these numbers represent the order in which I rank the three candidates, they do not act as a measure of my preference. If, for example, I consider that A is 100 times better than B and that C is only $1/10,000$ worse than B, then I should be allowed to write A 100, B 1, C 0.9999.

My ranking of a candidate and my appreciation of his merit compared to each of his opponents are two such distinct ideas that I can hardly believe they have ever been confused. The rank varies according to the number of candidates, but their relationship is constant, and neither adding nor withdrawing a few candidates can alter it. If I consider that B is worth half as much as A, the relationship does not change when I fill the space between A and B with several intermediaries. Whether I place C, D, E, and F before or after A or B, I still consider that A is precisely twice as good as B; no more and no less. The line of merit is infinitely divisible, and the distance between two unchanging points on this line is the same even when all the divisions have been made.

To see how unreasonable it is to express relative merit by signs of rank, we need only apply the considerations we have been applying to moral questions to purely physical quantities instead. The heights of a six foot man and a five foot one are in the ratio 6:5. The numbers 6 and 5 express a constant ratio, and as long as we are dealing with just these two men, no one would be tempted to express their relationship by the numbers of their rank, that is by the numbers 2 and 1, which signify that the first is double the second. But if there are an additional eight men, giving a total of ten men to compare, substituting ranks for ratios produces very strange results. If the eight newcomers all measure between five and six foot, then the first two will be ranked at the two extremes and assigned the numbers 10 and 1 respectively to show that six foot is worth ten times more than five foot. If, on the other hand, the eight newcomers are all shorter than five foot, then the first two would be assigned numbers 10 and 9 and would appear to differ from one another by just a tenth. And if some of the newcomers are more than six foot and some less than five, the ratio between being six foot tall and being five foot could be expressed by several of the various combinations of the numbers 2, 3, 4, 5, 6, 7, 8, and 9, taken two by two.

This is the confusion, inconsistency, and error which using such an inaccurate measure of the intensity of preference would introduce into an election. I rank *A* first, *B* second, and *C* third while you rank *A* last, *C* second, and *B* first. You prefer *B* to *A* while I prefer *A* to *B*, but you claim that your preference is worth more than mine, that it is more intense, that *B* is worth three times more than *A* whereas on my ballot paper, *A* is not even worth twice as much as *B*. How can you make such strange claims? Why should the fact that I prefer *B* to *C* be relevant? It does not stop me from considering that there is a huge difference between *A* and *B*, a difference greater even than the entire difference you perceive between both *B* and *C*, and *C* and *A*. Imagine instead of *A*, *B*, and *C*, that Despréaux is stating his preferences between Racine, Quinault, and Pradon. In his eyes, Quinault and Pradon are nothing. He judges the former so severely, so unjustly if you like, that he would be tempted to rank him with the latter and to declare that there is no worse degree of mediocrity. Racine, on the other hand, is everything to him. He prefers him to the other two as genius to weakness and light to shadows. Despite finally ranking Quinault in second place, he still considers that Racine is so superior to him that this superiority could not be measured, and could certainly not be expressed by the numbers 2 and 3. Expressing this vote simply by the signs of the ranks attributed would hardly take into account its intensity, or indeed its immensity. And if someone from the Hotel Rambouillet produces a ballot paper preferring Pradon to Racine and Quinault to Pradon, could we really claim that this does more for Quinault against Racine than Boileau had wanted to do for Racine against Quinault? We know that it is impossible for anyone to prefer Quinault to Racine more totally than Boileau prefers the author of *Britannicus* to the author of the *Astrate*.[2]

---

2. [Quinault, Philippe (1635–1688), French dramatist whose works include *Astrate* (1665).

Boileau, Nicolas, called Boileau-Despréaux (1636–1711), French writer and champion of great literature whose satires attacked all whose work he considered in bad taste or badly written.

Racine, Jean (1639–1699), celebrated dramatist whose works include *Britannicus* (1669).

Pradon, Jacques (1644–1698), French dramatist who attempted to rival Racine.

Hotel Rambouillet, the salon founded by Catherine de Vivonne, marquise de Rambouillet (1588–1665).

The *Biographie Universelle, Ancienne et Moderne* (Paris: Michaud, 1852) relates the following tale in Boileau's own words. One day when he was in the Versailles gallery with Valencour and Racine, they were "accosted by three or four young people from the court who were great admirers of Quinault and of Benserade. One of them asked if it was true that we rated these two poets a long way below Homer and Virgil. Why not ask if I prefer the crown jewels to those made in the Temple [a street market], I replied."

While no one disputes Boileau's respect for Racine, he is sometimes reproached for having so fiercely attacked Quinault. In the preface to the last edition of his works (1713), Boileau himself wrote "When I attacked M. Quinault, we were both very young and he had not yet written many of the works that have since justified the respect in which he is held." Pradon, however, seems to be universally disregarded, and Racine once wrote of his self-appointed rival, "The only difference between myself and Pradon is that I know how to write."]

But the decisive point seems to be that if we take the numbers of the ranks to express the intensity of the preferences, the general result depends on the scope or limits of the list of candidates. If the election is between just *A* and *B*, and *A* obtains the majority of votes, he is elected, since in this case we pay no attention to their intensity. If a third candidate is introduced, the voters' opinions about him alter the established relationship between the first two and may decide the election in favor of *B*. If a fourth appears who, on many papers, is ranked after *A* and before *B*, then *A* will regain the influence which the appearance of a fifth candidate may remove and a sixth restore, these bizarre variations clearly contradict the nature of all elections, since there must be a general opinion on the question of which of *A* and *B* is better which cannot be continually erased, restored, and distorted by questions about the other candidates.

Morales's Argument

In 1797, M. Morales, a Spanish writer, published and presented to the National Institute a paper on the calculus of opinions in elections.[3] In it he adopts the system I have just attacked, basing this choice mainly on an assumed difference between elections and debates. I venture to ask the nature of this difference.

In the first place, deliberations in which one or the other of just two opposing opinions must be adopted and elections in which one of two candidates must be chosen are so similar that M. Morales himself applies to both, without distinction, the maxim which states that the general will is that expressed by the greatest number of voters, without regard to the intensity of their votes. But surely an election between more than two candidates is just the same as a debate about a complex question which could have more than two solutions? In the same way, is not a debate designed to choose between four or five plans which have all been proposed together—between four or five taxes, for example, or four or five election methods—really just an election?

On the one hand we are presented with candidates, one of whom must be elected, and on the other with propositions, one of which must be adopted. The two processes seem to me to be equally deliberative and equally elective. While I accept that the subject matter is different, I cannot imagine how the processes could not be the same.

If a distinction has to be made, the only possible one seems to be between simple questions which can have just two solutions and those which could have more. But nothing in this distinction could authorize us to use two

---

3. *Memoria matematica sobre el calculo de la opinion en las elecciones* por el Dr Jos. Isid. Morales, Madrid, imprenta R[e]al. 1797 in 4°. [Our chapter 10. A copy of Morales's paper is still to be found in the library of the Institute. It was translated into French (published 1829) by D. A. Bourgeois, who was unaware of Daunou's work.]

completely contradictory procedures. When there are just two candidates, we look simply at the number of votes; why should we do anything else when there is more competition?

Because, says M. Morales, the general choice in matters of opinion and not of will is the result of *compensation*, by which he means the calculation of degrees of merit attributed by each voter to each candidate.

M. Morales therefore agrees that the will of the smallest number should never carry more weight than that of the greatest number and that *wills can be counted*. But he also thinks that *opinions can be measured*, because, he claims, the general opinion may be distributed unequally between the various debaters.

I still do not see what can be inferred from this distinction between opinions and wills. When a voter considers the relative merits of several candidates and this results in his preferring one of them to the others, this is undoubtedly an opinion. But, like all opinions which are linked to actions, it also incorporates a positive will, that is, the election of that candidate. Whatever the number of candidates and whatever the number and type of propositions, the direct effect of each voter's opinion is a personal will which is part of the general will. Is he suggesting that when there are just two options, we ask the debaters what they want and that in more complicated questions, we ask them simply what they think? After a ballot between candidates A, B, and C could we announce to the voters that while the general will was for A, the general opinion was for one of the other two? What justification could we have for such strange procedures? What secret means do we have of distinguishing my will from the opinion I want to express?

It is of course desirable to find an effective means of obtaining impartial votes based simply on an appreciation of merit and with no interference from other considerations. But, I repeat, no election method, whatever its form, should be designed to meet this goal, and it will certainly never be met by calculating the intensity of votes.

If we consider the voters trustworthy, then all distinctions between their opinions and their wills disappear, since they will want only to express their true opinions, and the inaccurate method of calculating the intensity of preferences by the numbers of the ranks assigned to the candidates is no more than a means of replacing their constant will with false and random opinions.

If the voters have a tendency to vote against their consciences, grading the votes will only increase the injustice by giving them the means to repel merit more effectively, the more obvious it is.

Conclusion

The only case in which the intensity of votes could be taken into account is when extremely enlightened and sincere voters express the degrees of their preferences not by the sequence of natural numbers, nor by any other fixed progression, but by the free and indefinite use of all possible numbers. And as we are no doubt agreed that this is impracticable, I conclude that we must abandon the unjust idea of considering the intensity of votes as an element of the general will and limit ourselves purely and simply to counting them. I therefore feel it my duty to continue with the maxims I have brought together and according to which we shall declare faulty all election methods

—which have a tendency to correct the election results rather than just counting them,

—or which take into account the supposed intensity of the votes, instead of taking them all to be equal and simply counting them,

—or which allow the election of a candidate decisively rejected by an absolute majority of the voters,

—or which make no distinction between cases in which there is an absolute majority and cases in which there is not,

—or finally which allow or facilitate the victory of a minority candidate over one preferred by an absolute majority to all others, taken together or individually.

In part two of this paper, I shall use these maxims to judge the various election methods which have so far been implemented or suggested.

Part Two: Examination of the Election Methods Hitherto Implemented or Suggested

Past Methods

Very few traces remain of the election methods used in ancient times. In democracies, the common will was almost always determined by strong, widespread, and sudden impulses and usually had such a burst of support that little uncertainty could remain. When the Greeks and Romans thought of supervising these large popular debates, it was less to check their results than to influence their quality, for people hardly imagined that verifying them could pose serious problems. Votes in Rome were cast out loud until the year 614,[4] and when the voting became secret, there is no evidence of any statute exclusively to do with ways of finding the general will. Even the ancient philosophers who made a fairly thorough study of social institutions do not appear to have examined this question.

---

4. [Daunou means 614 *ab urbe condita* (AUC), that is (counting forward from the supposed foundation of Rome in 753 B.C.), 140 B.C. These dates are no longer accepted by classics scholars.]

The first ecclesiastical elections were conducted by acclamation, and there was consequently no method of checking them. It was only when the aristocratic system was introduced into the church and into several Italian states that the decrease in the number of voters highlighted the need, and brought attempts, to make electoral acts subject to more precise laws. And these laws dealt primarily with the qualifications for the electorate and candidates and with exclusions and limitations by lot, that is, with guaranteeing impartial choices rather than with counting, comparing, and evaluating the votes. But we can see in them the germ of some of our ideas about actual election methods, for example of the need to decide some elections by a qualified majority, and of the distinction between principal votes and secondary or supplementary ones.

Elections have made little progress in England and America, where the representative system seemed to be ideally suited to perfecting them. The literary bodies established in the last two centuries made more noticeable progress: not only have they used tests, ballots, and the balancing of positive and negative votes, but they have also carried out frequent, careful experiments on the different methods. Some of their members have noticed the problems and tried to find more exact procedures.

A chronological account of all the election methods which have been implemented or suggested would be tiresome and repetitious and would simply make this discussion, which is already tiring in itself, vague and confusing as well. Rather than examine them chronologically, I have therefore set out the different methods by type.

Classification of Methods

All known election methods can be divided into two groups: individual elections and elections from a list. The latter involve either one list or several, or supplementary lists, or even comparative lists.

Individual Elections
When, in order to fill a single place, each voter writes the name of just one candidate on his ballot paper, the election is individual. The result can be assessed in two ways, depending on whether the voters have agreed to abide by a simple relative plurality or to make one or more attempts to obtain an absolute majority, after which an election will be conducted between the two candidates with the most votes.

I do not consider it necessary to prove the inaccuracy of individual ballots by a simple relative plurality: they may clearly lead to the election of the candidate who is wanted least by the absolute majority of voters.

The methods of making further attempts to obtain an absolute majority or choosing between just two candidates do not make the result any more certain. I examine the defects of this method only because we constantly resort to it.

We have a strange idea of probability if we say, "30 voters chose the first candidate, 19 the second, and just 18 the third, so we can presume that 200 or 300 voters who did not vote for any of the three prefer one of the first two to the last one."

Since we realize that the candidate with 19 votes may beat the one with 30, we should realize also, perhaps more clearly still, that the candidate with 18 votes could beat the one with 19. The ballot therefore proves nothing, except that one of the two candidates is disliked a little less by the absolute majority. Nothing ensures that the absolute majority would not prefer to reject them both, nor even that there is no third candidate whom they would have preferred to the ones between whom you force them to choose.

Elections from Lists

A single list election is one where several places are to be filled at once and each voter writes the same number of names on his paper as there are places to be filled. Candidates who obtain a relative plurality in the first round, or after several attempts, are elected. The results from this kind of method clearly become more suspect as the numbers of candidates and voters increase.

As we have seen, the methods we have examined, whether individual or from a single list, are so inaccurate that not only do they fail to reveal which candidates are really preferred but they often produce results which are directly contrary to the majority will. To prevent this problem, elections have sometimes been modified by negative votes, where each voter is given the chance both to positively elect candidates and to vote for the exclusion of others. However many positive votes a candidate obtained, they had no effect if he was rejected by more than half of the voters; and candidates were elected only if they were not excluded and in addition obtained a majority, whether relative or absolute after one or more attempts, and with or without balloting. This method could surely in certain circumstances have political drawbacks. I shall not deal with this question here, as I am concerned only with the verification of the general will. In this regard, this method seems to offer if not a positive advantage, then the absence of a crucial defect. It is just as unsatisfactory as the preceding methods as far as obtaining accurate results is concerned, but it does effectively dispose of the most inaccurate results.

When each voter writes two, three, or four times (etc.) as many names on his ballot paper as there are places to be filled, it is called a multiple list election. This method can be used both to fill several places at once and to elect just one person. The result is determined either by an absolute majority or, if attempts to obtain this are unsuccessful, by a simple relative plurality.

Analysis of List Methods

The inventors of multiple lists had two motives. They felt that multiple lists would make it easier to obtain an absolute majority and claimed also that they could influence the intrinsic goodness of choices by forcing each voter to base the votes remaining after friendship, favor, and partisan feelings had been accounted for, on considerations of merit.

The futility of the first reason is only too clear. The only true absolute majority is that which emerges naturally and is not contrived. Any absolute majority which results simply from the election method is never anything but a relative plurality, no matter how well it is disguised. It is both empty and misleading and could easily lead to the election of a candidate whom the general will, had it been better consulted, would have ranked below many others. How can we claim that I have been elected by more than half of the voters when it is not certain that a quarter or a tenth of them actually support my election? The true absolute majority consists in six votes out of ten; and we are placing it in six votes out of 20, 30, 40, or more.

The other reason contradicts the first maxim I am trying to establish, that is, that we should try to obtain accurate choices not by the election method itself but by rules external to it. We agreed that it was perverse to divert the means established to find the true result in order to supposedly improve these results; this kind of solution serves neither purpose.

We will not obtain the true result in this way. In fact, we are abandoning all hope of doing so by attempting to obtain a better one than that which results from completely free, natural, and spontaneous votes.

Nor is this any way to ensure good choices, for, on the one hand, we must often remain content with a relative plurality, sometimes a very small one which by no means guarantees the merit of the candidates elected. And on the other hand, the false majorities which are sometimes produced are so vague and circumstantial that we can regard them as virtually fortuitous. Besides, the more usual and probable results of this confusion favor the mediocre candidates who fill the bottom places on all the lists, while the worthier candidates, ranked first on a great many of these lists, are excluded from all those governed by intrigue and partisan feelings.

Our attitude toward a ballot in which each voter is forced to favor equally the candidate for whom he has very little respect and the one he considers the worthiest should be perfectly clear. It is this radical defect of purely multiple lists that first led people to resort to supplementary lists and then comparative ones.

Supplementary List Method

When the main vote is distinguished from the supplementary one, it is called an election by supplementary list. Each voter's paper is divided into two columns. In the first, he writes the same number of names as there are places to be filled, listing the names of the candidates he prefers. The second column is for the candidates whom the voter would choose after the first one and has either precisely the same number of names as the main column or twice or three times as many, and so on, depending on what has been agreed. When all the papers have been completed in this way, the votes in the main columns are counted. If one or more candidates obtain an absolute majority, they are elected. If no absolute majority results from the first columns, the supplementary columns are taken into account; we add up the votes obtained by each candidate in each column and elect those who obtain more votes than half the number of voters.

This is the kind of vote referred to by the scheme proposed by Condorcet at the beginning of 1793.

In this plan, the election began with an introductory ballot designed solely to form, by relative plurality, a list of three times as many candidates as there were places to be filled, if more than one candidate was to be elected at once, and of thirteen names if there was just one place to fill.

The final election would be conducted among only those candidates whose names appeared on these presentation lists and would be on ballot papers with two columns.

If several places were to be filled at once, there would be the same number of names in the supplementary column as in the main one.

If there was just one place to be filled, the main column would contain just one name, while the supplementary column would contain six.

This method can be reduced to a multiple list election, conducted on a list of candidates limited in such a way that as many candidates as there were places to be filled necessarily had to obtain a number of principal or supplementary votes equal to more than half of the voters. It is easy to see that an absolute majority of this kind is a sham; it is artificial and forced, necessitated by the election method and not produced by the free will of the voters.

While this method certainly has a very great advantage over purely multiple lists, where the main votes are not distinguished from secondary votes, this advantage only really exists for cases in which there is an absolute majority of main votes. As soon as we have recourse to adding or assimilating the votes from the different columns, it is reduced to no more than an ordinary multiple list election, where the chances of candidates the voters tolerate and those they prefer become equal.

When one place is to be filled by Condorcet's method, thirteen candidates are put forward and each voter must choose seven. In fact, it would be more exact to say that each voter rejects six, for our electoral powers are reduced to simple rights of rejection when we are forced to accept more than half of the candidates presented. Does this process enable us to contribute positively to the election of one of the candidates? Is it not more of a compromise than a choice?

There is, however, one important advantage to this method which appears in few others: that the candidate expressly rejected by an absolute majority can never be elected. But this is the only point in its favor. The greater the influence of the supplementary columns, the less likely it becomes that the candidate elected will be the one whom this majority would have successively preferred to each of the others.

Suppose that there is an active, scheming minority faction among the voters. The circumstances in which this method was suggested make this hypothesis only too plausible, and Condorcet expressly intended it to protect elections from minority intrigues. While I accept that his plan would have fairly effectively prevented a faction leader from being elected, it left too much scope either for some of the less odious faction members to be elected or for the nomination of the most distinguished members of the majority to be obstructed. I repeat, the general effect of multiple list elections is to favor characterless candidates with no personality, who provoke no real feelings either of hatred or respect. They fill the supplementary columns as if by right and are consequently elected whenever the main columns do not give an absolute plurality to a sufficient number of better candidates. But obtaining an absolute plurality in the main columns requires a degree of agreement between the greatest number of voters which majorities, becoming more confident and inconsistent as they increase in size, rarely seek or succeed in establishing between the votes of their members.

Changing the Majority Requirement

None of the election methods we have discussed therefore satisfies the conditions laid out in part one of this paper. Nor do they satisfy them any better when they require a majority which is greater than absolute than when they require just half of the voters, plus one; that is when they require one of the candidates to obtain votes from more than two-thirds or three-quarters, etc., of the voters. This method, while appearing to give a better guarantee of obtaining true results is in fact simply a means of falsifying the expression of the general will by making the positive will of the smaller number prevail over the positive will of the greater.

Suppose that 75 out of 100 voters nominate candidate N and that the remaining 25, determined to reject N, distribute their votes between two or three of his opponents. Suppose also that it has been agreed that 76 votes, that is more than three-quarters, are required before a candidate can be elected. The opposition persevere and gradually weaken the will of the 75, or at least of some of them. Unable to obtain their preferred candidate, they have to agree to choose only between the candidates they do not prefer. In this way, a sufficient number of votes are eventually obtained by another candidate, and the election method has forced the exclusion of the candidate who was truly elected.

People will argue that this is not the triumph of a positive minority will but of a negative one. The minority do not want candidate N.

This argument would be acceptable if it was not essential to elect someone. But since we must eventually elect someone, to require two-thirds or three-quarters is really to award a prize for stubbornness or intrigue. Either the election method or the will of some voters must give way, or else there will be no result. This is why this type of ballot has sometimes been accompanied by strange and despicable measures to make the voters progressively more uncomfortable as their meeting goes on, measures which tell us all we need to know about any election method which needs to use them. If it is the minority who will eventually give in, then we should have been content with seventy-five votes. But it is more likely that the majority will be destroyed, because minorities are by nature more consistent and because it is easier to find twenty-five stubborn men than seventy-five.

People argue in favor of this type of election that it is useful for cases in which the candidate elected must be in regular social contact with the voters. They claim that if he is elected by the minimum absolute majority he will both resent and be resented by almost half of the members of the society.

Without entering into a discussion of secret votes, which is the most natural and effective means of resolving this problem, let me stress that as soon as this kind of consideration is taken into account, we are no longer trying to obtain true results but useful ones. Besides, there are other considerations, which I shall not examine here: is the idea of a useful result properly understood, would the candidate elected have the strong support of voters who nominated him through exhaustion or coercion, and would he be indebted to them? And finally, whose situation would be better, a candidate who was decidedly preferred to all others by the majority of society members or the one whose election resulted only from their being forced to decide?

Comparative Lists: Borda's Method

And now to comparative lists, which may not have existed or been tried out before Borda. The method he invented is one of those ingenious ideas which deserve the praise even of those who refute them and whose simplicity we can admire though we contest their accuracy.

When this method was put into practice in the Institute, and especially in the divisions of the Institute, the abuse that can be made of it became apparent. The voters could favor their preferred candidate not only by ranking him first, which is just, but also by deliberately ranking his most dangerous opponents last.

People seem to feel that this quite accidental drawback, resulting from the partiality of a few voters, is the only criticism that could be made of a method which is considered both exact in itself and rigorously deduced from the nature of elections. But let us examine Borda's method assuming that all the ballot papers faithfully express votes of conscience. We shall see that it has also the very serious drawback of making the will even of a fairly small minority prevail over the clear will of an absolute majority.

Suppose that out of 36 voters, 22 rank candidate A top, while just 14 rank B in first place. The difference is quite striking, and anyone acting upon his most basic and also most infallible notions would declare A elected rather than B. But in Borda's method, B could win by 6 points if there were just 3 candidates, by 20 if there were 4, by 34 if there were 5, and so on, with this number increasing for each additional candidate by the same quantity as the number of first place votes obtained by B. Why should 14 voters, however sincere their rankings of the different candidates, have the right to destroy the natural power of 22 decisive first place votes in favor of A?

If, in this example, we had only to choose between A and B, A would be elected without any difficulty. Borda expressly states this in his paper, which appears among those of the 1781 Academy. "When the election is between just two candidates," he says, "the candidate with the plurality can be legitimately elected." But how can the intervention of another candidate alter or reverse the relationship established by the voters between these two candidates? When asked which of A and B we prefer, should we really have to make a distinction in our answer and say "if the choice is between just A and B, then we categorically prefer A, but if it is between A, B, and also C, then we consider that B beats not only C but A as well."

When we ask which of A, B, C, D, and E is preferable, this complex question is made up of ten simple ones, and an absolute majority of first votes in favor of A only really answers four of them. But it makes the answer to the remaining six useless, or at least superfluous as far as candidate A is concerned. Once we have ascertained that candidate A beats B, C, D, and E at once, his fate is decided and no uncertainty about his position can be caused by the judgments to be made solely about the respective relationships of his opponents.

Borda's method therefore jeopardizes the clear election of a candidate who is preferred by an absolute majority to all the others taken together. And it offers no guarantee of the very real, if less obvious, election of a candidate preferred by different absolute majorities to each of his opponents one by one. Suppose that there are 36 voters. 10 rank A in first place, and on 10 of the remaining 26 ballot papers, A, though not ranked first, is still preferred to B.

This would produce 20 votes in favor of *A* against *B* and just 16 in favor of *B* against *A*. And if 20 voters should have more influence than 16, then *A* should beat *B*. But Borda's method may give *B* two points more than *A* if there are three candidates, 18 more if there are four, 34 more if there are 5, and so on, this difference increasing by 16 points with each additional candidate.[5]

In any case, it is quite obvious that any method which pays more attention to the intensity of the individual votes than to their number in order to determine the general will is bound to deny the majority will its influence. Suppose that you prefer *C* to *D* while I prefer *D* to *C*, but that you rank *D* immediately below *C* whereas I rank several other candidates below *D* and above *C*. From this we conclude that my vote for *D* against *C* is worth twice, three times, four times as much as your vote for *C* against *D*. 5 or 6 voters who vote as I do would therefore do more for *D* than 10, 15, or 20 voters voting as you do could for *C*. We are no longer dealing with the quantity of votes but with their values, which, if there is some degree of truth in the points I presented at the end of part one, is both inaccurate and fundamentally unjust.

Various other drawbacks to Borda's method were noted shortly after it was published. In his 1785 essay on the probability of plurality decisions, Condorcet uses several examples to show the inaccuracy of this method: he shows how it leads to choices which are not only actually false but also inherently bad and above all that when two out of five candidates are considered worthy and the remaining three completely unworthy by more than half of the voters, one of the three rejected by the majority can easily obtain the greatest total.

But in fact a careful reading of Borda's paper itself is enough to show that his method is based on imprecise and incomplete observations and that it produces very inaccurate results. From the very beginning, it is clear that he is going to disregard completely the crucial distinction between the absolute greatest number and the relative greatest number. He confuses them both under the name of plurality, and pointing out that certain, that is, relative, pluralities can be obtained in ordinary elections by candidates who are not truly elected, he concludes without further discussion that the results of such elections are always suspect whenever there are more than two candidates. Are we then mistaken in following the maxim which declares the election of the candidate preferred by an absolute majority in the first round of the election to all others taken collectively? He should at the very least have explained his criticisms of this maxim, which has until now been generally accepted as a direct consequence of the very hypothesis of a deliberation between voters with equal rights.

---

5. [Daunou seems to have made an arithmetical error. The values for the extreme case should be 12, 28, 44, etc.]

Borda then notes that any election method will be defective if the candidates put forward have not all been compared two by two. I do not dispute that it is often necessary to make all these comparisons in order to conduct an accurate check on the general will, but instead of distinguishing cases in which these comparisons are indispensable from those in which they are not and cases in which they produce results from those in which they produce only contradictions, the author simply shows that in his method each voter presents a complete opinion on all the candidates, which is indeed the case, and quickly concludes from this that we obtain the same result by adding up numbers as by conducting individual votes between all the candidates taken two by two. This conclusion is untenable, and Condorcet demonstrates its falsity as follows.

> Suppose that there are [just] 3 candidates, A, B, and C, and 81 voters, and that each voter ranks the candidates in order of merit. 30 voters rank them ABC and one ranks them ACB. 10 rank them CAB and 29 BAC. 10 rank them BCA and 1 ranks them CBA. The proposition "A is better than B" therefore obtains 41 votes to 40, "A is better than C" obtains 60 votes to 21, [and "B is better than C" obtains 69 votes to 12]. The decision is therefore in favor of A. Now let us compare A and B using the method we have been examining here {Borda's one} . . . B . . . has 8 points more than A.[6]

But we do not even need examples to see that adding up numbers must produce different results to making pairwise comparisons between candidates. The results obtained by adding up the votes of two candidates vary according to the number of opponents and to the ranks obtained by these opponents above, below or between the first two, whereas the comparison of two candidates or the preference given to one over the other is, both in each voter's and in the general opinion, a simple, constant, and fixed relationship, independent of all others.

Borda, however, illustrates the application of his method with a few examples and then immediately takes this method as a sort of standard by which the very nature of elections should be judged. And drawing from this so-called principle the consequences it indeed entails, he established three rules which are to be permanently applied to all elections. These are

1. that when an election is conducted between two candidates, it is

---

6. Essay on the probability of decisions . . . p. clxxvii. Paris, imprimerie royale 1785 in 4°. [Daunou's quotation is more or less accurate but omits some of Condorcet's original text. We have inserted our translation of the passages omitted by Daunou in brackets. The phrase in braces is Daunou's.]

sufficient for a candidate to obtain half of the votes, plus one, in order to be elected;

2. that one of three candidates can be legitimately elected only by two-thirds of the votes;

3. that three-quarters of the votes are necessary if there are four candidates, four-fifths if there are five, and so on, so that the denominator is always equal to the number of candidates and the numerator is that same number, minus one, and so that unanimity is required if there are the same number of candidates and of voters.

I do not understand why obtaining such strange consequences did not impress upon the mathematician the need to make a more thorough examination of the method which produced them. It is absurd to claim that when a division at the Institute elects a president—that is, when there are the same number of candidates and of voters—no one could be truly and *legitimately* elected and no election could be duly ascertained unless the votes all supported the same member, so that if the elected candidate had not chosen himself, his election would be suspect! This would undoubtedly be the case with Borda's method; equal totals can be obtained by a candidate with thirty-nine first place votes and by a candidate with just one, and it is quite likely that a candidate with thirty-three first place votes will be declared inferior to someone with only three or four. These, and all similar, points clearly prove something either against the maxim of the superiority of absolute majorities or against Borda's method. But until this superiority has been proven contrary to the theory of voting,[7] I shall continue to believe that we must judge the method by the maxim and not the maxim by the method.

As we have just seen, Borda limited himself almost exclusively to explaining how his method would be implemented, without explaining the motives behind it. These were shown for the first time by citizen Laplace in one of his lessons for the colleges of education [for a citation to the French original see chapter 14 note 1; for a translation of this passage see Sommerlad and McLean 1991, 282–86.].

"Suppose," said this wise teacher,

that we give each voter an urn containing an infinite number of balls, so that he can express every nuance of the degrees of merit he attributes to each candidate. Suppose that he takes from his urn a number of balls proportional to the merit of each candidate, and suppose that this number is written on his ballot paper, beside the candidate's name. If we find the sum of all the numbers relating to each candidate on each ballot paper,

---

7. [French *théorie des délibérations*. This is the earliest use of this phrase we have found.]

then clearly the candidate with the largest total will be the one preferred by the Assembly, and the order of preference between the candidates will be the order of their individual totals.

Citizen Laplace admits that this hypothesis is true only if we suppose that the voters act in complete good faith. An equally necessary condition would be that the voters could judge different degrees of merit so perfectly that chance would play no part in the number of balls taken out of the urn for each candidate. Given these two conditions, we shall accept citizen Laplace's proposition, although we could still raise against it most of the points which aim to prove that the general will is always that of the greatest number of voters, with no regard for the intensity of their votes.

But in Borda's method, the ballot papers do not show the number of balls each voter has given each candidate. If this were the case, a single voter could, for instance, sometimes decide the election of a candidate ranked last by ninety-nine others, simply by giving 1,000 balls to him and less than 10 to his opponents, while the other ninety-nine voters expressed their preferences using only numbers lower than 11.

What then do Borda numbers represent? They show simply, says citizen Laplace, that the first candidate obtained more balls than the second, the second more than the third, and so on. We need to decide whether this second method can represent the first, that is, assuming that the first reveals the candidate with majority support, can we attribute the same advantage to the second?

In order to prove this, citizen Laplace points out that whatever the number of balls obtained by the first candidate on a given ballot paper, all combinations of lower numbers which satisfy the preceding conditions are equally admissible. And he adds that "the number of balls obtained by each candidate can be found by making a total of all the numbers given to him by each combination and by dividing this total by the total number of combinations."

This can be reduced to assigning a candidate a middle term in the various numbers below that assigned to the candidate immediately above him; so that if the first candidate has twenty, the second will have ten. In fact, this second candidate could be assigned any one of the terms of the natural series from 19 to 1. If we divide 190, the sum of all the terms of this arithmetic progression, by the number of combinations, that is by 19, we obtain 10 as a quotient. Generally, when the first candidate has n, the second will have $n - 1$ combinations, from the number $n - 1$ itself to unity; giving $(n^2 - n)/2$ as the total of the various numbers which this candidate can have, and $n/2$, that is half the number assigned to the first candidate, as the quotient of this sum divided by the number $n - 1$ of combinations. Similarly, there would be $n/4$ for a third candidate, $n/8$ for a fourth, and so on, so that there would be $n/2^{t-1}$ for a candidate ranked t.

But why substitute this average term for the precise will of the voters? In order to defend Borda's method, we start with the maxim that when the voters are able to express all the nuances in their opinions on the relative merit of the candidates, calculating these nuances reveals the general will, and yet we immediately deprive the voters of this possibility by setting up an average scale and fixing invariable numbers. Despite promising the voter complete freedom and indefinite scope to express the extent of his esteem, as soon as he represents one of these levels by twenty, we insist that the position immediately below it must be ten—no more and no less. While this number is certainly midway between the two extremes he could have chosen, it is after all just one of the nineteen equally probable terms between which he had to decide. While we might claim that it is a legitimate compromise between voters who would have used numbers lower than ten and those who would have used greater ones, it is debatable whether compromises of this kind are consistent with the nature of elective votes. When we conduct a ballot, is not our aim to replace the more or less probable result that we can predict with a confirmed, positive vote? Far from trying to obtain average terms, are not we in fact trying to recognize whether the results we obtain will not be precisely those that are most unexpected and most extreme?

By forcing the voters to use a given progression, we are attacking the very elements we consider to form the general will—that is, the number of voters and the intensity of their votes. On the one hand, the candidate elected by the smallest number may win, and in fact often does; and on the other, the votes are graded artificially, more or less contrary to the opinions of the voters.

However, the average scale n, $n/2$, $n/4$, etc., which results directly from citizen Laplace's statement that "the number of balls obtained by each candidate can be found by making a total of all the numbers given to him by each combination, and by dividing this total by the total number of combinations" [Sommerlad and McLean 1991, 283] is not even the same as that used by Borda. Instead of a geometrical progression, with 2 as a quotient, Borda simply uses the arithmetic progression 1, 2, 3, 4, 5, etc. This method not only differs greatly from that explained by citizen Laplace but also frequently produces different results. However, citizen Laplace points out that when there are a great many or an infinite number of balls and combinations, as we must suppose to be the case here, the average scale does indeed become n, $n - 1$, $n - 2$, etc., that is, simply the numbering of the ranks assigned to the candidates. As I have tried to prove, these numbers are an extremely inadequate means of representing degrees of esteem.

Majority Selection under Borda's Method

Before ending my examination of Borda's method, I feel I ought to mention the fact that if we use this method, the candidate with the smallest total is never the one the absolute majority prefers to all the others. He may well not be ranked last in the general opinion, he may even be considered second best; but he is certainly never the one considered to be the best. The truth of this remarkable fact, the most constant result of this method, can be seen from the following calculation.

This calculation is based on the following facts.

1. The numbers on each ballot paper form an arithmetic progression, limited at one end by unity and at the other by the number of terms, that is, the number of candidates. Since the sum of the terms of this progression is equal to the sum of the limits multiplied by half the number of terms, it follows that the sum of the numbers on each ballot paper can be found by multiplying the number of candidates plus one by half of the number of candidates. So if the number of candidates is n, the sum of the numbers on each paper will be $(n^2 + n)/2$.
2. If we multiply this quantity by the number of voters, the product will represent the sum of all the numbers on all the ballot papers. If the number of voters is p, the general total of these numbers can be expressed by $(pn^2 + pn)/2$.
3. Finally, if the general sum of the numbers were divided among all the candidates in equal shares, each candidate's share would be the quotient resulting from the division of this total sum by the number of candidates. Each share would therefore be $(pn + p)/2$.

Using these facts as a base, we see that if one candidate's total is assumed to be lower than each of the others', his share will necessarily also be smaller—even if just by one unit—than the average share $(pn + p)/2$.

We can easily convince ourselves that the candidate preferred by an absolute majority to all the others always has a total which is larger than the average.

The worst possible case for him is if he has the highest number on half plus one of the papers and the lowest—that is just one—on the remainder. It is true that if the absolute majority of voters prefer him to his opponents taken individually and not collectively, then he will not have precisely half plus one of the highest votes. However, if he is to be truly preferred, as I am assuming here, his top and bottom votes must be balanced in such a way that for every first place vote less than the half plus one required, he must also have one bottom vote less than the half minus one acceptable. His intermediary votes must make up in detailed preferences for what he lost in collective ones, and after all this counterbalancing, his total must be on the one hand at least equal to half of the voters minus one and on the other to half of the voters plus one multiplied by the number of candidates, that is,

1. $(p/2) - 1$ and

2. $n (p/2 + 1)$

giving in total $(pn + p + 2n - 2)/2$.

Thus, on the one hand the candidate with the lowest total necessarily has a total score of less than $(pn + p)/2$, while the candidate preferred to all his opponents by an absolute majority could not have a total of less than $(pn + p + 2n - 2)/2$. This last total is greater than the average share by $(2n - 2)/2$, which is the equivalent of $n - 1$, that is of the number of candidates minus one. And since the candidate with the lowest total is always at least one point below the average, it follows that the difference between him and the candidate preferred by the majority in favor of the latter is always at least equal to the number of candidates.

This result cannot be contested, but it is also the only one on which we can rely, for the candidate preferred by the absolute majority to all the others, even collectively, may very well obtain only the second lowest total, and the candidate with the lowest total may in fact be the one that the majority actually ranked in second place.

These two propositions can be shown in general terms at least for all cases where there are more than twice as many voters as candidates, that is when $p \geq 2n + 1$, which is usually the case.[8] Since the total obtained by candidate A, who has half plus one first votes and half minus one last votes, is $(pn + p + 2n - 2)/2$, let us suppose that candidate B, who has the lowest total, has half plus one last votes and half minus one second lowest, that is $p/2 + 2 (p/2 - 1) + 1$ or $(3p - 2)/2$. If we deduct these totals, that is $(pn + p + 2n - 2)/2$ and $(3p - 2)/2$, from the general total $(pn^2 + pn)/2$, then the remainder $(pn^2 - 4p - 2n + 4)/2$ is the total to be divided among the remaining $n - 2$ candidates, so that

$$\frac{pn^2 - 4p - 2n + 4}{2 (n - 2)}$$

or $(pn + 2p - 2)/2$ is the average share of each. If we delete the common terms $pn + p - 2$ from $(pn + p + 2n - 2)/2$ and $(pn + 2p - 2)/2$, then we obtain on the one hand $2n/2$ or n and on the other $p/2$. If $p > 2n$, the first of these will be smaller. Thus when there are more than twice as many voters as candidates, candidate A's total, greater than that of candidate B, may be lower than that of all of the others.

Suppose now that A has half plus one first place votes and half minus one second last ones, that is, $(pn + 2p + 2n - 4)/2$, and that B has half plus one second place votes and half minus one last ones, that is, $(pn + 2n - 4)/2$. If we deduct the sum of these two totals, that is $(2pn + 2p + 4n - 8)/2$, from $(pn^2 + pn)/2$, then the remainder $(pn^2 - pn - 2p - 4n + 8)/2$, when divided by $n - 2$, will give as the average share of each of the remaining candidates $(pn + p - 4)/2$. By deleting the common terms $pn - 4$ from $(pn + 2n - 4)/2$ and $(pn + p - 4)/2$, we obtain, as above, on the one hand $2n/2$ or n and on the other $p/2$. Thus, if $p > 2n$, B's total, already lower than A's, could also be lower than all of the others'. But examples will be enough here.

Suppose that there are 100 voters and ten candidates. The total number on each ballot paper will be 55, the general total 5,500, and the average share 550. As we have seen, the share of the candidate preferred by the majority may be just 559. It is possible that this total may be the second lowest, for one of the nine other candidates may have just 149, that is 51 times 1 and 49 times 2. If we subtract the two individual totals of 559 and 149 from the general total and divide the remaining 4,792 between the other eight candidates, the average share for each becomes 599, giving a fairly high chance that the candidate who obtained 51 times 10 and 49 times 1 will be ranked second from bottom.

With the same numbers of voters and candidates as above, suppose now that 51 papers give A 10 and B 9, and 49 give A 2 and B 1. This would mean that the absolute majority preferred B, certainly not to A but to the eight remaining candidates taken together. Yet in Borda's method, B could be declared the last of all. A's and B's totals added together come to 1,116. If we subtract 1,116 from 5,500 and divide the remaining 4,384 by 8, each of the remaining eight candidates has an average share of 548, which is 40 more than B's total of 508.

The only conclusions that can be drawn from a Borda count are that the candidate preferred by the absolute majority is neither the one with the smallest total, nor any of those whose totals are lower than $(pn + p + 2n - 2)/2$. The only way that this method could therefore be used to obtain accurate results is to eliminate the candidates with totals lower than $(pn + p + 2n - 2)/2$, and to conduct another ballot or count between the remaining candidates and to find the elected candidate by successive elimination. However, these procedures, which are so exhausting and time-consuming for the voters, or at least for the scrutineers, could not be applied when there was no kind of absolute majority and would be unnecessary when the general will was immediately obvious by the absolute majority of first place votes. We could only be tempted to use it, in order to find the majorities obtained by one individual candidate over each of the others; and, as we shall see, there are far simpler ways of finding this.

I shall conclude my examination of Borda's method by distinguishing the drawing up of the votes from their evaluation.

If the points I have just developed are valid, then the method of evaluating the votes by adding up numbers and considering the difference in their totals is fundamentally flawed.

But provided that it was understood that the numbers on the ballot paper were not going to be added up and that they served only to express the voter's opinion on all of the candidates taken two by two, the papers would be perfectly acceptable. A ballot paper giving A 3, B 2, C 1 would mean simply that the voter preferred A to B, A to C, and B to C and would contain clear, precise, distinct, and complete answers to each of the simple questions contained in the complex question of the election. Presenting the votes in this way is not only very useful but is also highly preferable to the ways used in other election methods. It is here that the enormous value of Borda's method lies.

Condorcet's Method

In his *Essay on the Application of Analysis to the Probability of Decisions Rendered by a Plurality of Votes* [1785; our chapter 6], Condorcet proposed a comparative ballot that was far more exact than that suggested by Borda. Since this essay aims primarily to find the probability of the intrinsic goodness of these decisions, it is not always possible to apply its theory directly to simply recognizing the positive truth of the results. It could even be said that the confusion of these two aims has made several parts of this work rather obscure. Nevertheless, we can extract the parts exclusively to do with checking the reality of the general will and present Condorcet's method as follows.

Suppose that ballot papers are drawn up as in Borda's method. They are sorted not by adding up the numbers but by counting the number of votes which prefer A to B or B to A, then those which prefer B to C or C to B, and so on until all the pairwise combinations of the candidates have been exhausted.

If, when there are three candidates, an absolute majority declares that A is better than B and also that A is better than C, then we can declare A to be elected, regardless of whether B beats C or C beats B.

But when the three propositions with absolute majority support are $A >
B$, $C > A$ and $B > C$, then any one of them contradicts the consequence of the other two. These three propositions, taken two by two, produce three systems, the first of which gives a result in favor of C, the second in favor of B, and the third in favor of A.

Taking only the propositions $A > B$ and $C > A$, we obtain a result in favor of C.

Taking only the two propositions $C > A$ and $B > C$, the result will be in favor of B.

And taking just the propositions $B > C$ and $A > B$, the result is the election of A.

If it is absolutely necessary to elect someone and we cannot abandon the election altogether, Condorcet advises us to consider as elected the candidate whose election results from the system with the support of the larger majorities.

Suppose that with sixty voters, we have twelve papers with the order ABC and nine with ACB, twenty with BCA and ten with CAB, nine with CBA and none with BAC.

The three propositions with majority support are $A > B$, $C > A$, and $B > C$, with majorities of 31, 39, and 32 respectively.

Suppose now that we form three systems out of these three propositions taken two by two. The system $A > B$ and $C > A$, which decides in favor of C, will obtain 70 votes; the system $C > A$ and $B > C$, which supports B, 71 votes; and the system $B > C$ and $A > B$, which supports A, 63 votes.

It is these three numbers, 70, 71, and 63 which Condorcet considers important, and as the largest—that is, 71—is attached to the system which supports B, it is B who is elected.

It is strange to note that in this example, Condorcet's method, Borda's method, and the conventional method of individual elections all produce different results.

In Condorcet's method, B is elected because his election results from the system with the most votes.

In Borda's method, C is elected because he has the largest total.

And A is bound to be elected in the conventional method because once A and B have obtained relative pluralities in the first round, A then obtains the absolute majority in the ballot held between them.

These three contradictory results not only vividly prove the inaccuracy of at least two of the three methods but also serve to highlight the very real problems caused by this situation and all those which resemble it. In this case, there is no general will and no majority preference for one of the candidates over the others, and as long as we do not have to obtain a result, the only proper solution is to avoid declaring any result at all.

But I stress, as did citizen Laplace, that even when it is absolutely necessary to elect someone, it would be quite wrong and completely futile to conduct another election at once. There is no reason at all why the voters should change their votes just because of the results of the first election. If they continue to vote in the same way, the results will remain the same and any changes in them brought about by fickleness, lack of thought, or intrigue hardly deserve to decide the outcome of an election. We must therefore obtain a result from the first comparative election.

Personally, I consider it best to elect the candidate with the most first place votes: for as soon as we have ascertained that there is no absolute majority, whether clear or hidden, in favor of any of the other candidates, it seems perfectly just to give the authority of this majority to the simplest, most direct, and clearest relative plurality. If A obtains 21 first place votes, B 20, and C 19, I would not hesitate to declare A elected, if it is absolutely necessary that someone should be. Nor would I demand that a ballot be held between A and B, partly because this ballot has already been conducted and partly because I could just as reasonably demand one between B and C, and this would be to repeat the whole comparative election which produced no result with absolute majority support.

Quite apart from the objection that Condorcet's method could only really be used for elections with a very limited number of voters, and especially of candidates, and that it would make the scrutineers' job both quite awkward and very time-consuming, I am not convinced that it is fundamentally sound.

Condorcet gives the system "A is better than B" and "C is better than A" 70 votes, and the system "B is better than C" and "A is better than B" just 63. But in fact, the first of these systems was directly supported by only 10 voters—that is, by those who adopted the order CAB—while the second, represented by the order ABC, was supported by 12. Condorcet similarly finds that the system which supports B is only one-seventy-first better than that which supports C, whereas in fact 20 positive votes simultaneously support the two propositions which form the first system and just 10 the two which form the second.

Condorcet obtains the numbers 71, 70, and 63 by taking into account for each of the three conclusions the votes given to each of the propositions from which it is deduced. I am not entirely sure that this kind of addition is sufficiently consistent with the nature of debates, or even of human reasoning. It seems to me that someone who accepts one premise but rejects the other is by no means voting for the conclusion. In fact, I doubt whether we could even claim that he supports it more than a voter who rejected both premises. If I categorically deny that Molière is worse than Térence, then it is completely irrelevant that I prefer Térence to Plautus, and my opinion is just as consistent and inflexible as if I had ranked Térence below Plautus. Why should my preferences between Térence and Plautus gain influence as part of a system which produces a result against Molière? And yet this is precisely what happens in the method advised by Condorcet. Using my assent for one of the premises, he manipulates the votes I have given so that I appear to support a conclusion I actually reject. This is not how debates work. The only propositions I have truly approved are those which I have expressly formulated or which are entailed by my votes alone, without the interference of votes which are not mine or which contradict mine.

Having said that, Condorcet's method is undoubtedly the most accurate of all those we have examined so far. It is completely accurate whenever there is an absolute majority, because it allows that majority to work when it is clear and reveals it when it is hidden. The only possible criticism is that when we must be content with a relative plurality, it strays too far in its search for this plurality and determines it by procedures which are both uncertain and laborious.

An Institute Proposal

I shall end part two of this paper by discussing a voting plan suggested to the Institute in its general meeting of the 5 floréal, an VIII [25 April 1800]. While this method, which is individual, really belongs in one of the categories I have already discussed, I wanted to discuss it separately as it is of special interest.

Article 7 of the plan establishes that if there is no absolute majority after the third round of the election, we must conclude from this that the division feels that no candidate has a sufficiently pronounced advantage over his opponents for them to make a choice and that consequently the formation of the list will be adjourned.

Two points should be made here.

First, the role played by a division in the Institute's elections was not precisely to select the candidate who was markedly superior to all the others but to designate three candidates who were more or less worthy of the votes.

In 1672, neither Boileau nor La Fontaine were members of the Académie Française. Nor were Racine, who had produced *Andromaque* and *Britannicus*, or Molière, who in fact never became a member of this body. Now it seems to me that while the Academy could certainly have been permitted to hesitate between such candidates, the members required to present a list of candidates could not have been permitted to announce that there was no need to replace Godeau or Salomon.[9]

The second point concerns the election method itself.

We feel able to conclude from the fact that the three first rounds of an individual election have not revealed any absolute majority that the division feels that no one candidate has a marked advantage over the others. But this hasty conclusion goes far beyond the facts on which it is based. Only by a

---

9. [Boileau, Racine, see footnote 2 to this chapter. La Fontaine, Jean de (1621–1695), French poet; best known for his *Fables* (1668–1678); With Racine, Boileau, and Molière formed the salon of the rue du Vieux Colombier, ca. 1665; Blocked for membership of the Académie française in 1682 and 1683 because his nomination was opposed by Louis XIV. Molière, pseudonym of J.-B. Poquelin (1622–1673), French actor and dramatist; writer of famous satirical comedies of manners (*Tartuffe*, *Le Bourgeois Gentilhomme*, *Le Malade Imaginaire*); died soon after the opening of *Le Malade Imaginaire*, in which he had been playing the role of the imaginary invalid. Godeau, Antoine (1605–1672), bishop and writer. Salomon, François-Henri (1620–1670), man of letters.]

comparative ballot between all of the candidates taken two by two can we ascertain that no candidate is preferred to each of the others taken individually. Dividing the question up like this may reveal that two-thirds, three-quarters, or four-fifths of the division actually have a preference for one of the candidates. As we have seen, this will happen whenever most of the voters who do not rank this candidate in first place rank him second.

Article VIII runs as follows: "Once the first name has been placed on the list in this way [by an absolute majority], a second individual election shall be held and the two names which obtain the most votes shall be placed on the list in second and third places."

The unreliability of the second part of this clause is only too clear, partly because a relative plurality proves nothing if we have not first ascertained that there is no absolute majority, and partly because deriving two results at once from a single individual ballot prevents us even from checking the relative plurality. Since he can write only one name on the ballot paper, each voter is answering only part of the complex question up for debate, and this part decreases as the number of candidates increases. He has no influence, no vote, and no power to act on the rest of the question. Suppose that there are just five or six candidates and just twenty or thirty voters, as may be the case in a division of thirty to forty because of absentees. If the votes are divided more or less equally between the candidates, we can almost regard the two results as completely the result of chance. In this respect, the plan seems worse than conventional elections, which at least give the voter a double vote when they are aiming to fill two places at once.

Article XI states that when the ballot is conducted between three candidates, a candidate who obtains a majority of more than half of the voters will be elected. But if no clear majority results from this individual ballot, then with no attempt to examine more thoroughly whether one of the candidates is not in fact preferred by an absolute majority to each of the other two, taken individually, the rule proceeds to a ballot between the first candidate and whichever of his opponents received the relative highest number of votes in the first round.

Bearing in mind everything I have said so far, it is quite clear that a method of this kind is very far from guaranteeing true results. In my opinion, a learned society should adopt a stricter one.

Part Three: Adjustments Which Could Be Made to the Various Election Methods

It remains for me to discuss the adjustments which could be made to the various methods I have just examined. But first I must make a few points specifically about the rules relating to the intrinsic goodness of choices.

I shall not discuss whether individual votes should be secret or public. It seems quite superfluous, at least in the current circumstances and the current climate of opinion, of customs and characters, to prove that public votes would have very serious drawbacks both in the French Republic and in the Institute itself.

Nor shall I discuss whether it is useful to leave chance some influence over the elections. Rousseau and other philosophers recommended a mixture of voluntary acts and determination by fate. They believed that a blind, but impartial, power could sometimes rectify the errors in our thought and aberrations caused by our personal affections, confound intrigue, and repress evil ambitions. But as far as I can see, chance could only ever be usefully applied to preliminary reductions in the number of candidates or voters. Using it in the final stages and solution of the election to decide the final result would be to disregard both the authority and advantages of human debate.

More important, indeed essential, are the rules which determine the number, qualifications, influence, and functions of the voters. The voters must always be selected from among those who will be directly exposed to the drawbacks or dangers which would result from a bad choice. But in addition to this particular, direct, and personal interest in obtaining good results from the elections, they must also have sufficient knowledge both of the nature of the posts they are filling and of the personal qualities of the candidates between whom they must choose.

The conditions which must be met by the members of an electoral body do more than just guarantee intrinsically good choices. They also make elections easier to conduct because they tend to decrease the number of voters, or to distinguish their functions and to divide between them the various tasks which make up an election.

The same is true of rules about the numbers, eligibility, and presentation of the candidates. As long as votes can be given to candidates whose suitability can in no way be assumed or be spread over an indefinite number of eligible candidates, it would be foolhardy to hope for a good result and difficult to obtain a true or even probable one. Only limiting the list of candidates allows some degree of precision in drawing up and counting the votes.

Having a great many candidates presents a far greater obstacle to precision than having a great many voters. It is easier to use a strict method for an election between just five candidates with 300, 400, or 500 voters, than for one with 60 voters and nine or ten candidates. This is because increasing the number of voters just makes the process more time-consuming without complicating it, whereas an additional candidate brings as many new questions as there were candidates before him.

So, before choosing an election method, we need to know the nature and circumstances of the election that is to be conducted; we need to consider the results of any rules concerning the voters and the candidates; and we need to know to what extent these rules have reduced both the number of voters and, more importantly, the number of candidates.

Types of Elections

We can therefore distinguish two types of election.

1. Those in which there are both more than seven candidates and more than fifty voters.
2. Those in which there are either not more than fifty voters or not more than seven candidates.

Exact, precise, and rigorous election methods are applicable to the second type of election but would hardly suit the first type.

The divisions between the two types could of course be different, but we can at least use seven and fifty as an example. I chose them because an eighth candidate immediately increases the number of questions to be answered from twenty-one to twenty-eight, giving an extra 385 votes if there are just fifty-five voters.

Many Candidates and Voters

If, when there are more than seven candidates, there are also a great many voters, we are more or less condemned to using imperfect methods.

Among the election methods which offer no guarantee of finding the candidate actually preferred to the others by the general will, I consider the least faulty to be those which prevent the election of candidates who are actually rejected by this will. We have found two methods which do this, that is, the one which allows negative votes and the supplementary list method suggested by Condorcet in 1793. Both undoubtedly have drawbacks. The first is quicker and simpler but, it is claimed, may cause and nourish resentment between those who are excluded and those they imagine excluded them. The second uses the same exclusions but cleverly conceals this fact and is therefore more complicated. There are more stages to it, and they are more time-consuming and more difficult. And the results it produces are often unsatisfactory because, as we have seen, it generally favors the election of mediocre candidates.

But the fundamental drawbacks of the other methods are more striking even than these. It seems absurd to assemble voters, to claim to be looking for the general will, and then to declare results which have been refused and rejected by more than half of them. While it is conceivably acceptable not to do precisely what they want most, because their positive will is very difficult to determine, doing in their name what we can easily see they do not want at all is, in my opinion, a breach of public trust and a sort of blasphemy. Suppose that 300 votes are divided between many candidates. Anytus receives 20 and Melitus 18, and no other candidate obtains as many as either of these two. If we consult the 262 voters who voted for neither of these candidates, they will say that they would consider the election of Melitus or of Anytus a disaster and that they would prefer any other candidate instead. We announce that we have heard enough, that this is their option, and that they must exercise their sovereign right to choose between two evils. Tomorrow one of the candidates they reject will become their representative, claiming that he has their backing to proscribe innocence and to destroy the world.

Besides, negative votes, double columns, and above all conventional methods are so faulty that they should be used only to reduce the number of candidates to seven. If we decide not to use negative votes, we should not present the voters with two candidates between whom they must choose but must instead find the seven who obtained a relative plurality and use a strict method to conduct an election between them.

Few Candidates and Voters

When there are seven candidates or fewer, we can use the following very simple method, which seems to result from the points I have presented in this paper.

Each voter has only to draw up one ballot paper according to Borda's method. Everything else is done by the scrutineers.

They first of all check whether any candidate has obtained an absolute majority of first place votes. If so, they declare him elected.

If not, they check how many times each candidate is preferred to each of his opponents, and if an absolute majority prefers one candidate to each of the others taken individually, that candidate is elected.

If there is still no result, they examine whether any candidate is ranked below all of the others either collectively or individually, on an absolute majority of ballot papers. If so, they eliminate him.

Then, they work out which of the candidates who have not been eliminated obtained the relative plurality of first votes, and this candidate is elected if it is absolutely necessary to elect someone.

With this method, we would not need to recall the voters for new ballots even when several places were to be filled at once. Having determined which candidate was elected first, we could then remove his name from all of the papers, and consider only the remaining names in order to elect the second, and then the third, and so on.

This method satisfies all our conditions. It guarantees both the negative and positive rights of the absolute majority and only takes the relative plurality into account after having ensured that there is no absolute majority, whether positive or negative, clear or hidden.

It might perhaps be useful to explain, with examples, how this method works and the results it produces. For added clarity, I shall apply it to the situation with which we are most familiar—the system of voters and eligible candidates which has so far been used in the National Institute.

I do not need to examine whether the necessary presentations by section, the additional presentations by other members, the reduction of the list of candidates by the division, and the final choice by the Institute were good or bad arrangements in themselves as I am simply taking them as hypotheses. But with regard to my subject alone, I can at least say that they made the election process considerably easier and seemed to promote the use of the strictest and most precise method.

National Institute Elections

An election in the National Institute was conducted in three stages, the first by section, the second by division, and the third by the general assembly.

There were just six voters in the section, and sometimes just five, when the election was to replace one of the section members. But there was an indefinite number of candidates, which would immediately have caused problems if these five or six voters had not always been more or less in agreement. It would have been unnecessary and difficult to make a rule to cover such rare problems, which always resolve themselves. However, if we consider the theory of this method and take the worst possible case—that in which each of the six voters persists in nominating five completely different candidates to those nominated by each of the others—we find that the list would still be made up of just thirty names. If the section then ranked the candidates by the Borda method, it would not be too difficult, given the very small number of ballot papers, to use the counting method I have suggested in order to find the five candidates to be put forward.

Each member of the class had the right to nominate other candidates, and the class as a whole had the right to accept or reject each of these additional nominations. This could of course have made the list of eligible candidates so big that counting the votes by adding up the numbers would have been very dangerous. In my method, however, it would simply have required a little more attention in the count, when the additional nominations increased the total number of candidates to more than seven. They could easily have been reduced to this number by conducting a preliminary ballot among the additional nominations purely to eliminate those who had obtained the fewest votes and could therefore be considered less nominated than the others. Since there were no more than seven candidates and between thirty and sixty voters, my method of counting the votes would have been no more difficult or tiring for two or three scrutineers than the countless tiring additions required by Borda.

In the general assembly, which had simply to elect one of three candidates, the counting method I have suggested would be far easier than that which was used. We would have been able to see at once whether or not there was an absolute majority of first place votes for one of the candidates. If there was not, it would not have taken long to look for distributed majorities; whatever the number of voters, we would have needed simply to check their answers to the three questions: which is better, A or B, A or C and B or C? This check could even be conducted without being written down, for the six different combinations of the three terms A, B, and C could produce just six types of ballot paper. We could simply place all those of the same kind on the same pile and then count the papers in each pile. Finally, if we were quite certain that there was no absolute majority of any kind, we could have seen at a glance which candidate had the relative plurality of first votes.

This method would reveal that the absence of an absolute majority for any candidate produces the system of votes in which each of the propositions with majority support contradicts the consequence of the other two. I repeat that when this is the case, it is best to adjourn the election for a fairly long period. Only when it cannot be adjourned or when adjourning it could do more harm than a choice based on chance should we decide it by the relative plurality of first votes.

Final Comments

There are of course, in the field of moral and political science, many far more important matters than that to which I have, perhaps for too long, directed the attention of the National Institute. In this field, there is no such thing as excessive precision or an inconsequential error or a truth not worth searching for. Besides, in free countries, the general will is so sacred that no amount of checking it could be excessive.

The areas of social science which, like elections, offer some scope for strict calculations will undoubtedly be perfected first. But it must be stressed that however good the mathematical procedures are in themselves, applying them to moral ideas only works properly when these ideas have to some extent been prepared for calculation by a recognition of the facts from which they derive and the elements of which they are formed. If our principles are false, our explanations of the facts incomplete, and our definitions obscure; if we make any mistakes in our observation of the facts, omit anything, or use ambiguous language, then calculations based on them will simply develop a series of perfectly linked errors, and the mathematical apparatus will simply inspire great respect for illusions.

Part 3
The Nineteenth Century

CHAPTER 12

C. L. Dodgson [Lewis Carroll]

A Discussion of the Various Methods of Procedure in Conducting Elections, 1873

The following paper has been written and printed in great haste, as it was only on the night of Friday the 12th that it occurred to me to investigate the subject, which proved to be much more complicated than I had expected. Still I hope that I have given sufficient thought to it to escape the commission of any serious mistake.

I commence by considering certain known Methods of Procedure, in the case where *some* candidate *must* be elected, proving that each Method is liable, under certain circumstances, to fail in giving the proper result.

I then consider the question of 'Election or no Election?' proving that the two ordinary Methods of deciding it are unsound.

And I conclude by describing a Method of Procedure (whether new or not I cannot say) which seems to me not liable to the same objection as have been proved to exist in other cases.

C.L.D.

CH. CH., DEC. 18, 1873.

Contents

Chapter II
On the failure of certain Methods of Procedure, in the case
where it is allowable *to have 'no Election'*

Chapter III
On a proposed Method of Procedure

Chapter IV
Summary of Rules

Chapter I: On the failure of certain Methods
of Procedure, in the case where an Election
is necessary

§ 1. *The Method of a Simple Majority*

In this Method, each elector names the *one* candidate he prefers, and he who gets the greatest number of votes is taken as the winner. The extraordinary injustice of this Method may easily be demonstrated. Let us suppose that there are eleven electors, and four candidates, *a, b, c, d;* and that each elector has arranged in a column the names of the candidates, in the order of his preference; and that the eleven columns stand thus:

---

1. [This section was printed separately; Dodgson intended it to be added to the pamphlet. It is bound in with the Bodleian Library's copy of *Suggestions* . . . , where the catalogers were misled by the fact that *Suggestions* . . . has five numbered sections. We have restored it to its correct place in the text, added this reference in the contents list, and added the column of figures headed "§6" in the table in Chapter III (correcting a mistake in Dodgson's arithmetic). This column, and the other additions to the printed text recorded in notes 2 and 3 below, were added by Dodgson in his own copy of *A Discussion* . . . This, the only known copy, is in the collection of Dodgson's papers acquired from M. L. Parrish by Princeton University Library. We have worked from the reverse photocopy provided to Christ Church Library by Robin Farquharson in 1954. We have silently corrected a small number of typographical mistakes in all three pamphlets.]

Case $(\alpha)^2$

a	a	a	b	b	b	b	c	c	c	d
c	c	c	a	a	a	a	a	a	a	a
d	d	d	c	c	c	c	d	d	d	c
b	b	b	d	d	d	d	b	b	b	b

Here *a* is considered best by *three* of the electors, and second by all the rest. It seems clear that he ought to be elected; and yet, by the above method, *b* would be the winner—a candidate who is considered *worst* by *seven* of the electors!

§ 2. *The Method of an Absolute Majority*

In this Method, each elector names the *one* candidate he prefers; and if there be an absolute majority for any one candidate, he is taken as the winner.

Case (β)

b	b	b	b	b	b	a	a	a	a	a
a	a	a	a	a	a	c	c	c	d	d
c	c	c	d	d	d	d	d	d	c	c
d	d	d	c	c	c	b	b	b	b	b

Here *a* is considered best by nearly half the electors (one more vote would give him an absolute majority), and never put lower than second by any; while *b* is put last by *five* of the electors, and *c* and *d* by three each. There seems to be no doubt that *a* ought to be elected; and yet, by the above Method, *b* would win.

2.	a	a	a	a	a	a	a	b	b	b	b
	c	c	c	c	c	c	c	d	c	c	c
	d	d	d	d	d	d	d	a	a	a	a
	b	b	b	b	b	b	b	c	d	d	d

agrees with opposite, both in marks, & in votes on pairs. [Manuscript note by Dodgson on blank page opposite Case α. In Case α, *a* is the Borda winner (see the table in Chapter III of *A Discussion . . .*) but not the relative majority winner. In the case in this note, *a* wins by any reasonable procedure. The Dodgson matrices, and hence the Borda and Condorcet/Copeland scores, of the two cases are identical; *a* is of course the Borda and Condorcet winner in each case. Dodgson presumably wrote this note some time after abandoning the Borda rule and rediscovering the Condorcet rule in 1874.]

§ 3. *The Method of Elimination, where the names are voted on by two at a time*

In this Method, two names are chosen at random and proposed for voting; the loser is struck out from further competition, and the winner taken along with some other candidate, and so on, till there is only one candidate left.

Case (γ)

a	a	a	a	a	b	b	c	d	d	d
c	c	c	c	d	a	a	b	b	b	b
b	d	d	d	c	c	c	a	a	a	a
d	b	b	b	b	d	d	d	c	c	c

Here it seems clear that *a* ought to be the winner, as he is considered best by nearly half the electors, and never put lower than third; while *b* and *d* are each put last by *four* electors, and *c* by *three*. Nevertheless, by the above Method, if (*a*, *b*) were put up first for voting, *a* would be rejected, and ultimately *c* would be elected. Again, if (*a*, *c*) were put up first, *c* would be rejected, and if (*a*, *b*) were put up next, *d* would be elected—but if (*a*, *d*), *b* would be elected.

Such preposterous results, making the Election turn on the mere accident of *which* couple is put up first, seem to me to prove *this* Method to be entirely untrustworthy.

§ 4. *The Method of Elimination, where the names are voted on all at once*

In this Method, each elector names the *one* candidate he prefers: the one who gets fewest votes is excluded from further competition, and the process is repeated.

Case (Δ)

b	b	b	c	c	c	d	d	d	a	a
a	a	a	a	a	a	a	a	a	b	c
d	c	d	b	b	b	c	c	b	d	d
c	d	c	d	d	d	b	b	c	c	b

Here, while *b* is put last by *three* of the electors, and *c* and *d* by *four* each, *a* is not put lower than second by any. There seems to be no doubt that *a*'s election would be the most generally acceptable:[3] and yet, by the above rule, he would be excluded at once, and ultimately *c* would be elected.

§ 5. *The Method of Marks*

In this Method, a certain number of marks is fixed, which each elector[4] shall have at his disposal; he may assign them all to one candidate, or divide them among several candidates, in proportion to their eligibility; and the candidate who gets the greatest total of marks is the winner.

This Method would, I think, be absolutely perfect, if only each elector wished to do all in his power to secure the election of *that candidate who should be the most generally acceptable,* even if that candidate should *not* be the one of his own choice: in this case he would be careful to make the marks exactly represent his estimate of the relative eligibility of *all* the candidates, even of those he *least* desired to see elected; and the desired result would be secured.

But we are not sufficiently unselfish and public-spirited to give any hope of this result being attained. Each elector would feel that it was *possible* for each other elector to assign the entire number of marks to his favorite candidate, giving to all the other candidates zero: and he would conclude that, in order to give his *own* favorite candidate any chance of success, he must do the same for him.

This Method is therefore liable, in practice, to coincide with 'the Method of a Simple Majority', which has been already discussed, and, as I think, proved to be unsound.

§ 6. *The Method of Nomination*

In this Method, some one candidate is proposed, seconded, and the votes taken for and against. This Method is fair for those electors *only* who prefer that candidate to *any* other, or else *any* other to him. But any other elector might say 'I do not know whether to vote for or against *a* till I know *who*

---

3. *a* beats *b* by 8 to 3.

   a beats *c* by 8 to 3.

   a beats *d* by 8 to 3.

[Manuscript note by Dodgson. Thus *a* is the Condorcet winner as well as the Borda winner (for which see the table in Chapter III of *A Discussion* . . . in our chap. 12). As with note 2 above, Dodgson may have written this later on coming to see the importance of the Condorcet criterion. He has not annotated case *β*, where the Borda and Condorcet winners are different.]

4. [The printed text has "candidate," an obvious slip for "elector."]

would come in if he failed. If I were sure *b* would come in, I would vote against *a:* otherwise, I vote *for a.*'

If this Method leads to a *majority* of votes being obtained for the proposed candidate, it is identical with 'the Method of an absolute Majority,' which was discussed in § 2. If a *minority* only is obtained, it may be thus represented:

b	*b*	*c*	*c*	*d*	*d*	*a*	*a*	*a*	*a*	*a*
a	*a*	*a*	*a*	*a*	*a*	*b*	*b*	*c*	*c*	*d*
c	*c*	*b*	*b*	*b*	*b*	*c*	*c*	*b*	*b*	*b*
d	*d*	*d*	*d*	*c*	*c*	*d*	*d*	*d*	*d*	*c*

Here there seems no doubt that *a* ought to be elected; and yet, by the above Method, he would be rejected at once, and, *whichever* candidate came in, *nine* of the electors would say 'We would rather have had *a*.'

Chapter II: On the failure of certain Methods
of Procedure, in the case where it is allowable
to have 'no Election'

§ 1. *The Method of* commencing *with a vote on the question*
'Election or no Election?'

This Method has the strong recommendation that if 'no Election' be carried, it saves all further trouble, and it *might* be a just method to adopt, provided the electors were of two kinds only—one, which prefers 'no Election' to *any* candidate, even the best; the other, which prefers *any* candidate, even the worst, to 'no Election.' But it would seldom happen that *all* the electors could be so classed: and any elector who preferred certain candidates to 'no Election,' but preferred 'no Election' to certain other candidates, would not be fairly treated by such a procedure. He might say 'It is premature to ask me to vote on this question. If I knew that *A* or *B* would be elected, I would vote to *have* an election; but if neither *A* nor *B* can get in, I vote for having none.'

Let us, however, test this Method by a case—representing 'no Election' by the symbol '0'.

Case (ϵ)

a	*a*	*b*	*b*	*c*	*c*	0	0	0	0	0
0	0	0	0	0	0	*a*	*a*	*b*	*b*	*c*
c	*c*	*a*	*a*	*b*	*b*	*d*	*d*	*c*	*c*	*b*
d	*d*	*d*	*d*	*d*	*d*	*b*	*c*	*a*	*a*	*a*
b	*b*	*c*	*c*	*a*	*a*	*c*	*b*	*d*	*d*	*d*

Here there seems no doubt that 'no Election' would be the most satisfactory result: and yet, by the above Method, an Election would take place, and, *whichever* candidate came in,[5] *nine* of the electors would say 'I would rather have had no Election.'

§ 2. *The method of* concluding *with a vote on the question*
'*Shall X (the successful candidate) be elected, or shall there be*
no Election?'

Here again a voter who preferred certain candidates to 'no Election', but preferred 'no Election' to certain other candidates, would not be fairly treated. He might say 'If you had taken *A* or *B*, I would have been content, but as you have taken *C*, I vote for no Election,' and his vote might decide the point: while the other electors might say 'If we had only known how it would end, we would willingly have taken *A* instead of *C*.'

But let us test this Method also by a case.

Case (ζ)

b	b	b	b	b	0	a	a	a	a	a
a	a	a	a	a	b	0	0	0	0	0
c	c	c	c	c	a	b	b	b	b	b
d	d	d	d	d	c	c	c	c	c	c
0	0	0	0	0	d	d	d	d	d	d

Here there seems to be no doubt that the election of *a* would be much more satisfactory than having no Election: and yet, by the above Method, *b* would first be selected from all the candidates, and ultimately rejected on the question of '*b* or no Election?' while *ten* of the electors would say 'We would rather have taken *a* than have no Election at all.'

The conclusion I come to is that, where 'no Election' is allowable, the phrase should be treated exactly as if it were the name of a candidate.

Chapter III: On a proposed Method of Procedure

The Method now to be proposed is, *in principle,* a modification of No. 5, viz. 'The Method of Marks,' since it assigns to each candidate a mark for every vote given to him, when taken in competition with any other candidate.

Suppose that, in the opinion of a certain elector, the candidates stand in

---

5. [Dodgson substituted the phrase ", *whichever* candidate came in," in his copy for the following in the printed text: "in all probability *b* would be elected, a candidate regarding whom." His second thoughts are more general than his first.]

the order *a, b, c, d:* then his votes may be represented by giving *a* the number 3, *b* 2, *c* 1, and *d* 0.

Hence all that is necessary is that each elector should make out a list of the candidates, arranging them in order of merit.

If 'no Election' is allowable, this phrase should be placed somewhere in the list.

If the elector cannot arrange all in succession, but places two or more in a bracket, a question arises as to how the bracketed names should be marked. The tendency of many electors being, as explained in Chap. I, § 5, to give to the favorite candidate the maximum mark, and bracket all the rest, in order to reduce their chances as much as possible, it is proposed, in order to counteract this tendency, to give to each bracketed candidate the same mark that the *highest* would have if the bracket were removed. This plan will furnish a strong inducement to avoid brackets as far as possible.

In order to illustrate this process, let us apply it to the various 'Cases' already considered.

	α	β	γ	δ	§6	ϵ	ζ
a	25	27	23	24	27	21	37
b	12	18	15	15	17	21	33
c	20	11	14	14	14	20	16
d	9	10	14	13	8	10	5
0						38	19

It will be seen that in each case the candidate, whose election is obviously most to be desired, obtains the greatest number of marks.

Chapter IV: Summary of Rules

1. Let each elector make out a list of the candidates, (treating 'no Election' as if it were the name of a candidate), arranging them as far as possible in the order of merit, and bracketing those whom he regards as equal.
2. Let the names on each list be marked with the numbers, 0, 1, 2, &c., beginning at the last.
3. Whenever two or more names are bracketed, each must have the mark which would belong to the highest, if there were no bracket.
4. Add up the numbers assigned to each candidate.

The *first* Rule is all with which the electors need trouble themselves. Rules 2, 3, 4 can all be carried out by one person, as it is merely a matter of counting.

Suggestions as to the Best Method of Taking Votes, Where More than Two Issues Are to Be Voted On, 1874

In the immediate prospect of a meeting of the Governing Body, where matters may be debated of very great importance, on which various and conflicting opinions are known to be held, I venture to offer a few suggestions as to the mode of taking votes. On this subject I printed a paper some little time ago, but have since seen reason to modify some of the views therein expressed. Especially, I do not now advocate the method, there proposed, as a good one to *begin* with. When other means have failed, it may prove useful, but that is not likely to happen often, and, when the difficulty does arise, the question what should next be done may fairly be debated on its own merits.

C.L.D.

CH. CH., JUNE 13, 1874.

§ 1. *Votes to be taken in writing*

The method here suggested is to divide a sheet of paper into as many columns as there are issues to be voted on, and place the name of each at the head of a column. The paper is then passed round, each voter placing his name in the column he prefers.

The only objection to this method, that I can think of, is that it takes rather more time than voting *vivâ voce;* and even *this* is not always the case, as it is by no means unusual for a doubt to arise as to the result of a *vivâ voce* vote, which makes it necessary to take the votes over again.

Its advantages are, that it enables the division-list to be put on record, which I think should always be done when an important matter is voted on, except in elections of Students, in which case there are obvious objections to the names of the voters being recorded.

At the end of a meeting, it should be settled which of the division-lists, if any, are to be entered on the minutes; and the other lists might then be destroyed.

§ 2. *A list to be made of all the issues to be voted on*

This should be done before *any* vote is taken at all. The list should contain every issue which is proposed, and seconded, for entry on it. The *general negative* issue ('that there be no election', or, 'that nothing be done') should, I think, find a place on this list (provided of course that it be proposed and seconded), and should not be voted on separately—a course sometimes adopted, but which I think I have shown, in a former paper on this subject, to be unsound.

§ 3. *The first vote to be taken on all the issues collectively*

This course is suggested in the hope that it may give an absolute majority (or such a majority as may be previously declared to be binding), so as to settle the question at once.

§ 4. *Failing a settlement by this method, the issues to be then voted on two at a time*

This course is suggested in the hope that by it some one issue may be discovered, which is preferred by a majority to every other taken separately. For this purpose, any two may be put up to begin with, then the winning issue along with some other, and so on. But no issue can be considered as the absolute winner, unless it has been put up along with *every* other.

§ 5. *Failing a settlement by this method also, further proceedings may be then debated on*

If no settlement has been arrived at by § 3 or § 4, it will at least prove that the matter is one on which the meeting is *very evenly divided in opinion.* Such a state of things is of course very difficult to deal with, but the difficulty, though possibly not diminished, will certainly not have been increased by adopting the process I have here suggested.

A Method of Taking Votes on More than Two Issues, 1876
March 1876
Not yet published

(*As I hope to investigate this subject further, and to publish a more complete pamphlet on the subject, I shall feel greatly obliged if you will enter in this copy any remarks that occur to you, and return it to me any time before . . . .*)[6]

§ 1. *Proposed Rules for Conducting an Election*

I

Each elector shall write down the issue he desires ('no Election' being reckoned as an issue) and hand in the paper folded, with his name written outside:

---

6. [This blank is filled in with the words "June 1876" in Dodgson's hand in the copy at Christ Church. Another copy has "April 1878" (Williams et al. 1979, 89). This, in addition to

and the Chairman, or some one appointed by him, having before him a list of the electors, shall enter these issues against their names.

II

If the Chairman find any issue having an absolute majority of votes, he shall communicate the list to the meeting. This issue shall then be formally moved, and, if none object, the Chairman shall declare it carried.

III

If the Chairman shall find no issue having an absolute majority of votes, he shall communicate to the meeting the list of issues only, without stating who vote for each, and shall return the papers, that each elector may add the other issues, arranged in his order of preference. The Chairman shall enter these on his list, and then communicate the whole to the meeting.

IV

If an issue be found which has a majority over every other taken separately, it shall be formally moved as in Rule II: but if none be found, the majorities being 'cyclical,' opportunity shall be given for further debate. In ascertaining which of any pair of issues is preferred to the other, any elector whose paper contains one only of the two shall be reckoned as preferring that one, and any whose paper contains neither shall be considered as not voting.

V

If the issues cannot be all arranged in one cycle, but form a cycle and a set of issues each of which is separately beaten by each of the cycle, it shall be formally moved that this cycle be retained and all other issues struck out, and, if none object, this shall be done.

VI

If, a formal motion having been made that a certain issue be adopted, or that a certain cycle be retained and all other issues struck out, any one object, he may move as an amendment that a division be taken between the issue he desires and the issue so to be adopted, or any one of the cycle so to be re-

what Black calls Dodgson's "cyclostyled sheet" of December 1877 soliciting comments on *A Method . . .* (Black 1958, 234), suggests that Dodgson tried for nearly two years to get Oxford colleagues to comment on the paper. It rather implies that he failed.]

tained. If every such amendment be lost on a division, the Chairman shall declare the original motion carried: but, if any such amendment be carried, by some voting contrary to their written papers, they shall be required to amend their papers, and the process shall begin again.

VII

When the issues to be further debated consist of, or have been reduced to, a single cycle, the Chairman shall inform the meeting how many alterations of votes each issue requires to give it a majority over every other separately.

VIII

If, when the majorities are found to be cyclical, any elector wish to alter his paper, he may do so: and if the cyclical majorities be thereby done away with, the voting shall proceed by former Rules: but if, when none will make any further alteration, the majorities continue cyclical, there shall be no election.

§ 2. *The Legal Conditions*

In any election, when there are only *two* issues to vote on—for instance (there being only one candidate), 'shall *A* be elected or not?' or again (there being only two candidates, and it being understood that there is to be an election) 'shall *A* or *B* be elected?'—and when the Chairman is able to give a casting vote, it is clear that there *must* be a majority for one or other issue, and in this case open voting is the obvious course.

But wherever there are three or more issues to vote on, any one of the following three cases may exist in the minds of the electors:

(α) *There may be one issue desired by an absolute majority of the electors.*

(β) *There may be one issue which, when paired against every other issue separately, is preferred by a majority of electors.*

(γ) *The majorities may be 'cyclical,'* e.g., *there may be a majority for* A *over* B, *for* B *over* C, *and for* C *over* A.

The words of the Ordinance are **'That Candidate for whom the greatest number of votes shall have been given shall be deemed elected.'**

It seems to me that this may be complied with by either of two modes of election:

In case (α) *If a candidate be declared elected who, when all are voted on at once, has an absolute majority of votes.*

In case (β) *If a candidate be declared elected who, when paired with every other separately, is preferred by the majority of those voting.*

But that it is *not* complied with by the following mode:

In case (γ) *If a candidate be declared elected, though it is known that there is another who, when paired with him, is preferred by the majority of those voting.*

Mode (α) needs no discussion. Failing this, it seems clear that mode (β) would be a satisfactory result, as any one who preferred some other candidate might be allowed to take a division between the two.

If modes (α) and (β) both fail, it shows that the majorities on the separate pairs are 'cyclical,' and if, after all possible discussion, this continues to be so, any election that may be arrived at *must* introduce mode (γ). My own opinion is that, under these circumstances, there ought to be 'no Election': two other courses might be suggested, which I will now consider.

§ 3. *Courses that have been suggested for the case of 'Cyclical Majorities'*

(1) *That all candidates should be voted on at once, and the one who has the greatest number of votes should be elected.*

This might be thought to fulfill the *letter* of the law, if after the words 'shall have been given' we supply the words 'in the final voting.'

Let us suppose that there are 11 electors, and 4 candidates, *a, b, c, d;* and that each elector has arranged in a column the names of the candidates in the order of his preference; and that the 11 columns stand thus:

a	a	a	a	b	b	b	c	c	c	d
d	d	b	b	c	c	d	b	b	b	c*
c	c	d	d	a	a	c	d	d	d	b*
b	b	c	c	d	d	a	a	a	a	a

FIG. 1.

Here the majorities are cyclical, in the order *a d c b a*, each beating the one next following.

Moreover, if we make a table of majorities in the separate pairs, in which the numerator of each fraction represents the number voting for the issue which stands at the top of that column and the denominator the number voting for the issue which stands at the end of that row, and in which every division, where the issue at the top of the column is beaten, is distinguished by placing the fraction in a parenthesis, we have

	a	b	c	d
a		$^7/_4$	$^7/_4$	$(^5/_6)$
b	$(^4/_7)$		$^6/_5$	$(^3/_8)$
c	$(^4/_7)$	$(^5/_6)$		$^6/_5$
d	$^6/_5$	$^8/_3$	$(^5/_6)$	

Fig. 2.

Here *a* and *d* each need 4 changes of votes to win, but *b* and *c* each need one only: for instance, the interchange of the two issues which are marked * would make *b* win. It seems clear that *a* has much less claim to be elected than either *b* or *c* (observe that he is put *last* by nearly half the electors, and only needs *one* interchange of votes to cause him to be beaten by *every* other candidate separately), and yet by the above course he would win.

Again, let there be 13 electors and 4 candidates.

a	a	a	a	b	b	b	c	c	c	d	d	d
b	b	b	b	d	d	d	d	a	a	b	b	b
c	c	c	c	c	c	c	a*	b	b	c	c	c
d	d	d	d	a	a	a	b*	d	d	a	a	a

Fig. 3.

Here the majorities are cyclical, in the order *a b c d a;* the table of majorities being:

	a	b	c	d
a		$(^6/_7)$	$^9/_4$	$^7/_6$
b	$^7/_6$		$(^3/_{10})$	$(^4/_9)$
c	$(^4/_9)$	$^{10}/_3$		$(^6/_7)$
d	$(^6/_7)$	$^9/_4$	$^7/_6$	

Fig. 4.

Here *a, c, d* each need 4 changes of votes to win, while *b* needs only one, for instance, the interchange of the two issues marked *. Yet by the above course *a* would win—a candidate whom this single interchange would cause to be beaten by *every* other candidate separately.

(2) *That all candidates should be voted on at once, and the one who has the smallest number of votes should be struck out, and the process repeated till only two are left.*

a	a	a	a	b	b	b	b	c	c	c
b	b	c	c	c	c	c	c	b	a	a
c	c	b	b	a	a	a	a	a	b	b

Fig. 5.

Here the majorities are cyclical, in the order *a b c a*. Moreover, *a* beats *b* (6 to 5), *b* beats *c* (6 to 5), but *c* beats *a* (7 to 4).

If any one is to be elected, it would seem that *c* has the strongest claim; but by the above method *a* would win—a candidate who is put last by nearly half the electors.

Again, let there be 15 electors and 4 candidates:

a	a	a	a	b	b	b	b	c	c	c	c	d	d	d
d	d	d	d	c	c	c	c*	d	d	d	d	a	a	b
b	b	b	b	d	d	d	d*	a	a	b	b	c	c	c
c	c	c	c	a	a	a	a	b	b	a	a	b	b	a

Fig. 6.

Here there is a cyclical majority, in the order *a b c d a;* therefore by above Rule *d* is excluded: we now have

a	a	a	a	b	b	b	b	c	c	c	c	a	a	b
b	b	b	b	c	c	c	c	a	a	b	b	c	c	c
c	c	c	c	a	a	a	a	b	b	a	a	b	b	a

Fig. 7.

Here there is again a cyclical majority, in the order *a b c a;* therefore *c* is excluded.

The candidates are now reduced to *a* and *b,* and *a* wins by a majority of 8 to 7.

But if we tabulate the majorities thus—

	a	b	c	d
a		($^7/_8$)	$^9/_6$	$^{11}/_4$
b	$^8/_7$		($^6/_9$)	$^{11}/_4$
c	($^6/_9$)	$^9/_6$		($^7/_8$)
d	($^4/_{11}$)	($^4/_{11}$)	$^8/_7$	

Fig. 8.

we see that *a* needs 6 changes of votes to win, *b* 5, *c* 2, and *d* only 1. It seems clear that d ought to win; yet he is the very first to be excluded by the above course.

Lastly, let us take a case in which these two courses bring in different candidates, neither of them being the one that ought to win.

Let there be 23 electors and 4 candidates.

a	a	a	a	a	a	a	b	b	b	b	b	b	c	c	c	c	c	c	d	d	d	d
b	b	c	c	c	c	d	d	d	d	d	d	d	b	b	b	b	b	b	b	b	c	c*
d	d	b	b	b	b	b	a	a	a	a	a	a	a	a	a	a	a	d	a	a	b	b*
c	c	d	d	d	d	c	c	c	c	c	c	c	d	d	d	d	d	a	c	c	a	a

FIG. 9.

Here the majorities are cyclical in the order $a\ d\ c\ b\ a$. The table of majorities is:

	a	b	c	d
a		$16/7$	$(8/15)$	$(11/12)$
b	$(7/16)$		$12/11$	$(5/18)$
c	$15/8$	$(11/12)$		$13/10$
d	$12/11$	$18/5$	$(10/13)$	

FIG. 10.

Now, by course (1) a wins.

By course (2) d is excluded; but we still have a cyclical majority $a\ c\ b\ a$; we then exclude a, and c wins.

But, if we reckon how many changes of votes each needs to win, we find that a needs 5, c needs 6, and d needs 8; whereas b needs only 1—a single interchange, such as the two marked *, would give him a clear victory.

Note also that this single interchange would cause c (who is brought in winner by course (2)) to be beaten by *every* other candidate separately.

The instances I have taken seem to show that neither of these courses can be relied on to give a satisfactory result. But there is a stronger, and as I think a fatal, objection to both; namely, that any elector, who had not consented to this course being adopted, would have a very strong ground of appeal against the election if he were able to say 'A was declared elected, and yet he had not "the greatest number of votes" given for him, since he was beaten when paired against B.'

The conclusion I come to is that, in the case of persistent cyclical majorities, there ought to be 'no Election.'

I am quite prepared to be told, with regard to the cases I have here proposed, as I have already been told with regard to others, 'Oh, *that* is an extreme case: it could never really happen!' Now I have observed that this answer is always given instantly, with perfect confidence, and without any examination of the details of the proposed case. It must therefore rest on some general principle: the mental process being probably something like this—'I have formed a theory. This case contradicts my theory. *Therefore* this is an extreme case, and would never occur in practice.'

§ 4. *Reasons for beginning with a vote on all issues at once*

One reason for this is that it *may* show an absolute majority for some one issue, and so save all further trouble. But another, and a stronger, reason is that, when a division is taken first of all between a certain pair of issues, there will very often be some of the electors who will not know which way to vote. I am not speaking of electors who are willing to vote contrary to their real opinion, but of electors generally.

An example or two will make this clear.

Suppose there are two vacancies, but that it is not necessary to fill both: and that a division is taken first of all on the question 'Shall both vacancies be filled, or only one?' An elector might reasonably say 'I wish to elect *A* alone. If I were sure he would come in, I would vote for electing *one* only: but if *B* is preferred, then, rather than lose *A*, I would vote for electing *two*.' And another might say '*I* wish to elect *A* and *B*, but I strongly object to *C*. If I were sure *A* and *B* would come in, I would vote for electing *two*: but if that would result in *A* and *C* coming in, then I vote for *one* only.' How much simpler to allow the one to write down '*A* alone,' and the other '*A* and *B*.'

Again, suppose it settled that two are to be elected, and a division to be taken between *B* and *D*. An elector might reasonably say 'I wish to elect *A* at any rate: the other to be *B* or *C*, I do not care which: but I object to *D*. I would vote for *B*, if I were sure that *A* would be elected as the other. But if I knew that *C* would beat *A* on a division, I should wish to get *C* and *A* elected, and this *might* be effected by voting for *D*. I happen to know that *C* and *A* can each beat *D*, so that he has no real chance. My voting for him would not mean that I wish to bring him *in*, but that I wish to keep *B* out, and so to get *C* and *A* elected, instead of *C* and *B*.' How much simpler to allow him to write '*A*, and then *B* or *C*.'

§ 5. *Reasons for allowing 'no Election' to be reckoned*
among the other issues

Evidently an elector who desires 'no Election' ought to have *some* opportunity of voting on the question. And if it be not reckoned as an issue, it must be voted on, as a separate question, at the beginning or the end of the proceedings.

(1) *The method of* beginning *with a vote on the question 'Election or no Election?'*

This Method has the strong recommendation that if 'no Election' be carried, it saves all further trouble, and it *might* be a just method to adopt, provided the electors were of two kinds only—one, which prefers 'no Election' to *any* candidate, even the best; the other, which prefers *any* candidate, even the worst, to 'no Election.' But it would seldom happen that *all* the electors could be so classed: and any elector who preferred certain candidates to 'no Election,' but preferred 'no Election' to certain other candidates, would not be fairly treated by such a procedure. He might say 'It is premature to ask me to vote on this question. If I knew that *A* or *B* would be elected, I would vote to *have* an election; but if neither *A* nor *B* can get in, I vote for having none.'

(2) *The method of* ending *with a vote on the question 'Shall X be elected, or shall there be no Election?'*

Here again a voter who preferred certain candidates to 'no Election,' but preferred 'no Election' to certain other candidates, would not be fairly treated. He might say 'If you had taken *A* or *B*, I would have been content, but as you have taken *C*, I vote for no Election,' and his vote might decide the point: while the other electors might say 'If we had only known how it would end, we would willingly have taken *A* instead of *C*.'

The conclusion I come to is that, where 'no Election' is allowable, the phrase should be treated exactly as if it were the name of a candidate.

§ 6. *Reasons for having a preliminary voting on paper and not open voting*

Suppose *A* to be the candidate whom I wish to elect, and that a division is taken between *B* and *C;* am I bound in honor to vote for the one whom I should *really* prefer, if *A* were not in the field, or may I vote in whatever way I think most favorable to *A*'s chances? Some say 'the former,' some 'the latter.' I proceed to show that, whenever case (α) fails to occur, and there are among the electors a certain number who hold the latter course to be allowable, the result *must* be a case of cyclical majorities.

Let there be 3 candidates, *A, B, C,* each preferred by about one-third of the electors; and suppose that, when a division is taken between *A* and *B*, *A* wins. A division is now taken between *A* and *C*, which of course depends on the votes of the *B*-party; perhaps a majority of them *really* prefer *A*, and if they voted accordingly *A* would win under case (β); it might need only two or three to vote contrary to their real opinion to turn the division in favor of *C*. We have now got '*A* beats *B*, *C* beats *A*,' and of course a division must be taken between *B* and *C;* this depends on the votes of the *A*-party, and, as before, it may only need two or three to vote contrary to their real opinion to prevent C winning the election. Thus we get 'A beats B, C beats A, B beats C.'

This principle of voting makes an election more of a game of skill than a real test of the wishes of the electors, and as my own opinion is that it is better for elections to be decided according to the wish of the majority than of those who happen to have most skill in the game, I think it desirable that all should know the rule by which this game may be won. It is simply this: 'In any division taken on a pair of issues neither of which you desire, vote against the most popular. There *may* be some one issue which, if all voted according to their real opinion, would beat every other issue when paired against it separately: but, by following this rule, you *may* succeed in getting it beaten *once,* and so prevent its having a clear victory, by introducing a cyclical majority. And this will give, to the issue you desire, a chance it would not otherwise have had.'

Now, it is impossible to prevent such votes being given: and even if a preliminary voting on paper should seem to lead to case (α) or (β), it is impossible, when it comes to the final formal vote, to prevent votes being given contradictory to previous votes.

The advantages of having the preliminary voting taken on paper and not openly are, first, that each elector, not knowing exactly how the others are voting, has less inducement to vote contrary to his real opinion, so that a more trustworthy estimate is arrived at of the real opinion of the body of electors, and cyclical majorities are less likely to occur, than with open voting; and secondly, that if cyclical majorities do *not* occur in this process, they cannot occur in the formal voting except by some one or more of the electors giving votes inconsistent with their written opinions, and I think it desirable that in such a case the body of electors should know who they are that have so voted—a result which this method would secure.

I do not suppose that any one would be so unwilling to have it known that he has so voted that this publicity would *prevent* an artificial cyclical majority—for I am sure that those who do so believe it to be an honorable course to take, and so have no motive for desiring concealment—but I think it would increase the sense of the responsibility incurred by those who thus exercise their right of voting, and so make its occurrence less likely.

These written lists will also be, in many cases, a great saving of time. An example will best show this. Suppose there are 2 vacancies to be filled, and 3 candidates, all recommended on various grounds by the examiners, and that the electors are divided among the following 6 issues, 'A B,' 'B A,' 'A C,' 'C A,' 'B C,' 'A alone.' These, taken two and two, give 15 pairs: that is, it might require 15 divisions to be taken to get the information which the written lists furnish at once.

CHAPTER 13

Charles L. Dodgson [Lewis Carroll]

The Principles of Parliamentary Representation, 1884

Preface

Through all the dust and din of the present controversy, four things, at least, are surely clear to all thinking men:—

First, that it would be an unmitigated evil to have a General Election with the new Franchise, but without a new Distribution of Seats;

Secondly, that there would be no difficulty in avoiding all risk of such a catastrophe, *PROVIDED THAT* a clause were added to the Franchise-Bill, enacting that it "shall not be put into operation until a Redistribution-Bill has also been passed";[1]

Thirdly, that there would be no difficulty in both parties agreeing to such a clause, *PROVIDED THAT* each felt secure against the other party obtaining an unfair advantage in the Redistribution;

Fourthly, that there would be no difficulty in making this secure, *PROVIDED THAT* some general principles, making it impossible for either side to obtain any such advantage, could be discovered and accepted by both parties.

It is in the profound conviction that such principles exist, and that they can be as clearly formulated, and as fully proved, as the principles of any other Science, that I venture to address these pages to all interested in the matter.

C. L. D.

Ch. Ch., Oxford,
Nov. 5, 1884.

[This is the first edition. In February 1885 Dodgson produced a second edition in which the mathematical arguments were relegated to the back. Whether or not this succeeded in making the pamphlet easier for the lay reader, it obscures things for the well-informed reader, so we reproduce the text of the first edition. With, or soon after, the second edition, Dodgson produced a supplement and postscript to the supplement dealing with his arguments against the Hare scheme and a rebuttal of points made by its defenders. These are too specialist to reproduce here but will be found in Black forthcoming.]

1. [This demand was successfully made by Salisbury in the weeks that followed. Dodgson and Salisbury had discussed it in their correspondence earlier in 1884.]

Chapter I: Desiderata

The chief *desiderata* seem to be as follows:—

(1) That each Elector should have the same chance of being represented in the House. (Under *any* system, *some* Electors must be left unrepresented.)

(2) That each Elector, who is represented at all, should be represented by the same fraction of a Member. Or (which is the same thing) that each Member should represent the same number of Electors. Or (which is the same thing) that the number of Electors, needed to secure the return of a Member, should be uniform throughout the Kingdom.

(3) That the number of unrepresented Electors should be as small as possible.

(4) That the proportions of political parties in the House should be, as nearly as possible, the same as in the whole body of Electors.

(5) That the process of voting should be as simple as possible.

(6) That the process of counting the votes, and announcing the result, should be as simple as possible.

(7) That the waste of votes, caused by more votes being given for a Candidate than are needed for his return, should be as far as possible prevented.

(8) That the result of a local Election should depend as much as possible on the wishes of the Electors in that District, and as little as possible on chance.

(9) That the Electors in a District should be, as far as possible, uninfluenced by the results of Elections in other Districts.

Chapter II: Principles to be observed in forming
electoral Districts, and in determining, for each District,
how many Members it shall return

§ 1. *Number of Members in House.*

There seems to be no sufficient reason, *a priori,* for any change in this particular. It would probably be best to take 660 as the number to be generally aimed at, though holding ourselves free to modify this as circumstances might require.

§2. *Number of electoral Districts; whether to be equal
or unequal; &c.*

The two extreme cases are (1) to have as many Districts as Members, each to return one Member, in which case the Districts should of course be equal; (2) to form the whole Kingdom into one District.

In the first case (a method that has been much advocated) it is only a bare majority in each District who are represented. For it must not be supposed that all who vote for a Member are duly represented by him. If a District contains 20,001 Electors, so that 10,001 are enough to return a Member, all additional votes are absolutely wasted: hence only 10,001 Electors in that District are represented in Parliament; the other 10,000, whether they vote for the successful Candidate, or for a rival, or even if there be no contest at all, are unrepresented. This method, then, leaves nearly half the whole body of Electors unrepresented.

The injustice of this method may be illustrated from two points of view. Suppose a bare majority of the Electors to be of one party, and the rest of the opposite party; e.g., let 6-11ths be 'red' and 5-11ths 'blue.' Then, as a matter of abstract justice, about 6-11ths of the House ought to be 'red,' and 5-11ths 'blue.' But practically this would have no chance of occurring: if the 'reds' and 'blues' were evenly distributed through the Kingdom, a 'red' would be returned in every District, and the whole House would be of one party! Yet this distribution is, by the Laws of Probability, more likely than any other one distribution, and, the nearer the distribution to the most probable one, the nearer we come to this monstrous injustice.

The other way of looking at it is almost as telling. Suppose the House to have been elected, and that 6-11ths of the Members are 'red,' and 5-11ths 'blue': all we could learn from this, as to the views of the Electors, would be that 6-22ths (about 28 p. c. [percent]) are 'red,' and 5-22ths (about 23 p.c.) 'blue': as to the other 49 p. c., we should know absolutely nothing—if they were all 'red' (i.e., if 3-4ths of the Electors were 'red'), or all 'blue' (i.e., 7-10ths of the Electors 'blue'), it would make no difference in the House.

Taking this first extreme, then, as yielding the *maximum* of injustice which can be effected by arrangement of Districts, and observing that, if each District returned 2 Members, only 1-3rd of the Electors (on the assumption that each Elector has only one vote—an arrangement whose justice we shall hereafter prove) would be unrepresented, if 3 Members, only 1-4th, and so on, we see that the fewer and larger the Districts, i.e., the greater the number of Members which, on an average, each District returns, the fairer the result: till we come to the other extreme, where the whole Kingdom is formed into one District returning 660 Members, in which case only 1-661th of the whole body of Electors would be left unrepresented. A general Election, with so gigantic a District, would of course be impracticable: and probably Districts, returning 6 Members each, would be about as large as could be conveniently dealt with: but very small Districts should be, as far as possible, avoided.

I find, in the *Standard* for October 10, 1884, a very good instance of the injustice done by subdividing large electoral Districts. "The Birmingham Conservatives are, a Correspondent telegraphs, keenly discussing the Government Redistribution Scheme. The clause which apportions 6 Members to

Birmingham gives much dissatisfaction in Conservative circles. It is contended that, if the borough is to be divided into three electoral Districts, each District to have 2 Members, the Liberals could so manipulate the voters as to be certain of returning the whole of the 6 Members." Now, assuming that each Elector is to have one vote only, the Liberals could only do this by mustering more than two-thirds of the votes in each District; i.e., they must be 67 p. c., or more, of the whole body of Electors in Birmingham. But, if the three Districts were made one, it would need about one-seventh of the whole (i.e., 14 and 2-7ths p. c.) to return one Member. Hence 67 p. c. could only return 4 of the 6 Members: it would require 71 p. c. to return as many as 5; and they could not return all 6, unless they were 86 p. c. of the whole body.

Taking it as proved, then, that single-Member Districts should be in all cases avoided, and that all such should be grouped together, so as to form Districts returning at least 2 Members each, and, wherever it is possible, 4 or 5 or even more, we need only add, as a general remark, that, the more we equalize the Districts, the more we equalize the chance that each Elector has of being one of those represented in the House. Thus, in a District, returning 2 Members, the chance is 2-3ds; with 3 Members, it is 3-4ths; and so on.

§ 3. *Formula for determining, for each District, how many Members it shall return.*

A preliminary question must here be asked, viz. are we to count population, or Electors only? I do not think it matters much which, as they probably vary nearly together, i.e. a District having twice the population of another would probably have twice as many Electors. The Formula can best be determined for the number of *Electors:* but if, in using it, the number of population be substituted, it will make no important difference in the result.

The formula will of course have to be modified for each case, if it be agreed to give political weight to differences in rateable property, or to the distinction between town and country voters: and for this purpose rules would have to be laid down.

Now, taking 'e' to represent, for any one District, the number of Electors, and 'm' the number of Members to be assigned to that District, and assuming that each Elector has only one vote, we require a formula giving m in terms of e. This formula must evidently be such as will secure that every Member in the House shall, as far as possible, represent the same number of Electors.

Now, whatever be the quota of recorded votes, which is necessary and sufficient, *before the poll is closed,* to make it certain that 'A' will be returned, that is the number of Electors whom A will represent in the House. He cannot represent *less,* for this number is *necessary;* and he cannot represent *more,* for it is *sufficient,* so that all additional votes are superfluous. Let us call this necessary and sufficient quota 'Q.'

Now, in order that Q may be *sufficient,* it must not be possible for m other Candidates to obtain Q votes each; i.e., $(m + 1) \cdot Q$ must be greater than e; i.e., Q must be greater than $e/(m + 1)$. Also, in order that Q may be *necessary,* it must be the whole number *next* greater than this fraction. Hence, approximately, $Q = e/(m + 1)$; i.e. $m = e/Q - 1$.

This, then, is the formula required. An example will make it clear. Suppose the universal quota to be 6,000: then a District containing 50,000 Electors would have 7 Members assigned to it.

We have yet to find a formula for determining Q. Let 'e_1' be the number of Electors in District No. 1, 'e_2' the number in No. 2, and so on; let 'm_1' be the number of Members assigned to District No. 1, 'm_2' the number assigned to No. 2, and so on; also let 'E' be the total number of Electors in the Kingdom, 'M' the number of Members in the House, and 'D' the number of Districts. Then we have

$$(m_1 + 1) \cdot Q = e_1,$$

$$(m_2 + 1) \cdot Q = e_2,$$

&c.

$$\therefore (M + D) \cdot Q = E; \quad \text{i.e., } Q = \frac{E}{M + D};$$

$$\therefore m = e \cdot \frac{M + D}{E} - 1.$$

§ 4. *Tables calculated by the preceding Formulæ.*

Let us suppose the 2,000,000 new Electors to be already enfranchised, thus making the total Electorate about 5,000,000. Let us further assume the number of electoral Districts to be 180, so that each will return, on an average, 3 and 2-3ds of a Member.

Let M = No. of Members in House = 660.
$\quad D$ = No. of Districts = 180.
$\quad e$ = No. of Electors in a District.
$\quad E$ = total No. of Electors = 5,000,000.
$\quad p$ = population in a District.
$\quad P$ = total population = 36,000,000.
$\quad Q$ = universal quota, to be aimed at.
$\quad m$ = No. of Members assigned to a District.

Then $E/(M + D)$ = 5,000,000/840 = about 6,000;

$$\therefore m = \frac{e}{6,000} - 1 \dots\dots\dots\dots\dots\dots\dots\dots\dots\dots\dots\dots\dots\dots (a)$$

It will be worthwhile to contrast with this the 'rough and ready' method of assigning Members in proportion to the number of Electors, so that $M:e::M:E$. This gives us

$$m = e \cdot \frac{M}{E} = e \cdot \frac{660}{5,000,000} = \frac{e}{7,600} \dots\dots\dots\dots\dots\dots\dots\dots (b)$$

In the following Table [1], the second column gives the number of Members to be returned by a District, the first the number of Electors by Formula (a), and the third the same by Formula (b).

The numbers, in the first and third columns, have been calculated by giving to m, in the preceding Formulæ, the successive values one-half, 3-halves, 5-halves, &c. Hence we see that, by Formula (a), a District containing between 9,000 and 15,000 Electors must have between one-half and 3-halves of a Member (i.e., must have *one* Member) assigned to it; and so on. If a District contained almost exactly 15,000, it could not fairly be determined, by this

TABLE 1.

e, by (a)	m	e, by (b)
9,000		4,000
	1	
15,000		11,000
	2	
21,000		19,000
	3	
27,000		27,000
	4	
33,000		34,000
	5	
39,000		42,000
	6	
45,000		49,000
	7	
51,000		57,000
	8	
57,000		65,000
	9	
63,000		72,000
	10	
69,000		80,000

Table, whether it ought to return one Member, or two. In such a case, it would be best to change the boundaries of the District, so as to increase or diminish the number of Electors by 2,000 or so.

Comparing the results of the two Formulæ, we see that, for Districts whose population[2] is about 27,000, it matters very little which Formula we use: but, for small Districts, Formula (*b*) assigns too many Members, and, for large Districts, too few; e.g., 13,000 Electors ought to return only one Member—Formula (*b*) gives them two; 60,000 ought to return 9—Formula (*b*) gives them 8.

We will now examine the effect of counting the population of a District, and not the Electors only.

Here, for $E/(M + D)$, we must substitute $P/(M + D)$; i.e., 36,000,000/ 840, i.e., about 43,000.

Hence Formula (*a*) becomes

$$m = \frac{e}{43,000} - 1 \dots\dots\dots\dots\dots\dots\dots\dots\dots\dots\dots (c)$$

Also Formula (*b*) becomes

$$m = e \cdot \frac{660}{36,000,000} = \frac{e}{54,500} \dots\dots\dots\dots\dots\dots\dots (d)$$

Comparing this with Table 1, we see that, provided only it be true that the number of Electors in a District is always about 5-36ths of the population, the substitution of number of population for number of Electors will suffice for all practical purposes; and, seeing that there is evidently a tendency to go by population, and that it is much more easy to take the population of a District than to estimate what will be the number of its Electors when the Franchise-Bill is passed, the first column of Table 2. is probably the best to employ.

Chapter III: Principles to be observed in conducting Elections

§ 1. *Number of Votes each Elector may give.*

The two extreme cases are (1) to let each Elector give as many votes as there are Members to be returned by the District; (2) to let him give one vote only.

The effect of each of these methods, and of the intermediate methods

---

2. ["Population" should read "electorate."]

TABLE 2.

e, by (c)	m	e, by (d)
64,000		27,500
	1	
107,000		82,000
	2	
150,000		136,500
	3	
193,000		191,000
	4	
236,00		245,500
	5	
279,000		300,000
	6	
322,000		354,500
	7	
365,000		409,000
	8	
408,000		463,500
	9	
451,000		518,000
	10	
494,000		572,500

which lie between them, will be best understood by considering the following Tables of percentages.

We will first find general formulæ for determining what number of Electors, in a given District, is necessary and sufficient to secure the return of one Candidate, of 2, of 3, &c.

Let e = No. of Electors in the District,
m = ... Members assigned to it,
v = ... votes each Elector can give,
s = ... seats it is desired to fill,
x = ... Electors required.

Also let it be assumed that an Elector may not give 2 votes to the same Candidate. (N.B. 'cumulative' voting is discussed at p. 312.)

Now, in order that x may be *sufficient* to fill s seats, it must be large enough to make it impossible for the other $(e - x)$ Electors to fill $(m + 1 - s)$ seats; since the two events are incompatible, so that, if the latter were possible, the former would be impossible. To effect this, each of the s Candidates must have more votes than it is possible to give to each of $(m + 1 - s)$ rival Candidates.

In order that *x* may be *necessary,* it must be only *just* large enough for the purpose.

It will be necessary to consider the following 4 cases separately. Observe that > means 'greater than,' ⧁ means 'not greater than,' and ∴ means 'therefore.'

Case (*a*) *v* is ⧁ *s*, and also ⧁ (*m* + 1 − *s*);
Case (*b*) ... > *s*, but ⧁ (*m* + 1 − *s*);
Case (*c*) ... ⧁ *s*, but > (*m* + 1 − *s*);
Case (*d*) ... > *s*, and also > (*m* + 1 − *s*).

In case (*a*), the *x* Electors can give *vx* votes, which, divided among *s* Candidates, supply them with *vx/s* votes apiece. Similarly, the (*e* − *x*) Electors can give *v* · (*e* − *x*) votes, which, divided among (*m* + 1 − *s*) Candidates, supply them with

$$\frac{v \cdot (e - x)}{m + 1 - s}$$

votes apiece. Hence we must have

$$\frac{vx}{s} > \frac{v \cdot (e - x)}{m + 1 - s},$$

where *v* divides out;

$$\therefore x \cdot (m + 1 - s) > se - sx;$$

$$\therefore x \cdot (m + 1) > se;$$

$$\therefore x > \frac{se}{m + 1}.$$

In case (*b*), each of the *x* Electors can only use *s* of his *v* votes, since he can only give *one* to each Candidate: hence the *x* Electors can only give *sx* votes, thus supplying *s* Candidates with *x* votes apiece. But the (*e* − *x*) Electors can, as in case (*a*), supply (*m* + 1 − *s*) Candidates with

$$\frac{v \cdot (e - x)}{m + 1 - s}$$

votes apiece. Hence we must have

$$x > \frac{v \cdot (e - x)}{m + 1 - s};$$

$$\therefore x \cdot (m + 1 - s) > ve - vx;$$

$$\therefore x \cdot (m + 1 - s + v) > ve;$$

$$\therefore x > \frac{ve}{m + 1 - s + v}.$$

In case (c), the x Electors can, as in case (a), supply s Candidates with vx/s votes apiece. But each of the $(e - x)$ Electors can only use $(m + 1 - s)$ of his votes: hence the $(e - x)$ Electors can only give $(m + 1 - s) \cdot (e - x)$ votes, thus supplying $(m + 1 - s)$ Candidates with $(e - x)$ votes apiece. Hence we must have

$$\frac{vx}{s} > e - x;$$

$$\therefore vx > se - sx;$$

$$\therefore x \cdot (s + v) > se;$$

$$\therefore x > \frac{se}{s + v}.$$

In case (d), the x Electors can, as in case (b), supply s Candidates with x votes apiece. And the $(e - x)$ Electors can, as in case (c), supply $(m + 1 - s)$ Candidates with $(e - x)$ votes apiece. Hence we must have

$$x > e - x;$$

$$\therefore 2x > e;$$

$$\therefore x > \frac{e}{2}.$$

Tabulating these results, we have the following formulæ [fig. 1].

By these formulæ the following Table is calculated. It shows, for a given District, what percentage of the Electors is necessary and sufficient to secure the return of *one* Candidate, of 2, of 3, &c.

The 2nd line in the 3d section represents the well-known "three-cornered

	Data.	Formulæ
(a)	$v \not> s$ $\not> m + 1 - s$	$x > \dfrac{se}{m + 1}$
(b)	$v > s$ $\not> m + 1 - s$	$x > \dfrac{ve}{m + 1 - s + v}$
(c)	$v \not> s$ $> m + 1 - s$	$x > \dfrac{se}{s + v}$
(d)	$v > s$ $> m + 1 - s$	$x > \dfrac{e}{2}$

[Fig. 1]

constituency."[3] Observe (by comparing it with the next line) that it makes it too hard for a minority to fill *one* seat, and too easy for a majority to fill *all*.

In examining this Table, we notice, first, the uniformity of the *upper* line in each section (i.e., the percentages required when each Elector can give as many votes as there are seats to fill). Here, in every case, more than half the Electors must agree, in order to fill one single seat: but, when once this number have mustered, they have it in their power to fill *all* the seats! '*C'est le premier pas qui coûte.*'

This absurdity diminishes gradually, from line to line, as we look down each section; the lowest line (i.e., the percentages required when each Elector can give one vote only) being always the most reasonable. One of the most startling anomalies is the 4th line of the 6th section. Here we see that, out of 100 Electors, we must muster 34 in order to fill *one* seat: with four more Electors, we can fill the second seat: with five more, the third: but 'then comes the tug of war'; to win the fourth seat, we actually need *fifteen* more Electors!

Lastly, comparing together the lowest lines of the several sections, we notice that they gradually improve as we move down from section to section, requiring a smaller percentage to fill *one* seat, thus giving a minority a better chance of being represented, and a larger percentage to fill *all,* thus leaving a smaller number unrepresented. This last figure (the right-hand end of each

---

3. [By "the well-known 'three-cornered constituency,'" Dodgson means the constituencies such as Manchester and Birmingham in which the limited vote had been in operation since 1867. They were three-member seats in which each voter had two votes. See the discussion of the limited vote in the Introduction.]

TABLE 3.

No. of Members Ret. By District	No. of Votes Each Elector Can Give	No. of Seats It Is Desired To Fill					
		1	2	3	4	5	6
1	1	51					
2	2	51	51				
	1	34	67				
3	3	51	51	51			
	2	41	51	61			
	1	26	51	76			
4	4	51	51	51	51		
	3	43	51	51	58		
	2	34	41	61	67		
	1	21	41	61	81		
5	5	51	51	51	51	51	
	4	45	51	51	51	56	
	3	38	43	51	58	63	
	2	29	34	51	67	72	
	1	17	34	51	67	84	
6	6	51	51	51	51	51	51
	5	46	51	51	51	51	55
	4	41	45	51	51	56	61
	3	34	38	43	58	63	67
	2	26	29	43	58	72	76
	1	15	29	43	58	72	86

lowest row) represents the percentage of the Electors in the Kingdom who would be represented in the House, supposing all the Districts similar to the one under consideration: and this percentage we find to rise, from 51 in the case of single-Member Districts, to 86 in the case of six-Member Districts.

The obvious conclusion is—let the Districts be as *large* as possible, and let each Elector give *one* vote only.

The effect, on the composition of the House, will be yet more clearly seen by considering the following three Tables, which are calculated on the assumption that, in any District, all proportions, between 'red' and 'blue,' are equally probable, and that 6-11ths of the House are 'red' and 5-11ths 'blue." Table 4 gives the percentage of the whole body of Electors represented by the 'red' Members, Table 5 the percentage represented by the 'blue,' and Table 6 the percentage unrepresented:—

By inspecting these Tables, we see two things:—

TABLE 4.

Number of Members Assigned to Each District	Number of Votes Each Elector Can Give					
	6.	5.	4.	3.	2.	1.
1.	—	—	—	—	—	28
2.	—	—	—	—	28	37
3.	—	—	—	28	36	42
4.	—	—	28	35	40	44
5.	—	28	33	39	43	46
6.	28	32	36	40	44	48

TABLE 5.

Number of Members Assigned to Each District	Number of Votes Each Elector Can Give					
	6.	5.	4.	3.	2.	1.
1.	—	—	—	—	—	23
2.	—	—	—	—	23	31
3.	—	—	—	23	30	34
4.	—	—	23	29	34	37
5.	—	23	28	32	36	38
6.	23	27	30	34	37	38

TABLE 6.

Number of Members Assigned to Each District	Number of Votes Each Elector Can Give					
	6.	5.	4.	3.	2.	1.
1.	—	—	—	—	—	49
2.	—	—	—	—	49	32
3.	—	—	—	49	34	24
4.	—	—	49	36	26	19
5.	—	49	39	29	21	16
6.	49	41	34	26	19	14

First, that the fewer and larger the Districts, i.e., the greater the number of Members returned (on an average) by each District, the more equitable the result. This conclusion we have already arrived at, from general considerations. (See p. 301, line 32.) We observe, further, that the advantage, in fairness of result, increases rapidly at first and more slowly afterward. For instance, in Table 6, if each Elector be allowed one vote only, the change from single-Member to two-Member Districts changes the percentage of unrepresented Electors from 49 to 32 (i.e., deducts about 1/3); whereas the change, from 5-Member to 6-Member Districts, only changes the percentage from 16 to 14 (i.e., deducts only 1/8). The conclusion is that *the* important point is to have as few single-Member, and even as few 2-Member, Districts as possible; but that, when we have got as far as to Districts returning 4 or 5 Members each, it is hardly worthwhile to go further.

Secondly, we see that the fewer the number of votes (down to the least possible, viz. '*one*') that each Elector is allowed to give, the more equitable the result. We observe, further, that the advantage, in fairness of result, increases slowly at first and more rapidly afterward. For instance, in Table 6, if 6 Members be assigned to a District, the change from 6 votes to 5 only changes the percentage of unrepresented Electors from 49 to 41 (i.e., deducts less than 1/6); whereas the change from 2 votes to one changes it from 19 to 14 (i.e., deducts more than 1/4). We observe, further, that the system of allowing each Elector as many votes as there are seats to fill produces, in *every* case, the same result, (the most inequitable that it is possible to produce by any variation in these data,) viz. that it leaves about 49 p. c. of the Electors unrepresented. The system (already discussed at p. 301) of "equal electoral Districts, each returning one Member" is only a particular instance of this general law.

The method of 'cumulative voting' (where an Elector can give two or more votes to the same Candidate) will usually have no other effect than to increase the 'specific gravity'—so to speak—of a vote. Let each Elector have 4 votes, with permission to 'lump' them if he chooses, and in the end you will find most of the votes given in lumps of 4, and the result much the same as if each Elector had had *one* vote only.

The conclusion is that *the* important point is to let each Elector give *one* vote only.

§ 2. *Formula for determining, after the poll is closed, the quota of Votes needed to return a Member.*

By a process, exactly similar to that employed at p. 303, we may prove that, if 'r' be the number of recorded votes, and 'm' the number of Members to be returned, the quota must be just greater than $r/(m + 1)$. For example, if

55,000 votes had been given, and the District had to return 6 Members, the quota needed to return one Member would be just greater than 7,857 and 1-7th: i.e., a Member, having 7,858 votes, would be returned. Similarly, anything just greater than 15,714 and 2-7ths would be enough (if the votes could be reckoned *en masse*) to return 2 Members: i.e., if 2 Members of the same party had 15,715 votes between them, both could be returned. We shall prove, further on, that such reckoning of votes is equitable and ought to be provided for.

This quota must be carefully distinguished from the one discussed at p. 303. If a District, returning one Member, contains 10,001 Electors, the quota needed, *before the poll is closed,* to make it certain that '*A*' will be returned, is 5,001; but, if only 8,001 vote, the quota needed, *after the poll is closed,* to return him, is only 4,001. For the purpose of *assigning Members to a District,* it is fair to proceed as if *all* the Electors were sure to vote; but, for the purpose of *returning Members,* we can count only the votes that are actually recorded.

§ 3. *Method for preventing waste of Votes.*

Assuming it to be agreed that each District is to return 2 or more Members, and that each Elector is to give one vote only, we have now to consider what is to be done when 2 or more Candidates of the same party have got, among them, enough votes to be returned, but when some have got more than the quota, and others less. It is obviously not fair that the party should fail in bringing in their rightful number of Members, merely by an accidental disarrangement of votes; but how to make an equitable transfer of the superfluous votes is by no means so obvious.

Various methods have been proposed for this: of which I will consider two:—

(1) "The Proportional Representation Society" proposes to let each Elector hand in a list of Candidates, marked in the order of his preference; and that his vote, if not required for his No. 1, should be transferred to his No. 2, and, if not required for him, then to No. 3, and so on. One great objection to this method is the confusion it would cause in the mind of an ignorant Elector who, though quite able to name his favorite Candidate, would be utterly puzzled if told to arrange 5 or 6 names in order of merit. But a much stronger objection is the difficulty of deciding to *which* of the remaining Candidates the surplus votes shall go: e.g., if 8,000 be the quota needed to return a Member, and if 6,000 lists be headed '*A B,*' and 4,000 '*A C,*' *which* 2,000 are to be transferred? Mr. J. Parker Smith, in a Pamphlet entitled "Preferential Voting," says (at p. 2), "The course which is exactly fair to *B* and *C* is that the votes which are transferred should be divided between them in the same proportion

as that in which the opinions of the whole number of A's supporters is divided." (This would require, in the above instance, that 3-5ths of the 2,000, i.e., 1,200, should be taken from the 'A B' lists, and 2-5ths, i.e. 800, from the 'A C' lists.) He adds, "This principle avoids all uncertainty, and is indisputably fair." He then proceeds to show that if, instead of counting and arranging the surplus votes, they be taken "in a random order," the chances are very great that they will come out nearly in this proportion. And he further adds (at p. 4), that "the element of chance will not be of importance as between the different parties, but only as between different individual Candidates of the same party." Now all this rests on the assertion that this mode of dividing the surplus votes, whether effected by counting or left to chance, is "indisputably fair:" and this assertion I entirely deny. The following instance will serve the two purposes, of showing that this method may easily lead to gross injustice, and of showing that the difficulty may easily arise between candidates of opposite parties.

Take a town of 39,999 Electors, returning 3 Members, so that 10,000 votes will suffice to return a Member; let there be 4 'red' Candidates, A, B, C, D, and one 'blue,' Z; and let there be 21,840 lists "A B D," 10,160 "A C B," and 7,999 "Z." There can be no shadow of doubt that, as a matter of justice, A, B, C ought to be returned, since there are more than two full quotas who put 'A B' first, and, over and above these, more than one quota who put 'A C' first. Let us see what, under the Society's present rules, would be the most probable result.

The 32,000 lists headed "A" are of two kinds, bearing to each other the ratios of the numbers 273, 127. Hence the certain event, if the lists are divided by rule, and the most probable event, if they are divided at random, is that the 10,000 lists, used in returning A, will contain 6,825 "A B D" and 3,175 "A C B." Erasing "A" from the remaining lists, we have now in hand 15,015 "B D," 6,985 "C B," and 7,999 "Z"; so that B is returned. Erasing "B" from the remaining lists, we now have 5,015 "D," 6,985 "C," and 7,999 "Z"; so that Z is returned with a majority of more than 1,000 over C. And the 'reds' must derive what consolation they can from the reflection that their rejected Candidate really had 2,161 more supporters than the successful 'blue'!

While fully agreeing, then, with the Proportional Representation Society as to the propriety of allowing only one vote to each Elector, I think I have sufficiently proved the fallacy of its method for disposing of surplus votes.

(2) A mechanical method of recording votes was suggested, in a letter signed "F. R. C.," in the *St. James' Gazette* for Aug. 1. Each Elector is to pass (unseen) through one of a set of turnstiles, (each Candidate having a separate turnstile), which will mechanically record his vote. The records are to be periodically examined, and the results placarded outside, in order that Electors, on seeing that a Candidate has already got votes enough to secure his

return, may cease to vote for him. Several objections, each by itself fatal, may be made to this method. One is that, if the periods were short enough to prevent waste of votes, the inspection would destroy the secrecy of the ballot, as it would be known who had just voted, and the result of his voting would be at once placarded; whereas, if the periods were long enough to avoid this, time would be allowed for large waste of votes. Another is that, as the quota, necessary to return a Candidate, could not be fixed till the poll had closed, it would be impossible to know, during the Election, whether a Candidate had or had not received votes enough to secure his return. Another is that, if part of the machinery went wrong, so as (for instance) to record a total of votes greater than the number of Electors, the mistake could not (as it can with voting-papers) be rectified, but the Election would have to be held over again.

Having proved, then, that the method of arranged lists will not serve fairly to dispose of surplus votes, and yet that we cannot prevent such votes being given, we have now to find, if possible, a fair method for disposing of them. Clearly *somebody* must have authority to dispose of them: it cannot be the Elector (as we have proved); it will never do to refer it to a Committee. There remains *the Candidate himself, for whom the votes have been given.* This seems to solve the whole difficulty. The Elector must understand that, in giving his vote to *A,* he gives it him as his absolute property, to use for himself, or to transfer to other Candidates, or to leave unused. If he cannot trust the man, for whom he votes, so far as to believe that he will use the vote for the best, how comes it that he can trust him so far as to wish to return him as Member?

§ 4. *Method for preventing the Electors in one District from being influenced by the results of Elections in other Districts.*[4]

That Electors are liable to such influences may be proved both *a priori* and *a posteriori.* On the one hand, it is a tendency of human nature, too well-known to need proving, to surrender one's own judgment in order to be on the winning side. In the words of the immortal Mr. Pickwick, "it's always best on these occasions to do what the mob do." "But suppose there are two mobs?" suggested Mr. Snodgrass. "Shout with the largest," replied Mr. Pickwick. On the other hand, no one, who has ever watched the progress of a General Election, can need to be reminded how obviously the local Elections of the later days have 'followed suit,' under the irresistible influence of those of the earlier days. "The secret of success," it has been well said, "is to succeed"

---

4. [In the nineteenth century, general elections were staggered over several days. Thus, as in modern national elections in the United States, early results were known to voters in late contests.]

and there can be little doubt that the party, which fails in carrying a majority of the local Elections at first, is heavily handicapped during the rest of the contest.

Supposing it admitted that such an influence does exist in General Elections as now managed, and that it is an influence to be avoided, the remedy is not far to seek: let the local Elections be so arranged that all, or nearly all, the results may be announced at the same time.

This arrangement would no doubt be unwelcome to certain 'pluralists,' who are now able to vote in several different Districts. Possibly, in such exceptional cases, voting-papers might be allowed. But, even if no remedy could be found, the justice of allowing one Elector to vote as if he were, "like Cerberus, three gentlemen at once," seems so doubtful that the objection hardly deserves serious consideration.

§ 5. *Conduct of Elections.*

The practical working of the principles, which have now been demonstrated, would be as follows:—When the poll is closed, let the total number of votes recorded be divided by the number of Members to be returned increased by one, and let the returning-officer announce the whole number next greater than the quotient as the quota needed to return *one* Member. Similarly, the whole number next greater than twice the quotient will be the quota needed to return *two,* and so on.

Let him further announce the number of votes given for each Candidate, and also announce as "returned" any Candidate who has received the quota needed to return *one.* If there are still Members to return, let him appoint a time and place for all the Candidates to appear before him; and any two or more Candidates may then formally signify that they wish their votes to be clubbed together, and may nominate so many of themselves as can be returned by the votes so clubbed. They must of course include in their nomination any of themselves who have been already declared to be returned. Let the returning-officer add together the votes of these Candidates, and, if the amount be not less than the necessary quota, let him declare to be duly returned the Candidates so nominated.

As an example, suppose that a District is to return 5 Members, and that there are 4 'red' Candidates, *A, B, C, D,* and 3 'blue,' *X, Y, Z.* Then the returning-officer might announce as follows [fig. 2]:

The Candidates might then appear before the returning-officer, and *B, C, D* might formally declare that they wished to club their votes; and, as the sum total of their votes is 30,501, they would be declared to be "returned": similarly, *X, Y, Z* might club their votes, naming *X* and *Z* as the Candidates to be

Votes given for

C	·	15,000
X	·	9,000
D	·	8,001
Z	·	8,000
B	·	7,500
A	·	6,500
Y	·	6,000

6 60,001

10,000 and 1-6th.

Quota needed to return

1 Member ·	·	10,001
2 Members	·	20,001
3 Members	·	30,001
4 Members	·	40,001
5 members	·	50,001

I hereby declare C to be duly returned.

Four vacancies remain to be filled.

(Signed)

_____

[Fig. 2]

returned; and, as the sum total of their votes is 23,000, X and Z would be declared to be "returned."

Such Candidates would have to sign some such paper as the following [fig. 3]:

This method would enable each of the parties in a District to return as many Members as it could muster the proper quota for, no matter how the votes were distributed. There would be no risk of a seat being left vacant through rivalry between two Candidates of the same party: an unwritten law would soon come to be recognized—that the one with fewest votes should give way. With Candidates of two opposite parties, such a difficulty could not arise at all: one or other of them could always be returned by the surplus votes of his own party. The only exception to this would be the occurrence (a very rare one) of an exact balance of votes. This might happen, even in the case of a single-Member constituency, if each of 2 Candidates got exactly half the votes. Of course, in such a case, somebody must give a casting-vote.

We, the undersigned, for whom the recorded votes, as stated below, amount to _____ , which is not less than _____ , the quota announced as needed to return _____ Candidates, hereby declare that we desire the said votes to be clubbed together. And we nominate, as Candidates whom we desire to be returned by the said votes, in addition to _____

_____ , who have been already declared to be duly returned, _____

_____ .

	Names	Votes
Signed,		
	Sum total of votes	

[Fig. 3]

Chapter IV: Final Summary

The main points, which I claim to have made good in this little treatise, are as follows:—

(1) That electoral Districts should be so large as to return, on an average, 3 or more Members each: and that single-Member Districts should be, as far as possible, done away with.

(2) That Members should be assigned to the several Districts in such numbers that the quota, needed to return a Member, should be tolerably uniform throughout the Kingdom.

(3) That each Elector should give one vote only.

(4) That all votes given should be at the absolute disposal of the Candidate for whom they are given, whether to use for himself, or to transfer to other Candidates, or to leave unused.

(5) That the Elections in the several Districts should terminate, as nearly as possible, at the same time.

As a practical conclusion to this treatise, I venture to suggest the following ideal Schedule of General Resolutions, such as might fairly be agreed on by all parties, and thus tend to the peaceful termination of this deplorable controversy.

(N.B. The *numbers* here suggested are merely tentative, and capable of being modified *ad libitum*.)

General Resolutions.

1. The House shall consist of 660 Members.
2. There shall be 180 electoral Districts.
3. No District shall contain less than a population of 60,000, or more than 500,000.
4. A District, whose population is between 60,000 and 105,000, shall have one Member assigned to it; between 105,000 and 150,000, two Members; and so on, in accordance with the following Table [fig. 4]:
5. If the population of a District be very near to one of the above-named numbers, its boundaries shall be altered so as to increase, or diminish, the population, by not less than 10,000.

Population	Members
60,000	
	1
105,000	
	2
150,000	
	3
195,000	
	4
240,000	
	5
280,000	
	6
320,000	
	7
365,000	
	8
410,000	
	9
455,000	
	10
500,000	

[Fig. 4]

6. If it be agreed to give political weight to differences in rateable property, or to the difference between town and country voters, this shall be done by modifying the number of Members assigned by the above Table.

7. The procedure at a local Election shall be as follows:—Each Elector shall give one vote only. When the poll is closed, the number of recorded votes shall be divided by the number of Members to be returned increased by one, and the returning-officer shall announce the whole number, next greater than the quotient, as the quota needed to return one Member; the whole number, next greater than twice the quotient, as the quota needed to return two Members; and so on. He shall also announce the number of votes recorded for each Candidate, and shall declare to be duly returned any Candidate who has obtained the quota. If any vacancies remain to be filled, he shall appoint a time when the Candidates shall appear before him, and any two or more of them may then formally signify their desire to club their votes, and may nominate, as Candidates to be returned by those votes, so many of themselves as the votes suffice for: provided always that they include, in such nomination, any of themselves who have been already declared to be returned. And, if the sum total of the votes so clubbed be not less than the quota needed to return the Candidates so nominated, the returning-officer shall declare to be duly returned all of them who have not been already so declared.

8. The local Elections shall be so arranged that their results may be announced, as nearly as possible, at the same time.

CHAPTER 14

E. J. Nanson

Methods of Election, 1882
(Read October 12, 1882.)

If there be several candidates for an office of any kind, and the appointment rests in the hands of several persons, an election is held to decide who is to receive the appointment. The object of such an election is to select, if possible, some candidate who shall, in the opinion of a majority of the electors, be most fit for the post. Accordingly, the fundamental condition which must be attended to in choosing a method of election is that the method adopted must not be capable of bringing about a result which is contrary to the wishes of the majority. There are several methods in use, and none of them satisfy this condition. The object of this paper is to prove this statement, and to suggest a method of election which satisfies the above condition.

Let us suppose, then, that several persons have to select one out of three or more candidates for an office. The methods which are in use, or have been put forward at various times, may be divided into three classes.

The first class includes those methods in which the result of an election is arrived at by means of a single scrutiny.

The second class includes those in which the electors have to vote more than once.

The third class includes those in which more than one scrutiny may be necessary, but in which the electors have only to vote once.

In describing these methods, the number of candidates will in some cases be supposed to be any whatever, but in other cases it will be assumed, for the sake of simplicity, that there are only three candidates. The case in which there are only three candidates is the simplest, and it is of frequent occurrence. I propose, therefore, to examine, for the case of three candidates, the results of the methods which have been proposed, and to show that they are erroneous in this case. This will be sufficient for my purpose, for it will be easily seen that the methods will be still more liable to error if the number of candidates be greater than three. I shall then discuss at some length the proposed method in the case of three candidates, and afterward consider more briefly the case of any number of candidates.

Methods of the First Class

In the first class three methods may be placed, viz., the single vote method, the double vote method, and the method of Borda. In these methods the electors have only to vote once, and the result is arrived at by means of a single scrutiny.

The Single Vote Method

This is the simplest of all methods, and is the one adopted for Parliamentary elections in all English-speaking communities in the case in which there is only one vacancy to be filled. As is well known, each elector has one vote, which he gives to some one candidate, and the candidate who obtains the greatest number of votes is elected. This method is used for any number of candidates; but in general the larger number of candidates the more unsatisfactory is the result.

In this method, unless some candidate obtains an absolute majority of the votes polled, the result may be contrary to the wishes of the majority. For, suppose that there are twelve electors and three candidates. A, B, C, who receive respectively five, four, and three votes. Then A, having the largest number of votes, is elected. This result, however, may be quite wrong, for it is quite possible that the four electors who vote for B may prefer C to A, and the three electors who vote for C may prefer B to A. If this were the case, and the question

> That A is to be preferred to B

were put to the whole body of electors, it would be negatived by a majority of two, and the question

> That A is to be preferred to C

would also be negatived by a majority of two. Thus the single vote method places at the head of the poll a candidate who is declared by a majority of the electors to be inferior to each of the other candidates. In fact, if A and B were the only candidates B would win; or if A and C were the only candidates C would win; thus B and C can each beat A, and yet neither of them wins. A wins simply because he is opposed by two men, each better than himself.

Thus the single vote method does not satisfy the fundamental condition. It appears also not only that the best man may not be elected, but also that we are not even sure of getting in the second best man. It is clear that if any candidate obtain an absolute majority of the votes polled this error cannot occur. All we can say, then, about the single vote method is that if any candidate obtain an absolute majority the method is correct, but if no one obtains such a majority the result may be quite erroneous.

These results are well known, and consequently in elections under this plan great efforts are generally made to reduce the number of candidates as much as possible before the polling day, in order to avoid the return of a candidate who is acceptable to a small section only of the electors. This reduction can, in practice, be made only by a small number of the electors, so that the choice of a candidate is taken out of the hands of the electors themselves, who are merely permitted to say which of two or more selected candidates is least objectionable to them.

The Double Vote Method

In this method each elector votes for two candidates, and the candidate who obtains the largest number of votes is elected. This method is erroneous, for it may lead to the rejection of a candidate who has an absolute majority of votes in his favour, as against all comers. For suppose that there are twelve electors, and that the votes polled are, for A, nine; for B, eight; for C, seven, then A is elected. Now, in order to show that this result may be erroneous it is merely necessary to observe that it is possible that each of the seven electors who voted for C may consider C better than A and B; that is to say, an absolute majority of the electors may consider C to be the best man, and yet the mode of election is such that not only does C fail to win, but in addition he is at the bottom of the poll. This is an important result; we shall see presently the effect it has on other methods of election.

In the case in which there are only three candidates this method is, in fact, equivalent to requiring each elector to vote against one candidate, and then electing the candidate who has the smallest number of votes recorded against him.

Borda's Method

This method was proposed by Borda in 1770, but the first published description of it is in the volume for 1781 of the "Memoirs of the Royal Academy of Sciences." For some remarks on the method see Todhunter's "History of Probability," p. 433, where the method is described. In the case of three candidates, it is as follows: Each elector has three votes, two of which must be given to one candidate, and the third vote to another candidate. The candidate who obtains the greatest number of votes is elected.

In order to show that this method may lead to an erroneous result, suppose that there are twelve electors, of whom five prefer A to B and B to C, whilst two prefer A to C and C to B, and five prefer B to C and C to A. Then the votes polled will be, for A, fourteen; for B, fifteen; for C, seven. Thus B is elected. It is clear, however, that this result is wrong, because seven out of the whole twelve electors prefer A to B and C, so that, in fact, A has an absolute majority of the electors in his favour. Hence, then, Borda's method does not satisfy the fundamental condition, for it may lead to the rejection of a candidate who has an absolute majority of the electors in his favor.

It may be observed that the result of the poll on Borda's method may be obtained, in the case of three candidates, by adding together the corresponding results in the polls on the methods already described.

If there be n candidates, each elector is required to arrange them in order of merit; then for each highest place $n - 1$ votes are counted; for each second place, $n - 2$ votes, and so on; $n - r$ votes being counted for each rth place, and no votes for the last place. The candidate who obtains the greatest number of votes is elected.

Borda does not give any satisfactory reasons for adopting the method. Nevertheless he had great faith in it, and made use of it to test the accuracy of the ordinary or single vote method, and arrived at the extraordinary conclusion that in any case in which the number of candidates is equal to or exceeds the number of electors, the result cannot be depended upon unless the electors are perfectly unanimous. This in itself is sufficient to show that Borda's method must be capable of bringing about a result which is contrary to the wishes of the majority.

There is, however, another objection which is of great importance. Borda's method holds out great inducements to the electors to vote otherwise than according to their real views. For if an elector strongly desires the return of a particular candidate, he not only gives his two votes to that candidate, but he also takes care to give his remaining vote to the least formidable of the other candidates. The effect of this is to give a great advantage to second-rate candidates. Thus not only does Borda's method fail to interpret the true wishes of the electors, supposing that they vote honestly, but it holds out great inducements to them to vote otherwise than according to their real views.

Laplace discussed the question of the best mode of electing one out of several candidates, and by an analytical investigation was led to Borda's method.[1] He states distinctly that this method is the one indicated by the theory of probabilities. He then proceeds to point out the objection just stated, and expresses the opinion that the method would, without doubt, be the best if each elector would write the names of the candidates in what he thinks the order of merit. We have seen, however, that this is far from being the case.

---

1. *Journal de l'Ecole Polytechnique* cahiers vii and viii, pp. 169–70; *Théorie analytique des probabilités* pp. 101, 299; Todhunter [1865] pp. 547–48. [These passages from Laplace are translated in part in Sommerlad and McLean (1991). For more detail on Laplace's arguments see Black (1958, 180–83), and Daunou's criticism of them in chapter 11.]

Methods of the Second Class

The simplest method of the second class is the French method of double elections. In this method each elector has one vote, as in the single vote method, already described. If, however, no candidate obtain an absolute majority of the votes polled, a second election is held. For this second election only the two candidates who obtained the largest number of votes at the first election can be candidates. The result is that the successful candidate is returned by an absolute majority of those who vote at the second election, so that it would appear, at first sight, that the successful candidate represents the views of a majority of the electors. We must not lose sight, however, of two facts, first, that all the electors who vote at the first election may not vote at the second election; second, that those who do so vote merely have to choose between the two remaining candidates, and that, consequently, they may not be represented in any sense by the candidate they vote for; they may merely be in the position of having a choice of evils.

This plan has frequently been proposed for adoption in England, and quite recently it has been proposed by more than one speaker in the Legislative Assembly of Victoria. The method is indeed a great improvement on the present system of single voting, and if the election be merely a party contest, and neither side runs more than two candidates, the result cannot be wrong. But if these conditions be not satisfied, the method may easily lead to an erroneous result. The method may be used whatever be the number of candidates; but it is sufficient to show that it is erroneous in the case of three candidates only. This is at once done by a further consideration of the example already given in discussing the single vote method. For in that example C is at the bottom of the poll, and, according to the present system, he is rejected, and a second election is held to decide between A and B, because no one has an absolute majority at the first election. The result of the second election is, for A, five votes; for B, seven votes; so that B wins. In order to show that this result be erroneous it is only necessary to suppose that the five electors who voted for A prefer C to B. For then, if the question

That C is to be preferred to B

was put to the whole body of electors, it would be carried by a majority of four. Now, we have already seen that the question

That C is to be preferred to A

would be carried by a majority of two. Hence, then, this method leads to the rejection of a candidate who is declared by a majority of the electors to be superior to each of the other candidates. This method, then, clearly violates the condition that the result must not be contrary to the wishes of the majority.

We may consider this example from a slightly different point of view. In discussing it under the single vote method, the important result arrived at was that A was inferior to each of the other candidates, and, therefore, ought to be at the bottom of the poll, instead of being at the top, as he was, in consequence of his being opposed by two good men, B and C. Thus, instead of excluding C, as in the French method, A is the one who ought to be excluded. Having arrived at the result that A is to be excluded, the whole of the electors have now a right to decide between B and C. On putting this question to the issue, we find that C is preferred by the electors.

We see, then, that the French method may lead to error through throwing out the best man at the first election. And this is the only way in which it can err; for if there be a best man, and he survive the ordeal of the first election, he must win at the second, seeing that he is, in the opinion of the electors, better than each of his competitors.

Comparing the French method with the single vote method, we see that in the case of three candidates the worst candidate may be returned by the single vote method, but that it would be impossible for such a result to be brought about by the French method. By that method we are at least sure of getting the second best man, if we fail to get the best.

There is, however, a grave practical objection to this method. It is that a second polling may be necessary. This is of great importance; for in the case where the number of electors is large, as in a political election, great expense has to be incurred, not only by the authorities in providing the necessary machinery, but also by the electors themselves in coming to the poll again. Besides this, the excitement of the election is kept up much longer than it would be if the whole matter could be settled by a single polling. There can, I think, be little doubt that this objection has been one of the chief obstacles with which the advocates of this method have had to contend. Accordingly, we find that the single vote method is employed, as a rule, in those cases in which there are some hundreds of electors, and it would be inconvenient to hold a second election. On the other hand, when the number of electors is small, so that they can all meet together, and remain till a second or third election has been held, the number of candidates is generally reduced to two by means of a preliminary ballot or ballots. This very fact shows that the defects of the single vote method are recognized, because in those cases in which it is considered to be practicable to do so a preliminary election is held, so as to try to avoid the glaring defect of the single vote method—that is, to avoid returning a candidate who is acceptable to a small section only of the electors. It is a mistake, however, to suppose that it is not practicable to hold one or more preliminary elections when the number of electors is large. It is generally thought that in order to do so a fresh set of voting papers must be used for the second election, and that this second election cannot be held till the result of the first is known, so that the electors have the expense and trouble of going to the poll a second time. This, at all events, appears to be the practice in France, Germany, and Italy. This, however, is not necessary: for, by a very simple expedient, any number of preliminary elections, on any plan whatever, may be held by means of a single set of voting papers, and without troubling the electors to vote more than once. The expedient is to require each elector to indicate his order of preference amongst all the candidates. Once get this information from the electors, and we can tell how any elector will vote on any question that may be put as to the merits of the candidates. It is here assumed that an elector will not change his opinion during the course of the election. This expedient of making each elector indicate his order of preference among all the candidates is necessary in order to carry out Borda's method, which has been described above: indeed, it was suggested by Borda himself. But Borda does not appear to have noticed that it might be made use of for a series of elections without requiring the electors to vote again; this appears to have been first pointed out by Condorcet. The idea of a preferential or comparative voting paper is one of the fundamental ones in Hare's system of proportional representation. We are not concerned with this subject here, as the only question under consideration is that of filling a single vacancy. It is, however, worthy of notice that the preferential voting paper which is such an important feature in Hare's system, is of such old origin, and that it was suggested by Condorcet as a means of filling several vacancies, which is the very question considered by Hare. The method of Condorcet, however, is quite different to that of Hare.

If the expedient here described were adopted, the French system would be free from the practical objection which has been indicated. It would still, however, be open to the objection that the result of the election might be contrary to the views of the electors. Notwithstanding this, the method would be a good practical one for elections on a large scale; it would be very suitable for party contests, and if neither side ran too many candidates, the result could not be wrong. The method, however, would be altogether unsuitable if there were three distinct parties to the contest. Under any circumstances, however, the method would be very little more complicated than the present system of single voting, and it would give much better results. If, however, it be considered desirable to reform the present electoral system so far as to introduce this French system of double elections, it would be as well to at once adopt the method of Ware, described below. This is the same, in the case of three candidates, as the French method, but in other cases it is a trifle longer. No difference whatever would be required in the method of voting, but only a little more labor on the part of the Returning Officer. The results of this method would be much more trustworthy than those of the French method.

Other Methods of the Second Class

Before passing on to the methods of the third class, it may be stated that each of the methods described under that heading may be conducted on the system of the second class. In order to do so, instead of using a preferential voting paper, as in the methods of the third class, we must suppose a fresh appeal made to the electors after each scrutiny. This, of course, would make the methods needlessly complex, and, in the case of a large number of electors, totally impracticable. This, however, is not the only objection to the methods of the second class. For if the electors be allowed to vote again after the result of one of the preliminary elections is known, information is given which may induce an elector to transfer his allegiance from a candidate he has been supporting to another candidate whom he finds has more chance of success. A method which permits, and which even encourages, electors to change their views in the middle of the contest cannot be considered perfect. This objection does not apply to those cases in which there are only three candidates, or to any case in which all but two candidates are rejected at the first preliminary election, as in the French system.

There is another objection, however, which applies to all cases alike; it is that, at the first preliminary election, an astute elector may vote, not according to his real views, but may, taking advantage of the fact that there is to be a second election, vote for some inferior candidate in order to get rid, at the first election, of a formidable competitor of the candidate he wishes to win. If this practice be adopted by a few of the supporters of each of the more formidable competitors, the result will frequently be the return of an inferior man.

On account of these objections, I consider it unnecessary to enter into any further details as to the methods of the second class.

Methods of the Third Class

In the methods of the third class each elector makes out a list of all the candidates in his order of preference, or, what comes to the same thing, indicates his order of preference by writing the successive numbers, 1, 2, 3, &c., opposite the names of the candidates on a list which is supplied to him. Thus one voting only is required on the part of the electors. These preferential or comparative lists are then used in a series of scrutinies; and the methods of the third class differ from one another only in the way in which these scrutinies are conducted. Three different methods, which may be called Ware's method, the Venetian method, and Condorcet's practical method, have been proposed for use, and these will now be described.

Ware's Method

This method is called Ware's method because it appears to have been first proposed for actual use by W. R. Ware of Harvard University.[2] The method was, however, mentioned by Condorcet,[3] but only to be condemned. This method is a perfectly feasible and practicable one for elections on any scale, and it has recently been adopted by the Senate of the University of Melbourne. It is a simple and obvious extension of the French system, and it is obtained from that system by two modifications, viz.:—

(1.) The introduction of the preferential or comparative method of voting, so as to dispense with any second voting on the part of the electors.

(2.) The elimination of the candidates one by one, throwing out at each scrutiny the candidate who has fewest votes, instead of rejecting at once all but the two highest.

In the case in which there are three candidates only, the second modification is not necessary. It will, perhaps, be convenient to give a more formal description of this method. The mode of voting for all methods of the third class has already been described; it remains, therefore, to describe the mode of conducting the scrutinies in Ware's method.

At each scrutiny each elector has one vote, which is given to the candidate, if any, who stands highest in the elector's order of preference.

The votes for each candidate are then counted, and if any candidate has an absolute majority of the votes counted, he is elected.

But if no candidate has such an absolute majority, the candidate who has fewest votes is excluded, and a new scrutiny is proceeded with, just as if the name of such excluded candidate did not appear on any voting paper.

Successive scrutinies are then held until some candidate obtains on a scrutiny an absolute majority of the votes counted at that scrutiny. The candidate who obtains such absolute majority is elected.

It is obvious that this absolute majority must be arrived at sooner or later.

---

2. See "Hare on Representation," p. 353. [Hare (1873): i.e., the fourth edition, appendix M. The appendices, some first added in the third edition and some, including this one, in the fourth, contain a large amount of undigested material about PR overseas, much of it implying criticisms of the Hare scheme that Hare did not address.]

3. *Oeuvres* 1804, vol. xiii, p. 243 [Arago and O'Connor (1847, vol. 8). This is the *Essay . . . on provincial assemblies*, translated in part in chapter 7. Condorcet attacks the double-ballot and Ware (alternative vote) schemes in a number of places but was powerless to prevent the French Republic from adopting them. It has retained them ever since.]

It is clear, also, that if on any scrutiny any candidate obtain a number of votes which is greater than the sum of all the votes obtained by those candidates who each obtain less than that candidate, then all the candidates having such less number of votes may be at once excluded.

Ware's method has been shown to be erroneous for the case of the three candidates in the remarks on the French method, of which it is in that case a particular form. It is easy to see that if there be more than three candidates the defects of this method will be still more serious.

The objection to this method, concisely stated, is that it may lead to the rejection of a candidate who is considered by a majority of the electors to be better than each of the other candidates. At the same time, the method is a great improvement on the single vote method; and the precise advantage is that whereas the single vote method might place at the head of the poll a candidate who is considered by a majority of the electors to be worse than each of the other candidates, it would be impossible for such a candidate to be elected by Ware's method.

To illustrate fully the difference between the two methods and the defects of each, suppose that there are several candidates, A, B, C, D, . . . , P, Q, R, and that in the opinion of the electors each candidate is better than each of the candidates who follow him in the above list, so that A is clearly the best, B the second best, and so on, R being the worst, then on the single vote method R may win; on Ware's method, A, B, C, D, . . . , P, may be excluded one after another on the successive scrutinies, and at the final scrutiny the contest will be between Q and R, and Q, of course, wins, since we have supposed him better than R in the opinion of the electors. Thus the single vote method may return the worst of all the candidates; and although Ware's method cannot return the worst, it may return the next worst.

A great point in favor of Ware's method is that it is quite impossible for an astute elector to gain any advantage for a favorite candidate by placing a formidable competitor at the bottom of the list. On account of its simplicity, Ware's method is extremely suitable for political elections. In cases of party contests, the strongest party is sure to win, no matter how many candidates are brought forward. The successful candidate, however, will not always be the one most acceptable to his own party.

The Venetian Method

For the sake of simplicity, I describe this method for the case of three candidates only. Two scrutinies are held; at the first scrutiny each elector has two votes, which are given to the two candidates, one to each, who stand highest in the elector's order of preference. The candidate who has fewest votes is then rejected, and a final scrutiny is held between the two remaining candidates. At the final scrutiny each elector has one vote, which is given to that one of the remaining candidates who stands highest in the elector's order of preference. The candidate who obtains most votes at the final scrutiny is elected.

This method is very faulty; it may lead to the rejection of a candidate who has an absolute majority of the electors in his favor. For we have seen, in discussing the double vote method, that such a candidate may be rejected at the first scrutiny. In fact, unless the candidate who has fewest votes at the first scrutiny has less than N votes, where 2 N is the number of electors, we cannot be sure the result is correct. For, for anything we can tell, the candidate who is rejected at the first scrutiny may be, in the opinion of an absolute majority of the electors, the best man for the post. If, however, the candidate who has fewest votes on the first scrutiny has less than N votes, then the method will certainly give a correct result. For, since there are only three candidates, to require an elector to vote for two candidates comes to exactly the same thing as to ask him to vote against one candidate. Now, if with the two votes any candidate got less than N votes, it is clear that there are more than N votes against him, for each candidate must be marked first, or second, or third on each paper. Thus, in the opinion of an absolute majority, the candidate is worse than each of the other candidates, and, therefore, ought not to be elected. Unless, therefore, the lowest candidate has less than N votes, this method violates the fundamental condition.

I do not know that the method has ever been used in the form here described; but in the still more objectionable form of the second class, which differs from the one just described only by dispensing with the preferential voting paper, and allowing the electors to vote again after the result of the first scrutiny is known, it is exceedingly common, and is frequently used by Committees. An instance, which was fully reported in the Melbourne papers, occurred some time ago in the selection of a candidate to stand on the constitutional side at the last election for Boroondara. It is fair, however, to say that the result of the method appears to have been correct in that case; but that was due to accident, and not to the method itself.

If there be more than three candidates the method is very complicated, and the defects are more serious. It seems, however, hardly worthwhile going into any details in the cases.

Condorcet's Practical Method

This method was proposed in 1793 by Condorcet, and appears to have been used for some time at Geneva. It is described at pp. 36–41 of vol. xv of "Condorcet's Collected Works" (edition of 1804), and may be used in the case of any number of candidates for any number of vacancies. We are at present concerned only with the case of a single vacancy; and for the sake of simplicity I describe Condorcet's method for the case in which there are only three candidates.

Two scrutinies may be necessary in order to ascertain the result of the election in this method. At the first scrutiny, one vote is counted for each first place assigned to a candidate, and if any candidate obtains an absolute majority of the votes counted he is elected. But if no one obtain such an absolute majority a second scrutiny is held. At the second scrutiny one vote is counted for each first place, and one vote for each second place, exactly as in the first scrutiny on the Venetian method, and the candidate who obtains most votes is elected. At first sight we might suppose that this method could not lead to error. Comparing it with the Venetian method, described above, we see that Condorcet supplies a remedy for the obvious defect of the Venetian method—that is to say, the rejection of a candidate who has an absolute majority is now impossible. A little examination, however, will show, as seems to have been pointed out by Lhuilier,[4] that the method is not free from error. For, let us suppose that there are sixteen electors, of whom five put A first and B second, five put C first and B second, two put A first and C second, two put B first and A second, and two put C first and A second. Then the result of the first scrutiny will be, for A, B, C, seven, two, seven votes respectively. Thus, no one having an absolute majority, a second scrutiny is necessary. The result of the second scrutiny will be—for A, B, C, eleven, twelve, and nine votes, respectively. Thus B, having the largest number of votes is elected. This result, however, is not in accordance with the views of the majority of the electors. For the proposition, "B is better than A," would be negatived by a majority of two votes, and the proposition, "B is better than C," would also be negatived by a majority of two votes, so that in the opinion of the electors B is worse than A and also worse than C, and, therefore, ought not to be elected.

Summing up the results we have arrived at, we see that each of the methods which have been described may result in the return of a candidate, who is considered by a majority of the electors to be inferior to each of the other candidates. Some of the methods—viz., the double vote method, the method of Borda, and the Venetian method—may even result in the rejection of a candidate who has an absolute majority of votes in his favor as against all comers. It would, however, be quite impossible for such a result to occur on the single vote method, or the methods of Ware and Condorcet.

Method Proposed

Having pointed out the defects of the methods in common use, it now remains to describe the method proposed for adoption, and to show that it is free from

---

4. See Montucla [1802] vol. iii, p. 421.

these defects. It consists merely in combining the principle of successive scrutinies with the method of Borda, and at the same time making use of the preferential voting paper, so that the proposed method belongs to the third-class. I propose, first, to describe and discuss the method for the case of three candidates, and then to pass on to the general case in which there may be any number of candidates.

Let us suppose, then, that there are three candidates, A, B, C. Each elector writes on his voting paper the names of two candidates in order of preference, it being clearly unnecessary to write down a third name. If we prefer it, the three names may be printed on the voting paper, and the elector may be required to indicate his order of preference by writing the figure 1 opposite the name of the candidate of his first choice, and the figure 2 opposite the name of the candidate of his second choice, it being clearly unnecessary to mark the third name. In order to ascertain the result of the election two scrutinies may be necessary.

At the first scrutiny two votes are counted for each first place and one vote for each second place, as in the method of Borda. Then if the two candidates who have the smallest number of votes have each not more than one-third of the whole number of votes, the candidate who has most votes is elected, as in the Borda's method. But if one only of the candidates has not more than one-third of the votes polled (and some candidate must have less), then that candidate is rejected, and a second scrutiny is held to decide between the two remaining candidates. At the second scrutiny each elector has one vote, which is given to that one of the remaining candidates who stands highest in the elector's order of preference. The candidate who obtains most votes at the second scrutiny is elected.

The method may be more briefly described as follows:—

Proceed exactly as in Borda's method, but instead of electing the highest candidate, reject all who have not more than the average number of votes polled. If two be thus rejected, the election is finished; but if one only be rejected, hold a final election between the two remaining candidates on the usual plan.

In order to show that the proposed method is free from the defects above described it is necessary and it is sufficient to show that if the electors consider any one candidate, A, say, superior to each of the others, B and C, then A cannot be rejected at the first scrutiny. For if A be not rejected at the first scrutiny he cannot fail to win at the second scrutiny. Let therefore the whole number of electors be 2N, and let the number who prefer B to C be $N + a$, and consequently the number who prefer C to B be $N - a$; similarly, let the number who prefer C to A be $N - b$, and therefore the number who prefer A to C be $N - b$, and let the number who prefer A to B be $N + c$, and therefore the number who prefer B to A be $N - c$. Then it is easy to see that the numbers of votes polled by A, B, C at the first scrutiny will be

$$2N - b + c, 2N - c + a, 2N - a + b$$

respectively. For if the compound symbol A B be used to denote the number of electors who put A first and B second, and similarly for other cases, it is clear that A's score at the first scrutiny will be

$$2AB + 2AC + BA + CA.$$

Now this expression can be written in the form

$$(AB + AC + CA) + (AC + AB + BA),$$

and it is clear that the three terms in the first pair of brackets represent precisely the number of electors who prefer A to B, which number has already been denoted by $N + c$. In the same way the remaining three terms represent the number of electors who prefer A to C, which number has been denoted by $N - b$. Hence the score of A on the first scrutiny is $2N - b + c$. In exactly the same way it may be shown that the scores of B, C are $2N - c + a$ and $2N - a + b$ respectively. The sum of these numbers is 6N, as it ought to be. Thus 2N is the mean or average of these three numbers, and consequently the highest of the three candidates must have more than 2N votes, and the lowest must have less than 2N votes. Now, let us suppose that a majority of the electors prefer A to B, and likewise that a majority prefer A to C; then c must be positive, and b must be negative. Hence the score of A, which has been shown to be $2N - b + c$, is necessarily greater than 2N, for it exceeds 2N by the sum of the two positive quantities—b and c. Thus A has more than 2N votes, that is, more than one-third, or the average of the votes polled. He cannot, therefore, be rejected at the first scrutiny, so that B or C or both must be rejected at the first scrutiny. If either of the two, B and C, be not rejected, A must win at the second scrutiny, for there is a majority for A against B, and also against C. Hence, then, it has been demonstrated that if the opinions of the electors are such that there is a majority in favor of A as against B, and likewise a majority in favor of A as against C, the method of election which is proposed will certainly bring about the correct result; whereas it has been shown by the consideration of particular examples that the methods in ordinary use may easily bring about an erroneous result under these circumstances. Thus the proposed method cannot bring about a result which is contrary to the wishes of the majority, so that the proposed method satisfies the fundamental condition.

The method which is proposed has, I think, strong claims. It is not at all difficult to carry out. The result will, as often as not, be decided on the first scrutiny. We simply require each elector to put down the names of two of the three candidates in order of preference. Then for each first name two votes are counted, and for each second name one vote is counted. The number of votes for each candidate is then found. The third part of the sum total may be called the average; then all candidates who are not above the average are at once rejected. The lowest candidate must, of course, be below the average. The second is just as likely to be below as above the average. If he is below, the election is settled; but if he is above the average, a second scrutiny is necessary to decide between him and the highest candidate.

Cases of Inconsistency

We have now to consider what is the result of the proposed method in those cases in which there is not a majority for one candidate against each of the others. The methods which have been described have been shown to be erroneous by examining cases in which either one candidate has an absolute majority of the electors in his favor, or a candidate A is inferior to B and also to C, or a candidate A is superior to B and also to C. Now it is not necessary that any of these cases should occur. If a single person has to place three candidates in order of preference he can do so, and it would be quite impossible for any rational person to arrive at the conclusions—

B is superior to C	..	..	..	..	..	(1)
C is superior to A	..	..	..	..	..	(2)
A is superior to B	..	..	..	..	..	(3)

When, however, we have to deal with a body of men, this result may easily occur, and no one of the candidates can be elected without contradicting some one of the propositions stated above. If this result does occur, then, no matter what result any method of election may give, it cannot be demonstrated to be erroneous. We have examined several methods, and all but the one now proposed have been shown to lead to erroneous results in certain cases. It may fairly be urged, then, that that method which cannot be shown to be erroneous in any case has a greater claim to our consideration than any of the other methods which can be shown to be erroneous. On this ground alone I think the method proposed ought to be adopted for all cases.

We can, however, give other reasons in favor of the method proposed. We have seen that it gives effect to the views of the majority in all cases except that in which the three results (1), (2), (3) are arrived at. In this case there is no real majority, and we cannot arrive at any result without abandoning some one of the three propositions (1), (2), (3). It seems most reasonable that that one should be abandoned which is affirmed by the smallest majority. Now, if this be conceded, it may be shown that the proposed method will give the correct result in all cases. For it is easily seen that the majorities in favor of the three propositions (1), (2), (3) are respectively $2a$, $2b$, $2c$. Hence, then, in the case under consideration, a, b, c, must be all positive. Let us suppose that a is the smallest of the three. Then we abandon the proposition (1), and consequently C ought to be elected. Now let us see what the proposed method leads to in this case. B's score at the first scrutiny is $2N - c + a$, and this is necessarily less than $2N$, because c is greater than a, and each is positive. Again C's score is $2N - a + b$, and this is necessarily greater than $2N$, because b is greater than a, and each is positive. Thus B is below the average, and C is above the average. Therefore, at the first scrutiny B goes out and C remains in. If A goes out also, C wins at the first scrutiny. But if A does not go out, C will beat A at the second scrutiny. Thus C wins in either case, and therefore the proposed method leads to the result which is obtained by abandoning that one of the propositions (1), (2), (3) which is affirmed by the smallest majority. We have already seen that in the case in which the numbers a, b, c are not all of the same sign, the proposed method leads to the correct result. Hence, then, if it be admitted that when we arrive at the three inconsistent propositions (1), (2), (3) we are to abandon the one which is affirmed by the smallest majority, it follows that the proposed method will give the correct result in all cases.

We have, then, arrived at two results. First, that if the electors affirm any two of the propositions (1), (2), (3), and affirm the contrary of the remaining one, and so affirm three consistent propositions, then the result of the method of election which is here proposed, will be that which is the logical consequence of these propositions, while the methods in ordinary use may easily give a different result. Second, that if the electors affirm the three propositions (1), (2), (3) which are inconsistent, then the result of the method proposed is that which is the logical consequence of abandoning that one of the three propositions which is affirmed by the smallest majority.

Another way of applying Proposed Method

The method may be stated in another form, which may sometimes be more convenient. For each first place count one vote; then, if any candidate has an absolute majority, elect him. But if not, count in addition one vote for each second place; then, if the lowest candidate has not got half as many votes as there are electors, reject him and proceed to a final scrutiny between the remaining two. But, if not, take the aggregate for each candidate of the results of the two counts; then reject all who have less than one-third of the votes now counted, and, if necessary, proceed to a final scrutiny.

This process will give the same final result as the method already described. This is readily seen as follows: 1st, if any one has an absolute majority on the first places, the election is settled at the first scrutiny, and the result is manifestly correct, and therefore the same as that of the proposed method. 2nd, if no one has an absolute majority on the first places, but some one has on first and second places less than half as many votes as there are electors, it is manifest that more than half the electors consider that candidate worse than each of the others, so that he ought to be rejected, and hence the result of the final scrutiny will be correct, and therefore in accordance with that of the proposed method. 3rd, if neither of the above events happen, we take the aggregate. Now (as has already been remarked) the result of taking the aggregate is to give us exactly the same state of the poll as in the first scrutiny of the proposed method. Thus the second way of applying the method will give the same final result as the proposed method. This second way is very convenient, for if there be an absolute majority for or against any candidate, it is made obvious at the first or second count, and the election is settled with as little counting as possible. The two counts are conducted on well known plans, and if the circumstances are such that either of these necessarily gives a record result, that result is adopted. But if it is not obvious that a correct result can be arrived at, then we take the mean, or what comes to the same thing, the aggregate of the two counts. This might appear to be a rule of thumb, and on that account may perhaps commend itself to some persons. This is not the case, however; and it is remarkable that that which might suggest as a suitable compromise in the matter should turn out to be a rigorously exact method of getting at the result in all cases. The view of the proposed method which has just been given shows exactly what modifications require to be made in Condorcet's practical method in order to make it accurate.

Laplace's Objection

It may be said that the proposed method is open to the objection raised by Laplace to the method of Borda. To this I think it a sufficient answer to say, that if we have a method which will truly interpret the wishes of the electors, as expressed by their voting papers, we need not trouble ourselves whether they vote honestly or not; that is their own concern. If we provide a method which will bring out a correct result for honest electors we need not try to go further, and endeavor to construct a method which will force dishonest electors to vote honestly. Nevertheless, it may be pointed out that Laplace's objection is not of so much force in this case as in the case of Borda's method. For if an elector vote otherwise than according to his real views it will be at the risk of having his vote at the final scrutiny counted against the candidate whom he considers most fit for the office to be filled. This risk would be sufficient to deter most electors from voting otherwise than according to their real opinions. If, in spite of this risk, an elector persists in voting otherwise than according to his real views we must take him at his word. To illustrate this objection, let us suppose that B and C are two formidable candidates, and that A is in reality inferior to each of them, but that the voting is as follows, BA = 5, CA = 4, AB = 1, AC = 1; so that B's supporters, in their anxiety to defeat C, put A second, and C's supporters, in their anxiety to defeat B, put A second. The result at the first scrutiny is A 13 votes, B 11 votes, C 9 votes. Thus C is rejected and A wins in the final scrutiny. A wins because the whole of C's supporters put him second. Had one of C's supporters voted according to his real views, and put B second, the result would have been different.

If the preferential mode of voting were not employed this objection would be of great force; for then the supporters of each candidate would put his most formidable opponent at the bottom of their list at the first scrutiny, knowing that they would have at the second scrutiny an opportunity of reviewing their vote.

A Modification of Proposed Method

It may be mentioned that there is another, but in general a more tedious, method of getting at a result, which cannot be shown to be erroneous in any case. This method has been adopted by the Trinity College Dialectic Society. It is as follows:—In the method proposed above, instead of rejecting all the candidates who are not above the average, reject the lowest only. It is obvious from what has been said above that this cannot lead to error. But a second scrutiny will always be required, whereas in the proposed method one scrutiny only may be necessary. There is another disadvantage: the result will not in all cases agree with that of the proposed method. For, let us suppose that a, b, c are all positive, and that a is the least of the three, and at the same time that $2c$ is less than $a + b$. On the method proposed, as we have already seen, C would be elected, but on the method now under discussion B would be elected. For the scores of A and B at the first scrutiny are $2N - b + c$. $2N - c + a$, respectively, and the first of them is the smallest, because $2c$ is less than $a + b$, and therefore $c - b$ is less than $a - c$. Thus A would be thrown out at the first scrutiny, and a second scrutiny would be held to decide between B and C, and B would win because a is positive. Thus the result is that which would follow from abandoning the proposition "A is better than B," which is affirmed by a majority of $2c$, whereas the result of the proposed method is that which would follow from abandoning the proposition "B is better than C," which is affirmed by a majority of $2a$, which is smaller than the former majority.

There is, however, one point in favor of the modified method. The first scrutiny will at once give us the values of the three differences $b - c$, $c - a$, $a - b$. From these, of course, we cannot find a, b, c. In the modified method, however, a second scrutiny is always necessary and this will at once give us the value of one of the three a, b, c. Having already found the three differences, we can at once find each of the quantities a, b, c, and thence we can ascertain if the result is demonstrably correct. Thus if the modified method be used, we can always ascertain by a simple calculation, whether the result is perfectly satisfactory or not. The same remark applies to the proposed method in those cases in which two scrutinies are necessary.

Before leaving the case in which there are three candidates only, it may be of interest to give a short algebraical analysis of the question. As before, let the compound symbol AB stand for the number of electors who put A first and B second, and similarly for other cases. Let us suppose, as is clearly possible, that six quantities, a, b, c, α, β, γ, are found from the following equation:—

$$AB = \beta + c \qquad BC = \gamma + a \qquad CA = \alpha + b$$

$$AC = \gamma - b \qquad BA = \alpha - c \qquad CB = \beta - a$$

Also let us suppose that 2N denotes the whole number of electors, which is clearly equal to $2(\alpha + \beta + \gamma)$, then the states of the poll on the different modes of election which have been discussed are as shown in the following Table [14.1]:—

In the first column is set out an analysis of the votes. In the second is the result of the poll on the single vote method. For instance, in the first line we have the quantity $\beta + \gamma - b + c$, which is the sum of AB and AC, *i.e.*, it denotes the number of electors who put A first. In the third column is the result of the poll on the double vote system, in which each elector has two votes. For instance, in the first line we have N + α, or what is the same, $2\alpha + \beta + \gamma$ and this is equal to AB + AC + BA + CA, *i.e.*, it denotes the number of electors who put A first, or second. In the fourth column is the result of the poll on Borda's method. For instance, in the first line we have $2N - b + c$, and this is equal to 2AB + 2AC + BA + CA, as it ought to be. It is also seen

TABLE 14.1.

Analysis of Votes	Single Vote	Double	Borda	Condorcet		
A $\begin{cases} AB = \beta + c \\ AC = \gamma - b \end{cases}$	$\beta + \gamma - b + c$	$N + \alpha$	$2N - b + c$	*	$N - b$	$N + c$
B $\begin{cases} BC = \gamma + a \\ BA = \alpha - c \end{cases}$	$\gamma + \alpha - c + a$	$N + \beta$	$2N - c + a$	$N + a$	*	$N - c$
C $\begin{cases} CA = \alpha + b \\ CB = \beta - a \end{cases}$	$\alpha + \beta - a + b$	$N + \gamma$	$2N - a + b$	$N - a$	$N + b$	*
$2N = 2(\alpha + \beta = \gamma)$	2N	4N	6N	2N	2N	2N

at once that $2N - b + c$ is the sum of the two numbers in the first line in the second and third columns. This shows the truth of what was stated above, viz., that the poll on Borda's method is the aggregate of the polls on the single and double vote systems. In the fifth, sixth, and seventh columns, under the heading Condorcet, are set down the states of the poll on the supposition that each of the candidates, A, B, C, is excluded in turn. Thus, if A be supposed excluded for a moment, we have $N + a$ votes for B in preference to C, and consequently $N - a$ for C in preferences to B. For $N + a$ is equal to $AB + BC + BA$, as it ought to be. Thus it is clear that $2a$ is the majority for B as against C, so that the letters a, b, c, have the same meaning as in the previous part of this paper. It is clear too, as has been proved before, that the number in any row in the column headed Borda, is the sum of the two numbers in the same row in the columns headed "Condorcet."

The result of the method of election proposed in this paper depends solely upon the numbers a, b, c. The same is true of the method of Borda. On the other hand, the result of the double vote method depends solely on the values of α, β, γ. Consequently, whatever be the result of the proposed method or of Borda's method, we can clearly construct cases in which the result of the double vote method shall be what we please. The same is true of the single vote method; for although the result of the single vote method depends upon a, b, c as well as upon α, β, γ, it is easy to see that we can choose α, β, γ so as to eliminate the effect of the quantities a, b, c, whatever may be the values of the latter. The results of the Venetian method and of Ware's method depend on the values of a, b, c, as well as upon those of α, β, γ, so that although for given values of a, b, c, we cannot bring about any result we please, still we can choose α, β, γ so as to bring about a result different from the true one. This, of course, is to be done by choosing α, β, γ, so that the best candidate is thrown out at the first scrutiny. We have already seen that this is possible.

It is clear that no one of the quantities $\beta + \gamma, \gamma + \alpha, \alpha + \beta$ can be negative. For we have $\beta + \gamma = BC + CB$, and BC, CB can neither of them be negative. Again, $\beta + \gamma = N - \alpha$; thus α cannot be greater than N. So also β, γ can neither of them exceed N. Since $\beta + \gamma$ cannot be negative, β and γ cannot both be negative; thus one only of the three α, β, γ can be negative. If α be negative it is clear that the numerical value cannot exceed N, for $\alpha + \beta$ cannot be negative, and β cannot exceed N. So for β and γ. Thus no one of the three α, β, γ can numerically exceed N, and one at most can be negative.

The limits between which a, b, c must lie are at once found from the consideration that AB, AC, &c., must none of them be negative. Thus $a + \gamma$, $\beta - a$ can neither of them be negative; thus a cannot be less than $-\gamma$ nor greater than β. Hence, a fortiori, no one of the three a, b, c, can be numerically greater than N. This last result is obvious from the fact that no one of the numbers in the columns headed "Condorcet" can be negative.

Formal demonstrations will now be given of a few results.

(i.) If any candidate have less than N votes on the double vote method, he ought not to be elected.

This has already been seen, but the following proof is given. Suppose A has less than N votes; then a must be negative, and therefore c must be negative and b positive. Thus A is worse than B, and also worse than C.

(ii.) Even if every elector put A in the first or second place it does not follow that A ought to be elected.

For if A has no third places we must have BC = O and CB = O, thus $a = \beta = -\gamma$. Suppose β positive and therefore γ negative. Then by preceding case C ought to go out and A or B ought to win as c is positive or negative. Now c may be negative so that B may win; for the only conditions with reference to c are that c must be greater than $-\beta$ and less than a, and as is β positive it is clear that c may be negative.

(iii.) It is impossible to arrive at the true result by merely counting the number of first places, the number of second places, and the number of third places for each candidate.

This result seems obvious enough after what has been given. It may, however, be formally proved as follows:—

Let A_1, A_2, A_3 denote the numbers of first, second, and third places respectively for A, and let corresponding meanings be given to B_1, &c., C_1, &c. Then we have—

$$A_1 = \beta + \gamma - b + c$$

$$A_2 = 2\alpha + b - c$$

$$A_3 = \beta + \gamma$$

with corresponding equations for B's and C's. We see at once from these equations that it is impossible to find a, b, c even if A_1, A_2, A_3, B_1, &c., be all given. We can, however, find α, β, γ and the three differences $b - c$, $c - a$, $a - b$, viz., the results are—

$$\alpha = N - A_3, \ \beta = N - B_3, \ \gamma = N - C_3$$

$$b - c = A_3 - A_1, \ c - a = B_3 - B_1, \ a - b = C_3 - C_1,$$

$$\text{where } 2N = A_1 + B_1 + C_1 = A_3 + B_3 + C_3 \ \ldots \ldots \text{ (i)}$$

thus any five of the quantities A_1, B_1, C_1, A_3, B_3, C_3, may be chosen at pleasure; the sixth and N are then determined by the conditions (i) and A_2, B_2, C_2 are then given by the equations

$$A_2 = 2N - A_1 - A_3, \text{ &c.}$$

(iv.) If there be a demonstrably correct result, say A better than B and B better than C, so that c, a, are positive and b negative, then if Ware's method be wrong, Venetian method is right, and if Venetian method be wrong, Ware's method is right.

For if Ware be wrong A must be lowest on the single vote method, and therefore we must have

$$\alpha + \beta - a + b > \beta + \gamma - b + c$$

or

$$\alpha > \gamma + a + c - 2b$$

i.e., *a fortiori* $\alpha > \gamma$ because a, c are positive and b negative. Thus A cannot be lowest on double vote method, so that A will win on the Venetian method. Again, if Venetian be wrong, A must be lowest on double vote method, and therefore we must have $\gamma > \alpha$ and therefore $\beta + \gamma - b + c > \alpha + \beta - a + b$ because a, c are positive and b negative. Thus A cannot be lowest on single vote method, so that A will win on Ware's method.

(v.) If we agree to accept the proposed method as correct in all cases, then the conclusions of the last proposition will be true in all cases.

For, in the demonstration of the last proposition, the essential condition is that $a + c - 2b$ should be positive. Now, if we suppose as before that the accepted result is A better than B, and B better than C, we must have a, b, c all positive and b the smallest of the three, so that it is clear that $a + c - 2b$ is positive.

Comparing then Ware's method with the Venetian method, we see that both may be right, or one wrong and one right, but both cannot be wrong; so that, if these two methods agree, the result cannot be shown to be wrong. If, however, they do not agree, we cannot tell which is right without in effect having recourse to the proposed method.

(vi.) If $a = b = c$, single and double vote methods give different results.

For A's scores on the two methods will be respectively $N - \alpha$ and $N + \alpha$. Thus, if $\gamma > \beta > \alpha$, the candidates are in the order A, B, C on the single vote method, and in the order C, B, A on the double vote method. In this case Borda's method leads to a tie, and consequently the proposed method also.

Ware elects A or B as c is positive or negative, and Venetian method elects C or B as a is negative or positive. Thus, in this case, Ware and Venetian method give different results.

(vii.) If $\alpha = \beta = \gamma$, double vote method, and therefore also Venetian method, gives a tie; single vote method and Borda lead to same result; but Ware and proposed method will not necessarily lead to same result. If one only of the three, $b - c$, $c - a$, $a - b$, be negative, Ware and proposed method will lead to same result; but if two be negative the results may or may not agree.

(viii.) If AB = AC, BC = BA, CA = CB, all the methods will give the same result, and that result will be demonstrably correct.

This is the case in which the strong supporters of each candidate are equally divided as to the merits of the remaining candidates. In this case we have

$$a = \beta - \gamma, b = \gamma - \alpha, c = \alpha - \beta,$$

and A's scores on the single, double, and Borda's method are respectively 2α, $N + \alpha$, $N + 3\alpha$. Thus, if $\alpha > \beta > \gamma$, it is obvious that each of these methods will put A first, B second, and C third, and it is clear that this result is correct, for a, c are positive and b negative. It is at once seen that all the methods which have been discussed will lead to the same result in this case.

(ix.) If we suppose that

$$\alpha = \frac{N}{3} + p(b - c), \beta = \frac{N}{3} + p(c - a), \gamma = \frac{N}{3} + p(a - b),$$

then A's scores on the single, double, and Borda methods will be respectively

$$\frac{2N}{3} - (p + 1)(b - c), \frac{4N}{3} + p(b - c), 2N - (b - c).$$

Hence we see that—

If $p < 0$ and > -1, the results of all three methods will be the same.

If $p < -1$, double and Borda methods will give the same result, which will be opposite to that of single method.

If $p > 0$, single and Borda methods will give the same result, which will be opposite to that of double method.

Thus, if $p > 0$ or < -1, single and double methods will give different results. If we suppose that b, c are positive and a negative, and also that $2b < c + a$, then it may be shown that these different results will both be wrong.

Cases of More Than Three Candidates

It remains now to state and examine the method proposed for the case in which there are more than three candidates.

A series of scrutinies are held on Borda's system of voting, and all candidates who on any scrutiny have not more than the average number of votes polled on that scrutiny are excluded. As many scrutinies are held as may be necessary to exclude all but one of the candidates, and the candidate who remains uneliminated is elected.

The method proposed cannot lead to the rejection of any candidate who is in the opinion of a majority of the electors better than each of the other candidates, nor can it lead to the election of a candidate who is in the opinion of a majority worse than each of the other candidates. These results are an extension of those already proved for the case of three candidates, and they may be proved as follows:

As before, let 2N be the number of electors, and let the candidates be denoted by A, B, C, D, &c. Let the compound symbol ab denote the number of electors who consider A better than B, and let corresponding meanings be given to ac, ad, ba, &c., so that ba will denote the number of electors who prefer B to A, and we shall, therefore, have $ab + ba = 2N$. Now suppose that at the commencement of any scrutiny the unexcluded candidates are A, B, C, . . . , P, then the score of A on the scrutiny will be

$$ab + ac + ad + \ldots + ap.$$

For suppose that there are n unexcluded candidates, and consider a voting paper on which A now occupies the rth place. For this A gets $n - r$ votes. Now on this paper A stands before $n - r$ other candidates. Thus the $n - r$ votes which A receives may be considered each as due to the fact that A stands before one of the following $n - r$ candidates. Thus we see that on any one voting paper A receives one vote for every candidate placed after him. Summing up for all the voting papers, we see that A receives one vote for each candidate placed after him on each paper. Now ab denotes the number of times B is placed after A on all the papers, and similarly for ac, ad, &c. Thus it is clear that A's score is

$$ab + ac + ad + \ldots + ap.$$

This result was stated by Borda,[5] but proved only for the case of three candidates.

---

5. *Mémoires de l'Académie Royale des Sciences*, 1781, p. 663 [chapter 5 above].

The whole number of votes polled is

$$2N (1 + 2 + 3 + 4 + \ldots + n - 1)$$

or Nn ($n - 1$). Thus the average polled by all the candidates is N($n - 1$). Now let us suppose that there is a majority for A as against each of the other candidates, then each of the $n - 1$ numbers ab, ac, ad, $\ldots$, ap is greater than N; thus the sum of these numbers, which is equal to A's score, is necessarily greater than ($n - 1$) N, that is, greater than the average score. Thus A will be above the average on every scrutiny, so that he must win on the proposed method.

Next, let us suppose that there is a majority for each of the other candidates against A. Then each of the numbers ab, ac, $\ldots$, ap is less than N, and therefore their sum, which is equal to A's score, is less than ($n - 1$) N, that is, less than the average score. Thus A is below the average, and will, therefore, be excluded at the first scrutiny.

The results which have just been proved are particular cases of a more general theorem, which may be enunciated as follows:—

If the candidates can be divided into two groups, such that each candidate in the first group is, in the opinion of a majority of the electors, better than each of the candidates in the second group, then the proposed method cannot lead to the election of a candidate of the second group.

The results which have just been proved are obtained from the above by supposing: first, that the first group contains one candidate, and the second group all the rest; and second, that the first group contains all but one of the candidates, and the second group the remaining candidate.

Let the first group consist of the l candidates, A, B, C, &c., and let the second group consist of the m candidates, P, Q, R, &c., and let $l + m = n$, so that n is the whole number of candidates. Because each of the candidates A, B, C, &c., is better than each of the candidates P, Q, R, &c., each of the numbers ap, aq, ar, &c. $\ldots$, bp, bq, &c., $\ldots$, &c., is greater than N. Now the scores of A, B, C, D, &c., at the first scrutiny are respectively

$$* \quad ab + ac + ad + \&c. \ldots + ap + aq + ar + \&c.$$

$$ba \quad * + bc + bd + \&c. \ldots + bp + bq + br + \&c.$$

$$ca + cb \quad * + cd + \&c. \ldots + cp + cq + cr + \&c.$$

$$da + db + dc \quad * + \&c. \ldots + dp + dq + dr + \&c.$$

$$\&c. \qquad \&c. \qquad \&c. \qquad \&c.$$

If we add together all these numbers, we shall get the sum of the scores of A, B, C, D, &c. Now the numbers in the first l columns can be arranged in pairs, such as ab, ba, and $ab + ba = 2N$, and then are $\frac{1}{2} l (l - 1)$, of these pairs; thus, the sum of the first l columns is $Nl(l - 1)$. Again, the numbers in the last m columns are each greater than N, and there are lm of these numbers; thus, the sum of the last m columns is greater than Nlm. Thus, the sum of all the numbers is greater than $Nl(l - 1) + Nlm$; that is, than $Nl(l + m - 1)$; that is, greater than $Nl(n - 1)$. Thus the sum of the scores of the l candidates of the first group is greater than $Nl(n - 1)$. Hence the average score of the candidates of the first group is greater than $N(n - 1)$. Hence the candidates of the first group cannot all be rejected at the first scrutiny. By the same reasoning it follows that those of the first group who survive cannot all be rejected at the second scrutiny; and so on. Thus some candidate of the first group must win on the proposed method; or, in other words, no candidate of the second group can be elected.

If the candidates can be divided into two groups in the manner just indicated, it is quite clear that no candidate of the second group ought to win. At the same time, whichever of the candidates of the first group wins, the result cannot be shown to be erroneous. If the division into groups can be made in more than one way, it is clear that the last statement applies only to the smallest group of the first kind. Now, in the proposed method the successful candidate must belong to the smallest group of the first kind. Hence, then, it is clear that the result of the proposed method cannot be shown to be erroneous in any case.

It is clear that no candidate can have more than N $(2n - 2)$ votes on any scrutiny, n being as before the number of unexcluded candidates at the commencement of that scrutiny. For a candidate could only have this number by obtaining the first place on each voting paper.

Again, if any candidate obtain N $(2n - 3)$ votes on any scrutiny, there is an absolute majority in his favour, so that we can at once elect him. For if a candidate were not put first on half the papers, he could not have so many as $(n - 1)$ N $+ (n - 2)$ N votes, this being the number he would have if he were put first on one half of the papers and second on the other half. It is clear, too, that if any candidate has less than N votes there is an absolute majority against him; for if a candidate has less than N votes, he must be last on at least half of the papers. These results are not of much use except in the case of three candidates; for if there be more than three candidates, it is only in cases of remarkable unanimity that a candidate can have so many as N $(2n - 3)$, or so few as N votes. If, however, there be three candidates only, the above results may be stated as follows: The average is 2N; the largest number of votes any one candidate can have is 4N; if any candidate has 3N votes, or more, there is an absolute majority for him, and we can elect him at once, no matter whether the second candidate is above the average or not; if any candidate has less than N votes, there is an absolute majority against him, so that the result of the proposed method is demonstrably correct.

In the case of any number of candidates it will sometimes save a great deal of trouble if we first examine if there be an absolute majority for or against any candidate. This is easily done, and the results arrived at in the inquiry will be of use in carrying out the proposed method, if such be found necessary. For let A_1, A_2, . . . , A_n denote the numbers of papers on which A occupies the first, the second, . . . , the last or nth place, and let similar meanings be given to B_1, B_2, &c., C_1, &c. If A_1 be greater than N, there is an absolute majority for A, and we may at once elect him. If A_n be greater than N, there is an absolute majority against A, and we may at once exclude him. If neither of these results hold good for any candidate, we must use the proposed method in its general form. Now A's score on that method is

$$(n - 1)A_1 + (n - 2)A_2 + \ldots + (n - r)A_r + \ldots + A_{n-1}.$$

Thus to find A's score we must find A_2, A_3, . . . , A_{n-1}. Now to find these it is not necessary to count all the votes for A. For we have

$$A_1 + A_2 + A_3 + \ldots + A_n = 2N,$$

and A_1, A_n having been already found, we see that it is sufficient to calculate any $n - 3$ of the $n - 2$ quantities, A_2, A_3, . . . , A_{n-1}, and the remaining one can then be found from the above equation.

It would, however, in practice be better to calculate each of the n quantities, A_1, A_2, . . . , A_n, and then to use the above equation as a test of the accuracy of the counting of the votes. Similar remarks apply to the numbers B_1, B_2, . . . , B_n, C_1, C_2, . . . , C_n, &c.

We have also n equations of the former.

$$A_r + B_r + C_r + \ldots = 2N,$$

where r may have any one of the values 1, 2, 3, . . . , n. This gives us n independent tests of the accuracy of the enumeration of the votes. In fact, if we arrange the n^2 quantities, A_1, A_2, . . . , A_n, B_1, &c., in the form of a square array

A_1, A_2, A_3, &c.

B_1, B_2, B_3, &c.

C_1, C_2, C_3, &c.

&c., &c., &c.

the sum of every row and of every column ought to be 2N, so that we have altogether $2n - 1$ independent tests of the accuracy of the enumeration of the votes.

The proposed method is not so laborious as might appear at first sight. The number of scrutinies will not usually be large, for we may reasonably expect to halve the number of candidates at each scrutiny. At each scrutiny we reject all who are not above the average. Now, in the long run we may expect to find as many below as above the average on a poll. Thus, if there be eight candidates, we should not, on the average, require more than three scrutinies. There can be no doubt, however, that the method would be tedious if the number of electors were very large, unless the number of candidates was very small indeed. In cases where the number of electors is large Ware's method has great practical advantages, for in that method we only require to count one vote for each paper examined at each scrutiny, and at every scrutiny except the first the number of papers to be examined is but a small fraction of the whole number of papers.

Condorcet's Theoretical Method

A method of election was described by Condorcet in 1785, but on account of its complexity it was never proposed for actual use. On this account, and in order to distinguish it from Condorcet's practical method (which has been already described), I propose to call it Condorcet's theoretical method. This method is described by its author in the following terms:—

There exists but one rigorous method of ascertaining the wish of the majority in an election. It consists in taking a vote on the respective merits of all the candidates compared two and two. This can be deduced from the lists upon which each elector has written their names in order of merit.

But, in the first place, this method is very long. If there are only twenty candidates, in order to compare them two and two, we must examine the votes given upon 190 propositions, and upon 780 propositions if there are forty candidates. Often, indeed, the result will not be as satisfactory as we could wish, for it may happen that no candidate may be declared by the majority to be superior to all the others; and then we are obliged to prefer the one who is alone judged superior to a larger number; and among those who are judged superior to an equal number of candidates, the one who his either judged superior by a greater majority or inferior by a smaller. But cases present themselves where this preference is difficult to determine. The general rules are complicated and embarrassing in application. ("Œuvres de Condorcet," 15:28, 29.)[6]

By this method Condorcet showed that the single vote method and the methods of Ware and Borda are erroneous. I do not think, however, that any one has hitherto noticed that Borda's method may lead to the rejection of a candidate who has an absolute majority of the electors in his favor as against all comers. It has also been shown above by the help of this theoretical method that Condorcet's practical method is erroneous. Thus it will be seen that the theoretical method is of use in testing the accuracy of other methods. From the description which has been given above, however, it is not clear what the result of the theoretical method is, even in the simplest cases, when discordant propositions are affirmed, for if there be three candidates only, and with the notation already used, we have $a = 1$, $b = 2$, $c = 3$, each candidate is superior to one other candidate, and A is superior by most, whilst C is inferior by least. Thus, according to the above description, it is not certain which of the two, A or C, wins. In another passage, however,[7] Condorcet explains how he deals with any case of three candidates, and the process he adopts in the case of inconsistent propositions is to reject the one affirmed by the smallest majority. This is exactly the process which has been described above, and which was shown to be in accordance with the method proposed. Thus it is clear that in the case of three candidates the result of the proposed method will always be the same as that of Condorcet's theoretical method.

The general rules for the case of any number of candidates as given by Condorcet[8] are stated so briefly as to be hardly intelligible. Moreover, it is not easy to reconcile these rules with the statements made in the passage quoted above, and as no examples are given it is quite hopeless to find out what Condorcet meant.

---

6. [This is Condorcet's "Sur la forme des élections," 1789, quoted from section XV. Arago and O'Connor (1847, vol. 9). For translations see Sommerlad and McLean (1989, 167–93); McLean and Hewitt (forthcoming).]

7. *Oeuvres* vol. xiii, p. 259 [i.e., *Provincial Assemblies*. The passage Nanson cites states, "As we must reject one proposition adopted by the majority, it is more natural to abandon the one with the smallest majority."]

8. *Essai sur l'application de l'analyse* [. . . .], pp. 125–26 [for a translation, see Urken, Pinkham, and McClellan (1995) and chapter 6 in this volume.]

Comparison of Proposed Method with Condorcet's Theoretical Method

Comparing the method proposed in this paper with Condorcet's theoretical method, we see that, so far as any conclusion can be drawn from the votes of the electors, the two methods always agree. In those cases in which no conclusion can be drawn from the votes, the results of the two methods will not always be the same. It is equally impossible to prove either of these results wrong. Condorcet's method always shows whether the result is incapable of being proved wrong or not, but the proposed method gives us no information on this point. With the proposed method, however, there is no difficulty in arriving at the result in any case, whereas Condorcet's method is, by his own admission, so complicated as to be quite impracticable. Condorcet returns the candidate who is superior to the largest number of other candidates, without reference either to the number of votes by which the candidate is superior to those other candidates, or to the number of votes by which the candidate is inferior to the remaining candidates. Now, in the proposed method both these elements are taken into consideration. Each candidate is, in fact, credited with the numbers of votes by which he beats all candidates he is superior to, and is debited with the numbers of votes by which he is beaten by all candidates he is inferior to. All candidates who have the balance against them are excluded, and the election then proceeds as if the remaining candidates were the only ones eligible.

It seems clear, then, that the proposed method is quite as rigorous as that of Condorcet. It gives the same result as Condorcet's in the case of three candidates and it agrees therewith in all cases so far as any conclusion can be drawn from the votes. In those cases in which no valid conclusion can be drawn from the votes the two methods may not agree, and although nothing can be proved one way or another in these cases, the principles on which the proposed method is founded seem quite as sound as those of Condorcet's method. The proposed method has, however, great practical advantages over Condorcet's method, for the process of arriving at the result is the same in all cases; the operations throughout are of the same kind. The number of numerical results which have to be arrived at is much smaller than in Condorcet's method. For instance, if there be sixteen candidates we should expect, in the long run, to have four scrutinies, involving thirty numerical results, whereas Condorcet's method would require the computation of the votes for and against 120 different propositions. When the numerical results are arrived at there is not the slightest difficulty in applying them, whereas in Condorcet's method the rules are very complicated. It may be claimed then, that the proposed method has all the rigor of Condorcet's method and none of its practical difficulties.

Incomplete Voting-papers

There is a point of some practical importance to be considered in connection with the proposed method. If the number of candidates was large, some of the electors might not be able to make out a complete list of the candidates in order of preference. We have then to consider how voting papers, on which the names are not all marked in order of preference, are to be dealt with. Such a voting paper may be called incomplete. In order to examine this question, let us first suppose, for the sake of simplicity, that there are only three candidates A, B, C, and that the votes tendered are of one of the forms AB, BA, C, that is to say, that all the electors who put A first put B second, that all who put B first put A second, and that all who vote for C mark no second name. In accordance with the proposed method, for each paper of the form AB, two votes would be given to A and one to B; and for each paper of the form BA, two votes would be given to B and one to A. The question arises, however: Is a paper of the form C, that is, a plumper for C, to be counted as one vote or as two votes for C? If it be counted as one vote only, it is clear that C might be defeated even if he had an absolute majority of first votes in his favor. For if we suppose $AB = BA = a$, and $C = c$, it is clear that the scores of A and B will each be equal to $3a$, and that of C to c. Thus C will be defeated unless $c > 3a$; but if $c > 2a$, there is an absolute majority for C. Hence, then, we may be led into error if each plumper for C be counted as one vote only. If, on the other hand, a plumper be counted as two votes, it is clear that C might win even if there were an absolute majority against him. For the score of C will now be $2c$, and C will win if $2c > 3a$. But if $2c < 4a$, there is an absolute majority against C. Thus we should also be led into error if each plumper be counted as two votes. If, however, we agree to count a plumper as three halves of a vote, neither of these errors could occur. This course is readily seen to be the proper one in any case of three candidates, for it clearly amounts to assuming that the electors who plump for C are equally divided as to the merits of A and B. For if a^1, b^1, c^1 denote the numbers of plumpers for A, B, C respectively, and if we agree to consider all the electors who plump for A as being equally divided as to the merits of B and C, the effect of the a^1 plumpers for A would be to give $2 a^1$ votes to A, and $1/2 a^1$ each to B and C. Now, as we are only concerned with the differences of the totals polled for each candidate, we see that the result of the first scrutiny will be the same if we take away $1/2 a^1$ votes from each candidate. Thus the result will come out the same if we give $3/2 a^1$ votes to A, and none to B or C, so far as the plumpers are concerned. Similarly the results will not be altered if the b^1 plumpers for B be counted, as $3/2 b^1$ votes for B and nothing for C and A, and so for C's plumpers. Thus the final result will be in accordance with the views of the electors, if each plumper be reckoned as three halves of a vote.

The assumption that the electors who plump for A are equally divided as to the merits of B and C, appears to be perfectly legitimate, for the electors have an opportunity of stating their preference, if they have one, and as they have, in the case supposed, declined to express any, it may be fairly concluded that they have none.

At the final scrutiny (if held), all plumpers for the candidate who has been rejected will have no effect.

If there be more than three candidates, and incomplete papers are presented, we should have to make a similar assumption, viz., that in all cases where the preference is not fully expressed, the elector has no preference as regards the candidates whom he has omitted to mark on his voting-paper. Thus, for example, if there be four candidates, A, B, C, D, a plumper for A ought to count as two votes for A and none for B, C, D. Again, a voting-paper on which A is marked first and B second, and on which no other names are marked, ought to count as two and a-half votes for A and three halves of a vote for B. If there be more than four candidates the varieties of incomplete papers would be more numerous, and the weights to be allotted to each would be given by more complicated rules. Practically it would be best to count one vote for each plumper in the case in which only one candidate is marked on a voting-paper; one for the last, and two for the first, when two names only are marked on a voting-paper; one for the last, two for the next, and three for the first, when three names only are marked on a voting-paper, and so on giving in all cases one vote to the candidate marked lowest on any paper, and as many votes to the candidate marked first as there are names marked on the paper. By this means the rules for computing the votes would be the same in all cases and at all scrutinies. We have seen, it is true, that this method may lead to error. The error has the effect of decreasing the votes for the candidates who are marked on any incomplete paper, and it arises solely in consequence of the papers being incomplete. Thus, if the electors do not fully express their preference, the effect is to injure the chances of their favorite candidates. If, then, we adopt the plan just described for incomplete papers, it will be sufficiently simple for practical purposes, and its use will tend to elicit from electors a full statement of their various preferences.

Cases of Equality

No case of equality can occur in the proposed method except when all the candidates poll exactly the same number of votes on a scrutiny, for if less than the whole number of candidates have the same number of votes in any scrutiny, if that common number be not greater than the average, all the equal candidates are excluded. If it be greater no one of them is excluded; and in either case we pass on to another scrutiny.

If on any scrutiny all the candidates poll exactly the same number of votes, that number, of course, must be the average, and it is necessary that some one should have a casting vote. If it is thought proper to do so, one casting vote can then be made to settle the election, by allowing the casting vote to decide who is to win. But if it is thought that this is giving too much weight to the casting vote, then we may permit the casting vote to decide who is to be excluded, and then proceed to a fresh scrutiny between the remaining candidates. It will be observed, however, that the chance of a casting vote being required at any scrutiny except the last, when only two candidates remain, is very minute, seeing that it depends upon all the candidates polling exactly the same number of votes on a scrutiny.

Statement of Method

It is convenient to give here a formal statement of the method which it is proposed should be used when incomplete papers are presented.

Each elector is furnished with a list of the candidates in alphabetical order, upon which he indicates his preference among the candidates by placing the figure 1 opposite the name of the candidate of his first choice, the figure 2 opposite the name of the next in order of preference, the figure 3 opposite the next, and so on, to as many names as he pleases.

It is, of course, unnecessary to mark all the names; it is sufficient to mark all but one. In what follows, if all the names be marked, it is unnecessary to pay any attention to the name marked lowest in order of preference.

The mode of dealing with the papers is as follows:—For the lowest candidate marked on any paper count one vote, for the next lowest two votes, for the next three votes, and so on, till the highest is reached, who is to receive as many votes as there are names marked on the paper. The total number of votes for each candidate is then to be ascertained; and thence the average number polled. All candidates who have not polled above the average are then to be excluded. If more than one candidate be above the average, then another scrutiny must be held as between all such candidates.

In counting up the votes for the second, or any subsequent scrutiny, no attention must be paid to the names of any candidates who have been excluded.

As many scrutinies as may be necessary must be held, so that finally all the candidates but one are excluded, and the last remaining candidate is elected.

Practical Details

In order to show precisely the amount of labor which would be required to carry out the proposed method, it may be as well to state what appears to be the most convenient way of making up the result. As in the ordinary methods, it would be necessary to have a poll-book in which to keep a tally of the votes. In this book the names of the candidates should be printed from the same type as the ballot-papers are printed from. Each ballot-paper should be placed with the names in a line with the corresponding names in the poll-book, and the numbers written opposite to the names on each ballot-paper should then be copied into the successive columns of the poll-book. In this way the risk of error in transcription would be exceedingly small, and any error which was made would be at once detected on placing the ballot-paper side by side with the column in which its numbers are recorded. When this is done many of the columns would contain vacant spaces. In every vacant space in each column write a number greater by unity than the largest number copied from the voting-paper into that column. After doing this add up the figures in each row; then find the mean or average of the sums. Every candidate who has a sum *equal* to or *greater* than the average is to be excluded. A little consideration will show that this process will give the same result as the method described above. When the papers have once been copied into the poll-book as just described, all subsequent scrutinies that may be necessary can be conducted without handling the voting-papers again.

Cases of Bracketing

Under the head of "Incomplete Voting-papers" we have considered a case in which an elector does not fully express his preference. There is, however, another way in which an elector may fail to fully express his preference. An elector may have no difficulty in putting a number of candidates at the bottom of his list, and yet he may have considerable difficulty in deciding as to the precise order in which to place the candidates at the top end of his list. In such a case an elector might wish to put two or more candidates equal for the first, second, or some other place on his list. This may be called a case of bracketing. It is now to be shown that this system of bracketing can be permitted without causing any difficulty in the practical working of the system. Let us suppose that an elector brackets m_1 candidates for the first place, m_2 for the second place, and so on; so that $m_1 + m_2 + m_3 + \ldots = n$, the case in which one candidate only is put in the rth place being provided for by supposing $m_r = 1$. Then in the poll-book already described enter the number one for each of the m_1 candidates in the first bracket, the number two for each of the m_2 candidates in the second bracket, the number three for each of the m_3 candidates in third bracket, and so on. Suppose, for example, that there are seven candidates, A, B, C, D, E, F, G, and that an elector wishes to bracket B, E for the first place, and A, D, F for the second place, and that he does not care to say anything about C, G. Then he would mark his paper as shown below.

2A
1B
C
2D
1E
2F
G

As nothing is said about C, G, we should consider them as bracketed for the third or last place. Now in order to record this vote in the poll-book, it is merely necessary, as before, to copy the column of numbers on the voting paper into a column of the poll-book, taking care to write in two 3's in the two blank spaces opposite the names C, G. After copying the numbers from each ballot-paper into the poll-book and filling up all the vacant spaces, we should add up the different rows and proceed exactly as before to ascertain the result of the election. Thus it is clear that the method of dealing with the papers is exactly the same no matter how many or how few names be marked, nor how many are bracketed in the various brackets, and that there is very little risk of error in the process.

If this system of bracketing be permitted we at once get rid of the objection that the proposed method could only be used in a highly educated constituency, because it is only highly educated electors who can possibly arrange the candidates in order of merit. The method can easily be used by the most ill-informed electors. In fact, an elector, if he so pleased, could vote in exactly the same manner as in elections under the common "majority" system of voting in cases where there are several candidates—that is, the elector may simply cross out the names of all the candidates he objects to and leave uncancelled as many names as he pleases. In such a case the uncancelled names would all be considered bracketed for the first place, and the cancelled ones as bracketed for the second or last place.

Exactly as in the case of incomplete papers previously discussed, it is easy to see that the method just given is not strictly accurate, that the strictly accurate method would be too complicated for practical purposes, and that the error has the effect of decreasing the chances of success of the favorite candidates of the elector who resorts to bracketing. In fact it may be shown that the numbers which ought strictly to be entered in the poll-book for the candidates in the successive brackets are

$$0, \frac{m_1}{2} + \frac{m_2}{2}, \frac{m_1}{2} + m_2 + \frac{m_3}{2}, \dots \dots \dots \dots \dots \dots \dots \dots \dots \dots (1)$$

$$\frac{m_1}{2} + m_2 + m_3 + \dots + m_{r-1} + \frac{m_r}{2}, \&c.$$

Now the plan just described comes to the same thing in the end as entering instead of these the numbers—

$$0, 1, 2, \ldots , (r - 1), \&c. \dotfill (2)$$

and as no one of the numbers m_1, m_2, m_3, &c., can be less than unity, it is easy to see that no one of the numbers (2) can be greater than the corresponding one of the numbers (1), that when no bracketing occurs the two sets (1), (2), are the same, and that the two sets agree until the first bracket is reached. Now observe that the numbers entered in the poll-book are in reality negative votes, and we see at once that the moment an elector begins to bracket, he diminishes the influence of his own vote on the result of the election, and also decreases the chances of success of all candidates who on his own list are placed higher than the bracket. Each additional bracket will have precisely the same effects. Thus it is clear that the effect of the proposed method will be to discourage the practice of bracketing. If we do not wish to discourage this practice, we must resort to the accurate method, and use the numbers (1) instead of (2). This is not very difficult to do, but as it introduces a new method for the bracketed votes, it would give considerable extra trouble to the officers who make up the poll-books. The most convenient way of stating the accurate method would be as follows:—For each first place count one negative vote, for each second place count in addition $(m_1 + m_2)/2$ negative votes, for each third place count in addition to the last $(m_2 + m_3)/2$ negative votes, for each fourth place count in addition to the last $(m_3 + m_4)/2$ negative votes, and so. As before remarked, the numbers for the successive places would be the natural numbers 1, 2, 3, 4, &c., until a bracket was arrived at. When brackets do occur we shall in general have to deal with half-votes, but no smaller fraction could occur.

Another Method for Cases of Bracketing

Another plan might also be adopted for dealing with cases of bracketing. It is as follows: For each candidate in the first place count one vote; for each candidate in the second place count $m_1 + 1$ votes; for each candidate in the third place count $m_1 + m_2 + 1$ votes; for each candidate in the fourth place count $m_1 + m_2 + m_3 + 1$ votes; and so on. The plan now under consideration comes to the same thing as counting for the successive places the numbers 0, m_1, $m_1 + m_2$, $\ldots$, $m_1 + m_2 + \ldots + m_{r-1}$, &c., instead of the proper numbers (1). Thus the errors for the successive places are

$$0, \frac{m_1 - m_2}{2}, \frac{m_1 - m_3}{2}, \ldots , \frac{m_1 - m_r}{2}, \&c.$$

Hence we see that

1. If the same number of candidates be bracketed for each place, the plan is accurate.
2. If m_1 be greater than either of the numbers m_2, m_3, &c., that is, if more candidates are bracketed for the first place than for any other place—then the errors will be all positive, and the effect will be to give the elector more negative votes than he is entitled to, and, consequently, to increase unduly the chances of the candidates bracketed for the first place.
3. If m_1 be less than each of the numbers m_2, m_3, &c.—that is, if fewer candidates are bracketed for the first place than for any other place—then the errors will be all negative, and the effect will be to give the elector fewer negative votes than he is entitled to, and, consequently, to decrease unduly the chances of the candidates placed at the top end of the elector's list.
4. If m_1 be equal to the mean of the numbers m_2, m_3, &c., the elector will have just as many votes as he ought to have, but he will give more negative votes to some candidates and less to others than they ought to have.
5. If m_1 be not equal to the mean, then the elector will have more or less votes than he is entitled to, according as m_1 is greater or less than the mean.

The results just given apply to each scrutiny; but the numbers m_1, m_2, m_3, &c., will generally be altered at each scrutiny. Thus it is in general impossible to tell at the commencement of an election what will be the effect of different modes of bracketing. Sometimes the elector will get too many votes, sometimes too few. At some scrutinies the candidates at the top end of his list will get too many votes, and at others those at the lower end will get too many votes.

If there be one candidate only in each place, except the last, or, in other words, if the only bracket be for the last place, we have the case of incomplete papers discussed above. In this case the plan just described, and the method adopted above, agree; and the effect is, as has already been pointed out, to give the elector too few votes; and this would be the case at each scrutiny, until all but one of the candidates in the bracket are rejected.

If, however, an elector bracket a number of candidates for the first place and arrange all the rest in order of merit, he would get more votes than he is really entitled to, and this would be the case at each scrutiny until all but one of the candidates in the bracket are rejected. Electors would very soon find this out. Each elector would ask himself the question, "How must I vote in order to get as much electoral power as possible?" and the answer would very soon be seen to be, "I must bracket all the candidates I don't object to for the first place, and I must arrange all the rest in numerical order." Thus, instead of encouraging the electors to arrange all the candidates in order of merit, this plan would lead to each elector trying all he could to defeat objectionable candidates without expressing any opinion as to the relative merits of those he does not object to.

Rule for Forfeit

If the method which is proposed were adopted for Parliamentary elections, it is clear that the number of candidates would be very much greater than at present. In order to prevent the number becoming so great as to make the election unmanageable, it is necessary to provide some method for keeping the number of candidates within reasonable bounds. Such a provision exists for the method now in use. It is that any candidate who fails to obtain one-fifth of the number of votes polled by the lowest successful candidate forfeits the deposit which he has lodged with the Returning Officer. This rule is, of course, purely empirical, and we must fix upon some rule of the same kind for the proposed method. I will first state a rule for the method as first described, i.e., when positive votes are used. This rule is as follows:—

If at the first scrutiny any candidate has a number of votes which is less than half the number of votes polled by the candidate who is highest at the first scrutiny, he shall forfeit his deposit.

In the mode of applying the method which is most convenient in practice this rule takes a somewhat more complicated form, as follows:—

If at the first scrutiny any candidate has a number of votes which, together with a number which is equal to half the number of electors, exceeds half the number of votes polled by the candidate who has the smallest number of votes by the average for the first scrutiny, he shall forfeit his deposit.

Case of Several Vacancies

Hitherto we have supposed that there is only one vacancy to be filled. If there be more than one vacancy we have to settle a most important question before we can consider what method of election is to be adopted. This question is as follows: Is the majority of the electors to fill the whole of the vacancies, or are the successful candidates supposed to represent the different sections of the electoral body? The first case is that of the selection by a Board of Governors of officers to fill various offices. No question of representation is involved, but simply the selection of those persons most fit, in the opinion of the whole electoral body, to fill the different offices. The second case is that of the selection of representatives by a large electoral body. In the first case the whole electoral body has to decide for itself once for all, and the majority must rule. In the second case the electoral body has to select representatives, who are to decide and act for it in a variety of matters; and in order that the decision may be as far as possible in accordance with the views of the electoral body, it is necessary that all the different sections thereof should, as far as possible, be represented.

In the first case there is only one method of arriving at the correct result, and the method is to fill each vacancy separately. Thus one person must be elected by the method described above; then, by means of the same set of voting-papers, we must proceed to a second selection for the next vacancy, and so on till all the vacancies are filled. After each vacancy is filled we must of course suppose the name of the successful candidate erased from all the voting-papers.

The second case—that of the selection of representatives—has been considered by Hare, Andræ, and other writers. It is not proposed here to discuss this question beyond pointing out that it follows from the principles which have been established in this paper that the process of "elimination," which has been adopted by all the exponents of Hare's system, is not satisfactory.

References

Alcover, A. M., ed. 1914. *Obres originals del illuminat Doctor Mestre Ramon Lull.* Vol. 9. Palma: Comissió Editora Lulliana.

Alt, J. E., and K. A. Shepsle, eds. 1990. *Perspectives on positive political economy.* Cambridge: Cambridge University Press.

Andrae, P. 1926. *Andrae and his invention, The PR method.* Translated by V. Meisling. Copenhagen: P. Andrae.

Arago, M. F., and A. Condorcet O'Connor, eds. 1847. *Oeuvres de Condorcet.* 12 vols. Paris: Firmin-Didot.

Aristotle. 1984. *The Constitution of Athens.* Edited and translated by P. J. Rhodes. Harmondsworth: Penguin.

Arrow, K. J. 1951. *Social choice and individual values.* New York: Wiley.

Badinter, E., and R. Badinter. 1988. *Condorcet: un intellectuel en politique.* Paris: Fayard.

Baker, K. M. 1975. *Condorcet: from natural philosophy to social mathematics.* Chicago: University of Chicago Press.

Balinski, M. L., and H. P. Young. 1982. *Fair representation: Meeting the ideal of one man, one vote.* New Haven, CT: Yale University Press.

Barber, B. 1985. *Strong Democracy.* New York: Basic Books

Barry, B. 1986. Wasted votes and other mares' nests: A view of electoral reform. Pasadena, CA: Caltech Social Science Working Paper no. 612.

Bartholdi, J. J., III, and J. B. Orlin. 1991. Single transferable vote resists strategic voting. *Social Choice and Welfare* 8:341–54.

Bartholdi, J. J., III, C. A. Tovey, and M. A. Trick. 1989. Voting schemes for which it can be difficult to tell who won the election. *Social Choice and Welfare* 6:157–66.

Berg, S. 1992. Condorcet's jury theorem: Dependency among jurors. Paper for meeting of Society for Social Choice and Welfare, Caen, June.

Bill, E. G. W., and J. F. A. Mason. 1970. *Christ Church and reform, 1850–1867.* Oxford: Clarendon Press.

Black, D. 1958. *The theory of committees and elections.* Cambridge: Cambridge University Press.

———. 1967. The central argument in Lewis Carroll's "The principles of parliamentary representation." *Papers in Non-Market Decision Making* 3:1–17.

———. Forthcoming. *Lewis Carroll and proportional representation.* Dordrecht: Kluwer Academic Publishers.

Bonner, A., ed. 1985. *Selected works of Ramon Llull.* 2 vols. Princeton, NJ: Princeton University Press.

Brams, S. J., and P. C. Fishburn. 1983. *Approval Voting*. Boston: Birkhäuser.

Brams, S. J., and J. H. Nagel. 1991. Approval Voting in practice. *Public Choice* 71:1–17.

Cappon, L. J., ed. 1959. *The Adams-Jefferson letters: The complete correspondence between Thomas Jefferson and Abigail and John Adams*. Chapel Hill, NC: University of North Carolina Press.

Citrine, W. (Lord). 1952. *ABC of chairmanship*. London: NCLC Publishing Society.

Cohen, M. N., ed. 1979. *The letters of Lewis Carroll*. 2 vols, continuously paginated. London: Macmillan.

Collin, N. [1820] 1885. On Condorcet's application of the theory of probabilities to decisions depending on a majority of votes. Verbal communication, 3 November 1820. *Proceedings of the American Philosophical Society* 32, Pt. 3: 119.

Condorcet, M. J. A. N. de Caritat, marquis de. [1785] 1972. *Essai sur l'application de l'analyse à la probabilité des décisions rendues à la pluralité des voix*. New York: Chelsea Publishing Co. Facsimile reprint of original published in Paris by the Imprimerie Royale.

————. 1787. *Lettres d'un bourgeois de New Heaven à un citoyen de Virginie sur l'inutilité de partager le pouvoir législatif en plusieurs corps*. In [P. Mazzei], *Recherches historiques et politiques . . . sur les Etats-Unis*. 4 vols. Paris: Froullé.

————. [1788] 1847. *Essai sur la constitution et les fonctions des assemblées provinciales*. In *Oeuvres de Condorcet*, ed. M. F. Arago and A. Condorcet O'Connor, vol. 8. Paris: Firmin-Didot.

Cornford, J. 1963. The transformation of Conservatism in the late nineteenth century. *Victorian Studies* 7:35–66.

Cox, G. 1987. *The efficient secret: The Cabinet and the development of political parties in Victorian England*. Cambridge: Cambridge University Press.

Crépel, P. 1988. Condorcet, la théorie des probabilités et les calculs financiers. In *Sciences à l'époque de la Révolution française*, edited by R. Rashed, 267–328. Paris: Blanchard.

————. 1990. Le dernier mot de Condorcet sur les élections. Paris: Centre d'Analyse et de Mathématiques Sociales, Série "Histoire du calcul des probabilités et de la statistique," working paper no. 8.

Crépel, P., and C. Gilain, eds. 1989. *Condorcet: mathématicien, économiste, philosophe, homme politique*. Paris: Minerve.

Daston, L. 1988. *Classical probability in the Enlightenment*. Princeton: Princeton University Press.

Daunou, P. C. F. (an XI = 1803). *Mémoire sur les élections au scrutin*. Paris: Baudouin, imprimeur de l'Institut National.

de Grazia, A. 1953. Mathematical derivation of an election system. *Isis* 44:42–51.

Dodgson, C. L. [1876] 1958. Suggestions as to the best method of taking votes, where more than two issues are to be voted on. Privately printed, Oxford. In *The theory of committees and elections*, D. Black, 222–34. Cambridge: Cambridge University Press.

Doron, G., and R. Kronick. 1977. Single Transferable Vote: An example of a perverse social choice function. *American Journal of Political Science* 21:303–11.

Doyle, W. 1989. *The Oxford history of the French Revolution*. Oxford: Clarendon Press.

Droop, H. R. 1869. On the political and social effects of different methods of electing representatives. *Papers Read before the Juridical Society* 3:469–507.

Dummett, M. 1984. *Voting procedures*. Oxford: Clarendon Press.

Elster, J., and A. Hylland, eds. 1986. *Foundations of social choice theory*. Cambridge: Cambridge University Press.

Estlund, D. M., J. Waldron, B. Grofman, and S. Feld. 1989. Democratic theory and the public interest: Condorcet and Rousseau revisited. *American Political Science Review* 83:1317–40.

Farquharson, R. 1969. *Theory of voting*. Oxford: Blackwell.

Finley, M. I. 1973. *Democracy, ancient and modern*. London: Chatto & Windus.

———. 1983. *Politics in the ancient world*. Cambridge: Cambridge University Press.

Galbraith, G. R. 1925. *The constitution of the Dominican order 1216–1360*. Manchester: Manchester University Press.

Gardner, M. 1982. *Logic machines and diagrams*. 2d ed. Brighton: Harvester.

Gardner, M., ed. 1970. *The annotated Alice*. 2d ed. Harmondsworth: Penguin.

Gillispie, C. C., ed. 1981. *Dictionary of scientific biography*. 18 vols. New York: Scribners.

Granger, G.-G. 1956. *La mathématique sociale du marquis de Condorcet*. Paris: Presses Universitaires de France.

Green, R. L., ed. 1953. *The diaries of Lewis Carroll*. 2 vols, continuously paginated. London: Cassell.

Grofman, B., and S. Feld. 1988. Rousseau's General Will: A Condorcetian perspective. *American Political Science Review* 82:567–78.

Grofman, B., and G. Owen. 1986. *Information pooling and group decision making*. Westport, CT: JAI Press.

Guilbaud, G.-Th. 1952. Les théories de l'intérêt général et la problème logique de l'agrégation. *Economie Appliquée* 5:501–84.

Hahn, R. 1971. *The anatomy of a scientific institution: The Paris Academy of Sciences, 1666–1803*. Berkeley, CA: University of California Press.

Hamilton, A., J. Madison, and J. Jay. [1788] 1987. *The Federalist Papers*. Ed. I. Kramnick. Harmondsworth: Penguin.

Hare, T. 1873. *The election of representatives, parliamentary and municipal: A treatise*. 4th ed. London: Longmans Green.

Hart, J. 1992. *Proportional representation: Critics of the British electoral system 1820–1945*. Oxford: Clarendon Press.

Henry, C., ed. 1883. *Correspondance inédite de Condorcet et de Turgot 1770–9*. Paris: Charavay.

Honecker, M. 1937a. Lullus-Handschriften aus dem Besitz des Kardinals Nikolaus von Cues: nebst einer Beschreibung der Lullus-Texte in Trier und einem Anhang über den wiederaufgefundenen Traktat "De Arte Electionis." In *Gesammelte Aufsätze zur Kulturgeschichte Spaniens*, edited by H. Finke, P. I, § 6, pp. 252–309. Münster in Westfalen: Verlag der Aschendorffschen Verlagsbuchhandlung.

———. 1937b. Ramon Lulls Wahlvorschlag Grundlage des Kaiserwahlplanes bei Nikolaus von Cues? *Historisches Jahrbuch* 57:563–74.

James, E. J. 1896. *An early essay on proportional representation* [by Thomas Gilpin]. Philadelphia: American Association for Political and Social Science.

Johns, F. 1922. *Who's who in the Commonwealth of Australia*. Sydney: Angus & Robertson.

Jones, A. 1972. *The politics of Reform 1884*. Cambridge: Cambridge University Press.

Kallen, G., ed. 1964. *Nicolai de Cusa opera omnia*, vol. 14. Hamburg: Felix Meiner.

Kendall, M. G., and A. Stuart. 1950. The law of cubic proportion in election results. *British Journal of Sociology* 1:183–97.

Kuhn, T. S. 1970. *The structure of scientific revolutions.* 2d ed. Chicago: University of Chicago Press.

Lhuilier, S. [1794] 1976. *Examen du mode d'élection proposé à la Convention Nationale de France en février 1793, et adopté à Genève: présenté au Comité Législatif par Simon Lhuilier et imprimé par ordre du Comité.* Geneva: Comité Législatif. Facsimile reprint in *Mathématiques et sciences humaines* 54:7–24.

Libiszowska, Z. 1991. England-Poland during the 18th century. In *The Polish road to democracy: The constitution of May 3, 1791: Exhibition in the Polish Cultural Institute in London April 18–June 18, 1991*, 7–20. Warsaw: The Seym Publishing House.

Lijphart, A. 1992. Democratization and constitutional choices in Czecho-Slovakia, Hungary and Poland, 1989–91. *Journal of Theoretical Politics* 4:207–23.

Lines, M. 1986. Approval voting and strategy analysis: A Venetian example. *Theory and Decision* 20:155–72.

Lubbock, Sir J. 1885. *Representation.* London: Swan Sonnenschein.

Lull, R. [ca. 1285] 1914. *Blanquerna.* In *Obres originals del illuminat Doctor Mestre Ramon Lull*, edited by A. M. Alcover, vol. 9. Palma: Comissió Editora Lulliana.

———. [1299] 1937. De arte eleccionis. Cod. Cus. 83 Fol. 47V–48R. In *Gesammelte Aufsätze zur Kulturgeschichte Spaniens*, edited by H Finke, P. I, § 6, pp. 308–309. Münster in Westfalen: Verlag der Aschendorffschen Verlagsbuchhandlung.

———. [1311] 1985. Vita Coaetanea. In *Selected works of Ramon Lull*, edited by A. Bonner, vol. 1, pp. 13–48. Princeton, NJ: Princeton University Press.

Marchione, M., ed. 1983. *Philip Mazzei: Selected writings and correspondence.* 3 vols. Prato: Edizioni del Palazzo.

May, K. O. 1952. A set of independent necessary and sufficient conditions for simple majority decision. *Econometrica* 20:680–84.

McClellan, J. 1986. *Science reorganized.* New York: Columbia University Press.

McLean, I. 1991. Forms of representation and systems of voting. In *Political theory today*, edited by D. Held, 172–96. Cambridge: Polity Press.

———. 1992. Rational choice and the Victorian voter. *Political Studies* 40:496–515

———. 1993. Why does nobody in Britain pay any attention to voting rules? In *The British Elections and Parties Yearbook 1992*, edited by P. Norris, I. Crewe, D. Denver, and D. Broughton, 13–24. Hemel Hempstead: Harvester Wheatsheaf.

McLean, I., and F. Hewitt, ed. Forthcoming. *Condorcet: Foundations of social choice and political theory.* Cheltenham: Edward Elgar.

McLean, I., and J. London. 1990. The Borda and Condorcet principles: Three medieval applications. *Social Choice and Welfare* 7:99–108.

McLean, I., and A. B. Urken. 1992. Did Jefferson or Madison understand Condorcet's theory of social choice? *Public Choice* 73:445–57.

Michaud, P. 1985. *Hommage à Condorcet: version intégrale pour le bicentenaire de l'Essai de Condorcet*. Paris: Centre Scientifique IBM, étude F.094.

Mill, J. S. [1861] 1972. *Considerations on representative government*. Edited by H. B. Acton. London: Dent.

Miller, N. R. 1980. A new solution set for tournaments and majority voting: Further graph-theoretical approaches to the theory of voting. *American Journal of Political Science* 24:68–96.

Monjardet, B. 1976. Lhuilier contre Condorcet, au pays des paradoxes. *Mathématiques et Sciences Humaines* 54:33–43.

———. 1990. Sur diverses formes de la "Règle de Condorcet" d'agrégation des préférences. *Mathématiques, informatique et sciences humaines* 111:61–71.

Montucla, J. E. 1802. *Histoire des mathématiques*. Vols. 3 and 4. Paris: Agasse. Montucla died in 1799. Vols. 1 and 2 of this history were published in 1799, a revision of a book that had first appeared as long ago as 1758. Vol. 3 was compiled from Montucla's proofs and new material by J.-J. Lalande, an associate of Condorcet. Vol. 4 is entirely Lalande. The passage cited by Nanson in chapter 14 is from the part completed but not published by Montucla himself.

Morales, J. I. 1797. *Memoria matemática sobre el cálculo de la opinion en las elecciones*. Madrid: Imprenta Real.

Morris, A. C., ed. 1889. *The diary and letters of Gouverneur Morris*. 2 vols. London: Kegan Paul, Trench & Co.

Murray, A. 1978. *Reason and society*. Oxford: Clarendon Press.

Mynors, R. A. B., ed. 1966. *C. Plini Caecili Secundi Epistularum Libri Decem*. Oxford: Clarendon Press.

Nanson, E. J. [1882] 1907. Methods of election. Paper read to Royal Society of Victoria on 12 October 1882. Printed in *Reports . . . respecting the application of the principle of proportional representation to public elections*, Cd. 3501, pp. 123–41. London: HMSO.

Nohlen, D. 1984. Two incompatible principles of representation. In *Choosing an electoral system*, edited by A. Lijphart and B. Grofman, 83–89. New York: Praeger.

Ordeshook, P. C. 1991. The development of contemporary political theory. Paper for the Eighth International Symposium in Economic Theory and Econometrics, St. Louis, MO, May 22–25, 1991.

Peers, E. A., ed. 1926. *Blanquerna: A 13th century romance translated from the Catalan of Raymond Lull*. London: Jarrolds.

Pitkin, H. 1967. *The concept of representation*. Berkeley: University of California Press.

Plott, C. R. 1976. Axiomatic social choice theory: An overview and interpretation. *American Journal of Political Science* 20:511–96.

Popper, K. R. 1959. *The logic of scientific discovery*. London: Routledge, Kegan Paul.

Radice, B., ed. 1969. *The letters of the younger Pliny*. 2d ed. Harmondsworth: Penguin.

Rasch, B. E. 1987. Manipulation and strategic voting in the Norwegian parliament. *Public Choice* 52:57–73.

Rashed, R., ed. 1988. *Sciences à l'époque de la Révolution française*. Paris: Blanchard.

Riker, W. H. 1982. *Liberalism against populism*. San Francisco: W. H. Freeman.

———. 1986. *The art of political manipulation*. New Haven, CT: Yale University Press.

Rodewald, C., ed. 1975. *Democracy: Ideals and realities*. London: Dent.

Rousseau, J.-J. [1762] 1973. *The social contract and discourses*. Trans. by G. D. H. Cole, revised by J. H. Brumfitt and J. C. Hall. London: Dent (Everyman).

Ruffini Avondo, E. 1927. *I sistemi di deliberazione collettiva nel medioevo italiano*. Turin: Bocca.

Saari, D. G. 1990. The Borda dictionary. *Social Choice and Welfare* 7:279–317.

———. 1992. A fourth grade experience. Northwestern University, Departments of Mathematics and Economics. Unpublished paper.

Salisbury, 3d Marquess of. 1884. The value of redistribution: A note on electoral statistics. *National Review* 4:145–62.

Schama, S. 1989. *Citizens: A chronicle of the French Revolution*. Harmondsworth: Penguin.

Sigmund, P. E. 1963. *Nicholas of Cusa and medieval political thought*. Cambridge, MA: Harvard University Press.

———, ed. 1991. *Nicholas of Cusa: The Catholic Concordance*. Cambridge: Cambridge University Press.

Sommerlad, F., and I. McLean, eds. 1989. *The political theory of Condorcet*. Oxford University Social Studies Faculty Centre Working Paper 1/89.

———, eds. 1991. *The political theory of Condorcet II*. Oxford University Social Studies Faculty Centre Working Paper 1/91.

Taagepera, R., and M. S. Shugart. 1989. *Seats and votes: The effects and determinants of electoral systems*. New Haven, CT: Yale University Press.

Thucydides. 1972. *History of the Peloponnesian War*. Trans. by Rex Warner and intro. by M. I. Finley. Harmondsworth: Penguin.

Todhunter, I. 1865. *A history of the mathematical theory of probability from the time of Pascal to that of Laplace*. London: Macmillan.

Tullock, G., ed. 1981. *Toward a science of politics: Essays in honor of Duncan Black*. Blacksburg, VA: Virginia Polytechnic Institute and State University Public Choice Center.

Urken, A. B. 1988. Social choice theory and distributed decision making. *Proceedings of the IEEE/ACM Conference on office information systems*, Palo Alto, CA.

———. 1989a. Condorcet—Jefferson: un chaînon manquant dans la théorie du choix social? In *Condorcet: mathématicien, économiste, philosophe, homme politique*, edited by P. Crépel and C. Gilain, 107–18. Paris: Minerve.

———. 1989b. Condorcet's 1785 *Essai* and the origins of social choice theory. Paper presented at the Annual Meeting of the Public Choice Society, Tucson, AZ.

———. 1991. The Condorcet-Jefferson connection and the origins of social choice theory. *Public Choice* 72:213–36.

Urken, A. B., R. Pinkham, and J. McLellan, eds. Forthcoming. [Condorcet's *Essai*]. New Haven, CT: Yale University Press.

Urken, A. B., and S. J. Traflet. 1984. Optimal jury design. *Jurimetrics* 24:218–35.

Watson, J. D., and F. H. C. Crick. 1953. A structure for deoxyribose nucleic acid. *Nature* 171:737–38.

Williams, S. H., F. Madan, R. L. Green, and D. Crutch. 1979. *The Lewis Carroll handbook.* Folkestone: William Dawson.

Wills, G. 1978. *Inventing America: Jefferson's Declaration of Independence.* New York: Vintage Books.

Woollcott, A., ed. 1939. *The complete works of Lewis Carroll.* London: Nonesuch Press.

Young, H. P. 1988. Condorcet's theory of voting. *American Political Science Review* 82:1231–44.

Index

Iain McLean is Professor of Politics,
University of Warwick.

Arnold B. Urken is Professor of Political
Science, Stevens Institute of Technology.